Conflict and Change in EU Budgetary Politics

How does the European Union deal with conflict among member states and between institutions? This book provides an institutionalist analysis of an important feature of EU decision-making.

Focusing on the dominance of conflict in EU budgetary politics, the author introduces the key actors and issues in European budgetary decision-making and traces the main developments in EU finances since the introduction of own-resources and parliamentary co-responsibility in the 1970s. With its analytical emphasis on distributive and institutional conflict, the author reveals the strong impact that rules and procedures have on the ability of EU actors to resolve conflict. Moreover, with its rigorous use of social science methodology, it makes a valuable contribution to the institutional research agenda and presents testable propositions on the influence of institutions and the emergence of institutional change.

This book will be of considerable interest to students and researchers of European Union politics and those interested in institutionalist analysis.

Johannes Lindner is Counsellor to the Executive Board of the European Central Bank. He holds masters degrees from the University of Cologne and the London School of Economics, as well as a doctorate from the University of Oxford.

Routledge Advances in European Politics

Conflict and Change
in EU Budgetary Politics

Johannes Lindner

LONDON AND NEW YORK

First published 2006
by Routledge
2 Park Square, Milton Park, Abingdon, Oxon OX14 4RN

Simultaneously published in the USA and Canada
by Routledge
270 Madison Ave, New York, NY 10016

Routledge is an imprint of the Taylor & Francis Group

Transferred to Digital Printing 2009

© 2006 Johannes Lindner

Typeset in Baskerville by
Keystroke, Jacaranda Lodge, Wolverhampton

British Library Cataloguing in Publication Data
A catalogue record for this book is available from the British Library

Library of Congress Cataloguing in Publication Data
Lindner, Johannes, 1974–
    Conflict and change in EU budgetary politics / Johannes Lindner.—1st ed.
        p. cm. — (Routledge advances in European politics)
    Includes bibliographical references.
    1. Budget—European Union countries. 2. Finance, Public—European
    Union countries. 3. Debts, Public—European Union countries.
    4. Fiscal policy—European Union countries. I. Title. II. Series.
    HJ2094.L56 2005
    352.4′094—dc22
    2005011829

ISBN10: 0–415–35679–2 (hbk)
ISBN10: 0–415–49917–8 (pbk)

ISBN13: 978–0–415–35679–4 (hbk)
ISBN13: 978–0–415–49917–0 (pbk)

Contents

Figures and Tables

Figures

Tables

Boxes

Acknowledgements

Without the support of many individuals and numerous institutions I would not have been able to write this book.

First of all, I owe deep gratitude to the many officials of the European Commission, the secretariat general of the European Parliament, the secretariat general of the Council, national permanent representations, the UK Treasury, the German Federal Ministry of Finance and the German Bundesbank, as well as current and former members of the European Parliament and their staff, who gave their time to answer my questions. This book benefited greatly from their insights and their support during several visits to Brussels, London, Berlin and Frankfurt between 2000 and 2004 and three longer stays at European institutions, namely at the directorate-general budget of the European Commission (October to December 2000), at the secretariat general of the European Parliament (March 2001) and at the secretariat general of the Council (September 2001). Of the many people who helped me during this time I am especially indebted to Alfredo Defeo and his unit, Jens Schaps, Eric Paradis and his unit, Walter Deffaa, Michel Vanden Abeele, Otto Harnier and Juao Martins. I would also like to thank Jürgen Stark, Luis Romero Requena, Sir Nigel Wicks and Terry Wynn, MEP.

In autumn 2001, I had the privilege to spend three months at the European Centre of the Institute d'Etudes Politiques de Paris. I am thankful to the Centre's director, Renaud Dehousse, for inviting me to Paris and for his support during my research stay. In a lucky coincidence, Fritz W. Scharpf was also a visitor at the European Centre during this time. I benefited greatly from three inspiring talks he gave at the Centre and a long discussion I had with him about my application of his research approach to EU budgetary politics.

During the last five years, a number of colleagues and friends discussed and commented on my work. I want to thank Frank R. Baumgartner, Nicolas-Jean Brehon, Wouter Coussens, David Cameron, Patrick Dunleavy, Henrik Enderlein, Tue Rasmussen Fosdal, John Garry, Patrick LeGalles, David Levi-Faur, Sonia Mazey, Margaret McCown, Mark Pollack, Lorena Ruano, Kenneth Shepsle, Michael Shackleton, Jeffrey Stacey, Yves Surel, Amy Verdun and Helen Wallace. I am also indebted to Chavi Nana who read through the complete manuscript.

My special thanks go to my University supervisor, Jeremy Richardson, and to my colleague, Berthold Rittberger. Jeremy guided me through this research project and provided key personal and administrative support and invaluable academic advice. Most importantly, his strong encouragements helped me to gain confidence in the research project. Berthold and I shared much of the ups and downs of writing a dissertation during which he became my close adviser and friend. I have learnt a great deal from his thorough methodological approach to social science and I thank him for the many good comments and suggestions he made to my work. I am also grateful to my College supervisor, Alec Stone Sweet, whose focus on institutions and approach to life was a source of inspiration during these years.

While conducting my research as a Ph.D. student at Oxford University, I benefited greatly from the generous financial support of the German Academic Exchange Service (DAAD-Doktorandenstipendium im Rahmen des gemeinsamen Hochschulprogramms III), which had already financed my master's course at the London School of Economics, and of the British Economic and Social Research Council (ESRC-Grant R00429934276). Moreover, Nuffield College provided not only ideal research conditions and a very stimulating environment, but also funding for conference visits, language courses and research trips.

In the process of transforming the Ph.D. manuscript into a book, I was helped by a number of people. First of all, I would like to thank my examiners, Brigid Laffan and Iain McLean, as well as two anonymous referees for their encouragement and comments to improve the manuscript. I am also grateful that Brigid gave me the chance to co-author the chapter on the EU budget in the new edition of the Wallace and Wallace textbook on policy-making in the EU. A previous version of that chapter gave me in 1998, when I was applying for Ph.D. positions, the inspiration to focus on conflict and change in EU budgetary politics. The conclusions of my book build, in parts, on Brigid's and my assessment of recent developments in budgetary politics. At Routledge, I wish to thank Heidi Bagtazo and the editorial team for their support. Finally, I benefited from a very stimulating environment at the European Central Bank, where I could continue to think and work on topics and issues that are directly related to my research interests. Especially, joint work with Henrik Enderlein and other colleagues on the reform of the EU budgetary procedure was relevant for this book. However, the opinions expressed in this book are my own and do not necessarily reflect those of the European Central Bank.

I dedicate this book to my wife, Lucia Wülfing, and to my parents, Regine and Burkhardt Lindner. I want to thank them for their love and support. Without the help of my parents I would have never been able to start a Ph.D. dissertation, and without Lucia I might have never completed it. Elisabeth, our daughter, is much younger than this project; but her calls for 'Papa' and her smiles when I look at her have shown me that there are much more important things than writing about the EU budget and that, therefore, this project has to come to a close.

Johannes Lindner
Frankfurt am Main
September 2005

Publisher's note

The publishers would like to thank the following for permission to reprint their material: Blackwell Publishing for permission to reprint Figures 2.2 and 2.3 from Johannes Lindner and Berthold Rittberger: 'The Creation, Interpretation and Contestation of Institutions', *Journal of Common Market Studies*, 41 (2003), 3, pp. 445–473; Routledge/Taylor and Francis for permission to reprint a short part of Johannes Lindner: 'Institutional Stability and Change: Two Sides of the Same Coin', *Journal of European Public Policy*, 10 (2003), 6, pp. 912–935. http://www.tandf.co.uk; Routledge/Taylor and Francis for permission to reprint Figures 1.2 and 12.1 from Henrik Enderlein and Johannes Lindner: 'The EU Budgetary Procedure in the Constitutional Debate', Jeremy Richardson (ed.) (forthcoming): *European Union: Power & Policy-Making*, third edition, London: Routledge. http://www.tandf.co.uk; Oxford University Press for permission to reprint from Chapter 8 'The EU Budget', by Brigid Laffan and Johannes Lindner in Helen Wallace, William Wallace and Mark Pollack (eds) (2005): *Policy-Making in the European Union*, Oxford, Oxford University Press. www.oup.com. By permission of Oxford University Press.

Every effort has been made to contact copyright holders for their permission to reprint material in this book. The publishers would be grateful to hear from any copyright holder who is not here acknowledged and will undertake to rectify any errors or omissions in future editions of this book.

Abbreviations

CAP	Common Agricultural Policy
CDU/CSU	Christlich Demokratische Union/Christlich Soziale Union
COPA	Confederation of Professional Agricultural Organisations in the European Community
COREPER	Committee of Permanent Representatives
DEP/RDE	European Democratic Alliance
DG	Directorates-General
EAGGF	European Agricultural Guidance and Guarantee Fund
EC	European Community
EC/EU-Bull.	Bulletin of the European Communities/European Union
ECJ	European Court of Justice
ECOFIN	Council of Economic and Finance Ministers
ECSC	European Coal and Steel Community
ECU	European Currency Unit
EDF	European Development Fund
EMS	Economic and Monetary System
EMU	Economic and Monetary Union
EP	European Parliament
EPP	European People's Party
ERDF	European Regional Development Fund
GDP	Gross domestic product
GNI	Gross national income
GNP	Gross national product
IGC	Intergovernmental conference
IIA	Interinstitutional agreement
MEP	Member of the European Parliament
OJ	Official Journal of the European Communities
PDB	Preliminary draft budget
QMV	Qualified-majority voting
SEA	Single European Act
SPD	Sozialdemokratische Partei Deutschlands
SPE	Party of European Socialists
VAT	Value-added tax

1   Introduction

An institutionalist perspective on conflict and change in EU budgetary politics

Conflicts over 'who gets what and why?' and 'who pays?' have been at the heart of political developments for centuries and the trigger for fundamental institutional changes. The American Revolution was fought over the right to determine the level of taxation and over the ability to allocate the collected funds ('no taxation without representation'). In Europe, modern parliamentary democracy emerged from the continuous struggle between King and Parliament over the power to raise taxes and to determine the size and composition of the budget. Medieval kingdoms developed into potent nation states as they gradually centralised fiscal authority. Budgets provide the arena for conflicts over political priorities and the struggle for the power to govern the country.

In the European integration process, conflict over the budget in the 1970s and 1980s produced some of the most intense clashes among member states and between European parliamentarians and national ministers, seriously challenging the operation of European institutions. New member states, such as Great Britain, fought vigorously against the established distributive order and branded it as 'demonstrably unjust' (Margaret Thatcher 1979). Moreover, the European Parliament used its (new) budgetary powers to challenge the dominant position of national governments in European decision-making. Year after year, Parliament and Council failed to agree on budgets and fought over the power to determine European expenditure. Summit after summit, the European Council argued about British demands for a rebate and over the future of the Community's finances, culminating in a near collapse of the Community by the mid-1980s.

By the late 1980s, however, budgetary conflict seemed an issue of the past, and subsequent discussions over the Community budgetary have proceeded in a structured and orderly manner. Although distributive disputes still occur, they no longer challenge the ability of the Union to adopt annual budgets and to rely on a broad consensus over the distributive order of the European Union. This sudden disappearance of high levels of conflict in EU budgetary politics is unique for a political system with so many different and competing interests. It poses an interesting empirical puzzle that is still unresolved.

This book explains why the European Union (EU)[1] experienced such a stark variation in the level of conflict between the late 1970s, when budgetary disputes dominated European politics, and the 1990s, at which point actors were able to settle budgetary agreements peacefully. I argue that high levels of conflict in the 1970s and 1980s resulted primarily from the problematic institutional design of the 1970 budget treaty, which gave the Community its 'own-resources' and a largely supranational budgetary decision-making procedure. The key shortcomings of the new treaty provisions pertained to the exclusion of distributive and institutional interests of new member states and of the European Parliament (EP), and the scope of interpretation that allowed these actors to challenge dominant interpretations of the treaty provisions. Addressing these problems, a far-reaching reform in 1988 significantly reduced levels of conflict. It supplemented the treaty provisions with an institutional framework for multi-annual budget plans and clear rules for the budgetary procedure. The two pillars of this reform, the financial perspective and the interinstitutional agreement, were successfully renewed twice – in 1992/93 and 1999. Having identified institutional change as the trigger for reducing conflict, I will put particular emphasis on the 1988 reform. The bargaining power of the six member states that enacted the 1970 treaty, the institutional interdependence between subfields of budgetary politics, and the high switching costs (relative to the opportunity costs) prevented major institutional change in the 1970s and early 1980s. When these 'reproduction mechanisms' lost force, a reform became possible and a new institutional setting emerged in 1988.

This book therefore reveals a fascinating story of conflict and change. Budgetary conflict is primarily fought over distributive outcomes. It takes place within rules that structure the decision-making process. One of the key functions of rules is to manage and contain conflict. In failing to do so, they can themselves become an important source of conflict. For example, negotiations over how to distribute public finances get intertwined with debates over whose right it is to take these decisions and what kind of voting rule should apply. In this case, rules are not accepted as given, but heavily contested. Conflict within rules turns into conflict over rules and can eventually lead to institutional change. The mechanism of how distributive conflict may trigger institutional change depends to some extent on the functionality of the existing rules. Moreover, institutional change may often occur in culmination points, such as the 1988 reform. However, as this book shows, an explanation of institutional change that assumes that change occurs when rules fail to contain conflict and that focuses exclusively on key culmination points is too narrow. The book contends that in order to explain the occurrence of institutional change a thorough analysis of the preceding period of institutional stability is important. Such an analysis is likely to reveal that institutions are often 'sticky' and the timing and shape of institutional developments are not merely determined by the degree to which the existing institutional framework ensures an ordered decision-making process.

In this introduction, I will first sketch the empirical setting in which my story of conflict and change is told. In the following three sections, I will introduce the particular focus, the analytical tools and the data sources of the book. Finally, the outline of the book is presented.

The setting

EU budgetary politics

EU budgetary politics is a small but horizontal policy field that is interlinked with other policy fields. It is placed in a complex and evolving political system. I will briefly introduce the main features of EU budgetary politics and explain why – in my view – it is an interesting empirical field for research.

Given that welfare state policies still remain national competencies, the EU budget is not the key layer of budgetary activities in the European Union. Although it has increased significantly over the last 40 years, the budget accounts for only around 1 per cent of the EU's gross national income (GNI)[2] (see Figure 1.1; also Appendix No. 1: The EU budget in figures). Four-fifths of the budget is spent on two specific policy areas with a strong redistributive bent, namely agricultural and regional policies. On the revenue side, the EU budget was given its 'own-resources' in the 1970 budget treaty. These sources of revenue encompassed customs duties, agricultural levies and a uniform percentage rate of the VAT assessment base. The institutional overhaul of the budgetary procedure in 1988 brought the introduction of an additional 'fourth resource' which is calculated on the basis of member states' GNI in market prices and accounts in the meantime for two-thirds of the EU's revenue. The EU is obliged to keep the expenditure within the limits of the existing revenue as the treaty prohibits the adoption of a budget with a deficit.

The 1970 budget treaty introduced the treaty provisions for the annual budgetary procedure which, in principle, are still in place.[3] They were updated only once: the 1975 budget treaty introduced a number of minor revisions. Figure 1.2 illustrates the different steps of the budgetary procedure. It distinguishes between compulsory and non-compulsory expenditure: *compulsory expenditure* covers all spending that follows directly from treaty obligations (mainly agricultural spending), while *non-compulsory expenditure* encompasses the rest (in particular regional policy spending). Decision-making for both types of expenditure proceeds simultaneously but follows two different procedures. The Council can overrule parliamentary modifications for compulsory expenditure, but has to accept parliamentary amendments to non-compulsory expenditure. Yet, non-compulsory expenditure has to stay within a *maximum rate of increase*, which limits the extent to which Parliament can exceed the previous year's amount of non-compulsory expenditure.[4] The Commission calculates the maximum rate at the beginning of the year on the basis of indicators given in the treaty, i.e. the evolution of the EU's GNI, the average variation in the budgets of the member states, and the evolution of the inflation in the EU. The two arms of the budgetary authority, namely the Council and the Parliament, can alter the maximum rate of increase with a joint decision.

The treaty sets clear deadlines for the different stages of the budgetary procedure, limiting them to the time from 1 September to 31 December. In practice, however, a 'pragmatic' timetable has been applied by the three institutions since 1977:

- The Commission submits its preliminary draft budget (PDB) by no later than 15 June.

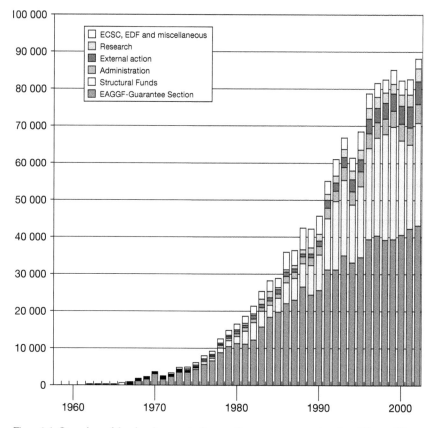

Figure 1.1 Overview of the development of expenditure at current prices in millions of Euros.
Source: European Commission (2003): *Financial Report 2002.*

- The Council establishes the draft budget in its first reading before 31 July.
- The EP holds its first reading in October.
- The Council conducts its second reading during the third week in November.
- The EP finally adopts the budget at its second reading in December.

When the Council and the EP fail to adopt an annual budget, the Commission enacts the system of provisional twelfths at the beginning of the financial year: EU spending is then limited per month to the one-twelfth of the previous year's budget.

Since 1988, annual budgetary decision-making has been supplanted by an institutional framework for multi-annual budget planning. The two pillars of the framework are the financial perspective and an interinstitutional agreement. The financial perspective is a multi-annual budget plan for originally five and now seven years which lays down the maximum amounts of both total annual expenditure and annual expenditure on specific policy headings. It also ensures a balance

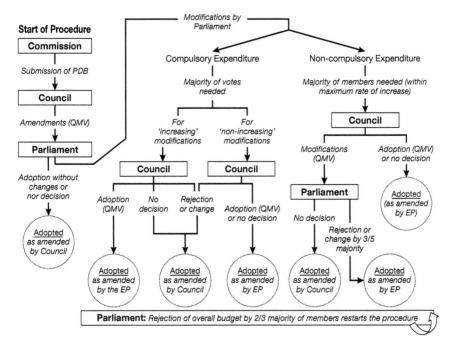

Figure 1.2 Overview of the annual budgetary procedure.

between the annual expenditure amounts and the overall revenue ceiling. The financial perspective is negotiated within the Council and adopted by Heads of State or Government. An institutional agreement between the Council, the EP and the Commission subsequently translates the financial perspective into a binding structure for annual budgets. In the negotiations over the interinstitutional agreement, the Commission and in particular the EP have the opportunity to demand concessions for accepting the financial perspective as adopted by the Heads of State or Government. These concessions take either the form of budgetary revisions of the financial perspective or they are institutional adjustments to the practice of annual budgetary decision-making. As a result, the financial perspective and the institutional agreement, which were renewed in 1992/3 and 1999, have radically altered the annual procedure without changing the rules of the treaty. In fact, they do not even have the status of enforceable law (Monar 1994). Except for the decisions on the revenue ceilings, their binding character stems chiefly from the political willingness of actors to adhere to the jointly agreed institutional and distributive framework.

Against the background of this brief sketch of the EU budgetary politics, the question arises: why is a focus on budgetary politics relevant to the study of the EU? In essence, I would argue there are four reasons.

First, the EU budget is – although limited in size – of high political importance. Key for the political importance of the EU budget is the fact that the EU spends most of its budget on the Common Agricultural Policy (CAP) and, since the late 1980s, also on Structural Funds. Hence, the budget is highly concentrated on two groups of recipients: farmers and less developed regions. Budgetary decisions, therefore, have a decisive impact on these two groups. In the case of farmers, the recipients are well organised and fiercely defend their distributive interests. They have political power far beyond their numerical strength and the potential to dominate the European agenda.

Moreover, the relationship between national contributions to the EU budget and gains from it plays an important role within the national discourse over the costs and benefits of EU membership. This is particularly true for countries, the so-called net-contributors, which contribute more than they gain (Appendix No. 3 on net-contributions). The visibility of budgetary figures gives the net-contributions a high symbolic value that goes far beyond their actual financial importance. Finally, the EU budget facilitates the progress of integration in other policy areas. Member states achieve unanimous decisions on new integration projects by financially compensating potential losers in the integration process. Without the possibility of side payments through the budget, a consensus on a deepening of European integration would be difficult to achieve, as the treaty revisions of the Single European Act and Maastricht amply demonstrated. Member states that fear the possible costs of further integration would be able to block any progress.[5]

Third, negotiations over the EU budget are linked to the question of what kind of Europe is evolving from European integration. Is it a political system that is oriented mainly towards providing a regulatory framework for a single market with the budget simply as the source for side-payments to facilitate integration; or is it a political community that regards equity and solidarity also as tasks and objectives of the European level?

Yet, beyond the direct political relevance of EU budget budgetary decision-making provides – as a fourth reason – a particularly telling case to examine a key characteristic of European integration: the necessity to balance national sovereignty with supranational authority and the tensions resulting from it. The 1970 budget treaty introduced a decision-making procedure that combined intergovernmental and supranational elements in a unique manner. On the revenue side, decision-making is exclusively intergovernmental. Council decisions, unanimously adopted and ratified by national parliaments, determine the general structure and the upper limit of the revenue. Yet, the exact amount of revenue follows from the level of the annual budget, which is determined by the supranational procedure for the expenditure side. Moreover, the so-called 'own-resources' underline their nominally supranational character.

This combination of intergovernmental and supranational elements in the 1970 budget treaty resulted from the needs and demands of the integration process. Money is a political issue that is very close to national sovereignty and is an area in which member states are reluctant to delegate authority to the EU level. As the European budget simultaneously gains in financial weight and political importance, however, supranational elements become necessary in order to ensure the effec-tiveness and legitimacy of budgetary decision-making: First, budgetary decisions are only effective when the central decision-making body has a degree of autonomy from national authorities, and adopts decisions under qualified majority voting rather than under condition of unanimity. Second, the strengthening of the central level and the introduction of qualified majority voting raises questions regarding the manner in which central spending decisions are legitimated. Member states tend to address this question by involving the European Parliament in the decision-making process (Rittberger 2005).

The conflictual nature of EU budgetary politics in the 1970s and 1980s demon-strates that the complex combination of supranational and intergovernmental elements embodied in the 1970 treaty failed to reconcile the tensions between national sovereignty and central authority. Parliament and Commission constantly sought to enhance the supranational character of the procedure, while member states focused on protecting their sovereignty. Only the 1988 reform finally bridged the gap and resolved tensions. Hence, this reform provides EU research with an interesting role model for the successful combination of supranational and inter-governmental elements.

Despite these interesting features of budgetary politics, the academic literature on the EU budget is mainly descriptive and relatively sparse compared to extensive coverage of other areas of European integration.[6] Thorough analysis of developments in budgetary decision-making and a convincing explanation of variations in the level of conflict has remained an elusive goal. Moreover, much of the existing literature on EU budgetary politics fails to draw on recent developments in social science theory, in particular the rise of new institutionalism. This stands in contrast to the enormous influence that new institutionalism has exerted in recent years over the study of the EU, in particular with regard to analyses of EU legislative politics (e.g. Tsebelis 1994; for literature review see Dowding 2000) and institutional change in the EU (e.g. Falkner 2002; Rittberger and Stacey 2003). My book seeks to close this gap and to present a theoretically informed explanation of variation in the level of conflict and the emergence of institutional change in EU budgetary politics.

The focus

Conflict and change

I draw on Morton Deutsch's classic, *The Resolution of Conflict* (1973), to guide my conceptualisation of conflict in this book. Deutsch regards conflict as a key feature of social interaction and characterises it as a combination of competition for resources, value differences and adversarial relationships. Differences in interests and values create the potential for conflict, the transformation of which into actions and articulated disputes makes it relevant for social interaction. Like Simmel (1955) and Coser (1956), Deutsch assumes that conflict is potentially of personal and social value. Conflict can be beneficial in that it can prevent stagnation, stimulate interest and reveal preference intensity. Conflict is the root of personal, social and institutional change; it aids in the establishment of group and personal identities. As external conflict, it also fosters internal cohesiveness. At the same time, conflict also has negative attributes. It exhausts time and resources, undermines cooperation and the achievement of joint objectives, destroys trust and mutual reliance, and endangers the operation of existing social systems. Ultimately, conflict can lead to violence.

Given the ambivalent role that conflict plays in social interaction, the main focus of Deutsch's inquiry is an emphasis on 'the conditions that determine whether a conflict will be resolved with constructive or destructive consequences' (1973: 8). Conflict has destructive consequences if participants are dissatisfied with the outcomes and if they feel they are net losers in the process. In contrast, a conflict has productive consequences if the participants are satisfied with the outcomes and feel they have gained as a result of conflict. For Deutsch (1973: 17), 'the point is not how to eliminate or prevent conflict but rather how to make it productive'.

In my application of Deutsch's work to conflict in EU budgetary politics, I assume that the difference between constructive and destructive effects of conflict is a question of degree. As long as conflict among actors is kept below a certain level, it plays a positive role in the budgetary process. It reveals the intensity of budgetary preferences and forces actors to find new solutions and to settle upon mutually acceptable compromises. Yet, when conflict escalates beyond a certain threshold, it unfolds its destructive potential. Budgetary actors are unable to fulfil the main function of the budgetary process, i.e. to adopt a stable budgetary agreement. Instead, they either enact budgets that are immediately contested by one of the actors or they do not settle on an agreement at all.

The prominence of conflict and the pressure to keep it at a low level are particularly high in budgetary politics (Rubin 1999).[7] First, budgetary decisions often have zero-sum character, by virtue of which the benefits of one group are the costs of another. The budgetary process has to constantly reinforce the benefits of cooperation, despite the existence of winners and losers. Second, the resulting pay-offs are visible, which intensifies the rivalry between competing interests. Third, the budget process operates according to a clear timetable. The budget is an administrative planning instrument that can only meaningfully fulfil its role when adopted before the beginning of the financial year. This means that space for extensive discussions is limited and pressure to settle high. Fourth, budgetary actors have to agree on a political compromise, as the system of provisional twelfths does not constitute a viable default solution. Hence, a strategy of postponing decisions is not feasible. Fifth, the budgetary process repeats itself every year, thus, unresolved conflict resurfaces annually. As I will illustrate in the following chapters, these characteristics of budgetary politics stimulate the emergence of special mechanisms to contain conflict. Where actors fail to create these mechanisms, conflict escalates and has immense destructive consequences for the functioning of the budgetary process.

In EU budgetary politics, political actors have to tackle conflict in the context of a political system, in which institutional architecture and political boundaries are more fluid than in most nation states. Between the early 1970s and the late 1990s, membership of the EU more than doubled, the political competencies of the central level drastically increased, and the different institutions took on significantly changed roles. Moreover, unlike many of its member states, the EU cannot rely on a unifying force, such as race, nation, language or religion. Where actors do not share a common identity, conflict resolution is difficult – in particular when costs and benefits are not evenly distributed, as in budgetary politics.

The measurability of conflict and its levels is only feasible on the basis of typologies that break conflict down into smaller units. Different types of conflict can be distinguished along three dimensions: the institutional fora, the actors, and the issues (see Table 1.1). Concerning the institutional fora involved, conflict takes place either within the annual budgetary procedure or outside, in an intergovernmental setting. Another typology of conflict is based on the actors involved. Interinstitutional conflict denotes disputes among European institutions, for instance between the EP and the Council. In contrast, intrainstitutional conflict relates to internal differences in the institutions, for instance conflict between member states or disagreements between parliamentary committees. Finally, conflict can also be differentiated on the basis of the conflictual issues themselves. In distributive conflicts, actors quarrel over budgetary outcomes; in institutional conflicts, actors disagree over the introduction of new rules or the interpretation of existing ones.

In this book, the distinction between conflict inside and outside of the annual budgetary procedure plays an important role in structuring the research. This is the case because, more than for the other typologies, a distinction along institutional fora allows me to measure the intensity and frequency of two types of conflict. In Figure 1.3, I concentrate on the destructive consequences of conflict that arose during the annual budgetary procedure. I measure the number of incidences in which actors failed to come to a joint budgetary decision within the given timetable. The measurement builds on four indicators:

- actors' inability to abide by the budgetary timetable, as laid down in the treaty (including the enactment of the provisional twelfths rule);
- actions taken before the European Court of Justice (against the EP);
- rejection of the general budget or a supplementary and amending budget by the EP; and
- member states' refusal to pay their share of the enacted budget.

Table 1.1 Types of conflict

Typology is based on	*Types of conflict*
Institutional forum involved	Conflict within the annual procedure. Conflict outside the annual procedure.
Actors involved	Interinstitutional conflict. Intrainstitutional conflict.
Issues involved	Distributive conflict. Institutional conflict.

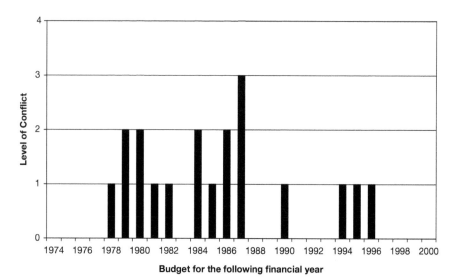

Figure 1.3 Indirect measure of the level of conflict in the annual budgetary procedures between 1974 and 2000.

If all four incidences occurred during a given budgetary procedure, that procedure is given a value of four for that year; conversely, a value of zero is assigned when none of these incidences arose. The picture that emerges from Figure 1.3 underlines the initial observation that between 1978 and 1987, high levels of conflict prevented the adoption of an uncontested budget within the given timetable (almost) every year. After 1988, the level of conflict decreased and the destructive effects became far more sporadic.

Figure 1.4 reveals a fairly similar picture. It measures the number of European summits that were dominated by budgetary questions over time. This measurement builds on the assumption that frequent negotiations over budgetary questions at the highest EU political level reflect the inability of governments to settle their differences (see Chapter 5 for detailed discussion of the measure used in Figure 1.4).

Overall, it can be concluded that there exists an eye-catching correlation between the reduction in the level of conflict and the reform in 1988. In more general terms, a link exists between budgetary conflict and institutional change: institutional change, defined as the introduction of new rules and/or new interpretations of existing rules, seem to have triggered a change in the level of budgetary conflict.

If the 1988 institutional reform was as significant as the data suggests, then it is relevant to identify the factors that led to its emergence, as well as the factors that – despite the high level of conflict in the 1970s and 1980s – fostered the stability of the institutional setting of the 1970 treaty. In this respect, an interesting additional link between conflict and change may emerge: institutional change may not only be a cause but also a consequence of budgetary conflict. As mentioned above,

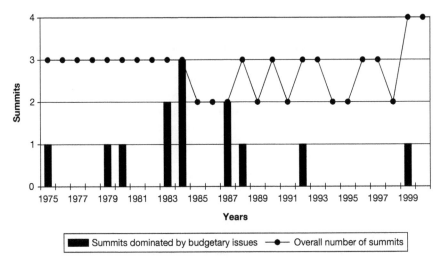

Figure 1.4 Indirect measure of the level of conflict over budgetary issues in the intergovernmental setting between 1975 and 2000.

conflict can often be an important source of change. Disputes over rules can trigger
changes in the rules. In the context of budgetary politics of the 1970s and 1980s,
conflict over the institutional framework will have put the existing rules under
pressure. Failure to accommodate the pressure may have invigorated conflict
further, thus contributing to the overhaul of the institutional framework in 1988.

The framework

Actors, institutions and time

Given the focus on budgetary conflict and institutional change, the book employs
a research framework that assesses the interrelation between actors, institutions and
time. Thereby, it combines 'actor-centred institutionalism', as introduced by Fritz
W. Scharpf (1997, 2000a), with an emphasis on the temporal dimension of political
processes, as advocated by Paul Pierson (2000a,b, 2004).

Scharpf links the level of conflict to three main variables: (1) preferences and
resources of *policy actors*, (2) the *institutional setting of the policy field*, and (3) the external
policy environment and the nature of the *policy problem*. His approach is actor-centred
in that he assumes that all political outcomes can be traced back to choices
and actions of individual or collective actors. At the same time, Scharpf is an
institutionalist in that he sees institutions exerting influence over the behaviour
of actors by setting incentives, shaping preferences, effecting capabilities and
facilitating decisions. As such, the term 'institution' stands for a set of rules that
structure interaction between political actors. It is used interchangeably with the

terms 'rules' or 'institutional settings'. The classic view of institutions as political organisations, e.g. the European Parliament as an EU 'institution', does not conflict with Scharpf's approach. For Scharpf, a differentiation between institutions as actors and institutions as rules is simply a question of perspective. A group of individuals becomes a parliament or a party through rules and procedures that structure their interaction. As political institutions, parliaments or parties are actors in decision-making processes that are governed by rules and involve other political actors.

The institutionalist approach suggests that, by focusing on the institutional setting, the researcher is able to identify factors that determine the level of conflict. Changes in the institutional setting are likely to lead to changes in the level of conflict, as they alter the strategies available to actors.

As much as such an institutionalist explanation is essential for understanding variation in the level of conflict, it constitutes only the first of a two-step process. The focus on institutions as independent variables assumes that institutions are stable within a given period of time and that they are set exogenously. In this formulation, however, the question how institutional change occurs remains unanswered. Over the recent years, institutionalist research has therefore realised that a logical second step is to take institutions as dependent variables and to analyse the factors that bring about institutional change. In order to clarify the two-step character of the research process, institutionalists distinguish between two levels: the *policy level*, at which actors interact within a given institutional setting and bargain over political outcomes ('games within rules'; exogenous rules), and the *institutional level*, at which actors interact and bargain over institutional settings ('games over rules'; endogenous rules) (early examples of this differentiation: Shepsle 1989 and Tsebelis 1990).

The structure of the book reflects this two-step approach. Part I concentrates on the interaction between actors within largely stable rule arenas. It contrasts two institutional settings and assesses their impact on the level of conflict. These two institutional settings correspond with two periods of budgetary politics with relatively stable, but different rules: the first period (1974–1988) was governed by the provisions of the 1970 and 1975 budget treaties, while the second (1988–2000) was structured by rules of the financial perspective and the interinstitutional agreement. Part II of the book performs the second step. It focuses on the stability of the two institutional settings and seeks to explain how actors, in 1988, adopted a far-reaching reform that replaced the original institutional setting of the 1970 treaty with the new rules of the financial perspective and the interinstitutional agreement.

However, inasmuch as the distinction between Part I and Part II relates to the separation between a focus on conflict within stable rules and a perspective on rule change, an important qualification of the two-step approach should be noted. Games within and over rules are often intertwined. Actors that interact within rules soon realise the effects that these rules have on distributive outcomes. Even if actors are not involved in the formal process of rule enactment, they are likely to interact over rules. They will seek to alter the impact of rules by presenting new interpretations or by simply disobeying them. Policy level and institutional level are even more closely connected when actors on both levels are largely identical. Political actors will play both games at the same time, seeking to maximise immediate and future benefits. This means that conflict occurs simultaneously as both distributive conflict and institutional conflict. Institutional change is likely to be preceded by intense distributive and institutional conflict.

This is the point where Pierson's emphasis on time becomes important. Pierson criticises that a rational choice focus on actors, preferences and institutions assumes that institutional choices can be analysed on the basis of a 'snapshot' of the situation when institutional change occurred. Such a perspective neglects the temporal dimension of institutions and the link between the causes and the effects of institutional change. Institutional settings evolve over time. Positive feedback mechanisms and self-reinforcing processes may lock-in existing rules ('path dependence') and create a high degree of 'stickiness' of institutions. The sequencing of events and processes often affects the design of institutions. Thus, Pierson advocates a shift in focus from discrete episodes of institutional 'selection' to an extended time-frame of institutional 'development'. Instead of a 'snapshot', institutionalist research should be based on a 'film' because '[j]ust as a film often reveals meanings that cannot be discerned from a single photograph, a view of Europe's development over time gives us a richer sense of the nature of the emerging European polity' (Pierson 1996: 127). Such a film perspective also prevents social scientists from falling into a common trap, as Pierson points out:

> As social scientists have sought to explain institutional outcomes, there has been a strong tendency to employ 'functional' interpretations in which institutional arrangements are explained by their consequences. In particular, what I term 'actors-based functionalism' typically rests on the claim that institutions take the form they do because powerful actors engaged in rational, strategic behavior are seeking to produce the outcomes observed.
>
> (2004: 14)

By taking into account the interaction between actors and institutions over a longer period of time, factors that lead to the change of institutions can be identified and the seemingly puzzling stability of 'dysfunctional' institutional settings, as one might want to describe the 1970 treaty might, can be explained.

In view of the link between the distributive and institutional conflict and of the temporal dimension of institutional change, Part I of the book does not limit itself to an analysis of distributive conflict on the policy level but includes conflict on the institutional level. It demonstrates that the rules (which govern the policy level and the procedure of rule enactment) are responsible for determining the degree to which institutional conflict accompanies distributive conflict. Subsequently, Part II focuses on the outcomes of institutional conflict. It assesses the extent to which conflict did (or did not) lead to institutional change.

The innovative contribution that the book makes to institutionalist research is rooted in the fruitful combination of the following two aspects. On one hand, the book adheres in its structure to the analytical separation between the effects of institutions and the development of institutions (i.e. 'games within rules' and 'games over rules'). This separation provides for an analytical clarity that a purely chronological perspective on the distributive and institutional developments in EU budgetary politics lacks. On the other hand, it acknowledges the linkage between the running of the institutions and their stability and change. In this latter respect, the book is in line with very recent institutionalist works that seek to overcome the deficiencies of focusing exclusively on discrete periods of institutional change (Pierson 2004; see also Mahoney and Rueschemeyer 2002; Greif and Laitin 2004; Streeck and Thelen 2005). This is particularly relevant for the EU context, where large-scale treaty revision represent only the tip of the iceberg and feedback mechanisms between the creation/reform of institutions and their effect on day-to-day politics exist (e.g. Stone Sweet *et al.* 2001; Falkner 2002; Rittberger and Stacey 2003).

In building on Scharpf and Pierson, the approach of this book is also innovative in another respect: it cannot be easily classified as being part and product of one of the different schools of institutionalism (see for example Hall and Taylor 1996; Schneider and Aspinwall 2001). It acknowledges that the different schools have strengths and weaknesses and advocates a pragmatic use of the different imageries. Moreover, the book keeps to Scharpf's assessment that there are essentially only two schools: rational choice institutionalism and sociological institutionalism. In contrast to Pierson, Scharpf (2000a: 770, Fn 4) views historical institutionalism not as a separate school, but rather as a group of authors who – although sharing a joint interest in the evolution of institutions and path dependence – lean either more toward rational-choice assumptions or toward social-constructivist interpretations.

Scharpf advocates a research design (for both the policy level and the institutional level perspective) that starts with a rational choice-approach and develops propositions based on rational actor assumptions. Taking these propositions as null hypotheses, the design should then account for the deviation between the propositions and evidence by up-dating the explanations on the basis of sociological institutionalism (Table 1.2).

It seems that – in the case of budgetary politics – rational choice institutionalism is particularly well equipped to provide explanations that leave only a small residual for clarification using the sociological method. Assumptions about rationality and self-interest are likely to carry high explanatory value in an area of politics, in which the distributive implications of choices are directly visible and the benefits of one actor are often the losses of another.[8]

The rational choice propositions take into account the specific setting of the political and institutional choice situation. They are based on three assumptions concerning the logic of action, the bases of preferences, and the definition of institutions.

Table 1.2 The up-dating approach to clarify previously unexplained variation in the dependent variable

Null hypotheses: Rational choice propositions	➡	Empirical assessment	➡	*Explaining the residual:* Up-dating of propositions on the basis of sociological institutionalism

1 *Logic of Action.* When making political or institutional choices, individual and composite actors act strategically and rationally following a '*logic of expected consequences*'. This does not mean that actors are always fully informed. Actors' rationality is bound by the complexity of choice situations, high costs of information and a limited time-horizon.

2 *Preferences.* Actors seek to maximise their *material self-interest*. Their preferences can change over time but they are stable within a given bargaining situation.

3 *Institutions.* Institutions constitute *explicit rules* that constrain and direct actors' behaviour. They can vary in the degree to which they are binding and precise, as well as in the extent that they delegate authority to a third party (Abbott *et al.* 2000, Stone Sweet *et al.* 2001). For the purpose of generating propositions, rules are only relevant when they are codified as legal texts or political agreements.

The sociological up-date of the propositions focuses on the perceptions and preferences of the actors. 'In doing so, it is often very useful – in the spirit of Lindenberg's (1990) "method of decreasing abstraction" – to begin by focusing on the institutionalised "norms of appropriateness" that are emphasised by sociological institutionalism (March and Olsen 1989), and to move on to searching for more idiosyncratic normative orientations and identity concepts only when the more stylised institutional hypotheses fail to explain choices' (Scharpf 2000a: 784). This means the definition of institutions is expanded to include informal rules and norms; actors' actions are linked to a 'logic of appropriateness'. This should enable the researcher to explain the residual that rational-choice propositions do not cover.

Method and data

The book focuses on budgetary politics between 1974 and 2000, using 1974, the year in which the new budgetary procedure of the 1970 treaty was first applied, as a logical starting point for a discussion of the contentious budgetary politics of this period. Data collection for this work ends in the year 2000. Though this decision was taken due to the practical need to set a deadline for the culmination of empirical research, the choice of the year 2000 is not completely arbitrary. Employing the year 2000 as a cut-off point allows me to analyse the experience of two annual procedures after the adoption of the 1999 interinstitutional agreement; this is important, as 1999 was a contentious year, and may have signalled the end of the period of low levels of conflict. By contrast, the 2002, 2003 and 2004 budget procedures would have added little to the analysis, as they followed the pattern of low levels of conflict. Current and very recent events, such as the adoption of the European Constitution and the negotiations over the new financial perspective for 2007 to 2013, will be covered in the Conclusion.

Although the book makes a general contribution to the literature on the EU and to institutionalist research, the explanations that I develop are oriented towards the specific empirical context of EU budgetary politics. The assessment of the propositions on budgetary conflict and on institutional change is done on the basis of inter-temporal comparisons. In Part I, the effects of the pre-1988 institutional setting are compared with the effects of the post-1988 institutional setting. In Part II, the stability (and eventual change) of the pre-1988 setting is compared to the continuous stability of the post-1988 setting. Such an inter-temporal comparison between two periods within the same policy field has the advantage of reducing the number of differences (other than institutional settings) for which the research design must control. This is the case because the main characteristics of the policy field and even the actors do not change. Yet, the downside of inter-temporal comparison is, of course, the fact that the two cases are not independent from each other and that actors under the second setting have the experience of the first. The book seeks to counterbalance this disadvantage of inter-temporal comparison by employing a method of 'process tracing'. This method provides a focus on 'the decision process by which initial conditions are translated into outcomes' (George and McKeown 1985: 35, quoted in King *et al.* 1994: 226). By dividing the two periods (namely 1974–1988 and 1988–2000) into shorter episodes, I analyse the mechanisms and trace the processes that determine the differential impact of various factors on the level of conflict (in Part I) and on institutional stability and change (in Part II).

The assessment of the propositions is based on four data sources: (1) interviews; (2) participatory observations; (3) 'hard primary sources' (namely archival material, budgetary and legislative acts and parliamentary debates); and (4) 'soft primary sources' (namely written accounts of the political developments and decisions from journalists, politicians and practitioners).[9]

In the course of the research projects, I conducted over 50 in-depth interviews (see Table 1.3). Many of my interview partners gave highly valuable, detailed and first-hand accounts of the budgetary developments of the 1990s. Yet, over two-thirds of these informants had little direct experience of the 1980s. As a result, they tended to overemphasise the intensity and relevance of current and recent budgetary conflicts. I have attempted to counterbalance this bias, supplementing it with existing written material on the 1970s and 1980s, and a few good accounts from interview partners that had participated in budgetary decision-making in the 1980s.[10]

As primary sources, I used the budget figures (published in the official journal and the EC bulletin), press releases, official decisions, resolutions and reports of the institutions, and parliamentary debates of the European parliament (and in one case of the German Bundestag). I also had access to internal working documents in the archives of the general secretariat of the Council and the European Parliament, as well as detailed coverage of the procedure for the 2000 and 2001 budgets by the Commission. Comprehensive descriptions written by practitioners, many of them published in the German year book *Jahrbuch für Europäische Integration* and the French journal *Revue du Marché commun et de l'Union européenne*, provided an additional, and essential source of information. Finally, budget chapters in the monthly EC/EU-bulletins, newspaper articles and notes from Agence Europe, as well as memoirs and analyses of politicians and officials, e.g. Delors (2004), Thatcher (1993), Howe (1994), Butler (1986), Tugendhat (1986) and Attali (1995), also provided insightful and thought-provoking points for further examination.

Table 1.3 Overviews of interviews

Institution	Position***	Number of interview partners *, **	Number of Interviews*
EP	MEPs.	4	4
	Assistants to an MEP or a parliamentary group.	3	3
	Officials of secretariat general.	6	11
Commission	Officials of the General Directorates.	14	20
	Officials from the cabinet of a Commissioner.	2	2
Council	Officials from the Permanent Representations of member states.	5	6
	Officials of the secretariat general.	1	3
	Officials of the ministry of finance based in the national capitals.	5	4
		Overall: 40	Overall: 53

* The figures for interview partners and interviews vary in some cases, because I sometimes undertook several interviews with one interview partner or (as in two cases) I had more than one interview partner in an interview.
** In three cases, interview partners are counted twice as they have moved from one institution to another and reported on the perspective of both.
*** This refers to the position that interview partners had during the times when they were involved in budgetary decision-making.

Outline of the book

The main structure of the book is based on the division between a focus on conflict in Part I and on institutional change and stability in Part II. As Table 1.4 illustrates, each part follows the above-mentioned up-dating approach and entails three components: the development, the empirical assessment and the final update of propositions.

In Part I, I argue that institutional design can be regarded as a key determinant of the level of conflict in EU budgetary politics. The institutional setting introduced by the 1970 treaty intensified conflict in two respects. First, it prompted conflict by cementing distributive outcomes that were favourable only to one group of actors. Second, it supported the use of confrontational strategies by offering a large scope of interpretation, and giving actors the opportunity to challenge the dominant interpretation of rules. Furthermore, it failed to accommodate distributive and institutional demands of the challenging actors. The 1988 reform, on the other hand, introduced an institutional setting that built on the unanimous support of all actors, limited the scope for interpretation, reduced the relevance of annual decision-making and provided forums for dialogue and regular reviews.

Part I is divided into six chapters. In Chapter 2, I develop a set of propositions about the level of institutional and distributive conflict, based on the assumptions

Table 1.4 Research design and structure

Task/Focus	1. Rational choice institutionalist propositions	2. Empirical assessment of the propositions	3. Up-date of propositions on the basis of sociological institutionalism
Part I: Level of conflict	*Chapter 2* Development of propositions on the level of conflict in EU budgetary politics	*Chapters 3 and 4* Conflict between EP and Council during the annual procedure before and after the 1988 reform Chapters 5 and 6 Conflict among member states in the inter-governmental setting before and after the 1988 reform	*Chapter 7*
Part II: Institutional change	*Chapter 8* Development of propositions on institutional stability and change in EU budgetary politics	*Chapters 9 and 10* Stability of the 1970 treaty setting, the 1988 reform, and the stability of the new institutional setting	*Chapter 11*

of rational choice institutionalism. Chapters 3 to 6 assess these propositions empirically. In each chapter, the value of the independent variable, i.e. institutional setting, is set constant. I assess the value of the dependent variable, i.e. the level of conflict, and subsequently analyse in detail the effect of different factors on the level of conflict. These factors are either control variables, unrelated to the institutional setting (e.g. the economic climate), or variables that are connected with institutional setting (e.g. the scope of interpretation). Such a detailed analysis enables me to analyse the mechanism determining the differential impact of various factors on the level of conflict.

Chapters 3 and 4 concentrate on conflict between the EP and the Council in the annual budgetary procedure. Chapter 3 assesses the level of conflict under the institutional setting of the 1970 treaty. It illustrates the impact of the institutional setting, as well as other factors, on the level of conflict, based on three case studies of annual procedures, namely the budget for 1979, 1982 and 1987. In line with the process-tracing approach, the three case studies illustrate as exemplary how the scope of interpretation (in the 1979 budget), the unity among Members of Parliament (in the 1982 budget), and disunity among member states (in the 1987 budget), incited conflict. Chapter 4 undertakes a similar assessment for the level of conflict under the rules of the financial perspective and the interinstitutional agreement presenting two case studies, namely the budgets for 1995 and 2000. These two cases are particularly challenging for the propositions that I developed in Chapter 2: the 1995 budget was an 'outlier' because the level of conflict briefly increased during the year contrary to the prediction of low levels of conflict. In addition, the 2000 budget is a 'hard case' because Parliament adopted a budget despite strong incentives for rejection. However, the detailed analyses reveal that these two cases are, nevertheless, in line with the propositions introduced in the theoretical chapter.

Chapters 5 and 6 focus on conflict among member states on issues of multi-annual budgeting that fall outside of the annual budgetary procedure. Chapter 5 takes the conflict over Britain's sizeable net-contributions as a case study for conflict under the institutional setting of the 1970 treaty. The British case was selected due to its character as an intensive budgetary conflict that paralysed European politics in the 1980s. Nevertheless, the mechanisms of conflict escalation that the case reveals were representative for budgetary conflict among member states before 1988. The chapter does not cover the full period until the 1988 reform, because the institutional change relevant for conflict over the UK problem occurred already in 1984. Chapter 6 contrasts the British case with the tensions over Germany's large net contributions, which emerged in the 1990s after German unification. The case of Germany's net-contribution is (again) a 'hard case': one would have expected that the level of conflict would rise significantly, because the German and the UK problems were similar in scope. Yet, Chapter 6 demonstrates how the institutional setting of the financial perspective channelled German discontent into the scheduled renegotiation point for the financial perspective and thus prevented the escalation that occurred in the UK case. Chapter 7 summarises the empirical results of the previous chapters and up-dates the rational choice propositions. It contends that the propositions cover large parts of the historical developments, but that informal institutions, such as norms and trust, also played a role in determining the level of conflict.

In Part II, I argue that the analysis of the 'reproduction mechanisms' that stabilised the institutional setting of the 1970s enables me to explain the occurrence of the 1988 institutional change. The bargaining power of the six member states that enacted the treaty, the institutional interdependence between subfields of budgetary politics, and the high switching costs (relative to the opportunity costs) prevented major institutional change for over a decade. When these factors lost force, a reform became possible and the new institutional setting emerged in 1988. Mechanisms similar to the ones that had stabilised the old setting started to strengthen the reformed rules after 1988. Yet, the new setting had an important advantage over the old one. It was functionally superior in that it channelled demands for change into minor institutional adjustments and thus produced outcomes that largely conformed to actors' preferences.

Part II is divided into four chapters. Chapter 8 develops rational choice propositions about institutional stability and change in EU budgetary politics. It is based on path dependence literature, which originates from the works of Brian W. Arthur and Paul David on network externalities (see e.g. Arthur 1994 and David 1985). I identify limits of the current literature and contribute to theory building by deducing testable propositions. I characterise the 1970 treaty and the 1988 reform as starting points of two separate institutional paths. Obviously, such a perspective is contestable, as the 1988 reform did not replace, but simply supplemented the treaty provisions. Yet, the 1988 reform changed fundamental characteristics of the rules governing budgetary decision-making. As such, this reform created a new institutional setting. Moreover, the path dependence approach demands a clear and narrow definition of paths, without which its explanatory power is too quickly reduced to the truism that the past influences the present.

Chapters 9 and 10 assess the propositions empirically. They analyse the impact of the 'reproduction mechanisms' on the stability of the respective institutional setting. Chapter 9 focuses on the stability of the institutional setting that the 1970 treaty introduced and illustrates how the pressure for change finally led to the 1988 reform. Chapter 10 provides with the 1988 institutional setting a comparable case of stability. Yet, it also reveals the extent to which the 1988 setting is better equipped than the 1970 institutional setting to accommodate pressure for change. Chapter 11 returns to theory, summarising empirical results and up-dating propositions. It shows that actors' rationality is often bounded, and that, under certain circumstances, individual politicians are able to 'manipulate' actors' choices.

Chapter 12 concludes the book. It builds on the detailed summaries of the findings in Chapters 7 and 11, and goes beyond the boundaries of the original research question. Linking the results of the book to latest developments in EU politics and in institutionalist research, the chapter discusses the relevance of non-institutional factors for the level of conflict and institutional stability and examines to what extent recent and current events, such as the adoption of the European Constitution and the negotiations over the financial perspective for 2007 to 2013 constitute a challenge to the stability of the 1988 institutional setting.

Part I

Variation in the level of conflict in EU budgetary politics

2   A rational choice-institutionalist explanation of conflict in EU budgetary politics

In this chapter, I develop rational choice-institutionalist propositions about conflict between budgetary actors. The chapter is divided into two sections. The first briefly introduces Scharpf's theoretical explanations of conflict in the policy process. The second will apply this framework to EU budgetary politics and derive a set of propositions.

A theoretical analysis of conflict in the policy process

In his work, Scharpf (1988, 1997, 2000a) analyses the ability of political actors to overcome conflict and to tackle problems imposed upon them by the policy environment. According to Scharpf, the policy environment and resultant problems are largely external to the policy process. Their impact on the level of conflict and policy outcomes is determined by three elements of interaction: actors' orientation and capabilities, actor constellations, and modes of interaction (see Figure 2.1).

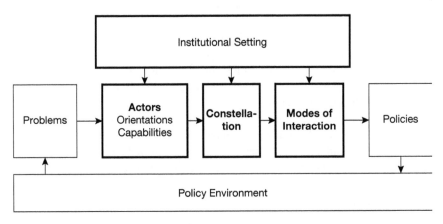

Figure 2.1 The domain of interaction-oriented policy research.
Source: Scharpf (1997: 44)

The policy environment and problems

Actors in the political process face different types of problems. Scharpf (1997: 70) distinguishes between: (1) *coordination problems*, where actors depend on each other to realise benefits; (2) *problems of externalities and collective goods*, when an actor's actions have negative (or positive) effects on other actors; the collective of all actors has an incentive to limit (or increase) the actor's actions to the level at which the aggregate benefits of all actors is highest; (3) *redistribution problems*, where actors lose benefits either through changes in the policy environment or due to political decisions that benefit other actors.

The policy environment impacts on the intensity and characteristics of the problem. Negative economic developments or increases in economic heterogeneity of actors, for example, are likely to intensify redistribution problems. At the same time, collective action problems might be easier to solve when the benefits of a collective action are very unevenly distributed and an actor with a strong interest provides a collective action, regardless of the free riding of others ('privileged group', Olson 1971). Another element of the policy environment is the embeddedness of the policy field within the political and institutional architecture of the political system and the linkage between different policy problems.[1]

Actor capabilities and orientation

Actor-centred institutionalism emphasises the importance of actors. Although institutions play a key role in influencing actors' preference and strategies, they do not determine them. Thus, after having mapped the problem, Scharpf focuses on identifying the relevant actors and on analysing their preferences and capabilities. For the development of rational choice propositions, I assume that material interest is the basic driving force of actors' behaviour. In addition to policy preferences, actors have institutional preferences. Actors prefer those institutional settings that promise to generate preferable distributive outcomes. The relationship between distributive or policy and institutional preferences depends largely on actors' time horizons. The longer the actors' time horizon (i.e. the lower the discount factors), the more dominant her institutional preferences (in comparison to the distributive preferences). Moreover, if the current institutional setting disadvantages the actor then she has a strong interest in altering it (see Knight 1992; Hix 2002). I will return to this issue in the next subsection.

The situation becomes more complex when focusing on composite, rather than individual, actors. Their ability to pursue their preferences depends on their internal cohesion and unity. They have to overcome internal tensions and to trade intertemporal, intersectoral, interpersonal losses and benefits.

Actor constellation

The actor constellation describes the level of potential conflict that exists between actors, given a certain distribution of preferences. Scharpf emphasises the usefulness of a game theoretic perspective: it forces the researcher to narrow the focus and to concentrate exclusively on the relevant actors and available behavioural options (e.g. cooperate or defect). Scharpf presents a series of different actor constellations: games of pure coordination (positive-sum), games of pure conflict (zero-sum), and mixed motive games (e.g. battle of the sexes, prisoner's dilemma and chicken game). In each case, the game matrix gives an indication of the choice and strategies of actors and suggests likely outcomes. Scharpf (1997: 105–107) acknowledges that game theory can rarely predict specific outcomes. Most of the time, multiple equilibria are possible because games entail more than one issue and/or they are repeated games. Yet, an important strength of game theory lies in its ability to specify conditions under which outcomes are likely to be stable and uncontested.

When actor constellations are modelled as repeated games or multi-issue games, the bargaining power and reputation of actors play an important role (Knight 1992). In repeated games, actors may trade the losses of one round against the higher benefits of a next round, gained by building up credible threats or a cooperative reputation. Such strategies depend on the time horizon (i.e. the discount factor of future benefits) and on the salience of the outcome of the current round compared with that of future rounds (i.e. the absolute values of the benefits of each round). Actors will apply similar calculations when considering their institutional preferences. Even if institutions are seen as external, actors might nevertheless try to alter them by linking the policy level ('games within rules') with the institutional level ('games over rules'). To illustrate this point, I briefly introduce here some of the content from the theoretical chapter on institutional change in Part II of this book.

Assuming that the games within rules and over rules are linked and outcomes are measured along two dimensions ('short-term distributive benefits and losses' and 'institutional losses and benefits'), it is possible to assess the impact of actors' time horizon on their strategies. Lindner and Rittberger (2003) show that strongly short-term oriented actors focus exclusively on the distributive outcomes of the current round, regardless of the outcome on the institutional dimension, while strongly long-term oriented actors concentrate only on the institutional outcomes, ignoring the short-term distributive consequences (Figures 2.2 and 2.3 illustrate this argument).[2]

Most actors have time horizons that lie between the two extreme cases. They concentrate on current distributive outcomes, but also aim at harvesting some institutional benefits. It is therefore more appropriate to look at the length of on actor's time horizon relative to that of other actors, rather than at absolute time horizons. In a situation with two actors (i.e. actors A and B), the actor with the longer time horizon, actor A, is likely to pursue a strategy of institutional contestation against actor B with a short time horizon and strong distributive interests (see second cell on the left in Table 2.1). Both actors will be able to settle their differences by agreeing on a compromise that grants A institutional advantages and B distributive gains.[3]

When both actors have similarly long/short time horizons, the potential for conflict is high. In the case of long time horizons, actors are likely to fight over institutional outcomes; while in the case of short time horizons the potential for distributive disputes dominates. Yet, often the two disputes coexist and are not

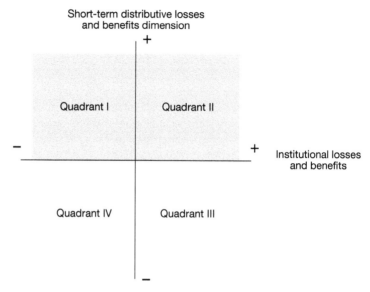

Figure 2.2 Short-term oriented actor.

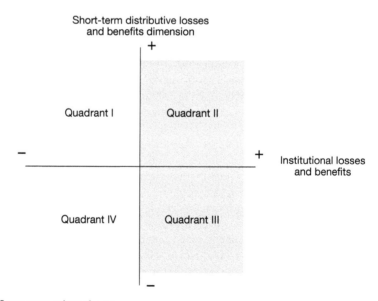

Figure 2.3 Long-term oriented actor.

Table 2.1 The impact of the length of actors' time horizon on the nature and potential of conflict

		Actor A Long-time horizon	Short-time horizon
Actor B	Long time-horizon	Institutional dispute most likely.	Settlement on institutional gains for B against distributive gains for A.
	Short time-horizon	Settlement on institutional gains for A against distributive gains for B.	Distributive dispute most likely.

easily separated, as distributive and institutional benefits are combined. Thus, a distributive dispute may appear to be an institutional conflict over a decision-making rule although both actors are only concerned with the immediate distributive consequences of the current round.

The likelihood of institutional conflict and the possibility of a linkage between the policy level and institutional level are also determined by the cost of institutional conflict and the degree to which actors at the policy level are identical with those at the institutional level. Actors are likely to contest an institutional setting when the benefits of institutional change exceed the costs of contestation. Thereby, the group of actors at the institutional level is not only composed of those who enacted the rules ('enacting coalition'). If the rules are vaguely defined and leave scope for alternative interpretations, actors at the policy level ('implementing coalition') gain power over the institutional setting and a low cost option of contestation. They can alter the rules by applying an 'opportunistic interpretation' that favours their institutional and distributive preferences. Alternatively, policy actors can lobby the group of actors that have the power and authority to alter the institutional setting. They may seek to use bargaining power at the policy level in order to gain support for their demands on the institutional level. Chapter 8 will return to these points.

Overall, the actor constellation indicates the potential for conflict between actors. It reveals the strategic options of actors and the likelihood of a stable and uncontested outcome. The time horizon and the cost of contestation are important factors that determine whether conflict on the policy level spills over to the institutional conflict.

Modes of interaction

Modes of interaction convert game constellations into policy outcomes. They are supposed to 'solve' the conflict that results from the actor constellation and to 'produce' outcomes. Scharpf (1997) differentiates between four modes: (1) unilateral actions; (2) negotiated agreements; (3) decisions by majority vote; and (4) hierarchy.[4]

These modes vary in the autonomy that they ascribe to the individual actor's ability to act unilaterally. In *negotiated agreements*, for example, each actor keeps her veto-power over the final agreement. Therefore, pure zero-sum game constellations cannot be solved within this mode of interaction. But even in positive-sum games, negotiated agreements face the problem of high transaction costs. These costs are associated with monitoring and guaranteeing the implementation of agreements, as well as with the need for simultaneous decisions on value-creation and value-sharing. Value-creation and value-sharing are often described as the tension between efficiency and distribution (Tsebelis 1990). Scharpf (1997: 117) illustrates that the actors' inability to agree on how to distribute the benefits from an efficiency-enhancing joint-action undermines their capacity to undertake the joint-action in the first place (see the 'Negotiator's Dilemma', Lax and Sebenius 1986). Transaction costs associated with overcoming this dilemma and with monitoring subsequent actions increase with the number of actors.

'Joint-decision systems' are a variation of negotiated agreements where 'parties are either physically or legally unable to reach their purpose through unilateral action and in which joint action depends on the (nearly) unanimous agreement of all parties involved' (Scharpf 1997: 143). Here, high transaction costs can turn a negotiated agreement into what Scharpf (1988) calls the 'joint-decision trap', where the beneficiaries of the status quo block attempts to reform the agreement. Often joint-decision systems combine interaction among actors that follows the unanimity rule, with internal procedures of each composite actor, based on majority voting.

Majority rule allows the majority to overcome the resistance of a minority. In contrast to negotiated agreements, decisions by majority vote have the capacity to overcome (re)distributive conflict. An increase in the overall efficacy of the decision-making system legitimates the overruling of the minority. Yet, majoritarian settings become problematic when a stable, self-interested majority rules on the back of a minority. It undermines the acceptance of the policy decisions among the minority and provokes resistance. Although this resistance does not lead to an immediate rise of the level of conflict because the minority cannot block decisions, it may in the long run radicalise the minority and motivate them to use means and ways outside the decision-making procedure. *Hierarchy* is a similar case. On the one hand, it keeps the level of conflict low and reduces decision-making costs. On the other hand, it may lead to resistance among actors that are permanently unsatisfied about the policy outcomes.

Overall, modes of interaction translate the potential for conflict into actual conflict and policy outcomes. Hierarchy and majority decisions are the modes that are likely to produce low levels of conflict. They depend, however, on the acceptance of the actors involved. This is only the case when policy outcomes do not systematically favour one group of actors. In contrast, negotiated agreements enjoy a higher degree of acceptance, as policy outcomes are the result of unanimous decisions. At the same time, the veto-power of each actor drastically complicates attempts to strike compromises, and may lead to long periods of high level of conflict. The situation intensifies the more actors and dimensions are involved in the negotiations.

Propositions on conflict in the EU budgetary decision-making process

In the following section, I apply Scharpf's theoretical explanations to EU budgetary politics and develop a set of rational choice propositions. The section is divided into three parts: first, I will describe the specific nature of the problems in EU budgetary decision-making and the policy environment. Second, I present the actors, their preferences, and the actor constellations in *inter*institutional conflict between the EP and the Council. Finally, in the third part I cease to treat Parliament and Council as unitary actors. Instead, I will focus on *intra*institutional conflict in the institutions and apply Scharpf's concept of 'modes of interaction'.

The policy environment and problems

EU budgetary politics forms part of the political and institutional architecture of the EU and its member states. As such, it is influenced by developments and changes that are external to the policy field. Most of these changes influence the characteristics of the policy problems that actors face, and can also directly affect the interaction of actors.

Actors in EU budgetary politics have to deal with all three types of problems identified by Scharpf: redistribution problems, coordination problems, and problems of collective goods. Budgetary actors have to decide to what extent they want to use the budget to alter the distribution of wealth among member states and among EU citizens. This redistribution problem is often linked to a coordination problem. In the discussion of whether to deepen integration, member states challenge the existing distribution of benefits and costs and demand the (re-)distribution of the benefits of integration. Finally, problems of collective action come into play when budgetary actors discuss whether the EU budget should take up a national policy responsibility that currently constitutes a disproportional financial burden for one member state, while benefiting the whole Union.

The policy environment impacts on these problems in different ways. First, *heterogeneity* among member states in the level of prosperity and in the net-benefits from European integration and the budget[5] is likely to intensify conflict over the existing distribution of wealth and benefits.[6] Heterogeneity can result from differences in economic development and the accession of new poor member states.[7] Second, *economic crises* are likely to increase tensions over distribution. As the EU budget cannot run a deficit, economic crises mean that there is less revenue to cover the expenditure. At the same time, crises in specific sectors of the economy where the European level bears special financial responsibility, e.g. in the agricultural sector, increase demands on the expenditure side. Third, the impact of *political and institutional architecture* of the EU on the characteristic of the problem and the interaction of actors is not uniform. It seems likely that linkages between integration decisions and the budgetary questions ease existing tensions over redistribution by turning a redistribution problem into a coordination problem. Logrolling between decisions on integration and on the budget facilitates budgetary agreements (Weber and Wiesmeth 1991). The budget is used as a source for side-payments, in exchange for support of an integration decision (Folkers 1994, 1998). Fourth, conflict in other policy fields might spill over to budgetary politics or it might detract attention from conflict in budgetary politics. The *link between legislative and budgetary decision-making* is particularly important. Traditionally the same actors control both arenas, because legislative decisions have budgetary consequences and vice versa (Discors 1997). When the actors in both decision-making procedures are not congruent and one actor, such as the EP, is represented in budgetary, but not in legislative decision-making, it seems likely that this actor will (1) protect the budgetary realm against the intrusion from the legislative realm, and (2) try to influence legislative decisions through budgetary decisions. Box 2.1 summarises the propositions.

Box 2.1 Propositions on policy environment and problems

1   Increases in *heterogeneity* with regard to the economic prosperity of member states and of their relative net-benefits from integration and the budget intensify conflict over (re)distribution.
2   *Economic crises* in Europe intensify conflict over (re-)distribution.
3   When linked to budgetary decisions, major *integration decisions* ease existing redistribution problems by turning them into coordination problems.
4   An *asymmetry in the decision-making powers* of the EP in the budgetary and legislative realm leads to clashes with the Council over the separation of the two decision-making procedures.

Interinstitutional conflict between the EP and the Council

The EP and the Council constitute the two arms of the budgetary authority. As such, they must reach a degree of consensus, in order to establish agreement on the budget plan for the following financial year.

Actors and their preferences

The EP has (1) a direct distributive interest (serving special constituencies), (2) a long-term systemic interest (strengthening of the European level in terms of policies delegated from the national level), and (3) an institutional interest (increasing the power of the EP in terms of influence in European decision-making) (Theato and Graf 1994). Within budgetary politics these interests translate into the following objectives: (1) The expansion of the budget, especially in areas in which the EU has not yet assumed political responsibility, mainly non-compulsory expenditure. As the EP does not have a direct responsibility for the revenue side and taxpayers' contributions are not clearly visible, the EP seeks to increase expenditure. (2) The increase of the role of the EP in budgetary decision-making, most importantly in an expansion of the classification of expenditure as non-compulsory and the abolition of the maximum rate of increase. (3) The use of the EP's existing budgetary powers as a lever to influence legislative politics, as long as the EP's power in this area is limited. The relative importance of each of these objectives is influenced by the time horizon of the EP. In selecting its strategy, the EP has to discount future distributive gains, i.e. an increase in its power, and compare it with the immediate benefits that would result from concentrating on financial demands of constituencies. As long as EU expenditure and pressure from constituencies on MEPs remain low, the EP can be assumed to have a long time horizon and a strong interest in enhancing its institutional powers in the decision-making process.

The aggregated preferences of the Council in annual budgetary decision-making are mainly oriented towards stability in the existing distribution of expenditure, i.e. compulsory expenditure, while seeking to minimise expenditure in new policy areas, i.e. non-compulsory expenditure.[8] Among national governments, European own-resources are still largely viewed as national contributions from national budgets. Money that is not committed in the EU budget plans goes back into the national coffers; the Budget Council, composed of national budget ministers, has a general interest in keeping the EU budget low. The Council's interest in institutional issues can be assumed to be lower than that of the EP. Finance officials experience stronger financial pressure from the domestic political arena than the EP and, thus, have a shorter time horizon where the immediate benefits are valued more than future benefits from institutional change. Moreover, the existing institutional setting is closer to the Council's ideal point than in the case of the EP because the Council negotiated the treaty provisions without much involvement of the EP.

Actor constellation

Given the rivalling objectives of the EP and Council, the conflict potential looms large in annual decision-making.[9] The EP wants to increase non-compulsory expenditure while the Council is eager to keep this expenditure low. It is the institutional design that frames conflict potential, and consolidates or accentuates it. According to the treaty, the EP has the last word on non-compulsory expenditure, but this power is significantly limited by the maximum rate of increase of non-compulsory expenditure, which can only be altered in consensus with the Council.[10]

Using the language of game theory, the constellation of the actors resembles that of the one-dimensional 'Battle of the Sexes' (Scharpf 1997: 75). The game is a positive-sum game, in which both actors prefer an agreement on a budget plan to a situation without an agreement.[11] However, the EP wants a high budget solution, i.e. an increase of the maximum rate of non-compulsory expenditure, while the Council seeks to achieve a low budget solution, i.e. no alteration of the maximum rate of increase. Both actors have full information. In contrast to the original 'Battle of the Sexes', the EP and Council do not move simultaneously; the Council makes the first move. As illustrated in Table 2.2, if the Council has opted for a low level

Table 2.2 'Battle of the Sexes' between Council and EP (in a non-iterated game)

		Council	
		High Budget	*Low Budget*
EP	*Reject*	1/1 No Budget	1/1 No Budget
	Accept	4/2 High Budget	2/4 Low Budget

budget and decided not to accept an increase in the maximum rate, the EP can either reject the budget altogether, or accept the low budget solution. In this situation, it will probably opt to accept the low budget, as this generates a higher pay-off. Yet, as the budgetary process can be characterised as an iterated game, which is repeated annually, the EP might opt for a rejection and thus trade lower pay-offs in one year for an overall increase in the credibility of the rejection threat.

The situation changes when the rules for application of the maximum rate and the classification of the expenditure leave scope for interpretation and allow the EP to unilaterally opt for a high budget solution. In circumventing the necessity for the Council's consent for a higher level of non-compulsory expenditure, the EP can adopt a 'high budget', even if the Council opts for a 'low budget'. Table 2.3 illustrates that the option of opportunistic interpretation is most attractive.[12]

However, the use of the opportunistic interpretation option hinges on several conditions: (1) the treaty is sufficiently vague that such an interpretation is possible; (2) the Commission is willing to follow the EP's interpretation and implements the adopted budget; (3) the European Court of Justice fails to limit the interpretation of Parliament and, most importantly; (4) the space for achieving a higher budget via interpretation is not significantly limited by the revenue limit. Figure 2.4 demonstrates the last point: when the gap between the maximum rate of increase and the own-resources does not leave space for achieving a higher budget, the EP is brought back to the original game of Table 2.2 because the balance budget rule prevents the credit-financing of additional expenditure. In this situation, it has a strong incentive to make the Council increase the revenue limit set by the VAT

Table 2.3 The interinstitutional battle when including the option of opportunistic interpretation

		Council	
		High Budget	*Low Budget*
EP	*Reject*	1/1 No Budget	1/1 No Budget
	Accept	4/2 High Budget	2/4 Low Budget
	Interpret	4/2 High Budget	4/2 High Budget

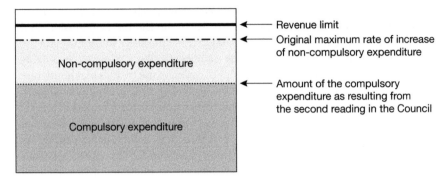

Figure 2.4 The structure of the annual budget and the limit imposed by the revenue
         side.

resources (or since 1988, by the GNP resource) in order to regain its space for the
interpretation option. It is most likely that the EP will try to achieve this by rejecting
the budget.

So far, I have assumed that the EP is mainly interested in relative short-term
distributive benefits. Yet, the longer its time horizon, the more it will trade short-
term distributive losses against longer-term benefits. As illustrated by the 'rejection-
option' in Table 2.3, the EP may be willing to accept a period of 'No Budget' in order
to strengthen the credibility of this option. The longer the time horizon of the EP
and the shorter the time horizon of the Council, the more the EP pushes for
institutional gains, even if they entail short-term distributive losses. The larger the
scope of interpretation offered by the treaty and left open by the ECJ, the more
the EP applies the 'interpretation option', not only in the area of classification and
maximum rate (where distributive and institutional benefits directly coincide), but
also in other areas in which it wants its role and powers enhanced, e.g. the impact
of budgetary decisions on the legislative realm.

Impact of the introduction of the financial perspective[13]

The introduction of the financial perspective in 1988 had a four-fold effect on annual
decision-making: (1) it increased the own-resources ceiling; (2) it limited compulsory
expenditure, which had previously eaten into the space left for non-compulsory
expenditure; (3) it fixed ceilings for five categories which replaced the maximum
rate of increase[14] and thus limited the scope of interpretation; and (4) with the
renegotiations of the financial perspective, it created a forum in which institutional
and distributive negotiations were combined. Not only did the effects of reform
satisfy some of the EP's distributive interests, it also transformed interinstitutional
relations by introducing an additional multi-annual game.

As the multi-annual budget plan is non-binding, its force relies on political
consensus between both actors. If only one or both actors during the annual

decision-making process cease to comply, the financial perspective breaks down. Non-compliance is articulated by adopting an amount that exceeds the ceiling of a category – without previous agreement between the EP, the Commission, and the Council to revise the ceiling. The EP has a strong incentive to comply with the financial perspective when the ceilings lay significantly above a budget obtainable through the 'ordinary' or 'interpretative' application of the treaty's maximum rate of increase. This is particularly the case at the beginning of the multi-annual period, when the financial perspective guarantees higher budgets for a period of several years. One could speculate whether actors at the end of a period of a financial perspective are tempted not to comply and thus to gain short-term benefits by pushing for a budget closer to their ideal point ('end game').[15] Yet, such behaviour could damage their reputation for subsequent renegotiations of the financial perspective. Overall, it seems likely that compliance by both actors constitutes a stable equilibrium.

Dominance of the compliance strategy is further strengthened by the institutional concessions that the financial perspective entails for the EP. When the difference between the treaty provisions and the institutional rights that the interinstitutional agreement grants the EP is considerable, the EP has an additional incentive to comply with the financial perspective. In the case of non-compliance, it would not only lose the distributive, but also the institutional benefits of the financial perspective.

Disregarding these institutional benefits, when the ceilings of the financial perspective come close to what is obtainable through the 'interpretative' or even the 'ordinary' application of the treaty's maximum rate of increase, compliance loses its dominant status. The EP then gains a credible threat. It can warn the Council that it would breach the financial perspective if the Council rejected parliamentary demands for an upward-revision of the financial perspective. As long as the ceilings of the financial perspective lie significantly above the maximum rate, parliamentary demands for a revision are weak, because the threat of non-compliance is not very credible (given the distributive and institutional advantages of the financial perspective), and the EP does not have the option of a unilateral increase in the ceiling, in form of an 'opportunistic interpretation' (given the precision of the institutional provisions of the financial perspective).

Treaty provisions that are not supplanted by the financial perspective provisions of the treaty, such as classification or the separation between legislative and budgetary decision-making, might still be the focus of opportunistic interpretation by the EP. Institutional interests, rather than direct distributive interests, would then motivate these attempts.

Box 2.2 summarises the arguments by presenting a set of propositions. In line with these propositions, the financial perspective is expected to have a conflict-reducing impact by reducing the scope of interpretation and making cooperation within annual decision-making a precondition for its application, and by providing for annual budgets significantly above a budget obtainable through 'ordinary' or 'interpretative' application of the treaty's maximum rate of increase. If the ceilings of the financial perspective do not lie significantly above a budget obtainable through the 'ordinary' or 'interpretative' application of the treaty's maximum rate of increase,

---

Box 2.2 *Propositions on interinstitutional conflict*

1   The stronger the distributive *differences in preferences* between the EP and the Council, the higher the likelihood of conflict.
2   The larger the *scope of interpretation* of the institutional framework, the more likely it is that an EP that is motivated by short-term distributive concerns will choose the '*interpretation option*', if it entails distributive benefits, or the as a second-best the '*rejection option*', if the '*interpretation option*' does not entail distributive benefits.
3   The larger the *scope of interpretation* and the longer the *time horizon* of the EP (relative to the Council), the more likely it is that the EP will choose the '*interpretation option*', even if it does not entail short-term distributive benefits.

---

the propositions suggest that compliance does not constitute the dominant strategy. The EP will either defect directly or issue credible threats that underline its demand for a revision of the financial perspective.

Intrainstitutional conflict and modes of interaction

So far, I have assumed that the EP and Council can be modelled as unitary actors. In the following subsection, I will relax this assumption and focus on internal coordination within these institutions. I will also draw on Scharpf's modes of interaction in order to predict the manner in which change in these modes affects the level of conflict.

EU budgetary decision-making is mainly dominated by the coexistence of two modes: intergovernmental negotiations and joint decision-making. As Figure 2.5 shows, *intergovernmental negotiations* encompass the treaty level, the revenue side, and a small part of the expenditure side, which is otherwise the domain of *joint decision-making*. Both modes have a distinct procedural character: joint decision-making decisions require consensus between the EP and the Council while internal decisions within these institutions are taken by majority vote (and to some extent by hierarchical decision-making). In contrast, intergovernmental negotiations exclude the participation of the EP and give each member state veto-power (unanimity vote).

Internal coordination in the EP

Internal unity of the EP is a prerequisite for conflict with the Council. When the EP fails to agree, the Council's budget is automatically adopted. Yet, unity is not easy to achieve in a Parliament that is (1) divided into different groups, committees, and nationalities; (2) suffers from a considerable level of absenteeism of MEPs in plenary votes; and (3) faces decision-making rules that demand a high degree of internal unity.

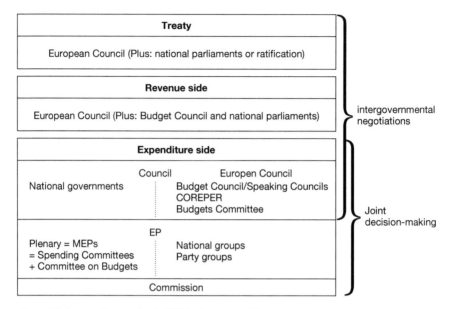

Figure 2.5 Interaction modes in EU budgetary politics.

The EP is composed of 732 MEPs and adopts all its decisions by plenary vote. Debates in plenary are prepared by committees and steered by the president of the EP. Party groups coordinate the work and votes of MEPs and keep them within the party line. MEPs are also part of national groups that exist either formally, as national sections of party groups, or informally, as the collective of all MEPs from the same member states. An MEP has to establish her position and allegiance within this maze of different groups.

Hix (2005: 89) argues that MEPs are motivated by a combination of the objective of reselection and reelection, and the objective of a European career.

The objective of reselection and reelection. Prerequisite for the continuation of an MEP's political career in the EP is reelection. Yet, MEPs face the problem that their work has very little impact on their chances of reelection because European elections are widely seen as second-order national elections, where national rather than European issues determine the outcome of elections (Hix 2005: 193–6). Thus, the reelection of MEPs depends largely on the rating of their national parties. Moreover, as European elections are based on proportional representation and closed lists,[16] one precondition for being reelected is reselection on a position high on the party list.[17] The establishment of this list is largely controlled by the leadership of the national party and based on an MEP's standing within the national party, rather than on its merits earned in Brussels. As long as national parties are largely uninterested in European politics and internal competition for seats is low, reselection is not a major concern for MEPs.

The objective of a European career. Once reelected, MEPs have an interest in enhancing their individual career in the EP ('office goal') and/or realising preferred political outcomes ('policy goal'). The 'office goal' is attractive because a career within the ranks of the EP to a position of a rapporteur, a committee chair, or of a (vice-) president of the EP brings power and prestige. The 'policy goal' is often linked to specific domestic or European constituencies. Such interest groups are important for an MEP as they offer perks and career options for the time after an MEP's retirement from Parliament. The realisation of both the office goals and the policy goals depends on an MEP's standing and work, first in her committee and second, in her EP party group. Therefore, MEPs focus mainly on their day-to-day activities in the committees and the parties.

In budgetary politics, the Committee on Budgets is the Parliament's key actor. It prepares all budgetary debates and decisions. While the Committee confines all of Parliament's budgetary expertise and develops the strategies of the EP, it only remains strong if it can count on the support of the plenary.[18] The prerequisites for support are very high: given the high degree of absenteeism of MEPs,[19] the Committee on Budgets needs a high level of consensus among MEPs in order to achieve the required majority for its proposals. This is especially the case for a proposal for rejecting the budget. Here, the treaty demands a three-fifth majority of votes and a majority of members. In order to achieve the support, the Committee on Budgets has to coordinate itself with the spending Committees and to include some of their distributive demands. It is therefore unlikely that the Committee on Budgets will put forward budgetary proposals that stand in stark contrast to the vested interests of dominant committees, such as the Committee on Agriculture. Moreover, given the consensus among MEPs on the institutional objective of enhancing parliamentary powers, conflict with the Council over institutional issues, such as the interpretation of the treaty, can help the Committee on Budgets to rally support among MEPs for the Committee's budget proposal. Therefore, the Committee emphasises the institutional dimensions of its proposals in order to gain the necessary majority in the plenary.

Two cleavages cut across the committee divisions and influence internal coordination in the EP. First, the relevance of national groups and the influence of national governments (and national parties) on MEPs are likely to complicate the negotiations among MEPs. Second, the impact of parliamentary party groups and the distribution of seats have an ambivalent effect. On the one hand, parties are important for ensuring stable majorities in plenary. On the other hand, the more pronounced the role of parties and political positions, the more difficult it is to gather the necessary majority, and the more important the distribution of seats for the choice of strategy in the EP, and subsequently for the level of conflict with the Council.

The conflict-reducing effect of the financial perspective becomes even more pronounced if the internal coordination in the EP is taken into account. Spending Committees are not willing to endanger the multi-annual period of guaranteed high budgets. Moreover, with the increase of legislative powers, MEPs lose interest in the institutional strategies of the Committee on Budgets.

Intrainstitutional conflict in the Council

Internal coordination in the Council is more complicated than in the European Parliament, because of the coexistence of, and rivalry between large numbers of political and bureaucratic actors. Within the joint decision-making system of the expenditure side, the Budget Council takes budgetary decisions on the basis of qualified majority voting. Before the budget plan reaches the Budget Council, it has gone through a hierarchy of preparatory stages. The Council's Budget Committee, consisting of the finance attachés from the national representations, discusses all budget lines and – in agreement with their superiors in the national finance ministries – delegates the outstanding issues to Coreper, which in turn leaves only highly contentious political decisions for discussion in the Budget Council. The institutional self-interest of the Budget Committee sets incentives for the finance attachés to clarify as many problems as possible on the Committee level, as this guarantees a high degree of autonomy from Coreper and the Budget Council (on Council committees, see Beyers and Dierickx 1998). On a horizontal level, the Budget Council competes with the spending Councils, which try to pre-commit budgetary decisions by legislative acts. Apart from the coordination mechanisms between finance ministers and spending ministers in the national governments, the Budget Council has little power over dominant spending Councils, such as the Agriculture Council, which are able to pre-commit budgetary resources through legislative decisions.

Only the European Council stands above the horizontal rivalry among the different Councils (Hayes-Renshaw and Wallace 1997). It frees issues from the grip of the specialists in the sectoral Councils and allows for the combination of different policy fields. Its impact on the expenditure side constitutes an intergovernmental 'interference' into joint decision-making. Given the zero-sum character of redistribution, the interference of the European Council ensures that decisions with a major redistributive impact are taken by unanimity. Through its position above the different policy fields, the European Council facilitates decisions through package deals. Thus, it transforms zero-sum budgetary decisions into positive-sum deals and combines value-sharing with value-creating. Decisions on the revenue side are also made exclusively within an intergovernmental mode,[20] as are agreements on the treaty level, where the institutional rules of the budgetary decision-making procedure are set and major delegation decisions are taken.[21]

However, these functional divisions in the Council should not blur the perspective on the important cleavage between national interests. Despite the introduction of own-resources and the European character of expenditure, member states form their preferences on the basis of net-benefits of the EU budget. As a result, major *intra*institutional conflict within the Council evolves between net-contributors and net-beneficiaries. Broadly speaking, member states that pay more into the budget than they receive (net-contributors) have a strong interest in reducing the budget while member states that receive more than they contribute (net-beneficiaries) have an interest in increasing the budget.

Aggregate budget figures give an indication, but do not provide the full picture of national preferences.[22] It is important to combine the national perspective with the functional divisions between finance ministers, spending ministers, and Heads of State or Government, as well as to assess the impact of different elements of the budget on domestic politics. As assumed above when describing the Budget Council's preferences, national finance ministers are generally driven by an interest in keeping the European budget low. All money that is spent as part of the European budget escapes the direct control of finance ministers and is therefore 'lost' for them (von der Vring 1996). Yet, finance ministers defend spending lines or programmes that disproportionately benefit their country in relation to the country's contribution to the EU budget. This money constitutes extra money that defuses the pressure on national budgets. It is easier for a country that bears a small share of the budget to reach this point than it is for a country that contributes a large share. So, finance ministers are likely to have a general bias in favour of keeping the budget low, but they have a selective interest in the spending programmes/budget lines that benefit their country and fiercely defend them.

The budget figures translate differently into national preferences when spending ministries are involved (see Scharpf's distinction between 'generalists' and 'specialists' 1988: 270–271). They are not concerned about their country's position as net-contributor or net-beneficiary. Largely captured by domestic interest groups, spending ministries in the sectoral Councils see European money as additional resources that must be guarded against cuts by Budget Council.

Heads of State or Government play a role that places them between their finance ministers on the one hand, and the spending ministers on the other. They are neither judged exclusively against their ability to control the national budget and to keep taxes low, as their finance ministers are, nor are they fully captured by interest groups, as their spending ministers might be. Their take of national preferences comes closest to Putnam's two-level game (Moravcsik 1993, 1997; Putnam 1988).[23] They have to balance the interests of domestic interest groups, especially those that are pivotal for reelection, against voter frustration that stems from high contribution to the EU budget.

Following Robert Putnam's two-level game model, domestic politics does not only determine national preferences, which the Head of State or Government represent in international negotiations, the government can also use domestic politics strategically (Putnam 1988). 'Tying one's hands' is a strategy through which a government commits itself domestically to the achievement of a specific political objective, e.g. reducing a country's contribution to the EU budget. This domestic commitment increases the bargaining power of the government in the international negotiations, because it can credibly claim that it cannot accept any outcome other than the one promised domestically (Moravcsik 1993; Schneider and Cederman 1994).

In general, national preferences are relatively stable, regardless of changes in government. Spending ministries remain captured by the same interest groups and the new finance minister is, as much as the old one, eager to establish her control over the budget. However, a newly elected Head of State or Government might shift the balance between different interests and favour those that are most pivotal for reelection. Elections also affect the time-horizon of member states. The closer the election date, the shorter the government's time-horizon.[24] Moreover, changes in a country's economic climate, in its socio-economic structure, and in the mobilisation of interest groups can alter national preferences. The structure of European decision-making also has an impact on national strategies. The member state that presides the Council has an incentive to subordinate its national preferences to the common interest of the Council for the period of its presidency (Hayes-Renshaw and Wallace 1997). The political benefits of a successful presidency outweigh the possible losses from not sufficiently defending the national preferences.

During the annual budgetary process, internal conflict among national governments does not weaken the Council, as long as the qualified majority can be secured by a stable coalition of member states. As Scharpf illustrates, such a stable majority can exploit a small minority. The problem arises when the minority gains the bargaining power that enables it to block qualified majority decisions. Then the majority loses its capacity to adopt decisions, while there is no new majority to replace the old. Although all member states prefer an agreement to no agreement, both sides try to steer the outcome towards their respective ideal points. This internal conflict can totally block the Council's internal decision-making process. In contrast to the EP, where disunity automatically leads to the adoption of Council's draft budget, failure of the Council to establish a draft budget in the first reading stops the annual budgetary procedure. Moreover, disunity among member states encourages the EP to pursue a confrontational strategy.

Conflict among member states also occurs outside the annual budgetary procedure in the intergovernmental setting. A member state that feels disadvantaged from the existing distributive order, but that does not have the bargaining power to block the majority of member states in annual decision-making will raise its demands in the intergovernmental setting, in particular at the European Council level, where decisions are largely based on consensus and unanimity. In linking its demands with a unanimous decision, the member states may gain the necessary veto-power to achieve distributive change. Decisions on treaty revisions and changes of the structure and limits of revenue sources provide the most conducive opportunities for these links. In the case of the revenue side, the joint decision-making system of the expenditure side clashes with the intergovernmental negotiation mode of the revenue side when the majority in the Budget Council accumulates expenditure decisions that exceed the revenue ceiling. Now, the majority depends on the unanimous agreement of all member states. In this situation, the previously disfavoured member state(s) gains a veto-power and the ability to demand distributive adjustments that have been rejected under qualified majority voting. The result can be a stalemate between a majority that is not willing or able to reduce its expenditure policy, and a minority (which, in an extreme case, consists of one member state) that refuses to accept an increase of the revenue (in form of an upwards correction of the VAT ceiling).

Impact of the financial perspective

The institutional and distributive setting of the financial perspective significantly alters the situation in the Council. It reduces intrainstitutional conflict by adjusting the relationship between the intergovernmental and the joint decision-making mode. The multi-annual budget plan, adopted by the European Council, strengthens the intergovernmental impact on the expenditure side and thus prevents a situation of persistent exploitation of a minority. It channels distributive demands to designated renegotiation points, namely the European summits, when the multi-annual budget plan is adopted and renewed. At the same time, it enables the joint decision-making system to regain its function of solving tensions on the expert level of Council Committee, as it reduces the significance of the annual decision-making. Brussels-based national finance attachés share an interest in finding a solution. Concerning the specific conflict situation of 1988, the financial perspective eased tensions because (1) it limited the rise of the expenditure for the Common Agricultural Policy by introducing an upper ceiling, (2) it satisfied the distributive demands of the minority, (3) it linked annual spending decisions with the revenue side and ensured the resources match expenditure.

The adjustment of the intergovernmental and the joint-decision-making mode in the 1988 reform also includes an interinstitutional dimension. The embeddedness of the financial perspective in an interinstitutional agreement between Commission, Council, and EP expands joint decision-making into the area of intergovernmental decisions. Although the EP has *de facto* only limited power to alter the financial perspective once the European Council has adopted it, the EP can *de jure* veto the expenditure categories and the own-resource ceilings. Thus, it gains the right of participation in the revenue side. Moreover, negotiations over the interinstitutional agreements give the EP an opportunity to codify its interpretation of the treaty provisions and to alter the institutional setting of the decision-making process, which *de jure* belongs to the confines of the intergovernmental treaty negotiations. Overall, in including the EP in the intergovernmental negotiation mode, the original tension between intergovernmental negotiations and joint-decisions-making is eased.

Box 2.3 summarises the arguments by presenting a set of propositions. In line with these propositions, the financial perspective is expected to reduce conflict by increasing unity in the Council and by weakening the unity among MEPs behind a confrontational strategy. It affects the unity of the Council positively through: (1) strengthening the intergovernmental impact on the expenditure side and thus preventing a situation of persistent exploitation and subsequent retaliation of a minority; (2) enabling the joint decision-making system to regain its function of solving tensions on the expert level of Council Committees; (3) linking the different subfields of budgetary politics, i.e. the CAP, the expenditures side and the revenue side, and centralising the decision-making process; and (4) channelling distributive demands into designated renegotiation points. Moreover, the financial perspective impacts negatively on the support within the EP for a confrontational strategy through extending the participation of the EP into the realm of intergovernmental decisions and through meeting the EP's distributive and institutional preferences.

Box 2.3 Propositions on intrainstitutional conflict

The European Parliament

1   Assuming a divergence of preferences between the two arms of the budgetary authority, the more *united* the MEPs, the more likely is conflict between EP and Council.

2   MEPs are likely to stand united behind a confrontational strategy when this strategy (a) concentrates on *institutional objectives* of the EP and (b) is in line with the *interests of the key spending committees*.

The Council

3   The stronger the *unity* among member states in the Council, the more difficult it is for the EP to succeed with a conflict strategy, and thus the less likely is conflict between the Council and the EP.

4   Conflict among member states within the *annual procedure* is prevalent when differences in *preferences* and *time horizons* among member states are pronounced and a *blocking minority* is able to prevent internal agreements.

5   Conflict among member states *outside the annual procedure* is prevalent when member states with *preferences* that differ strongly from those of the majority of member states have to establish a *veto-power* in the intergovernmental setting.

The role of the Commission

It is difficult to predict the impact of the Commission on the level of conflict from its institutional role. The Commission presents the preliminary draft budget and thus sets the agenda for subsequent negotiations between the Council and the EP. During the negotiations, the Commission acts as a mediator between the two sides and tables compromise proposals. However, the two arms of the budgetary authority do not have to take the Commission's advice and proposals into account. In contrast to legislative decision-making, the Commission cannot withdraw its budget proposals and the Council and the EP are basically free to adopt a budget of their choosing.[25]

This does not mean that the Commission is not influential in determining the budgetary outcomes. Large parts of the EU budget are allocated incrementally and adopted according to the wishes of the Commission. The key question is, however, can the Commission prevent an escalation of conflict over contentious spending lines by skilful agenda-setting and mediating? It seems that the answer lies with the reputation and credibility of the Budget Commissioner and her directorate-general. In areas of high uncertainty, when the link to the implementation of the budget is strong and technical knowledge is necessary, the Commission might be able to present proposals that are acceptable and convincing for both sides (Moravcsik 1999). The impact is highest when proposals have not yet reached the political stage, but remain on a bureaucratic level where close contacts among budget expert gives the Commission the opportunity to play on its information advantages. Alternatively, long-term reform proposals for the political stage allow the Commission to set 'focal points' for subsequent negotiations (on 'focal points', see Schelling 1960). In any case, assets such as information advantages and neutrality lose their value when national governments and the EP regard the Commission as partial and have reasons to question the accuracy of its figures and information.

The financial perspective strengthens the role of Commission as a long-term agenda setter and interinstitutional moderator. Concerning the first, the financial perspective gives the Commission the right of initiative for renegotiation proposals and for the revision proposals. It also grants the Commission a veto in the adoption of the interinstitutional agreement. Renegotiation proposals for the financial perspective is certainly an area of high uncertainty, in which the Commission not only influences actual political outcome, but can also reduce tensions between the two arms of the budgetary authority and among member states. Concerning the role as interinstitutional moderator, the influence of the Commission increases through the de-politicisation of budgetary annual decision-making and the strengthening of the role of experts, which is likely follow from the introduction of the financial perspective.

However, all this relies on the assumption that the Commission has a strong interest in reducing the level of conflict. This assumption seems justified, because, as the institution responsible for implementation, the Commission wants to start the financial year with an uncontested budget in order to cover its administrative expenses, and to fulfil the Union's expenditure commitments. Yet, interest in reducing conflict may conflict with the Commission's other distributive and institutional interests, which are usually close to the positions advanced by the EP. In determining the prevalence of these different interests for the strategy selection of the Commission, time-horizon is likely to play a role. At the end of its mandate, the college of Commissioners might be most oriented towards short-term interests (rather than building up the reputation as impartial mediator), although this largely depends on the individual Commissioner's career plans and prospects for a second term.[26]

Box 2.4 *Propositions on the role of the Commission*

1   When the Commission has gained a *reputation* of a credible and impartial mediator it can reduce the level of conflict.
2   When negotiations are kept on the *expert level* (rather than on the political level), the Commission can exert a large amount of influence on the decision-making process.
3   The higher the *uncertainty* and *technical speciality* of issues, the higher the potential that the Commission will play a mediating role.

Box 2.4 above summarises the arguments by presenting a set of propositions. In line with these propositions, the financial perspective is expected to reduce conflict by extending the rule of experts and by providing the Commission with the agenda-setting power for the multi-annual budget plan.

Conclusion

In this chapter, I developed propositions concerning the level of conflict among actors in EU budgetary politics. As summarised in Table 2.4, I identified different variables likely to affect the level of conflict. I argued that the introduction of the financial perspective significantly affected the values of these variables and thus reduced conflict.

In order to assess the explanatory power of this argument and the propositions derived from it, I will, in the following four chapters, closely analyse budgetary decision-making before and after the 1988 reform. I distinguish between two types of conflict. First, conflict between Parliament and Council within the annual budgetary procedure (in Chapters 3 and 4). Second, conflict among member states in the intergovernmental setting outside the budgetary procedure (in Chapters 5 and 6). The distinction between these two types is useful for the analysis, as they allow me to break down the overall level of conflict into smaller empirical phenomena, which I can attribute directly to the institutional fora in which conflict occurred.

Table 2.4 Variables that influence the level of inter- and intrainstitutional conflict

Variables	Correlation with conflict	Conflict-reducing impact of the financial perspective
The policy environment		
Heterogeneity among member states	+	
Economic crises and low prices on the agricultural markets	+	
Institutional structure of neighbouring policy fields and EU's overall political architecture	+/−	
Preferences and unity of actors		
Differences between EP and Council in preferences	+	Creates congruence by combining institutional and distributive negotiations at the renegotiation points.
Differences between EP and Council in time-horizon	−	Reduces unity as it guarantees expenditure for spending committees.
Internal unity of the EP	+	Increase unity because of commitment to unanimous decision.
Internal unity of the Council and linkage of the different expenditure elements	−	
Bargaining power for member states that demand distributive change	+/−	Forecloses the exploitation of minority by stable majority and directs distributive demands into renegotiation points where each member state has veto-power.
Credibility and reputation of the Commission	−	Provides opportunities for the Commission to gain credibility by granting agenda-setting power over the multi-annual budget plan and by increasing the rule of experts.
Institutional setting		
Scope of interpretation	+	Reduces the relevance of the maximum rate and the overall scope of interpretation.
Relevance of annual decision-making	−	Transfers key budgetary decisions outside the annual budgetary procedure.
The existence of a separate forum for conflict	−	Introduces forum for conflict-resolution.

3 Obstructing decision-making

Conflict between Parliament and Council in the annual budgetary procedure (1974–1988)

This is the first of four empirical chapters, in which I assess the explanatory value of the propositions introduced in Chapter 2. The preceding chapter focuses on conflict between Parliament and Council that occurred in the annual procedure between 1974 and 1988. It is divided into three sections. Each section covers a period of approximately five years: the first focuses on the introduction of the new budgetary procedure and the earliest experience with it (1974–1978); the second analyses the manner in which the first directly elected EP used its budgetary powers (1979–1983); the third concentrates on the developments between the second direct election in 1984 and the institutional reform in February 1988. The decision to take the two direct elections as a dividing line between the three separate periods is based on two assumptions. First, the division into several subclasses of annual budgetary procedures within the same institutional setting allows me to compare, and to assess in detail the impact of non-institutional variables on the level of conflict. Second, as the first direct elections in 1979 are usually seen as an important non-institutional factor that increased the level of conflict, a distinction between budgetary decision-making before and after 1979 is appropriate for assessing the actual impact of the direct elections. Although the second direct elections in 1984 were less relevant, they feature here as the starting point for the third period, because, for the sake of comparison, I wanted to have three periods of similar length.

The situation between 1974 and 1978

Tensions become conflict

Most analyses of budgetary conflict between the EP and the Council regard Parliament's first direct election in 1979 as the starting point of conflict (e.g. Theato and Graf 1994: 70; Commission 1995: 16). As Figure 3.1 illustrates, such a view fails to take into account tensions that occurred before 1979. The figure gives an indication of the level of conflict between 1974 and 1978 by measuring the ability of actors to settle their differences over the annual budget within the timetable of the treaty.[1] It shows that, by 1978, tensions between Parliament and Council had already led to the adoption of a budget that was contested by member states. However, inasmuch as Figure 3.1 invalidates standard accounts of EC budgetary

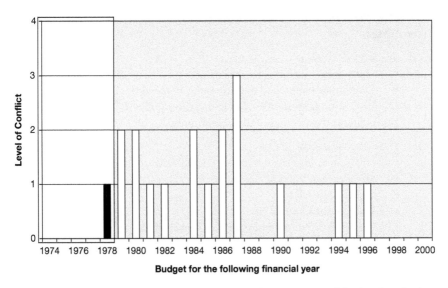

1978: Three member states refused to pay their share of own-resources following the adoption of the 1979 budget, which exceeded the maximum rate of increase.

Figure 3.1 Conflict in the annual budgetary procedure between 1974 and 1978.

politics, it also seems to challenge the institutionalist approach introduced in Chapter 2. This approach assumes that the high levels of conflict in the 1980s resulted from the institutional setting introduced by the 1970 budget treaty. Hence, we would expect conflict to dominate from the first application of the new decision-making procedure in 1974. In view of this, Figure 3.1 raises two questions: Why was the level of conflict lower during the years that immediately followed the introduction of the new procedure? And what triggered the adoption of the first contested budget in 1978 half a year before the direct election?

This section seeks to provide answers to these two questions, first assessing the values of the variables identified in Chapter 2, as well as their impact on the level of conflict. The assessment follows the sequence illustrated by Box 3.1. The section then turns to a detailed analysis of the procedure for the 1979 budget and explores the factors that triggered the escalation of conflict. The 1979 budget is examined due to its empirical relevance as first contested budget and because it illustrates the mechanisms through which a large scope of interpretation led to an escalation of tensions between budgetary actors. The section concludes with a brief summary and a discussion of empirical aspects unaccounted for by the propositions introduced in Chapter 2.

Box 3.1   Structure of the assessment of the different variables

(a)   *The policy environment*
- Heterogeneity among member states
- Economic climate and developments of the agricultural markets
- Institutional structure of neighbouring policy fields and overall political architecture of the Community

(b)   *Preferences and unity of actors*
- Differences in preferences between EP and Council
- Difference in the time horizons
- Unity of the EP
- Unity in the Council
- Credibility and reputation of the Commission

(c)   *Institutional setting*
- Scope of interpretation
- Relevance of annual decision-making
- The existence of a separate forum for conflict

Assessing the values of the variables and their impact on the level of conflict

THE POLICY ENVIRONMENT

Heterogeneity among member states, the economic climate in the Community, and the institutional structure of the neighbouring policy fields increased the potential for conflict. These factors also changed the actual level of conflict by affecting the unity of the Council and the preferences of member states.

The heterogeneity among member states in terms of absolute wealth and net-benefits from integration increased considerably with the accession of Ireland, Great Britain and Denmark in 1973. Most of the tensions resulting from this increase occurred within the intergovernmental setting outside the annual procedure (see Chapter 5). Nevertheless, they slightly weakened the Council's internal unity in negotiations with the EP. Great Britain joined Italy as an (temporary) ally for a strengthened regional policy, and as an opponent of the existing Common Agricultural Policy (CAP) (Wallace 1977). Both member states had a GDP per capita below the Community's average and benefited little from agricultural expenditure, Britain because of its small agricultural sector and Italy due to the CAP's bias towards Northern agricultural products.

The significant slow-down of economic growth and the rise in public debts that member states experienced after the mid-1970s had an impact on the preferences of finance ministers in the Council. They voiced a strong interest in keeping the rate of increase of the EC budget low. At the same time, low world market prices for agricultural products and growing levels of overproduction boosted the Community's agricultural expenditure.

The separation between budgetary and legislative decision-making procedures introduced by the 1970 treaty gave rise to significant tensions between Parliament and Council (Discors 1999). The institutions took opposing approaches towards the delineation between, and hierarchy of the two procedures. The Council regarded the legislative procedure as the key forum for decision-making, while the EP saw the budgetary procedure as a forum of equal political importance. The treaty's large scope of interpretation allowed both institutions to insist on their respective positions and led to repeated clashes over the issue (e.g. in the procedures over the 1977 budget and the 1978 budget, see Strasser 1977: Fn 21 and 1978: 24).

PREFERENCES AND UNITY OF ACTORS

The preferences and expectations of the EP and the Council diverged considerably. On the distributive level, the EP sought to adopt new spending policies and to adjust the balance between the expenditure of the CAP and the other parts of the budgets. Encouraged by the MacDougall Report (European Commission 1977), the EP regarded budgetary expansion as politically necessary and economically efficient. In contrast, the Council was very sceptical about budgetary expansion, which it viewed as additional pressure on already strained national budgets.

On the institutional level, the EP sought to extend and to strengthen its political powers. It condemned the limitations of its role in budgetary decision-making and demanded the delegation of further political powers, most importantly in the legislative realm. As long as Parliament was excluded from legislative politics, MEPs regarded their budgetary powers as a lever for influencing legislative decisions. Unsurprisingly, the Council did not share Parliament's institutional objectives. The Council did not foresee further transfers of power to the EP and it viewed the Parliament's role in budgetary politics as deliberately limited (Giraudy 1975). As previously mentioned, this translated into the Council's insistence on the superiority of the legislative realm, where it still exercised exclusive decision-making powers. Prerequisite of any budgetary act was, in the eyes of the Council, the existence of a legislative decision that introduced a legal base for the expenditure decision.[3]

In the procedure for the 1977 budget, the different approaches clashed. A parliamentary resolution strongly criticised that the Council acted as a 'book keeper' in the budgetary process. Using the budget as accounting device, the Council would simply note the budgetary consequences of decisions made in the legislative realm and would fail to regard the budget as a political instrument in its own right (EC-Bull. 9–1977: 74).

Despite the frustration among MEPs over the Council's stance, Parliament achieved, at least on the distributive level, some of its objectives. The actual rates of increase of non-compulsory expenditure lay considerably above the maximum rates of increase as calculated by the Commission at the beginning of each budgetary

Table 3.1 Actual rate versus original maximum rate of increase for non-compulsory appropriations for commitments *

Year (Budget)	Actual rate of increase of non-compulsory expenditure	Original maximum rate of increase as calculated by the Commission
1974 (1975 budget)	40.8%	14.6%
1975 (1976 budget)	44.29%	15.3%
1976 (1977 budget)	28.67%	17.3%
1977 (1978 budget)	23.35%	13.6%
1978 (1979 budget)	35.02%	11.4%

* This includes dissociated and non-dissociated appropriations of the general budget, as well as amending and supplementary budgets.

Source: Fugmann (1992: 399).

procedure (see Table 3.1). Yet, the rate related only to a small part of the budget, as the vast majority of expenditure was still classified as compulsory.

Another reason why distributive gains failed to satisfy Parliament was the prominence of institutional objectives among MEPs. Most MEPs understood themselves as supranational lobby, charged with strengthening the European level and the influence of Parliament (Kohler 1978; Coombes 1979: 33). They were less interested in the immediate effects of budgetary decisions. A European budgetary clientele had not yet emerged (with the exception of the agricultural lobby) and MEPs saw their seat secured through their membership in national parliaments. In contrast, governments were often slightly more short-term oriented. In 1978 budget, for example, the EP fought with the Council over expenditure for the regional fund. After intensive debates, the EP withdrew its distributive demands in exchange for a symbolic institutional concession from the Council (Strasser 1978: 18).

Institutional objectives also played an important role in unifying Parliament. The Committee on Budgets, which was the dominant committee in Parliament, used the unity on institutional issues strategically. In painting the picture of a common enemy, the Committee presented most budgetary disputes with the Council as institutional conflicts over the role of Parliament in EC politics. Already in the first application of the new procedure in 1974, budget experts portrayed the dispute over the classification of the regional fund as a 'defence of the rights of the EP' (Strasser 1975: 86; EC-Bull. 5–75: point 2402).

However, the Committee on Budgets could not build on unlimited unity. It faced internal opposition to its strategies, regarded by some MEPs as too confrontational. In the case of the procedure for the 1979 budget, for example, plenary did not endorse all aspects of the Committee's confrontational strategy (see the case study below). Occasional reluctance of MEPs did not, however, follow pressure of national governments, but tended to result from their own political preferences. Some MEPs, in particular the French and British, did not share the general enthusiasm for federalist ideas of a strong EP.

The Council managed to confront Parliament with a relatively united stand during most of the annual procedures. Tension over demands for correction mechanisms and the introductions of new spending policies were kept largely outside annual decision-making. However, tensions spilled over during the procedure for the 1979 budget when the UK and Italy took a stance against other member states and supported a parliamentary amendment that was in line with their distributive interests (see case study below). Moreover, the discrepancy between the flowery rhetoric of European summit declarations on the future of Europe and the actual decisions of the Budget Council, as well as the open ignorance of the Agriculture Council towards the austerity approach favoured by the Budget Council, provided Parliament with political ammunition for its distributive and institutional demands.[4]

While the intensity of interinstitutional relations between Parliament and Council gradually increased, the Commission had only limited influence on the level of conflict. Although its impact on the distributive outcomes was considerable, the Commission failed to bring Parliament and Council together or to close the gap between the different legal interpretations put forward by each side. Moreover, it did not manage to build up a reputation as a neutral and honest broker, encouraging the EP's distributive attacks out of sheer self-interest. It presented preliminary draft budgets that exceeded the maximum rate of increase and took sides with the EP against the results of the readings in the Council. To the applause of MEPs, the Budget Commissioner condemned final annual budgets as 'depressing', 'banal' or 'disappointing' every year after 1976 (Strasser 1977: 131). With regard to the institutional objectives of the EP, on the other hand, the Commission pursued an ambivalent strategy. The Commission criticised the interpretations put forward by the EP during the budgetary negotiations, but accepted and implemented the contested budget as soon as the EP adopted it (see the case study below).

INSTITUTIONAL SETTING

The wide scope for interpretation allowed by the treaty provisions was apparent soon after its first application. As the following overview illustrates (see Box 3.2), the scope of interpretation caused recurring annual tensions between the Parliament and Council that culminated in the adoption of the first contentious budget in 1978.

Despite these tensions, annual decision-making was the key forum for inter-institutional interaction between the EP and the Council; its importance transcended the realm of budgetary politics. For the EP, it was the only arena in which it could demonstrate its impact on European decision-making. Therefore, conflict in budgetary politics was a partial surrogate for Parliament's interest in challenging the Council in other areas of European decision-making. Yet, with regards to intrainstitutional conflict within the Council, discussions were largely kept outside annual budgetary decision-making and held at the intergovernmental level (see Chapter 5).

Case study: The adoption of the 1979 budget

The 1979 budget was the first budget process in which budgetary actors were unable to contain conflict within the boundaries of the annual procedure.[7] By the end of

---

Box 3.2 Overview of tensions over treaty interpretations (1974–1978)

1975 budget: The two arms of the budgetary authority found it difficult to agree on a joint interpretation of treaty provisions regarding classification and the maximum rate of increase for non-compulsory expenditure (Ehlermann 1975: 328–339). The disagreements centred on the classification of two issues: the regional fund and the contributions to the United Nations. The EP and the Council finally adopted a compromise, but evaded a permanent clarification on the classification question (Strasser 1975).

1976 budget: The EP opted for the first time for an 'opportunistic interpretation', as defined in Chapter 2. Based on an alternative interpretation of the provisions of expenditure classification, the EP went beyond the maximum rate of increase in the first reading. In its second reading, the Council moved towards the EP. Both sides agreed on a pragmatic solution that set an amount for the increase of non-compulsory expenditure. They did not, however, agree on an exact percentage, as this would have demanded a decision on classification (Strasser 1976). Hence, the Council prevented open conflict by 'legalising'[5] Parliament's 'opportunistic interpretation'.[6]

1977 budget: The EP argued that the maximum rate of increase was not applicable to commitment appropriations. The conciliation procedure brought an agreement in substance – again without clarifying the legal questions of classification and the maximum rate (Strasser 1977).

1978 budget: The Commission attempted to clarify the dispute over classification. The initiative did not bear fruit, as it was rejected by the EP and viewed with reluctance by the Council (Strasser 1978).

1979 budget: A new problem of the maximum rate of increase emerged. This time, it was not related to classification, but to the question of whether the Council could indirectly increase the maximum rate by adopting a budget that exceeded it. The questions opened a new gap in the treaty and offered the EP an attractive new variant of its strategy of 'opportunistic interpretation' (see case study below). For the first time, the two arms of the budgetary authority did not compromise at the end of the budgetary procedure. The EP insisted on its interpretation and adopted a budget that the Council contested.

1978, mounting institutional tensions turned into an intensive clash of rivalling interpretations.[8] The case study illustrates the exact mechanism by which the variables affected the level of conflict. First and most importantly, the scope of interpretation, which was particularly large that year, directly provoked the confrontational strategy of the Parliament. Second, disunity among member states weakened the Council and was responsible for the conflict-inducing effects of the large scope of interpretation. Third, due to the up-coming direct election, Parliament was determined to stand firmly by its treaty interpretation to a greater extent than it had been in previous years. Table 3.2 gives an overview of the different steps of the adoption process of the 1979 budget.

Conflict between Parliament and Council intensified during the *second reading in the Council (first part)*: Council rejected almost all modifications and amendments with which the Parliament had increased the budget beyond the maximum rate of increase for non-compulsory expenditure. However, member states did not assemble the required majority to reject a parliamentary amendment increasing the commitment appropriations for the Regional Fund, due to the objections

Table 3.2 Overview over the treaty provisions for the annual budgetary decision-making procedure and the developments during the adoption process for the 1979 budget

Annual budgetary procedure		*Adoption process of the 1979 budget*
Year: n–1	*Commission* prepares Preliminary Draft Budget.	Commission proposed significant increases in non-compulsory expenditure (NCE).
	First Reading in the Council: Council adopts Draft Budget.	The Council reduced NCE significantly.
	First Reading in the EP: EP tables amendments to NCE and modifications to compulsory expenditure (CE).	EP reinstated Commission proposals and raised NCE above the maximum rate of increase. It threatened the Council to reject the overall budget.
	Second reading in the Council: Council adopts CE and votes on NCE.	The Council had neither a majority for rejecting an increase of the Regional Fund as proposed by the EP nor a majority to adjust the maximum rate of increase accordingly.
	Second reading in the EP: EP votes on NCE (within the maximum rate of increase) and adopts/rejects the overall budget.	Interpreting the Council's failure to reject the EP's proposal as an implicit increase of the maximum rate, the EP adopted the budget. However, the Committee on Budgets failed to gain the necessary majority for a stronger line of conflict.
Year: n	*Commission* implements the budget.	The Commission implemented the budgets despite legal doubts and resistance from some member states.
		Council and EP agreed on a supplementary budget that ex-ante 'legalises' Parliament's adoption. The EP did not support proposals of the Commission for a further increase of the Regional Fund so as not to endanger the compromise with the Council.

of Italy and the United Kingdom, who were to receive more than two-thirds of the extra funds (one other member state – most likely Ireland – abstained). Consequently, the Council faced a situation in which, on the one hand, it had *de facto* adopted a budget that led to an increase in non-compulsory expenditure above the maximum rate of increase, while, on the other hand, the majority of the Council, most importantly Germany and France, was not willing to raise the maximum rate explicitly. As the EP immediately declared it would interpret the failure to reject its Regional Fund amendment as an implicit decision for a higher rate of increase, the Budget Council decided to postpone a final decision until the beginning of December, when the European Council was expected to discuss the financial endowment of regional policy at its summit meeting.

Second reading in the Council (second part)   In fact, the European Council did not agree on an increase in the provisions of the Regional Fund,[9] but adopted a loan scheme for less prosperous member states. This scheme was to be administered by the European Investment Bank with few monetary effects for the budget other than interest subsidies. Subsequently, the Budget Council remained unable to overcome its internal division on the Regional Fund issue and it signalled its willingness to Parliament to compromise on a new maximum rate of increase if the EP accepted the original endowment of the Regional Fund. For the Budget Council, the issue had gained an importance that transcended the mere distributive dimension. On the institutional dimension, the Council saw two important matters at stake. First, the EP was challenging the Council's general authority over the interpretation of treaty provisions on the setting of the maximum rate. Second, the EP's amendment for the Regional Fund deviated significantly from the annual provisions decided upon by the European Council in 1977. It thus undermined the authority of the European Council as a key forum for intergovernmental policy decisions. However, it became clear that despite the institutional importance, Council failed to act in a united manner towards the EP, because the member states that would benefit most from a higher Regional Fund pursued a short-term oriented strategy guided by distributive self-interest. They were unwilling to sacrifice their distributive gains for the long-term institutional interest of the Council.[10]

Second reading in the EP   The EP's rapporteur, Mr Bangemann, made it clear that Parliament stood by its interpretation: the Council had adopted the increase of commitment appropriations for the Regional Fund by failing to reject it. Therefore, the increase no longer conflicted with the maximum rate of increase. Mr Bangemann told the Council that, especially in the light of the coming direct elections, this interpretation was a matter of principle:

> We do not want a conflict; we have always tried to avoid conflict. We have done everything that might have served to prevent such a conflict. At this late hour we are still prepared to be flexible and reduce our figures. One thing we cannot do, Mr President, and that is to give up a legal position which involves at the same time Parliament's own position and a political opportunity and

also an opportunity to safeguard the Community's existence. That is what is at stake.[11]

For the EP, the Regional Fund was an ideal battleground with high symbolic value. On the distributive dimension, the Regional Fund symbolised Parliament's emphasis on European solidarity and the need to establish a truly supranational spending policy separate from the CAP. More importantly, on the institutional dimension, the Regional Fund had been a key issue on which the EP had defended its powers in previous years (Bangemann 1979: 177). Like the majority in the Council, the EP was willing to compromise on the distributive dimension (i.e. the specific amount for Regional Fund) as long as the legal conflict over the 'right' interpretation was won. Parliament had strong confidence in the legality of its own interpretation and saw the Council's approach as an attempt to encroach upon the EP's rights.[12] As the Council did not accept Parliament's position, it fell to the plenary to make a final decision on the budget.

The final debate in the plenary revealed that MEPs firmly supported the rapporteur's stance on the treaty interpretation concerning the Regional Fund amendment. Yet, the rapporteur failed to gain sufficient support for an (even) more confrontational strategy. Originally, he had proposed to pursue 'opportunistic interpretations' also concerning the classification of a number of budget lines and the application of Parliament's margin of manoeuvre. While the Committee on Budgets had endorsed these proposals, plenary was divided. A number of MEPs were reluctant to push the conflict with the Council too far.[13] In the end, the rapporteur withdrew his proposals of further 'opportunistic interpretations'. Parliament adopted the 1979 budget with the contested Regional Fund amendment.

Reaction (Commission) Although the Commission had tried to discourage the EP from pursuing its interpretation and had backed the Council's position during the debate, it immediately accepted and implemented the EP's adoption of budget. This was not without self-interest, given that, in principle, the Commission endorsed higher regional spending. In addition, of the three institutions, it was one least interested in a period of budgetary uncertainty. The Budget Commissioner, Mr Tugendhat, had warned throughout the debates that an enactment of the provisional twelfth's system would be the least desirable option.

Reaction (Council) The Council protested against the EP's decision and three member states (Denmark, France and United Kingdom)[14] paid only two-twelfths at the beginning of the year, calculated on the basis of the sums entered in the draft budget and not the budget adopted by EP. In order to prevent a recurrence of similar, internally divisive situations, eight member states agreed on an internal procedure that addressed the Council's voting process and committed the Council to a certain interpretation of the treaty.[15] However, despite these 'precautionary measures', the Council signalled its willingness to continue the discussion with the EP over a solution to the adoption of the 1979 budget.

Supplementary and amending budget No. 1/1979 In order to solve the interinstitutional dispute, the Commission took the lead and presented a supplementary and amending budget. It had feared EP pressure – backed by the threat of censure – to take Britain, France and Denmark to the European Court of Justice for failing to pay their full budget contributions (*Financial Times*: 6 February 1979). The Commission's proposal was a compromise between the two sides and included some new spending proposals favoured by the Commission. The Council accepted most elements of the supplementary and amending budget, while rejecting the Commission's new spending proposals. After taking these decisions, the Council endorsed a decision on the new maximum rate for non-compulsory expenditure.

The EP discussed and adopted the Council's draft of the supplementary amending budget without changes. During the debate, MEPs strongly criticised the influence of the European Council, both as regards the predetermination of figures for the Regional Fund in 1977, and also as regards the decision on the loans scheme in December 1978. The plenary followed the Committee on Budgets, which had – against demands of spending committees in the EP – proposed not to reinstate the Commission's new spending proposals, despite the fact that they were in line with the EP's distributive objectives. By approving further expenditure, the Committee feared that the EP would compromise its legal interpretation. The EP was thus willing to sacrifice possible short-term distributive gains for achieving an institutional accomplishment.

However, the closure of the budgetary procedure did not mean that both sides, the EP and the Council, had agreed on a joint interpretation of Article 203 or on the application of the maximum rate of increase. Instead, they had simply 'agreed to disagree'.

Summary: The belated outbreak

The assessment of the variables and the case study provide ample empirical evidence in support of propositions developed in Chapter 2. As expected, the scope of interpretation set the scene for conflict between Parliament and Council and prompted Parliament to opt for opportunistic interpretations. Parliament's alternative interpretations promised not only short-term distributive benefits, but also long-term institutional gains.[16] Moreover, the focus on institutional issues allowed the Committee on Budgets to strengthen Parliament's unity. Concerning the two questions from the beginning of this section (namely: Why was the level of conflict lower during the years that immediately followed the introduction of the new procedure? And what triggered the adoption of the first contested budget in 1978 half a year before the direct election?) the institutionalist account reveals that the 1978 escalation merely marked the culmination of tensions over institutional issues that had dominated the new budgetary procedure from the start. The disunity of the Council and the lack of clear treaty provisions for the specific problem that emerged in 1978 gave Parliament the opportunity to pursue a confrontational strategy.

However, this explanation does not fully explain why conflict did not escalate earlier. Three other aspects seem to have played an important role: (1) the willingness of MEPs to make the procedure work; (2) rivalling concepts of European governance in Parliament and the Council; and (3) the role of early and personal dialogue between the two arms of the budgetary authority.

Willingness During the first two or three years, both arms of the budgetary authority were clearly motivated to make the new budgetary procedure work. In particular, the EP sought close cooperation with the Council. This willingness faded when the gap between the expectations that Parliament had attached to the new procedure and the reality of budgetary decision-making became increasingly apparent. The resulting frustration among MEPs played a decisive role in the 1978 budget procedure, during which the first signs of a major conflict appeared. Finally, the upcoming direct elections encouraged MEPs to flex their muscles in the subsequent outbreak of conflict later in 1978.

Concepts of governance A declining willingness to cooperate was linked to a general dispute between the Parliament and the Council over the right concept of European governance. Parliament's based its vision on a powerful Parliament in a strong European centre. The strengthening of Parliament was justified as an act of democratisation, through which the European people could exercise direct influence over European decisions. In contrast, the Council's concept of governance was based on the vision of a strong representation for national governments in the European decision-making process. The concentration of power in the Council was justified by the idea that elected national governments were closest to citizens' interests. The concept of governance was viewed as particularly important in Parliament, where it constituted a strong focal point for the strategies and preferences of MEPs. It became a rhetorical frame that publicly reinforced the legitimacy of Parliament's demands. Moreover, it induced a heightened sensitivity among MEPs. Respect and the issue of being taken seriously as an 'equal partner' became a dominant benchmark against which the EP assessed Council's behaviour.

Dialogue The lack of formal and informal exchanges between budgetary actors played an important role in straining interinstitutional relations. Mr Bangemann (1979), the rapporteur for the 1979 budget, emphasised the relevance of dialogue, or lack thereof, in his analysis of conflict in EC budgetary politics. He argued that, during the first years of the 1970 budget treaty (prior to the 1979 budget procedure), personal contacts between members of Committee on Budgets and representatives of the Presidency of the Council already at an early stage of the procedure had been decisive for the elaboration of a common agreement. These contacts had introduced an element of indispensable flexibility into a procedure that had the tendency to reinforce opposition. When major tensions were not resolved at an early stage of the procedure, Bangemann argued, conflict became inevitable. Once the two arms of the budgetary authority had committed themselves publicly in their readings to divergent budgetary objectives, it was difficult to reconcile them. The existing provisions for dialogue at a later stage of the procedure proved useful solely in relation to non-fundamental measures and problems. Bangemann stressed that, during the 1979 budget procedure, Parliament and Council had failed to settle the fundamental distributive differences at the beginning of the procedure, due to the Council's inability or refusal to discuss the grand lines of the 1979 budget in spring 1978. Consequently, conflict over fundamental issues was shifted to the final stage. At this point, the procedure proved inadequate and forced actors into a tight corset of precise schedules and voting procedures. At this late stage, conflict had already escalated and actors were unable and unwilling to settle upon a compromise.[17]

The situation between 1979 and 1983

Conflict becomes dominant feature

From 1979 onwards, high levels of conflict and contested budgets became regular features of EC budgetary politics. The direct elections strengthened the self-confidence of MEPs and increased their determination to change the EC budget. At the same time, galloping agricultural expenditure and receding revenue deepened the antagonism between the distributive interests of Parliament and Council. As Figure 3.2 illustrates, all annual budgets between 1979 and 1983 (with the exception of the 1983 budget) were rejected or contested. While participants in 1978 had regarded the dispute over the 1979 budget as crisis of 'historic' dimension (see case study above), the inability of Parliament and Council to agree upon a joint budget started to become the norm.

The following section explores the development towards high levels of conflict as the dominant feature of annual budgetary decision-making. It first assesses the value of the variables identified in Chapter 2 and demonstrates their impact on the level of conflict, turning later to a detailed analysis of the 1982 budget procedure. The 1982 budget was selected mainly because it is representative for budgetary decision-making in the early 1980s. In contrast to the spectacular rejection of the 1980 budget, the procedure for the 1982 budget reflects the state of play at the time of annually re-emerging conflict, strong divergence in the preferences of Parliament and Council, and a large scope for rivalling treaty interpretation. The 1982 budget also reveals how Parliament unity and determination increased the level of conflict. The section concludes with a brief summary and a discussion of factors other than those described in Chapter 2 that played a role in determining the level of conflict between 1979 and 1983.

Assessing the values of the variables and their impact on the level of conflict

THE POLICY ENVIRONMENT

Heterogeneity among member states, the economic climate in the Community, and overlaps with the institutional structures of neighbouring policy fields increased slightly in comparison to the previous period. The 1981 Greek accession brought

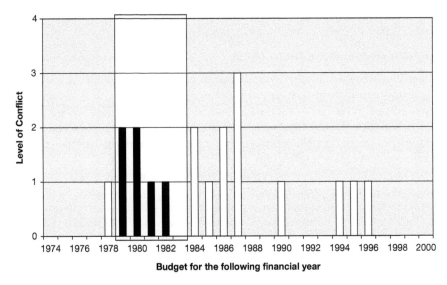

1979: Parliament rejected the 1980 budget and the Commission initiated the system of provisional twelfths.
1980: Parliament adopted the 1981 budget based on an opportunistic interpretation of the treaty provisions. Several member states refused to pay and took Parliament before the European Court of Justice.
1981: Parliament adopted a budget based on an opportunistic interpretation of the treaty provisions, which the Council challenged by taking the Parliament before the European Court of Justice.
1982: Parliament rejected the supplementary budget 1/1982.

Figure 3.2 Conflict in the annual budgetary procedure between 1979 and 1983.

a small, poor country with a strong interest in regional redistribution into the Community. Moreover, the termination of the transition period for UK budget contributions intensified the difference between net-contributors and net-beneficiaries in the Council.

Developments in the European economies and on agricultural markets between 1979 and 1983 increased the pressure on budgetary actors, but did not lead to the major economic crisis or the exhaustion of the own-resources that had been predicted in 1979. The GDP of the EC recovered in the early 1980s and world market prices for agricultural products and the exchange rate of the dollar led to high agricultural costs in 1980 and 1983, but allowed for temporary improvements 1981 and 1982. In 1983, the situation worsened and expenditure almost exceeded the available own-resources.

The institutional setting outside the budgetary procedure did not experience major changes. Clashes between Council and Parliament over the separation of the budgetary procedure from its legislative equivalent reoccurred annually, fuelled by the large scope of interpretation allowed by the treaty in this arena (Ehlermann and Minch 1981; Läufer 1990b: 119–121).

PREFERENCES AND UNITY OF THE ACTORS

The gulf between the distributive and institutional preferences of the EP and the Council widened. Budgetary actors defended their objectives with an increased determination. While member states felt mounting pressure on national budgets and their economies, the directly elected MEPs had campaigned on platforms that stressed the importance of their budgetary powers. They wanted to deliver on these election promises (Misch 1987: 19).

Although the EP had some distributive and institutional successes, it did not progress much towards realising its objectives. As Table 3.3 illustrates, the actual rate of increases for non-compulsory expenditure lay considerably above the original maximum rate. Yet, in contrast to parliamentary demands, the Council did not contain agricultural expenditure and did not agree on an increase of own-resources. On an institutional dimension, the EP achieved the recognition of the need for a clarification of the vague treaty provisions. The actual outcome, embodied in a joint declaration of Council, Parliament and Commission from 1982, however, did not entail significant concessions (see Case study below and Part II).

Institutional objectives strongly mobilised Parliament against the Council. The rejection of the 1980 budget over agricultural expenditure, for example, was mainly motivated by Parliament's interest in building up a reputation as a strong player in the budgetary procedure. Similarly, Parliament's attack on classification in the 1982 budget concerned institutional objectives and had limited distributive effect (see Case study below). Yet, it is difficult to assess the time-horizon of the new directly elected Parliament, because institutional and distributive objectives often coincided. And when the up-coming elections in 1984 cut the time-horizon of MEPs and reelection loomed large, they decided to (temporarily) reduce the confrontational element of their strategy, rather than shift from institutional to distributive objectives

Table 3.3 Actual rate versus original maximum rate of increase for non-compulsory appropriations for commitments*

Year (Budget)	Actual rate of increase of non-compulsory expenditure	Original maximum rate of increase as calculated by the Commission
1979 (1980 budget)	32.85%	13.3%
1980 (1981 budget)	24.4%	12.2%
1981 (1982 budget)	14.6%	14.5%
1982 (1983 Budget)	27.77%	11.8%
1983 (1984 budget)	16.97%	11.6%

Source: Fugmann (1992: 399)

* This includes dissociated and non-dissociated appropriations of the general budget, as well as amending and supplementary budgets.

(Misch 1987: 49). Parliament decided not to reject the 1984 budget, but opted for a less confrontational opportunistic interpretation (Strasser 1984; Goybet 1984).

Yet, member states were still more short-term oriented than the EP. They refused to embark on a long-term reform of EC finances partly because of the high switching costs involved in a reform (see Part II). At the same time, they recognised the distributive impact of institutional decisions and were therefore unwilling to trade institutional against distributive concessions with the EP.

The new directly elected Parliament was a highly unified group. A number of senior budget experts in the Committee on Budgets, who had served in the old Parliament,[18] had a strong grip on budgetary matters. Consensus on non-compulsory expenditure was relatively easy to achieve. The interest in initiating new policies through increases in non-compulsory expenditure combined institutional with distributive interests and was therefore supported by a large majority. Moreover, the EP carried no direct responsibility for the revenue side. The impact of a spending approach on the level of taxes for European citizens was blurred by its link to national taxation. Therefore, MEPs felt little direct motivation to restrain their demands for more distributive activities on the European level (Wallace 1987: 265).

Whenever tensions among MEPs arose, the Committee on Budgets presented the issues at stake as a question of institutional importance (Isaac 1980: 699–702). As in the previous period, conflict with the Council over institution questions was, therefore, a key instrument for overcoming internal differences among committees and national groups. As institutional victory would benefit the EP as a whole, MEPs were willing to subordinate their individual distributive interests to the institutional objective of the Parliament. As mentioned above, the attack on agricultural expenditure in the procedure for the 1980 budget was, for example, achieved through stressing its institutional dimension.

However, despite its dressing up as an institutional issue, agricultural expenditure remained a potential weak point in the unity of Parliament that was contained only through internal agreement among the Committee on Budgets and Committee on Agriculture. While EP budget experts and MEPs from non-agricultural constituencies wanted to reduce agricultural spending in order to free resources for non-compulsory spending, the agricultural lobby within the EP strongly defended the high levels of expenditure for the farming community. The CAP had more political resonance than any other spending policy. An alert public with a high degree of mobility followed agricultural decisions very closely and took to the streets when they saw their interests endangered. A considerable number of MEPs were highly sensitive to pressure from the farmers' associations, as they relied on the support of political and national groups with strong agricultural constituencies.[19] Realising this weakness, the EP developed a strategy for containing the internal differences over agricultural expenditure. It separated the budget and the CAP into two independent spheres of influence. Similar to the division between the Budget Council and Agricultural Council, the EP spoke with two different voices: depending on the occasion the EP spoke either as the 'Budget Parliament' or as the 'Agriculture Parliament' (Misch 1987: 32). Extant fragmentation in the decision-making processes over budgetary and agricultural issues helped the EP to institutionalise this

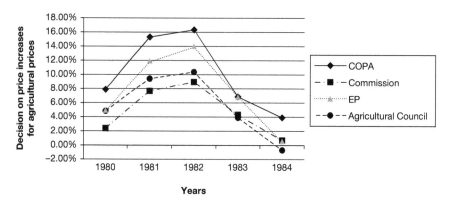

Figure 3.3 Profile of decisions on price increases for agricultural products (in percentages)*

Source: Misch 1987: 25.

*COPA is the acronym for 'Committee of Agricultural Organisations in the European Community'. It is the political representative of the European agricultural lobby, which publish its demands for increase in the price to the European institutions annually.

separation. Every spring, when the Council set the prices for agricultural products, the Agricultural Parliament demanded large increases (see Figure 3.3). In particular in 1981 and 1982, when high world market prices had reduced the costs for the CAP, MEPs went far beyond the proposals of the Commission. Yet, when the EP adopted its budgetary guidelines, also in spring, and in subsequent readings in the autumn, the EP usually stressed the importance of reducing agricultural expenditure.

This dualism was possible because the EP (wearing its agricultural hat) played only a consultative role in the setting of agricultural prices and (when wearing its budgetary hat) did not have much decision-making power over agricultural expenditure, which was classified as compulsory expenditure. Thus, neither the demands for higher prices nor proposals for significant cuts had an effect on the CAP, which remained Council's exclusive domain. Both sides of the EP saved face while internal conflict was significantly reduced. Given the strict majority prerequisite in the voting rules of the treaty and the high level of abstention among MEPs, budget and agricultural experts knew that they had to depend upon each other if they wanted Parliament to have a voice in the budgetary procedure and in discussions over agricultural prices.

Frequently, the limits of the compromise between agricultural and budgetary circles became apparent. Agricultural MEPs resisted whenever budget experts strayed beyond the boundaries of the compromise. The Committee on Budgets managed only once, during the above-mentioned 1980 budget procedure, to gather a sufficiently large majority for a serious attack on agricultural expenditure. Even in this case, however, the coalition against the CAP broke down soon after the rejection of the 1980 budget. In particular, MEPs from the European People's Party felt the 'hang-over' in the following months when they encountered strong protests from the agricultural lobby (Misch 1987: 36). They were not willing to repeat such a strong attack against agriculture expenditure. Moreover, the dualism undermined Parliament's political credibility as a whole, as the statements and actions of budget and agricultural experts were clearly incompatible. The limits of the compromise were fully revealed whenever budget experts tried to make the EP adopt reform proposals for the future of Community's finances.

The overall relatively united Parliament stood against a Council that increasingly felt the impact of its internal division. Although tensions among member states were still kept largely on the intergovernmental level, disunity spilled over frequently to annual decision-making. First, Greece's accession in 1981 strengthened the axis of poorer countries interested in redistribution, i.e. Italy and Ireland. Once they were able to win over one other member state, such as the Great Britain, they were able to block decisions.[20] It created the germ of a North-South-divide that became fully apparent in the Council after the Iberian accession. Second, the fragmentation of budgetary decision-making, which gave the Agriculture Council large autonomy, weakened the Budget Council. As in the procedure for the 1980 budget, eight of the nine delegations in the Budget Council had to concede that they shared the Committee on Budgets' interest in a containment of agricultural expenditure (Strasser 1980: 373), but that they were unable to change the legislative framework that determined agricultural spending. This weakened the Budget Council's political credibility and became a serious problem when, in 1983, galloping agricultural spending started to push expenditure towards the revenue limit (set by the existing own-resources). Third, intergovernmental negotiations over the British demands for compensation impacted repeatedly on annual decision-making. In the months after the Parliament's rejection of the 1980 budget, for example, the Council found it difficult to come to an agreement on the new budget proposal for 1980. Only when a preliminary solution to the British problem was found in the '30 May 1980 mandate' (see Chapter 5) could the member states adopt a budget.

While high levels of conflict between Parliament and Council dominated budgetary politics, the Commission had difficulties to position itself as an effective moderator between the two sides. Similar to the events of the previous period, the Commission significantly influenced budgetary outcomes and was able to present compromise proposals, but failed to prevent the emergence and escalation of conflict. In the dispute over the 1981 budget, for example, the Commission came into play only after the Parliament had adopted a contested budget. The Budget Commissioner rectified the situation by introducing an amending budget No. 1/1981, which skilfully combined the positions of Parliament and Council (Läufer 1981a,b). Yet, the Commission was only able to play this decisive role because EP and Council had in this particular case already signalled their willingness to find a compromise (Strasser 1981a+b).

INSTITUTIONAL SETTING

The large scope of interpretation continued to be the major source and arena of conflict (Glaesner 1981). As the following overview illustrates (see Box 3.3), conflict in all budget procedures between 1979 and 1983 centred on rivalling interpretation of treaty provisions, with the exception of the 1980 budget.

In each case, the Commission was supportive of Parliament's actions and the European Court of Justice did not intervene. The Commission implemented all adopted budgets, thereby significantly reducing the costs and risks involved in opportunistic interpretation. The EP could be sure that contested budgets would be implemented and, thus, that disputes did not lead to the enactment of the system of provisional twelfths. Moreover, Parliament could pursue opportunistic interpretations because the ECJ did not come to a ruling on the legal questions concerned. Although the Council filed complains against the EP before the ECJ twice (in 1981 and 1982), compromise agreements between the two arms of the budgetary authority prevented the intervention of the ECJ (see Part II).

In 1982, the Council recognised the problems that the vague treaty provisions posed for the budgetary decision-making process. It negotiated a joint declaration with the Parliament and the Commission in an attempt to clarify questions of classification and of the separation between legislative and budgetary powers (see Part II). However, the effect on the scope of interpretation was limited. Although interinstitutional cooperation increased temporarily (with some positive effect on the procedure for the 1983 budget, Strasser 1983), classification and the delineation of powers remained key issues of contention.

Case study: the adoption of the 1982 budget

The budgetary procedure for the 1982 budget was characteristic for the early 1980s, when strong tensions between the institutions over the adoption of the budget became a regular and dominant feature of budgetary politics.[22] Although the positive developments on the agricultural markets slightly eased the financial pressure, Council and Parliament failed to conclude the budgetary procedure with an uncontested budget and member states decided to take legal action against Parliament and Commission for the adoption and implementation of the 1982 budget. The case study illustrates how, after direct election in 1979, unity and determination in Parliament increased. MEPs proactively exploited the scope of interpretation of the treaty provisions. Table 3.4 gives an overview of the different steps of the adoption process of the 1982 budget.

Tensions over the classification of budget lines and the level of non-compulsory expenditure already occurred in the first period of the budget procedure. They increased during the *second readings in the Council and the Parliament*, at which point the Council accepted some of the modifications and amendments tabled by Parliament. Similar to the 1979 budget, tensions between the distributive interests of member states raised the adopted non-expenditure above the maximum rate of increase. As Council documents reveal, the new axis between Greece, Ireland and Italy had

Box 3.3 *Overview of tensions over treaty interpretations (1979–1983)*

1981 budget: The EP took the Commission's proposal for a second supplementary and amending budget to the 1980 budget as an opportunity to achieve an increase in non-compulsory expenditure, which the Council had rejected for the 1981 budget. Such a move was an opportunistic interpretation in a double sense. On one hand, it discounted the principle of annuality and the restriction of supplementary budget to extraordinary circumstances. On the other, it re-interpreted the maximum rates of increase of the 1980 and the 1981 budgets to allow for the increases in non-compulsory expenditure in both the supplementary budget and the annual budget (Strasser 1982).

1982 budget: The EP followed a strategy of opportunistic interpretation over expenditure classification. Based on reclassifications, the EP increased non-compulsory expenditure but stayed within the maximum rate of increase. The president of the EP was able to declare the budget finally adopted – although the Council had rejected the increase of non-compulsory expenditure (see case study below).

1983 budget: The EP repeated the strategy of opportunistic interpretation over classification and argued that its increases of non-compulsory expenditure complied with the existing margin of manoeuvre. In contrast to the previous year, the Council – after condemning the EP's move – settled on a compromise with the EP: the Council 'legalised' the opportunistic interpretation by increasing the maximum rate of increase.

1984 budget: The EP opted again for an opportunistic interpretation. It classified all compensation appropriations for the United Kingdom and Germany against the compromise found at the beginning of the year as non-compulsory expenditure and put it into reserve. In its final resolution, the EP told the Council that the compensation would only be de-blocked if the Council settled upon a permanent solution for the financing of the Community (EC-Bull. 12–1983: 91–93). Consequently, Parliament was able to increase the non-compulsory expenditure without altering its margin of manoeuvre (Strasser 1984: 342 and Table 8).[21] Council protested against Parliament's move in an official letter to the EP President (EC-Bull. 12–1983: 84). Yet, it decided not to take the EP to Court and settled the dispute with the EP in March 1984: the Council accepted the classification of the compensation payments as non-compulsory expenditure and Parliament unblocked the payments after the European Council had adopted a permanent solution to the UK problem (see Chapter 5).

Table 3.4 Overview of developments in procedure for the 1982 budget

Annual budgetary procedure		Adoption process of the 1982 budget
Year: n–1	First Reading in the Council	The Council cut – after internal discussions – the Commission's preliminary draft in the area of non-compulsory expenditure drastically.
	First Reading in the EP	The EP reinstated most of the Commission proposals and declared that it would only regard expenditure items as compulsory if all three institutions agreed unanimously on their classification as such.
	Second Reading in the Council	The Council accepted some of the modifications and amendments tabled by Parliament. Tensions between the distributive interests of member states raised the adopted non-expenditure above the maximum rate of increase. In the Council's view, this meant that a new maximum rate of increase would have to be fixed.
	Second Reading in the EP	The EP – applying its new expanded classification of non-compulsory expenditure – regarded a new maximum rate as unnecessary ('opportunistic interpretation') and adopted a budget with increased non-compulsory expenditure.
Year: n	Commission implements the budget.	The Commission decided to implement the budget. The Council introduced actions before the Court of Justice against the President of the EP for adopting, and against the Commission for implementing the 1982 budget. At the same time, it entered into an interinstitutional dialogue with the EP. In June, the EP, Council and Commission adopted an interinstitutional agreement that formally concluded the dispute over the 1982 budget and attempted to clarify institutional questions concerning the application of Article 203 EEC Treaty.

been able to gather sufficient additional support to prevent a rejection of some of Parliament's modifications and amendments (Council documents 11074/81). The resulting increase in non-compulsory expenditure above the maximum rate meant that a new rate had to be fixed. Therefore, the Council asked Parliament to enter into negotiations on a new rate. Parliament refused as long as the Council remained unwilling to combine them with a debate on classification. Applying a new expanded classification of non-compulsory expenditure, the EP regarded a new maximum rate as unnecessary ('opportunistic interpretation'). The Council did not accept Parliament's position; yet, it offered to enter a debate on classification only after the adoption of the 1982 budget. In its second reading, the EP maintained its position and applied the new classification (see Figure 3.4).

The Committee on Budgets gained sufficient support in plenary for an opportunistic interpretation, although a number of MEPs voiced resistance. In order to be consistent with its legal position, budget experts had to ensure that the reclassified non-compulsory expenditure items remained within the existing maximum rate of increase. Some of the spending committees had lobbied for stronger increases, and found their distributive interests upset. Moreover, members of the liberal group, of the European Democrats (namely the British Conservatives), and of the European Democratic Alliance (DEP/RDE) disputed the new classifications on institutional grounds. Mrs Scrivener from the French Liberals emphasised that the EP should not, as a matter of course, seek a trial of strength with the Council (EP debate from 14 December 1981). Despite these internal tensions, the EP adopted the budget.

Reaction (Commission and Council) Although the Budget Commissioner had originally criticised the strategy of the EP in the second reading, stating that 'we would not be able to support a tactic which seeks to boost Parliament's margin of manoeuvre by a device such as this' (15 December 1981: 40), the Commission implemented the 1982 budget at the start of the financial year. The Council strongly disapproved of Parliament's decision to adopt the budget without prior agreement and criticised the Commission for implementing it. Yet, the Council thought it best if member states coordinated their actions, unlike in 1979 and 1981, and accepted the integral payments on the basis of the budget adopted,

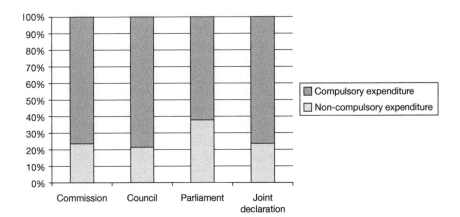

Figure 3.4 Different interpretations of expenditure classifications in the 1982 budget.
Source: Fugmann 1992: 386.

while opening the interinstitutional dialogue with the EP on the issue of classification. At the same time, the Council introduced – as a precautionary measure – actions before the Court of Justice against the Parliament for adopting, and against the Commission for implementing the 1982 budget.[23]

The 'Joint Declaration on various measures to improve the budgetary procedure' As a result of the interinstitutional dialogue, the EP, the Commission, and the Council agreed in June 1982 on a joint declaration that formally concluded the procedure for the 1982 budget and allowed the Council to withdraw its actions before the Court. The declaration not only covered the issue of classification, but also other aspects of the treaty provisions, in particular the delineation between budgetary and legislative powers. The final outcome constituted a compromise for both sides (see also Figure 3.4). Yet, the joint declaration did not significantly alter the institutional balance set out in the treaty and left most of the contentious issues unresolved (see Part II).

Compared to the 1979 budget, the EP was now a more proactive critic of the treaty provisions and the Council had started to accept the necessity to cooperate with Parliament on institutional matters. During the 1982 budget procedure, the EP initiated institutional conflict in reaction to the stark differences in distributive preferences between EP and Council, but also because of a heightened interest in institutional change.

Summary: The process of institutionalisation

The evidence presented largely supports the propositions put forward in Chapter 2. Parliament was relatively united and opted for opportunistic interpretation, facilitated by the large scope of interpretation and the Commission's willingness to implement contested budgets. The rejection of the 1980 budget and the decision not to reject in 1984 seem slightly surprising on the basis of these predictions, as they assume that an EP motivated by distributive interest would reject an annual budget that hits the revenue limit. However, the EP's moves are not completely out of place when taken in concert with the chapter's theoretical arguments. The 1979 rejection resulted primarily from Parliament's interest in establishing a reputation as strong negotiator (assuming that the annual budgetary decision-making was an 'iterated game'). The decision not to reject the 1984 budget, although it hit the revenue limit, was linked to internal disunity and the fear that voters would censure the use of a highly confrontational strategy so soon before the elections. Nevertheless, Chapter 2's institutionalist approach fails to account for certain additional elements of the interaction between EP and Council that affected the level of conflict.

Institutionalisation Budgetary conflict between Council and Parliament became the norm between 1979 and 1983, not only because Parliament chose 'opportunistic interpretation' as its dominant strategy, but also because actors in Council and Parliament saw conflict as inevitable ('institutionalised conflict', Grabitz *et al.*

1988: 164). Both sides lost their willingness to overcome tensions productively. A comparison with the 1970s is revealing. In a brochure of the London Information Office of the European Parliament from January 1979, two British MEPs gave a detailed account of the budgetary procedure of the EC. They stated:

> The procedure is complex; and is, indeed, evolving steadily. There are also several 'grey areas' where the precise competences of the different institutions are still in dispute, although these are gradually diminishing.
>
> (p. 13)

The optimism that the 'grey areas' would diminish was based on the assumption that the EP and Council would be willing to make the procedure work. Yet, this willingness faded as Council regarded Parliament's demands as excessive and as Parliament became increasingly impatient. The expectation that both sides would closely cooperate was successively undermined by the experience of failed attempts of cooperation. The repeated occurrence of conflict initiated a new behavioural pattern that became self-enforcing. A 'norm of conflict' emerged. Parliament and Council both assumed that the respective other side would opt for a confrontational strategy and thus, decided to be equally confrontational.

The 1982 joint declaration did little to change this logic. Except for the positive effect on the 1983 budget, the declaration failed to provide institutional clarifications and lasting positive momentum. Moreover, the norm of conflict was in line with the interests of key players. Not only did the confrontation promise larger budgets, conflict with the Council (in particular over institutional issues) gave the Committee on Budgets a very strong position within Parliament. Hence, budget experts had little incentive to cooperate with the Council, as this would have endangered their internal standing.

Focus on a specific issue Conflict often focused on specific and singular issues, rendering other issues less relevant.[24] The intensity of conflict over these issues exceeded their actual monetary importance.[25] The rationale behind this was the institutional and long-term importance of these issues. Parliament and Council assumed that whoever won the conflict would increase its overall reputation. Yet, there was also an element of randomness in the selection of these issues. The two arms of the budgetary authority, in particular the EP, seemed to take the next best opportunity for conflict. Once they had discharged their energy and gained sufficient publicity, they were willing to compromise. This matches the observation of the EP's general willingness to find a compromise at the beginning of the financial year, once the public showdown and muscle flexing in the second reading was over and the contested budget had been adopted. This element of randomness also corresponds with the criticism of political observers that Parliament failed to develop a coherent strategy that connected the contentious issues of the different annual procedures (Misch 1987: 47). It applied a 'guerrilla tactic' (ibid.), which meant it jumped on emergent budgetary issues that enhanced its preferences, but failed to engage in long-term planning towards reaching specific strategic objectives. As a result, it also failed to develop proper alliances with member states in the Council.

Internal dynamics of conflict Conflict with the Council also entailed an emotional dimension for MEPs, as they strove to become equal and respected partners in European decision-making. When they felt the Council would deny them this position, they opted for conflict. This emotionality was linked to internal dynamics, which reinvigorated the determination to fight the Council. The rejection of the 1980 budget illustrates the strong impact of these internal dynamics. Even MEPs with an interest in agricultural expenditure (who, therefore, did not share the distributive motivation of the rejection) could not resist the temptation to send a strong signal to the Council. Participants described the rejection as a 'happening' and a 'demo' (interview with former MEP). The Council employed a legalistic and strategic approach in the second reading, which outraged MEPs (*Neue Züricher Zeitung* 15 December 1979). MEPs, most of them newly elected and inexperienced,[26] were more shocked over the form than the content of the Council's proposals (Isaac 1984a: 700). The Council had miscalculated and thought it could bully the EP. When the Council finally realised its mistake and presented a compromise proposal on the morning before the vote, it was already too late. MEPs were set on their rejection course (interview with official of the general secretariat of the Parliament). As mentioned above, many MEPs from the European People's Party felt a 'hang over' after the rejection and regretted that they had voted against the distributive interests of their political clientele.

The situation between 1984 and 1988

The divide among member states further intensifies conflict

From the second direct election in 1984 to the budget reform in 1988, intrainstitutional conflict in the Council further intensified the conflict between Parliament and Council (see Figure 3.5). Member states were divided over how to tackle the problems of galloping agricultural costs and diminishing own-resources. Their incapacity to find a solution weakened the Council's position in annual decision-making. The situation deteriorated with the accession of Spain and Portugal, as the balance of power in the Council shifted, and a blocking minority exploited the annually recurring budgetary procedure to influence intergovernmental negotiations.

   This section explores the intensification of interinstitutional conflict as a result of the divide among member states. It first assesses the values of the variables identified in Chapter 2 and demonstrates their effect on the level of conflict, subsequently focusing on a detailed analysis of the 1987 budget procedure. The 1987 budget was selected because it illustrates in detail the extent to which the EP tried to exploit the heightened disunity of the Council. It was the first budget after the Iberian accession and the last budget before the adoption of the financial perspective in February 1988. The section concludes with a brief summary and discussion of factors, which,

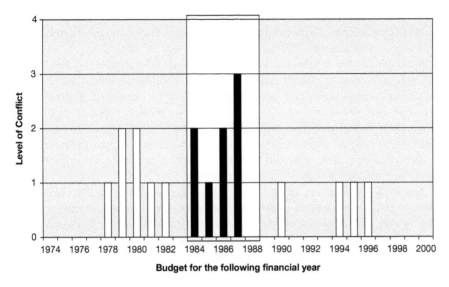

1984: Parliament rejected the 1985 budget and the Commission initiated the system of provisional twelfths.
1985: Parliament adopted a 1986 budget based on an opportunistic interpretation of the treaty, which the Council challenged by taking action against Parliament before the European Court of Justice.
1986: Parliament did not adopt a 1987 budget before the beginning of the financial year and the Commission initiated the system of provisional twelfths.
1987: Council failed to establish a draft budget for 1988 before the beginning of the financial year, Parliament took action against the Council before the European Court of Justice, and the Commission enacted system of provisional twelfths.

Figure 3.5 Conflict in the annual budgetary procedure between 1984 and 1988.

in addition to those introduced in Chapter 2, influenced the level of conflict between 1984 and 1988.

Assessing the values of the variables and their impact on the level of conflict

THE POLICY ENVIRONMENT

Heterogeneity among member states and the situation on the agricultural markets intensified and seriously challenged budgetary decision-making, in particular on the intergovernmental level. With the accession of Spain and Portugal in 1986, two new countries joined the EC. They had a level of economic development and prosperity that was significantly below the average of the Community. Although endowed with a large agricultural sector, they benefited little from the Common Agricultural Policy, which was still oriented mainly towards Northern agricultural products. Therefore, Spanish and Portuguese budget ministers joined their colleagues from Ireland, Greece and Italy, and demanded an expansion of the Community's regional policy. On the other hand, tensions over the 'UK problem' were finally resolved at the summit of Fontainebleau in 1984 through an agreement on a general rebate for the UK (see Chapter 5).

Although European economic development improved slightly (Tsoukalis 1993: 24), the own-resources of the Community were completely exhausted. Rising agricultural expenditure, new policy initiatives, and the accession of Spain and Portugal were pitted against falling revenues (Commission 1995: 19–20). The Community spent more than it actually had (Table 3.5). Member states tried to cover the revenue gap through increases of the VAT ceiling and repayable advances to the Community, but eventually realised that their piecemeal approach did not solve the problem (van Lier 1986; Magiera 1985).

Although the adoption of the Single European Act (SEA) in 1985 brought about considerable changes in the institutional and political architecture of the Community and induced a new momentum into intergovernmental negotiations on institutional reform (see Part II), the immediate effects on annual budgetary decision-making were limited. The new (modest) legislative powers of Parliament only came into effect in 1987 and thus, did not reduce tensions between Parliament and Council over the delineation of budgetary and legislative decision-making. Similarly, the new principle of cohesion, introduced in the SEA, did not have direct institutional consequences for the annual budgetary procedure. Yet, on a political level, the SEA's emphasis on cohesion helped Parliament and the poorer member states justifying their distributive demands for an expansion of regional expenditure.

PREFERENCES AND UNITY OF ACTORS

The differences in the preferences between Council and Parliament remained unchanged. The challenge of exhausting own-resources intensified the force with which each institution defended its position. Most of the member states regarded the exhaustion of own-resources as the result of an uncontrolled growth of expenditure that had to be tackled with an approach of budgetary discipline

Table 3.5 Budget approved and real costs (as % of VAT rate necessary for financing)

	1984	1985	1986	1987*
Expenditure set in the budgets	1.14	1.23	1.40	1.39
Expenditure not in the budget**	0.14	0.17	0.20	0.26
Overrun not covered by own-resources and non-refundable intergovernmental advances	0.20	0.17	0.20	0.25

Source: Com (87) 100, printed in EC-Bulletin Supplement Nr. 1/1987: 17).

* Estimates.

** It includes current deficits (i.e. EAGGF guarantee deficit and shortfall in traditional own-resources for 1986 and 1987), non-depreciation of agricultural stocks, and past costs (i.e. outstanding payment appropriations from commitment appropriations in the budget).

(Wallace 1987: 265). Given the legislative commitment for agricultural expenditure, such an austerity approach was directed mainly against non-compulsory expenditure, which was easier to cut. In contrast, Parliament, which did not have a political responsibility for the revenue side, was not willing to accept reductions in non-compulsory expenditure and regarded an increase of the VAT ceiling as the solution to the financial problems of the Community (Nicoll 1985). Moreover, Parliament had a strong interest in participating in the intergovernmental negotiations on the future of EC finances and it rejected Council attempts to enact unilateral measures affecting annual budgetary decision-making. In particular, the Council's internal agreement on budgetary discipline from December 1984 epitomised for MEPs the Council's unwillingness to cooperate with Parliament (Läufer 1985: 138; see also Chapter 9).

Parliament directly felt the impact of the Council's accord on budgetary discipline. Except for the 1986 budget, which included the initial costs for accession of Spain and Portugal (Nicoll 1986), Parliament realised increases in non-compulsory expenditure that lay only marginally above the maximum rate given in the treaty and were considerably lower than in previous periods (Table 3.6).[27] On the institutional front, the EP was similarly disappointed. It had to accept that the Single European Act did not change the institutional setting of the budgetary procedure and that its participation in the reform discussion on the intergovernmental level was very limited.

Parliament tried to benefit from the fact that the divide among member states made the Council increasingly short-term oriented. In the procedures for the 1985 budget and the 1986 budget, the EP charged the Council with attempting to mask the problem of exhausting own-resources through accounting tricks instead of adopting a long-term solution. It rejected the 1985 budget and considerably altered the 1986 budget on institutional grounds (Läufer 1985, 1986; Strasser 1985). Yet, short-term distributive and long-term institutional issues were so strongly intertwined that the difference in time-horizons between the two institutions did not lead to successful exchanges between distributive and institutional concessions. Moreover, intergovernmental negotiations entered a constructive stage in 1987, and totally overshadowed annual decision-making. Member states did not want to

Table 3.6 Actual rate versus original maximum rate of increase for non-compulsory appropriations for commitments*

Year (Budget)	*Actual rate of increase of non-compulsory expenditure*	*Original maximum rate of increase as calculated by the Commission*
1984 (1985 budget)	9.75%	9.0%
1985 (1986 budget)	approx. 20.0 %	7.1%
1986 (1987 budget)	8.2%	8.1%

Source: Fugmann (1992: 399).

* This includes dissociated and non-dissociated appropriations of the general budget, as well as amending and supplementary budgets.

precommit themselves in the annual procedure and sought to clarify the long-term issues first. Consequently, the 1988 budget was adopted only after member states had agreed on a budget reform in February 1988 (Siebert 1988).

The disunity of the Council stemmed mainly from the decision-making rules which gave every member state veto-power over decisions on the revenue ceiling, and from the accession of Spain and Portugal in 1986, which turned the anti-CAP coalition into a blocking minority and, at the same time, boosted demands for regional expenditure. In the procedure for the 1985 budget, the Council failed to adopt a draft budget in line with the pragmatic budget calendar and only just prevented a breach of the deadline spelled out in the treaty. The Council saw itself trapped by internal deadlock: the own-resources were exhausted but the Budget Council could neither agree on a reduction of agricultural expenditure, nor on the introduction of new financial means to cover the expenditure (Läufer 1985; Strasser 1985). This dilemma reoccurred in the procedure for the 1986 budget (Läufer 1986).

A split into two camps, an austerity camp and a spending camp, became increasingly apparent. The situation was further complicated by the autonomy of the Agriculture Council and the fact that even members of the austerity camp, such as France and Germany, were reluctant to support cuts in agricultural expenditure. The spending camp was strengthened after 1986, due to the accession of Portugal and Spain. The Southern member states and Ireland gained a blocking minority and henceforth prevented the austerity camp from adopting cuts in regional spending (Table 3.7). At the same time, Spain joined Greece and Great Britain in blocking increases in agricultural expenditure (interview with a former representative of the Spanish delegation).[28] Given the agricultural interests of the other

Table 3.7 Votes in the Council (Community of Twelve)

Member states	Votes
Belgium	5
Denmark	3
Germany	10
Greece	5
Spain	8
France	10
Ireland	3
Italy	10
Luxembourg	2
Netherlands	5
Portugal	5
United Kingdom	10
Total	76
Qualified Majority	54
Blocking Minority	21

Key members of the *Anti-CAP coalition*: UK (10) + Spain (8) + Greece (3) = 23 votes
Frequent additional members: Portugal (5), Netherlands (5).
Members of the *regional spending coalition*: Italy (10) + Spain (8) + Portugal (5) + Greece (3) + Ireland (3) = 29 votes

member states, the bargaining power of the blocking coalition was considerable, and coordination among the different groups became enormously difficult. The anti-CAP coalition blocked decisions on agriculture, while the austerity camp rejected increases in either regional expenditure or the own-resources, as possible solutions (interview with a representative of the Dutch delegation). Tension culminated during the procedure for the 1988 budget. The internal twist between the member states and the need for unanimity for any interim solution involving supplementary revenue prevented an agreement on a draft budget for 1988. Despite numerous meetings and intensive efforts on the part of the presidency, the Council failed to adopt a draft budget within the timetable provided in the treaty. As mentioned above, the Council concluded its first reading and transmitted a draft budget for 1988 to the EP only after an agreement on the financial reform was finally adopted in February 1988 (Siebert 1988).

The inability of the Council to find a permanent solution for the exhaustion of own-resources strengthened the unity of the EP. The Committee on Budgets was able to overcome distributive differences among MEPs by emphasising the institutional dimension of the conflict with the Council. The EP rejected the 1985 budget with an exceptionally clear vote (321 in favour, 3 against, and 16 abstentions) and followed the Committee on Budgets' proposals for an expanded 1986 budget – despite the initial unwillingness of Liberals and European Democrats (Läufer 1986). Moreover, tensions in the EP over agricultural expenditure decreased because the accession of Spanish and Portuguese MEPs weakened the agricultural lobby within Parliament (see below the case study of the 1987 budget).

However, the Committee on Budgets also encountered some reluctance towards its confrontational strategy, which explains why the EP did not use its right of rejection more often. In the vote on the supplementary budget No. 1/1987, for example, the Committee on Budgets had advised the plenary to reject the budget in order to increase the pressure on negotiations in the Council. Although a large majority voted in favour of the recommendation, the Committee on Budgets did not manage to secure the necessary majority of 260 votes (EC Bull. 7/8–1987: 99–100).

Although the Commission failed again to have direct conflict-reducing impact on annual budgetary decision-making, a change in Commission strategy, initiated by its new president, Jacques Delors, had important consequences for the role of the Commission in budgetary politics. In the long-run, it significantly reduced the level of conflict after 1988. The Commission loosened its ties with the EP and became less spending-oriented (Wallace 1987: 270). Previously an MEP and a French minister of finance, Delors recognised the fundamental character of the Community's financial problems. In contrast to the previous Commission, he emphasised that the solution had to be a major reform – not small adjustments during annual decision-making (interview with Commission official). Understanding that an increase in professionalism of the Commission was fundamental to the success of this new strategy, he brought in new personnel to the Directorate General of Budgets, and became personally involved in the budgetary politics. This move bore fruit: as budgetary actors recognised an increase in the quality of the Commission's budgetary figures and proposals, the Commission did, in fact, regain credibility (interview with Commission official; see also Part II).

THE INSTITUTIONAL SETTING

The scope of interpretation remained a dominant issue. As the following overview illustrates (see Box 3.4), budgetary actors pushed the scope of interpretation of the treaty provisions further than in previous years. Moreover, the Council actively reinterpreted the treaty for the first time in this period.

The annual decision-making procedure and intergovernmental negotiations on financial reform became increasingly intertwined. The inability of member states to adopt solutions on the intergovernmental level blocked decisions at annual budgetary level. Yet, the relevance of the annual procedure did not decline. Member states regarded the annual procedure as a continuation of intergovernmental negotiations. In particular, the Southern member states used the annual procedure to exercise their blocking power in order to gain concessions on the inter-governmental level. For the EP, the annual procedure kept its high relevance. It was the only forum in which the EP had the opportunity to influence political and institutional decisions on the future of the EC's finances.

Box 3.4 Overview of tensions over treaty interpretations (1984–1988)

1985 budget: The Council breached the treaty's principle of annuality by presenting a 10-month, rather than a 12-month budget. This gave the EP the opportunity to play the role as defender of the treaty and budgetary orthodoxy. Parliament rejected the budget on institutional grounds (Läufer 1985; Strasser 1985).

1986 budget: Parliament refused to accept the Council's draft budget, as it contained no financial provisions for the upcoming accession of Spain and Portugal. It did not reject the budget, but – exceeding its institutional powers – adopted a new considerably larger budget (Läufer 1986; Wallace 1987).

1987 budget: The ruling of the European Court of Justice in 1986 complicated the return to a classic opportunistic interpretation of the treaty provisions on issues of classification and maximum rate of increase, because the Court had annulled the 1986 budget. The EP, nevertheless, opted for this strategy, trying to pressure the Council into adopting a new maximum rate of increase (see case study below).

1988 budget: As the Council failed to complete the first reading until February 1988, a proper budgetary procedure could not unfold. Hence, the scope of interpretation did not play a role.

Case study: the adoption of the 1987 budget

The 1987 budgetary procedure was dominated by internal tensions in the Council, the exhaustion of the own-resources, and Parliament's insistence on increases in non-compulsory expenditure.[29] The Iberian accession in January 1986 gave the 'Southern' coalition of Italy, Greece, Spain, Portugal and Ireland a blocking minority and strengthened their demands for regional redistribution – at a time when the exhaustion of own-resource strengthened the determination of the austerity camp of 'Northern' member states. Parliament supported Southern member states and sought to undermine the Council's commitment to budgetary discipline. Yet, the ruling of the European Court of Justice that annulled the final adoption of the 1986 budget limited Parliament's room for manoeuvre (Glaesner 1987; Bieber 1986). The case study illustrates the impact of two important variables: first, disunity among member states, which had an increasingly paralysing effect on the Council after the mid-1980s; second, the economic crisis, which intensified the determination with which actors pursued their distributive and institutional objectives. Table 3.8 gives an overview of the different steps of the adoption process of the 1987 budget.

Decisive for the high level of conflict was the division among member states. In the *first reading in the Council*, the Council found it very difficult to establish a draft budget. In its July session, the Budget Council failed to settle upon an internal compromise, despite long and intensive debates. Similar to the cleavages in April, the blocking minority of 'Southern' member states, i.e. Italy (10 votes), Spain (8 votes), Greece (5 votes), Portugal (5 votes), and Ireland (3) demanded an extension of the maximum rate for non-compulsory expenditure.[30] The other seven member states insisted on budgetary discipline. Most of them were not willing to substitute existing agricultural expenditure for non-compulsory expenditure. The Budget Council continued its first reading in September, finally establishing a draft budget at this second meeting. The Council kept non-compulsory expenditure strictly within the maximum rate of 8.1 per cent. The austerity camp had managed to break up the Southern coalition by creating a reserve for unforeseeable financial consequences of the Southern enlargement, and by mitigating the reductions in the Integrated Mediterranean Programme. Consequently. Greece and Spain had voted for the draft, leaving Ireland and Portugal opposing, and Italy abstaining. The British Presidency had facilitated this compromise by agreeing that part of its rebate would not be claimed (Wallace 1987: 277).

While Parliament voted for significant increases and reclassified expenditure in its first reading, the *second reading in the Council* brought two decisions: first, the Council interpreted the EP's vote as a demand for a higher maximum rate and stated that it did not find a qualified majority to increase the rate. It accepted amendments of the EP only to the extent that stayed within the maximum rate of increase.[31] The Council rejected the classification applied by the EP in its second reading.

The second reading of the EP After unsuccessful conciliation and trialogue meetings, the EP met for its second reading in a situation very similar to the year before.

Table 3.8 Overview of the developments of the procedure for the 1987 budget

Annual budgetary procedure		*Adoption process of the 1987 budget*
Year: n-1	Preliminary Draft Budget of *Commission*	The Commission presented its preliminary draft budget (PDB), which did not entail large increases and exceeded the reference framework of the Council only in the area of non-compulsory expenditure.
	First Reading in the Council	The Council experienced great difficulties in the establishment of a draft budget. A blocking minority of Spain, Portugal, Ireland, and Italy demanded increases of non-compulsory expenditure above the maximum rate of increase. In contrast, the other seven member states insisted on an austerity budget. They finally managed to break up the Southern coalition and adopted a budget that stayed within the maximum rate of increase.
	First Reading in the EP	The EP re-established much of the Commission's PDB. It voted for significant increases in non-compulsory expenditure and applied classifications that differed from the ones employed by the Council. With regard to agricultural spending, the accession of Spanish and Portuguese MEPs facilitated a majority for reductions and a reform proposal.
	Second Reading in the Council	The Budget Council did not accept Parliament's proposals for agricultural expenditure, rejected the classifications applied by the EP, and accepted EP amendments only up to the maximum rate of increase.
	Second Reading in the EP	The EP opted for an 'opportunistic interpretation': it voted for an increase of non-compulsory expenditure that, following its classifications, remained within the maximum rate. MEPs knew that the ECJ ruling that year prevented the EP president from declaring the budget successfully adopted. Therefore, they acknowledged that the Council had a different opinion on classification and demanded that the Council consent to a new, slightly higher maximum rate.
Year: n	Further negotiations	The Commission enacted the provisional twelfths system. Internal debates among member states in the Council and between Council and EP continued. A compromise was finally found: non-compulsory commitment appropriations were raised above the maximum rate by 0.049% which provided 'pocket money' for the EP, but rounded down from 8.149% to

8.1%. The compromise allowed the EP and Southern member states to point at the slight increase of non-compulsory expenditure above the maximum rate and member states of the austerity camp to insist on a rejection of a new maximum rate.
The EP endorsed the result in a third reading.

The EP had three options: (1) it could accept the budget as it stood; (2) it could reject the budget; or (3) it could opt for an 'opportunistic interpretation'. The European Democrats and the Liberals favoured the first option, seeking to prevent another conflict with the Council. In particular the British conservatives within the group of European Democrats were eager to bring the budget procedure to a close. They feared the anger of the Thatcher government, which held the presidency at the time and was determined to achieve the adoption of an uncontested budget. Among them was the rapporteur, Mr Curry (European Democrats/UK), who stated in the final debate:

> We need a budget for two reasons. The first is the risk to new policies which would necessarily follow from the absence of a budget and the second is the very excellent reason that you [the British President of the Council, J.L.] gave, that the President of the Commission gave, that the Commissioners have given, concerning what lies over the mountain, as it were, in Community decision-making in terms of future financing, reform of the stuctural funds and reform agriculture (. . .) And yet, in normal circumstances, this would be an eminently rejectable budget, because it is a budget with gaping holes in it.
>
> (EP Debate 9.12.1986: 86)

The British Labour members in the Socialist group put forward the rejection option. Their main objective was to defeat the Tory rapporteur and the British presidency. Yet, the EP did not carry the proposal for rejection. In line with the rapporteur's argument against rejection, the EP regarded the 1987 budget only as a minor episode in the important debate over the future financing that was due to start in spring 1987. Most MEPs held that a rejection of the 1987 budget would not make the Council increase the own-resources (by an additional lifting of the VAT ceiling). At the same time, the upcoming negotiations on EC finances were also the reason why the EP was not willing simply to accept the Council's budget. It was important for the EP to underscore its institutional position. Thus, the majority of the Parliament supported the third option ('opportunistic interpretation'). They voted for an increase of non-compulsory expenditure that, following Parliament's contested classification, remained within the maximum rate. MEPs knew that, in contrast to the previous year, the ECJ's ruling prevented the president of the Parliament from declaring the budget as finally adopted. Therefore, they acknowledged that the Council had a different opinion on the classification and demanded that the Council consent to a new, slightly higher maximum rate.[32]

In search of a compromise As the Council was not willing to consent to a new maximum rate of increase and with the EP president's signature still pending, the Commission initiated the provisional twelfths regime. In parallel, it tabled a new compromise. While the EP signalled it could accept the Commission's compromise, the Council did not agree, and was again caught in a North-South divide. Southern member states supported the position of the EP and argued for an increase of non-compulsory expenditure. In February, the Council finally managed to find a compromise that was acceptable for the majority of member states and the EP. The agreement was based on a peculiar trick: non-compulsory commitment appropriations were raised above the maximum rate by 0.049 per cent, which provided 'pocket money' for the EP. This increase would round down from 8.149 per cent to 8.1 per cent. The compromise allowed the EP and Southern member states to point at the slight increase of non-compulsory expenditure above the maximum rate and member states of the austerity camp to maintain that no new maximum rate had been adopted.[33]

The third reading in the EP The compromise received the endorsement of large majority of MEPs (301 in favour, 41 against and 5 abstentions). In its resolution (Doc. A2–237/86), the EP noted with satisfaction that the maximum rate had been increased (which the Council, of course, denied). The EP also reminded the Council that the budget would probably not suffice to cover the whole year and that no agreement had been found on the issue of classification. The day before, Parliament had heard about a major plan for budgetary reform in the context of the Community futures financing from the president of the Commission. It was clear that the EP considered it as essential that the EC had a budget for 1987 and that it should now focus on the debate on the future of the financing of the Community.

Summary: Heightened frustration

The empirical material presented here provides strong evidence for the propositions detailed in Chapter 2. The increased disunity of the Council intensified high levels of conflict. The institutional separation between revenue and expenditure sides led to clashes between ever increasing spending commitments and shrinking revenue, which budgetary actors were unable to resolve. Following Chapter 2's propositions, it might seem surprising that the EP seldomly used its right to reject the annual budget in order to pressure member states into adopting an increase in revenue. Yet, a closer look reveals that the disunity among MEPs and the understanding that additional pressure on member states would not speed up negotiations in the Council over financial reform made Parliament opt for opportunistic interpretation, rather than rejection. In addition, the following aspect influenced the level of conflict:

The lack of dialogue and the dynamic of escalation Corbett *et al.* (2003a: 361) emphasise that the 'budget argument was conducted through a form of megaphone diplomacy with messages passed from a considerable distance'. This allowed conflict to escalate. Small sums gained enormous symbolic value. Frustrations, heightened sensitivities, and mutual provocations became self-enforcing. In the debate over the 1987 budget, even the very moderate British rapporteur was angry with the Council. He condemned the habit of the Council of 'putting inverted commas around "amendments" as if they were some form of illegitimate expression. Those are quibbles. Nonetheless they are quibbles which hide a substance about the attitudes taken into this negotiations' (Debate of 9.12.1986: 87). The lack of an effective dialogue on the administrative and political level made Parliament respond to the Council's rudeness 'in kind, with little or no attempt at getting minds to meet' (Corbett *et al.* 2003a: 364). As mentioned in a previous summary section, both sides saw their respective positions justified by a concept of governance. The EP regarded its concept of governance confirmed by the inability of the Council to find solutions. While, in the view of the EP, member states concentrated on national interests, 'Parliament saw itself as the conscience of the European Community on budgetary matters, with a duty to raise some of the uncomfortable dimensions of Community expenditure which are squeezed out by the bargaining amongst governments' (Wallace 1987: 264). Similarly, the Council's budgetary discipline approach was a product of its own concept of governance. The Northern member states in the Budget Council regarded the Council as the only directly legitimised representative of European taxpayers, which had to fend off a Parliament that, in their view, reacted to the pressing and dramatic budget crisis with irresponsible spending demands.

4 Facilitating decision-making

Cooperation between Parliament and Council in the annual budgetary procedure (1988–2000)

With the budgetary reform of 1988, the level of conflict declined sharply between the two arms of the budgetary authority in the annual budgetary procedure. Both institutions adopted annual budgets without major political clashes and persistent contestation. The two pillars of the institutional reform, the financial perspective and the interinstitutional agreement, were twice renewed, in 1992/93 and in 1999, and significantly changed EU budgetary politics.

Similar to the previous chapter, this chapter assesses the explanatory value of the propositions that were introduced in Chapter 2. It is divided into two sections: the first covers 1988 to 1994, the second 1995 to 2000. With this division into two subclasses of a similar institutional setting, I am able to account for the impact of non-institutional factors. I take the year 1995 as a dividing line between the two subclasses for two reasons. First and most important, the convergence of preferences of the two arms of the budgetary authority is often described as a decisive non-institutional reason for the reduction in the level of conflict in the 1990s. In this respect, 1995 marks an important shift in the attitude of Parliament towards the political positions of the Council. The self-proclaimed consensus on budgetary rigour turned the 1996 budget (adopted in 1995) into what the chairman of the Budgets Committee called a 'turning point' (Detlev Samland in European Parliament 1997: 6). It became clear for Parliament that the EU budget could not be exempted from the austerity pressure that the EMU convergence criteria of the Maastricht Treaty put on national budgets. Second, a division into periods of similar length is appropriate for the comparative analysis of subclasses. In this respect, 1995 is very useful dividing line, as it splits the time between 1988 and 2000 roughly in the middle.

The situation between 1988 and 1994

Actors work together within clear ceilings

Between 1988 and 1994, the level of conflict in annual budgetary decision-making was low. The financial perspective and the interinstitutional agreement reduced the scope of interpretation and set clear ceilings that lay above the maximum rate of increase. The importance of annual budgetary decision-making decreased and the preferences of Parliament and Council (slightly) converged. Although the Committee on Budgets was still a powerful committee in Parliament that enjoyed political autonomy over budgetary affairs, Parliament's interest in complying with the financial perspective, as well as the declining relevance of the budgetary politics, set clear boundaries for the conflict strategies of Parliament's budgetary experts. This does not mean that tensions did not arise. The two arms of the budgetary authority did experience tense negotiations, in particular as the economic climate worsened from 1992. Yet, these tensions did not endanger the ability of actors to adopt an uncontested budget within the given timetable. Only once, in 1994 (and to a much lesser extent in 1990), did the European Parliament use the remaining scope of interpretation and adopted a budget (and a supplementary budget) that was subsequently challenged by the Council in Court (see Figure 4.1).

This section explores the developments in annual budgetary decision-making between 1988 and 1994. Similar to the sections of the previous chapter, it first assesses the values of the variables identified in Chapter 2 and demonstrates their effect on the level of conflict. It then focuses on the procedure for the 1995 budget in a detailed case study. The 1995 budget is an important case because it constitutes an outlier in the sequel of uncontested budgets and low levels of conflict.[1] The intense debates between the Parliament and Council during the 1995 budget adoption process and the inability of the two arms of the budgetary authority to

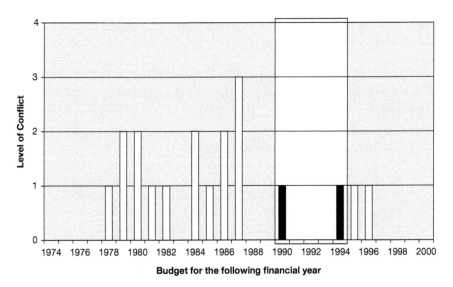

1990: Parliament adopted a supplementary and amending budget No 2/1990 with small corrections of the revenue side. This motivated the Council to take action against Parliament before the European Court of Justice.
1994: Parliament adopted a budget for 1995 based on a reclassification of agricultural expenditure, which the Council challenged at the European Court of Justice.

Figure 4.1 Conflict in the annual budgetary procedure between 1988 and 1994.

adopt an uncontested budget seem to challenge the main argument of the book, i.e. that the introduction of the financial perspective significantly reduced the level of conflict. Yet, a thorough analysis of the case reveals that the outlier is, in fact, in line with the book's theoretical explanation. The section concludes with a brief summary and a discussion of factors, which, in addition to the ones introduced in Chapter 2, influenced the level of conflict between 1988 and 1994.

Assessing the values of the variables and their impact on the level of conflict

When assessing the values of the variables introduced in Chapter 2, this section follows the same sequence as the previous chapter. Box 4.1 recaps the three groups of variables.

THE POLICY ENVIRONMENT

While economic heterogeneity among member states remained largely unchanged between 1988 and 1994, agricultural markets and European economies experienced a significant shift from initial boom to recession. Moreover, the institutional and political architecture underwent a considerable change with the Maastricht Treaty, the effects of which were, however, noticed in the annual budgetary decision-making only after 1994.

The heterogeneity of the distribution of wealth among member states declined slightly between 1988 and 1994. The payments from structural funds contributed to the general catch-up trend among poorer member states, pushing them towards

---

Box 4.1 Structure of the assessment of the different variables

(a) *The policy environment*
- Heterogeneity among member states
- Economic climate and developments of the agricultural markets
- Institutional structure of neighbouring policy fields and overall political architecture of the Community

(b) *Preferences and unity of actors*
- Differences in preferences between EP and Council
- Difference in the time-horizons
- Unity of the EP
- Unity in the Council
- Credibility and reputation of the Commission

(c) *Institutional setting*
- Scope of interpretation
- Relevance of annual decision-making
- The existence of a separate forum for conflict

the level of development in the wealthier European countries. Yet, Southern member states continued to demand expenditure increases for structural policy, in order to strengthen the positive trend. At the time of the renegotiation of the financial perspective in 1992, they were able to strengthen their demands by referring to the adoption of European Monetary Union in the Maastricht Treaty, which was expected to increase, at least temporarily, the heterogeneity among member states. The financial perspective significantly moderated the effect of heterogeneity on the level of conflict. It largely removed the redistributive demands of the poorer member states from annual budgetary decision-making, placing it in the designated arena of negotiations over the ceilings of the financial perspective. As the ceiling for structural expenditure adopted in the financial perspective had the special status of a spending target (Art. 16, IIA from 1988; Art. 21 IIA from 1993; see also Chapter 10), poorer member states, as well as less prosperous regions all over the EU, were guaranteed a fixed level of redistribution for the period of the financial perspective.

Positive economic developments in the years immediately following 1988 contributed significantly to the stabilisation of interinstitutional relations. The GNP of European countries experienced high growth rates between 1988 and 1991 (Commission 1995: 33). This affected the resources available to the European level through the link of own-resources with GNP established by the financial perspective. The institutions could adopt expenditure-increasing revisions of the financial perspective without alteration of the own-resource ceiling. Similarly, the positive development of agricultural prices on the world market (i.e. high market prices) and the strong dollar reduced the pressure on the agricultural sector.

As much as this boom reduced potential pressure on the ceilings and possible conflict resulting from necessary cuts, the financial perspective also mitigated the potentially negative effect of economic crises on annual budgetary decision-making. The introduction of ceilings on agriculture expenditure, set in the financial perspective and the agricultural guidelines, limited the automatism of agriculture expenditure. Even in the case of low world market prices, CAP spending could not exceed the ceiling without a unanimous decision on a revision of the financial perspective. Yet, the recession that hit Europe in 1992 did affect annual budgetary decision-making, in that it heightened finance ministers' interest in keeping the budgetary expenditure to a minimum.

Integration decisions and the treaty renegotiations had a limited impact on annual budgetary decision-making, but a considerable effect on multi-annual negotiations. Decisions on treaty reform and the Community's financial framework were linked and allowed member states to strike bargains over constitutional and distributive questions (Laffan 2000b; see also Chapter 7). With regard to the institutional structure of neighbouring policy fields and their effect on annual budgetary decision-making, the Maastricht Treaty continued a development initiated in the Single European Act. It increased the role of the EP in legislative decision-making. However, the consequences of the institutional change did not materialise before 1995, as the Maastricht Treaty came into effect in late 1993. Thus, tensions over the delineation of budgetary and legislative powers continued to remerge frequently.

In the procedure for the 1992 budget, for example, the EP challenged the amount that the Council had set in its legislative decision on the second and third research framework programme (Shackleton 1993a: 59; Timmann 1992; Corbett *et al.* 2003b: Chapter 13).

PREFERENCES AND UNITY OF THE ACTORS

The preferences of budgetary actors slightly converged and their intensity decreased between 1988 and 1995. On structural expenditure and foreign aid, Parliament and Council largely shared distributive objectives. The financial perspective recognised the distributive interests and the blocking power of the Southern coalition and established the ceiling of heading 2 (structural expenditure) as a spending target. The Southern coalition under the leadership of Spain ensured that the spending commitments were honoured. Thus, the Council had fulfilled a key distributive demand of the Parliament that dominated interinstitutional relations in the 1970s and 1980s.

In the procedures for the 1990, 1991 and 1992 budgets, the EP and the Council shared a strong interest in foreign aid (Nicoll and Lentz 1990; Läufer 1990a; Timmann 1991a; Fernandez-Fabregas and Lentz 1991, 1992). Reacting to the political development after the fall of the Berlin Wall and the Gulf War, they adopted budgets that entailed considerable aid programmes for Eastern Europe, the former GDR and the Gulf region. In line with demands from the EP, the Council agreed to facilitate these spending decisions through revisions of the financial perspective. In addition to the strong political and moral pressure for European involvement in the reconstruction of Eastern Europe, the Council sought to realise economies of scale by financing the reconstruction of Eastern Europe from the European budget (interview with Commission official). This was particularly the case for smaller countries, which did not have the capacity for individual aid programmes. The period of a strong joint-interest in foreign aid coincided with high growth rates in European economies and subsided when the effect of the recession was felt after 1992 (Fernandez-Fabregas and Lentz 1993).

Despite the convergence of preferences towards foreign aid and structural spending, Parliament still held distributive preferences that exceeded the Council's notion of the EC budget. Yet, the institutional setting channelled these distributive differences into debates over revisions of the financial perspective (and renegotiations of the interinstitutional agreement) as the ceilings set clear limits on expenditure. Moreover, the intensity of budgetary preferences declined because annual budgets lost a considerable part of their political relevance. First of all, the financial perspective and a rise of multi-annual programmes gave spending committees the assurance that their spending interests would be met. Second, the Single European Act had made the completion of the single market the key political project of the late 1980s and early 1990s. This shifted the interest to legislative politics, and away from the budget (interview with former MEP).

Institutional differences between Parliament and Council remained, in particular as budget experts in the EP increasingly focused on trading distributive concessions against institutional gains (interviews with officials from the secretariat general of the EP and with former MEP). As in previous years, Parliament was interested in extending its budgetary powers into the area of compulsory expenditure and the revenue side. The maximum rate of increase had lost its limiting role, replaced by ceilings for the different headings in the financial perspective. These institutional demands were largely channelled into the renegotiations over the interinstitutional agreement. Yet, where scope of interpretation still allowed, they erupted as disputes during the annual budgetary procedure, as in the case of the 1994 and the 1995 budget (see below).

The interinstitutional agreement and the financial perspective partly met the preferences of the Parliament. The 1988 and the 1992 financial perspective matched Parliament's interests in structural expenditure and a budget above the maximum rate of increase, but they left unfulfilled demands for increases in internal and external expenditure. The negotiations over the interinstitutional agreements offered the EP the opportunity to gain significant institutional concessions from the Council. Yet, Parliament failed to achieve a change of the treaty provisions (see Chapter 10).

The propositions in Chapter 2 predicted that Parliament would comply with the ceilings of the financial perspective when they lay considerably above the non-compulsory expenditure that would be obtainable through the application of the maximum rate of increase (or an 'opportunistic interpretation'). The ceilings fulfilled this condition between 1988 and 1994, with the exception of 1993. In the procedure for the 1994 budget, the EP could have obtained a higher budget by returning to the treaty provisions. An exceptionally high level of commitments in the 1993 budget offered the EP the option of increases for the 1994 budget that would have gone beyond the ceilings of the financial perspective. However, Parliament did not opt for non-compliance but successfully used the possibility of an above the ceiling budget as a credible threat for achieving a revision of the ceiling (Deffaa and Zangl 1994; Fernandez-Fabregas and Lentz 1994).[2]

The theory chapter also predicts that the EP would operate under incentives not to comply with the financial perspective in the final years of the multi-annual budget plan ('end game'). There is evidence that tensions were slightly heightened in the negotiations over the 1992 budget (Timmann 1992), but the impact of the 'end game' did not seem to be significant.

Overall, the financial perspective slightly led to a convergence of the time-horizons of Parliament and Council by structuring budgetary politics into multi-annual periods. Distributive negotiations over the financial perspective span the period of five to seven years. Moreover, the financial perspective synchronised institutional and distributive dimensions, because the institutional framework of the interinstitutional agreement was linked to the duration of multi-annual budget. This does not mean that there were no differences in the balance between distributive and institutional objectives, as illustrated by the negotiations over the interinstitutional agreement, where the EP gained institutionally because it accepted the multi-annual budget plan as the European Council had adopted it (see Chapter 10).

While the unity of the EP contributed significantly to the high levels of conflict in the 1970s and 1980s, unity among MEPs between 1988 and 1994 did not have the same effect. This resulted from two intervening factors: the relevance of annual budgetary decision-making and the preferences of the EP. The financial perspective massively reduced the relevance of annual budgetary decision-making. This strengthened the role of the budgetary experts during the decision-making process. The EP Committee on Budgets set the strategy and negotiated the compromises with the Council. Members of the Committee on Budgets worked together closely and shared similar institutional objectives that transcended party political or national group affiliations (interview with former MEP). Moreover, consecutive Socialist chairmen had a strong grip on their committee and were backed by the largest group in the EP, the Socialist Party of Europe (SPE). The hierarchical structure of the SPE and the consensus with the European People's Party (EPP) meant that recommendations of the Committee on Budgets were largely accepted in plenary (interview with official of the secretariat general of the EP). However, this apparent increase in internal unity was considerably counteracted by a shift in preferences among MEPs. The Committee on Budgets found it difficult to portray budgetary disputes with the Council as major institutional battles and important public events that needed the full support of the plenary. Spending committees saw their distributive interests largely satisfied and started to appreciate the stability provided by the financial perspective. In the light of this, the Committee on Budgets was clearly constrained. It knew that it could use its autonomy only as long as it stayed in line with the more moderate position of the plenary.

Therefore, it is no coincidence that the Committee on Budgets planned its major challenge of the classification of agricultural expenditure in 1994, the year of a European election. While Parliament was dissolved (for the election campaign and the summer recess) and re-established itself in a new composition, budget experts carefully planned their 'institutional attack' and then pushed it through plenary (see case study of the 1995 budget below).

Unity among member states, and between the different Councils during annual budgetary decision-making significantly increased with the introduction of the financial perspective. This had a clear conflict-reducing effect on interinstitutional relations. The main intergovernmental exchanges took place outside the annual procedure at the large negotiation table for the financial perspective. Here, national governments coordinated and reconciled their different positions and adopted, under unanimity, the financial perspective for the following years (see Chapter 6). The veto-power of each delegation ensured that distributive demands were met. Once the financial perspective was adopted, member states accepted the allocative structure and delegated the annual 'fine-tuning' to the budgetary experts (interview with representative of national delegation).[3]

Unity was institutionally created because ceilings and headings reduced the rivalry between different spending lines. The influence of the Agriculture Council was limited to its heading and separated from the rest of the budget by a clear upper ceiling. On the other side, structural expenditure was secured by its status of spending target. Expenditure totals were also pre-committed and linked with the revenue ceiling. A margin between own-resources ceiling and an aggregated total ensured that rising expenditure would not induce pressure on the revenue side.

Given this structure, the EP could no longer engineer division in the Council. The basis for the alliance between Parliament and the Southern member states in the 1980s had been their joint interest in increases of non-compulsory expenditure for structural operations. As the distributive demands of the Southern member states were largely met by heading 2 of the financial perspective, Southern member states lost interest in supporting EP demands for increases in non-compulsory expenditure, which the EP wanted to use for the headings 3 and 4. The financial perspective split the non-compulsory expenditure and satisfied the interest of Southern member states in one part of non-compulsory expenditure, while relegating the remaining non-compulsory expenditure to less well-endowed headings.

Annual decision-making reflected this pattern (interviews with official of the secretariat general of the Council and with representative of national delegation). The decisions in the Council were relatively predictable and taken without major tensions. In heading 1 (agriculture), the Council largely followed the forecast of the Commission, and minor tensions became apparent in this area only after the emergence of the austerity approach (see next section). In heading 2 (structural actions), the status of the ceiling as a spending target limited debates and the Southern member states, led by the Spanish government, fiercely defended 'their' expenditure lines – even though the backlog of utilised resources gave Northern member states the opportunity to adopt reductions. In heading 3 (internal policies), the member states did not quarrel. They mostly cut the Commission's preliminary draft budget and left the EP a margin for its priorities. Similarly, in heading 4 (external policies) Council largely left a margin to the EP, after having satisfied the clientele of member states, e.g. Latin America and Mediterranean third countries for Spain, and East Timor for Portugal. The Council was also fairly united in heading 5 (administrative expenditure).

Given this pattern, budgetary decisions were largely de-politicised and conducted on the expert level. Brussels-based civil servants in the Council's Budget Committee clarified the vast majority of the tensions between national positions before they even reached the level of Committee of Permanent Representatives (Coreper). Members of the Committee interacted on a very regular basis and developed a routine of joint decision-making. They shared the status of experts and the aspiration to keep the number of unresolved issues low (interviews with official of secretariat general of the Council and with representative of national delegation).[4] As a consequence, the readings in the Budget Council were considerably shorter than the marathon sessions of the 1980s, when large parts of the budget were left to the political level.[5]

The de-politicisation of budgetary negotiations in the Council significantly increased the role that the Commission played in annual budgetary decision-making. The more decisions were made at the administrative level, the more the Commission could fulfil the crucial role of the broker of compromises among member states and between Parliament and Council. Here, the technical expertise of the Commission came into full play (interview with Commission official). Moreover, the DG Budget was decisive in the early years of the financial perspective in ensuring compliance with the ceilings of the multi-annual budget plan. In contrast to the 1980s, when preliminary draft budgets usually went beyond the maximum rate of increase, it presented preliminary draft budgets that respected the ceilings of the financial perspective and did not fuel distributive interests within the EP (interview with Commission official).

INSTITUTIONAL SETTING

As mentioned above, the financial perspective reduced the relevance of the maximum rate of increase and replaced it with an institutional framework of headings and ceilings that left very little scope of interpretation.[6] This altered the pattern of distributive conflict between two arms of the budgetary authority in a decisive manner. The EP lost the option of increasing the budget unilaterally by pursuing a strategy of 'opportunistic interpretation' of the maximum rate of increase. The 'revision game' replaced the conflict constellation of 1970s and 1980s and introduced a situation, in which only mutual agreement (and not anymore unilateral deviation) could lead to increases above the ceilings (Läufer 1990a: 142). As discussed in Chapter 2, in the revision game the EP had to persuade the Council to consent to a revision. If the Council refused its agreement, the EP had no other option than to accept the Council's stance, or to reject the budget, which would have subsequently endangered the whole multi-annual financial perspective. It could not increase the budget above the ceiling by opportunistically interpreting the provisions of the interinstitutional agreement, as they were very clear in their categorisation of expenditure and allocation of explicit ceilings to the headings.

The 1990s witnessed a series of these revision games. During the first financial perspective, the Council was relatively open to Parliament's demands for revisions and consented to seven revisions of the financial perspective. This did not mean that the Council accepted all the demands of the EP. Yet, tensions did not escalate into major conflict. The most intense debate over revision at the time emerged during procedure for the 1992 budget (Shackleton 1991; Fernandez-Fabregas and Lentz 1992; Timmann 1992). The Council and the EP disagreed over whether aid to the Soviet Union should be covered within the existing, or within a revised ceiling. As the Council stood firmly by its refusal of a revision, the EP had to accept that the ceiling would remain unchanged.[7]

With regard to the conflict-reducing effect of the financial perspective, it is important to remember that the old conflict over the interpretation of the maximum rate of increase remerged when the actors returned to the full application of the treaty, i.e. during the 1993 budget procedure. This conflict was resolved only by the introduction of comfortable ceilings in the new financial perspective in December 1992 (Fernandez-Fabregas and Lentz 1993; Timmann 1993).

However, the financial perspective and the interinstitutional agreement did not close all scope of interpretation in the treaty provisions. Concerning the distinction between compulsory and non-compulsory, the existence of ceilings reduced the distributive motivation within the EP for challenging the existing interpretation. Yet, the EP was still interested in extending non-compulsory expenditure on institutional grounds. The EP took up the issue in the procedures for the 1994 and 1995 budgets. The existing scope of interpretation and the backing of the Commission (which implemented the contested 1995 budget) allowed the EP to challenge the dominant interpretation, which provoked the Council to take action against the EP before the ECJ (see case study below). Concerning the revenue side, the EP's interest in power over own-resources declined, since the financial perspective gave Parliament a limited veto-right on the overall expenditure and the corresponding own-resources ceiling. However, the EP took the chance during the procedure for the supplementary budget No. 2/1990 to adopt corrections on the revenue side (EC Bull. 7/8–1990: 125). The Council went immediately to the Court and reprehended the EP. The episode remained a minor and singular incident.

Overall, the reduction of annual conflict through the introduction of a multi-annual budget plan should not come as a surprise. Annual budgetary decision-making lost relevance, as large part of the annual distribution was already decided. Many of the tensions were bundled and transferred to a separate forum, where budgetary actors renegotiated the financial perspective and the interinstitutional agreement every five to seven years. The package character of the bargains at these renegotiation points helped actors to settle upon a compromise.

Case study: The adoption of the 1995 budget

The negotiations over the 1995 budget represent a budgetary procedure with the strongest 'institutional attack' of the EP between 1988 and 2000.[8] In its second reading, the EP adopted a budget that entailed reclassifications of originally compulsory agriculture expenditure, which the Council strongly disputed. Following the adoption, the Council took the EP to Court and gained the annulment of the budget. With its high level of conflict, the 1995 budget constitutes an outlier in the annual budgets of the 1990s. For this book it is, thus, an important budget, because it seems to contradict the book's argument that the institutional setting of the 1988 reform changed the interaction between budgetary actors and reduced the level of conflict.

However, the following detailed case study illustrates that the book's theoretical explanation of variation in the levels of conflict is able to account even for outliers like the 1995 budget. In line with propositions of Chapter 2, the 'institutional attack' of the EP was possible because of three factors. First, although the interinstitutional agreements of 1988 and 1993 closed much of the scope of interpretation and reduced the relevance of the treaty provisions, classification remained an issue over which competing interpretations existed. Second and probably most important, due to the European election in June 1994, MEPs were preoccupied with their election campaigns and Parliament's summer recess. This gave budgetary experts in Parliament the breathing space to prepare their institutional attack with little interference from other EP committees or the political groups. Third, Council and, in particular, its presidency, lacked the determination to contain the confrontational strategy of Parliament.

As Table 4.1 illustrates, two issues dominated the adoption process for the 1995 budget: the question of revision of the financial perspective on the occasion of enlargement and the above-mentioned dispute over classification (the 'institutional attack'). The first issue was, for large parts of the procedure, the more prominent bone of contention. On the one hand, it had elements of a classic revision game in which Parliament tried to convince a very reluctant Council to consent to changes of the ceilings. On the other, it was complicated by internal difficulties in the Council to adopt a decision on own-resources[9] and ratification of the accession treaties in the prospective new member states, namely Austria, Sweden, Finland, and Norway. Once the ratification process was concluded and it became clear that the own-resources decision would not come into force before the beginning of the following year, Parliament and Council quickly agreed on a revision of the financial perspective. Hence, tensions between the two arms of the budgetary authority on the issue were resolved before the second reading in Parliament.

Although the focus of the budgetary negotiations in 1994 shifted towards the dispute over classification only after the question of revision was resolved, budget experts in Parliament had long and carefully planned their 'institutional attack'. They wanted to undermine the long-resented distinction between non-compulsory and compulsory expenditure, and sought to extend their powers into the agricultural sector.[10] The Committee on Budgets had already concentrated on the agricultural sector in the previous year: it had addressed classification in the procedure for the 1994 budget and had gained a new *ad hoc* conciliation procedure on compulsory expenditure as a concession in the negotiations over the new interinstitutional agreement in 1993 (see Chapter 10).[11] The first year in which this new procedure would be applied was 1994, and budget experts sought to use it for a renewed institutional attack on the classification of certain expenditure lines in the agriculture sector.[12] Yet, the rapporteur, Mr Wynn,[13] was clear about the possible consequences of this attack. As an internal strategy paper of the Committee on Budget illustrates, he and the small circle of Committee members and Parliament officials who were behind the institutional attack wanted to risk neither a breakdown of the financial perspective, nor a refusal by the EP President to sign the budget on legal grounds (internal paper made available to the author, interview with MEP). They were, however, willing to risk the Council taking the EP to the European Court of Justice for allegedly violating the treaty provisions.

Council adamantly opposed changes in the existing classification of agricultural expenditure. Already before the first reading in the Council, Parliament had presented the Council with a list of budget lines in which it questioned the classification of certain budget lines as compulsory expenditure; the Council had been unwilling to discuss the issue. In the first reading in Parliament, MEPs criticised the Council's refusal and adopted some 150 amendments in the agricultural sector. Underscoring the institutional nature of the EP's attack on classification, the amendments concentrated largely on remarks on budget lines and left the amounts unchanged. As the Council rejected all these amendments in its second reading of

Table 4.1 Overview of the developments of the procedure for the 1995 budget

Annual budgetary procedure		*Adoption process of the 1995 budget*
Year: n–1	*Commission* prepares Preliminary Draft Budget	The Commission proposed a budget for twelve member states within an adapted revenue ceiling of 1.21% of GNP.
	First Reading in the Council	The Council adopted a draft budget for 12 member states within an unaltered revenue ceiling of 1.20% of GNP.
	First Reading in the EP	The EP tabled amendments and modifications that increased the budget to provide financial resources for an enlarged budget. The EP proposed cuts of expenditure lines with high importance for the Council in order to press the Council to consent to a revision, and to adopt the decision on the increase of the own resource ceiling. The EP reclassified certain expenditure in the agricultural sector.
		The Council finally adopted the own-resources ceiling and passed it onto the national parliaments for ratification.
	Second Reading in the Council	The Council largely confirmed its first reading and rejected the proposed reclassifications.
		After all applicant states had concluded the ratification process, the EP, the Council, and the Commission agreed on a revision of the financial perspective.
	Second Reading in the EP	The EP reinstated most of its amendments using the increase in the own-resources that resulted from the net-contributions of the new member states and an upwards correction of the economic forecast; but it stayed within the unaltered own-resource ceiling of 1.20%. The EP president declared the budget finally adopted, despite condemnations by the president of the Council of Parliament's reclassifications of agricultural expenditure.
Year: n	*Commission* implements the budget	The Commission implemented the budget, despite legal doubts within the Council. Council decided to take action against the final adoption of the budget before the ECJ. After the ECJ annulled the budget, the EP and the Council found an agreement on the 1995 budget and planned to settle their agreements in a permanent political solution.

the budget, it was then up to the MEPs to decide whether they would stand by their confrontational strategy and adopt a budget with contested classifications.

The second reading in the EP During the debate that preceded the vote, the German Council president told MEPs that the Council could not accept the classifications applied by the EP.[14] Yet, when challenged by the rapporteur, he was unwilling to specify how the Council would react to a budget that included reclassified agriculture expenditure lines.[15] In the final vote, MEPs supported the strategy of the Committee on Budgets and voted in favour of the reclassifications. Subsequently, the Council president restated its reservations and said that the Council's consent to the maximum rate of increase would remain pending until the question of classification was resolved. Three MEPs questioned the legality of the budget and demanded that the EP president not sign the budget, in order to prevent a conflict with the Council. The chairman of the Committee on Budgets and the rapporteur rejected these demands and insisted that Parliament had not breached the rules laid down in the treaty. The rapporteur told MEPs (Mr Wynn in EP debate 15.12.1994: 210):

> I wish to say to those who think the budget is illegal, ask the President-in-Office whether he wants the budget signed or not. Do not put him in that embarrassing position, because his answer will be 'yes'. The Council wants this budget signed, and I doubt whether it will challenge it. We are on very strong ground here, Mr President, and when you do sign it, we shall have a lot to be proud about.

Following this brief debate, the EP President declared that he would sign the budget.

In reaction to the signing of the budget, the (French) chairman of the Agricultural Committee in the EP issued a statement that condemned Parliament's decision on classification. He reproached the Committee on Budgets for having repeated its institutional *coup d'état* (that it had tried already in the procedure for the 1994 budget) and went so far as to hope that the Council would take the issue to the European Court of Justice. It was clear that the defenders of the CAP feared that Parliament's intrusion into the agricultural sector could result in a reduction of funding for this policy. The largest national group endorsing this defensive position in the Agriculture Committee had been the French. In the vote on the budget, even the French members of the two largest political groups in Parliament had voted with strongly anti-federalist groups against the recommendations of the Committee on Budgets or, as in the case of French Socialists, had abstained (Agence Europe, 16 December 1994, 6380: 13–14; Le Monde 17 December 1994). Yet, this opposition had not been able to prevent a parliamentary endorsement of the rapporteur's recommendations.

Given the reduced role that budgetary politics had become to play in the 1990s and the particular opposition from the agricultural lobby in the EP, final adoption of the reclassifications was a remarkable victory for the Committee on Budgets, which had worked hard behind the scenes to achieve it. One of the key factors that had facilitated this achievement was the European election in June 1994, which had strengthened the autonomy of a small circle of senior EP budget experts. The main internal decisions in the Committee on Budgets and the brief unsuccessful discussions with the Council over classification took place in summer, at a time when the Parliament was already dissolved (interview with official from secretariat general of the EP). The new Parliament, which was established in September, had a large percentage of new MEPs. This gave the Committee on Budgets the opportunity to pursue the issue without detailed coordination with the other committees. Meanwhile, a small group of senior members of the Committee on Budgets ensured that the political groups stood behind the position of the Committee on Budgets. In their groups, the budget experts emphasised the institutional importance, and the firm legal basis of the institutional challenge. However, this did not mean that internal discussions in the political groups were not intense. In the days before the budget vote, it was still unclear whether a majority would be achieved and whether the EP president, Mr Hänsch, would sign the budget once adopted in plenary – in particular as the legal service of the EP had advised the president not to sign it (interview with official from secretariat general of the EP).

Moreover, the Committee on Budgets benefited from a minor degree of disunity and weakness within the Council. The German Presidency condemned the reclassification and had refused to enter a dialogue on the issue during the budgetary procedure, but it failed to issue a clear warning to Parliament. This allowed the rapporteur to argue that the Council would probably not contest the budget (as quoted above).

Reactions of the Council and the Commission While the Commission stated that it would execute the budget as finally adopted by the EP, the Council discussed how to proceed from Parliament's decision on classification. France, which took over the Presidency in January, argued most strongly for court action against the EP.[16] Although this position was not shared by all member states, a majority in the Council finally decided to bring the issue before the European Court of Justice. In comparison to the conflicts of the 1980s, the Council's attitude was relatively tame and it simply sought to protect its authority over agricultural spending. Given the lack of immediate distributive consequences, it did not want its action to be seen as an obstacle to the implementation of the 1995 budget or as a questioning of the collaboration procedure in force (Agence Europe 23.01.1995, No. 6404).

The conflict continued into 1995 and led to a dispute over the supplementary and amending budget No. 1/1995. Yet, the *ad hoc* procedure for compulsory expenditure reduced the tensions in the negotiations over the 1996 budget. Finally, in December 1995, the Court annulled the act whereby the EP president had declared the 1995 budget finally adopted. As the EP and the Council had not agreed on a new maximum rate of increase, the EP president, so the Court's ruling, should not have concluded the budgetary procedure.

Summary: Bargaining within a new incentive structure

The empirical material presented largely supports the propositions of Chapter 2. The introduction of the financial perspective and the interinstitutional agreement changed the incentive structure of budgetary actors. It reduced the scope of interpretation and marginalised the maximum rate of increase. Therefore, opportunistic interpretation was no longer Parliament's dominant strategy. Distributive demands had to be satisfied within the existing ceilings of the financial perspective, or through a consensus with the Council on a revision of the ceilings. Institutional conflict also lost much of its mobilising force within the Parliament. MEPs saw their spending interests satisfied by the financial perspective and no longer regarded the budget as a key issue of integration. Hence, budget experts found it difficult to gain sufficient support in Parliament for institutional attacks. The fact that Parliament complied with the financial perspective even when the maximum rate of increase promised a larger amount seems at first glance surprising. Yet, as the empirical evidence reveals, budget experts used non-compliance as a bargaining chip in the negotiations with the Council over revision.

The previous chapter demonstrated that factors, which had not been predicted in Chapter 2, also influenced the level of conflict. It showed, for example, that the willingness of actors was particularly important in containing conflict in the first years of the new treaty procedure. The following paragraphs take up these factors and discuss their relevance for the 1988 and 1994 period.

The relevance of willingness In the early years of the financial perspective, the willingness of actors to make the new institutional setting work contributed to its positive effect on the level of conflict. Timmann (1989, 1992) describes how the close formal and informal contacts between the Commission, Parliament, and the Council during the negotiations over the 1988 interinstitutional agreement created this willingness. Yet, he also reveals that the willingness subsided after 1991. The political distance between Council and Parliament returned and led to fierce disputes over the revision of the financial perspective. This demonstrates that although willingness of actors was conducive for compliance with the financial perspective, its disappearance did not endanger the budgetary procedure. The new incentive structure was sufficiently robust in order to contain tensions between the two arms of the budgetary authority.

Close contacts Close contacts played an important role on the administrative level in the Council. As mentioned above, the de-politicisation of budgetary negotiations among member states gave the finance attachés in the budgetary working group increased autonomy. The increased number of contacts developed a climate in which finance attachés started to cooperate closely and to overcome national differences (within the given mandates from national capitals). Concerning administrative and political coordination between Parliament and Council, the negotiations over the 1993 interinstitutional agreement and the new *ad hoc* procedure strengthened formal and informal contacts. The effects of this development materialised after 1994, as illustrated in the next section.

The situation between 1995 and 2000

Actors agree on budgetary rigour

From 1995 until 2000, the levels of conflict continued to be significantly lower than in the 1980s. The financial perspective and the interinstitutional agreement structured annual budgetary decision-making and prevented the escalation of tensions into serious conflict. The only two issues over which legal disputes emerged were of minor importance, and did not threaten the functioning of the annual procedure (see Figure 4.2). Although the second half of the 1990s was quite similar to the first half (as described in the previous section), three particular developments contributed to lower levels of conflict: first, with the introduction of EMU convergence criteria for national budgets, Parliament joined Council's approach of budgetary rigour; second, the unity of the Parliament behind the Committee on Budgets decreased as the other parliamentary committees gained legislative powers; and third, national governments started to increase the pressure on MEPs.

The section explores the developments between 1995 and 2000 in three steps. It first assesses the value of the variables identified in Chapter 2 and demonstrates

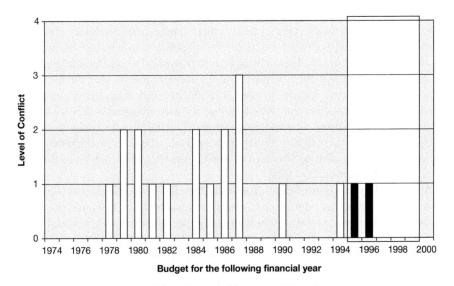

1995: Conflict over the Parliament's reclassification of agricultural expenditure in the 1995 budget spilled over to the adoption procedure for a supplementary and amending budget No. 1/1995. As Parliament was unwilling to withdraw its interpretation and adopted the budget with reclassifications, the Council decided to add proceedings against the adoption of the supplementary and amending budget to the case of the 1995 budget, which was still pending at the European Court of Justice.
1996: The Council took legal action against the Commission for implementing budget lines (that Parliament had adopted) without legal bases.

Figure 4.2 Conflict in the annual budgetary procedure between 1995 and 2000.

their effect on the level of conflict. It then focuses on the procedure for the 2000 budget in a detailed case study. The 2000 budget stands out as a very interesting case. First, it led to strong tensions between Council and Parliament, which were settled only at the last minute. The institutional fora for conflict settlement did not work as well as in previous years. Second and more important, it is surprising that budgetary actors settled at all on a 2000 budget within the framework of the new interinstitutional agreement. The EP experienced strong distributive incentives not to comply with the tight ceilings of the new financial perspective. Due to this second aspect, the 2000 budget is a 'hard case' for the book's theoretical explanation of the level of conflict. Yet, the thorough analysis reveals that the developments of the 2000 budget are, nevertheless, in line with the propositions introduced in Chapter 2. The section concludes with a brief summary and a discussion of factors, which, in addition to the ones introduced in Chapter 2, influenced the level of conflict between 1995 and 2000.

Assessing the values of the variables and their impact on the level of conflict

THE POLICY ENVIRONMENT

While heterogeneity among member states and developments on the agricultural markets did not greatly affect the level of conflict, changes in the institutional structure of neighbouring policy fields and the overall political architecture of the EU (induced by the treaties of Maastricht and Amsterdam) had a considerable impact.

The accession of new members in 1995 did not significantly alter the balance among member states. Austria, Sweden, and Finland were relatively prosperous countries and did not enter the Community with a strong interest in redistributive policies. On the contrary, their accession strengthened the austerity coalition in the Council and, in particular, the 'net-contributors club', the core of which became Germany, the Netherlands, Sweden and Austria (see Chapter 6; Appendix No. 3; Laffan and Shackleton 2000: 224).

With the introduction of the convergence criteria in the Maastricht Treaty, member states experienced strong pressure on national budgets. The position of the finance ministers within national politics was significantly strengthened and far-reaching cuts in national budgets were instigated. Although limited in size, the contributions to the EU budget also became a target point for finance ministers, in particular in the net-contributor countries. The political link was strong. At a time when national expenditure had to be scaled down drastically in order to facilitate the introduction of a European common currency, the European level could not continue to pursue an expansive spending approach. Hence, finance ministers sought to maintain a low budget expenditure level, regardless of the economic developments of the Union. The situation on the agricultural markets was conducive to this objective, leaving agricultural expenditure significantly below the (generous) ceilings of the 1992 financial perspective.

In contrast to the previous period, changes in the institutional architecture materialised fully in the shape of the Maastricht Treaty (and later, the Amsterdam

Treaty). In addition to the impact of EMU on the preferences of budgetary actors, the strengthening of Parliament in the legislative realm had a considerable effect on annual budgetary decision-making. Much to the disappointment of the Committee on Budgets, the new codecision procedure diverted interest further from budgetary politics and reduced the conflict potential over the delineation of budgetary and legislative decision-making, because it significantly reduced the asymmetry between the two procedures. Concerning the impact of legislative decision-making on the budgetary procedure, the Committee on Budgets found it difficult to sell its total opposition to the Council's practice of setting financial amounts in legislative decisions. As MEPs were now fully involved in legislative decision-making (at least in the areas to which the codecision procedure applied), Parliament budget experts could no longer brand this practice as undemocratic. Egged on by the institutional interests of the legislative committees, Parliament struck a deal with the Council and accepted the practice of setting financial amounts for all legislative decisions that were adopted under the codecision procedure ('Joint declaration on the incorporation of financial provisions into legislative acts' from 6 March 1995; see Chapter 10). With regard to the impact of budgetary decision-making on the legislative realm, the Committee on Budgets had to concede another of its traditional positions. The practice of using budgetary decisions to initiate new policies became untenable. Following a Court ruling in 1998, Parliament settled on a compromise with the Council, which clarified the limits of this practice ('Interinstitutional Agreement of 13 October on legal bases and implementation of the budget'; see Chapter 10).

PREFERENCES AND UNITY OF THE ACTORS

The preferences of budgetary actors over spending interests converged further between 1995 and 2000, although some differences remained. Most importantly, Parliament started to accept Council's emphasis on budgetary austerity. It was politically difficult for the EP to demand increases in the EU budget at a time when national budgets were under the strain induced by the EMU convergence criteria.

The EP presented the 1996 budget as a 'turning point' towards austerity (European Parliament 1996). The German chairman of Committee on Budgets, Mr Samland, was determined to free Parliament from its spending image. Answering to allegations from the Dutch national parliament, which was reluctant to ratify the own-resource decision in 1995, he declared:

> the decisions that the EP had taken during its vote on Thursday should persuade the Dutch to ratify this decision. They reproach the Parliament with not having sufficient budgetary rigour although this time the Parliament has been stricter than the Council.
>
> (Agence Europe 27.10. 1995, No. 6593)

The 1997 budget further strengthened the joint emphasis on budgetary rigour (Guth and Discors 1997). As 1997 was the reference year for fulfilment of the EMU convergence criteria, both arms of the budgetary authority had a strong interest in demonstrating that the EU level made similarly strong efforts as national budgetary authorities and adopted an 'austerity budget'. Figure 4.3 illustrates the new spending approach of the Parliament. From the 1996 to the 1999 budget, the EP kept the budgets below the ceilings in the headings 3 (internal policies) and 4 (external actions), where it had the last word. Thus, the EP restrained itself and did not use all the money to which it had access. The margins disappeared for the 2000 and 2001 budget, as the new financial perspective, in contrast to the previous one, set extremely tight ceilings for these headings.

A shift in the composition of the Parliament after the 1999 European elections further strengthened the focus on budgetary rigour. The Socialist Party of Europe (SPE) lost its role as the largest party to the European People Party (EPP). The EPP put 'value for money' at the centre of their budgetary strategy. New centre-right MEPs wanted to gain the profile of stern accountants fighting the image of a money-wasting European level (see interview with member of staff of the EPP parliamentary group). In the procedure for the 2001 budget, for example, the centre-right majority brought Parliament in line with the Council's rejection of a Commission proposal for a revision of the financial perspective (Grossir 2001). In previous years, the EP had always supported demands for revisions.

Parallel to the acceptance of budgetary rigour, the EP shifted its focus towards the implementation and management of the budget. This focus was not completely new. The EP had long criticised the tendency of member states to depart, in the implementation stage, from the budget lines adopted in the budget. However, the renewed emphasis on thorough implementation was a reaction to cases of fraud and mismanagement on the part of the Commission. Budgetary experts saw budget

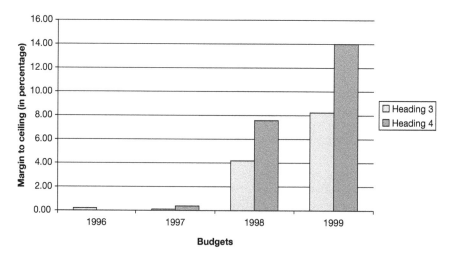

Figure 4.3 Increasing margins below the ceilings in Heading 3 and 4.
Source: Samland (1999).

control as an increasingly attractive field of influence and publicity, especially when annual budgetary decision-making lost political relevance. The new focus on management reduced the prevalence of the dualism between Council and EP and brought the Commission into the line of fire. It diverted attention away from traditional interinstitutional conflict. After the 1997 budget, the EP made use of budgetary reserves that were connected to conditions that the Commission had to fulfil. In particular, the EPP group in the Committee on the Budget was keen to put pressure on the Commission, as illustrated by the 2001 budget procedure. Here, extended discussions took place over a 'joint declaration on a progress report to be submitted by the Commission on 30 June 2001' (interviews with Commission officials and participatory observation).

Despite the convergence towards budgetary rigour and budget control, the EP nevertheless insisted on spending priorities. The EP did not want to lose its ability to imprint a specific emphasis on each year's budget. For MEPs it was very important to claim credit for budgetary decisions and to demonstrate their relevance in the budgetary process. This stood in contrast to the Council's interest in across the board cuts and incremental updating. The Council did not understand the need for annual priority projects, because it regarded annual budgeting as a largely administrative, rather than political act. It was not a fundamental disagreement over the necessity of budgetary rigour that divided the two arms of the budgetary authority. The EP simply wanted to have some money left for projects that would maintain Parliament's impact, such as employment initiatives or trans-European networks. The institutional dimension of this was clear. In the eyes of MEPs, budgetary powers of the EP would lose their relevance when there was no financial flexibility left to actually use them. This gained particular relevance in the discourse over the tight ceilings of the 1999 financial perspective (interview with MEP).

The unity of the EP on budgetary issues decreased over the years due to three factors: the influence of national governments; a shift in majorities in Parliament; and the declining importance of the Committee on Budgets.

First, the rise of the overall political importance of the EP made national governments and national party leadership more interested in the voting behaviour of MEPs. In contrast to the 1980s, they began to exert pressure on MEPs, and to ensure that MEPs considered national and party political interests when voting on budgetary items (Corbett *et al.* 2003a). This was particularly true for the Spanish and Greek MEPs, who strongly depended on the national leadership's support in the selection process for candidates, and did not want to endanger their position on the party list (interview with MEPs and member of staff of parliamentary group).

Second, the unity of the EP was further reduced by the victory of the EPP in the 1999 election. The EPP was less hierarchically structured and less cohesive than the SPE. Given the new position as largest group and the role as leading group, this weakness came into play and made decisions in plenary more unpredictable (interview with Commission official). Moreover, the EPP's self-declared objective was to politicise Parliament (interview with member of staff of EPP parliamentary group). Against the tradition of a consensual grand coalition in the EP, the EPP wanted to demonstrate to the electorate that its victory would have a significant impact on European politics. The political interests of the EPP became more important than the institutional interests of the EP.

Third, the Committee on Budgets lost its prominent role within Parliament. As mentioned in the previous section, this development had already started in 1988, but accelerated in the late 1990s. Corbett *et al.* (2003a) give three reasons for the decline: (1) the budget lost its role as a fundamental issue and became a managerial matter; (2) legislative committees influenced budgetary provisions through the codecision procedure; and (3) the legislative committees gained expertise in their policy field, making them unwilling to simply follow the recommendations of the budget experts.

Overall, budget experts in the EP experienced an interesting paradox. In the course of the 1990s, the EP gained significant political powers in legislative politics and strengthened its institutional position in the budgetary process. Yet, despite these powers, Parliament seemed weaker at the beginning new century than it had 20 years before. The increase in political prominence led to disunity among the committees, a politicisation of MEPs and intense pressure from national governments. The strong David became a weak Goliath!

In contrast to Parliament, unity among member states continued to be relatively high. The financial perspective set a clear financial frame and reduced the political importance of annual budgetary decision-making. During the Council's budget readings, junior ministers or civil servants represented national governments; the issues at stake were seen as too insignificant for the involvement of the finance ministers. Parliament bitterly complained about this development in the 1997 budget procedure (Agence Europe 11.12.1996, No. 6871). The chairman of the Committee on Budgets walked out of a conciliation meeting in protest over having to negotiate with junior ministers, who did not have the political autonomy to divert from their national briefs (interview with representative of national delegation). This changed slightly in subsequent years. Not only did the Ecofin get more involved, but exchanges between Council and Parliament, in particular the conciliation meetings before the Council's reading, which were strengthened in the 1992 and 1999 interinstitutional agreements, changed the character of the Council's readings and contributed to a modest de-bureaucratisation. The second reading of the Council and the preceding conciliation meeting started to become more time-intensive and developed into the key forum for debate between Parliament and Council. In several cases, as for example the 2001 budget and the 1998 budget, agreements at the conciliation meeting shortly before the second reading in the Council turned the second readings in the EP and the Council into formalities as both institutions simply implemented the compromise adopted at the conciliation meeting (Deffaa 2001).

Despite the generally high level of unity among member states, the orientation towards austerity induced some tensions between the Southern and Northern coalitions and increased the cohesion of these two blocs. The Southern coalition made it clear that structural expenditure was excluded from the austerity approach (see, for example, the internal debates over the 1997 budget and the 1998 budget;

Discors 1997 and Agence Europe 24.07.1997, No. 7022). At the same time, the Northern coalition of net-contributors sought to ensure that the austerity approach applied to all other headings. Although cooperation among the delegations of all member states in the budgetary working group of the Council was generally quite close, the coordination among net-contributors was particularly strong. Officials from ministries of finance of Britain, France, Germany, the Netherlands, Sweden and Austria met regularly in the capitals and discussed their strategies for a coordinated austerity approach (interviews with official from the secretariat general of the Council and with member of national delegation).

The presidency of the Council played an important role at all levels of budgetary decision-making in uniting the Council, in particular as the interaction with the EP increased over the years, and the Council had to speak with one voice at inter-institutional coordination meetings. Presidencies differed in their ability and willingness to fulfil this role. In the president's chair, small countries were often more willing than large countries to subordinate national interests to the Council's collective interest. They also tended to rely more on the help of the Council's secretariat general (interview with official from the secretariat general of the Council). The case study of the 2000 budget illustrates that presidency's inability to rally the member states behind a joint position caused a considerable prolongation of interinstitutional conflict (see case study below).

As mentioned in the previous section, increased contacts between Parliament and Council, in particular at the administrative level, increased the impact of the Commission on interinstitutional relations. Yet, the reputation and credibility of the Commission decreased slightly over the 1990s. The EP started not only to shift focus towards the implementation phase, it also questioned the role of the Commission in budgetary planning. During the procedures for the 1996 budget and 1997 budget, for example, the EP began to question the forecasts of the Commission for agriculture spending, and succeeded in demanding regular updates of spending forecasts for heading 1 (agriculture) (Discors 1998: 695). These developments weakened the Commission.

INSTITUTIONAL SETTING

The interinstitutional agreement continued to limit the scope of interpretation and to foreclose the option for opportunistic interpretation. Negotiations over revision replaced discussions over treaty interpretation. While Parliament had achieved eight revisions between 1988 and 1994, it failed to gain the Council's support for any revision after 1994. In order to free itself from the dependence on revisions, the Parliament gained a new 'flexibility instrument' in the 1999 interinstitutional agreement, which allowed an increase of expenditure above the ceiling (see also Chapter 10). Although it increased flexibility, the introduction of the new instrument weakened Parliament in the revision negotiations, as the Council referred Parliament to the use of the instrument when Parliament demanded a revision. This was the case in the procedure for the 2000 and the 2001 budget (see case study below; Grossir 2001).

Case study: The adoption of the 2000 budget

The adoption process of the 2000 budget presents a very interesting case that seems to challenge the book's theoretical explanation of variance on the level of conflict.[17] On one hand, negotiations were quite intense. Conflict centred on the question of how to finance reconstruction aid for Kosovo. While the EP demanded a revision of the newly adopted financial perspective, the Council wanted to keep the ceilings unchanged. A compromise was found only at the last minute: the two arms of the budgetary authority agreed to finance the aid out of the new flexibility instrument, and to reopen the discussion on revision in 2000. Hence, the case raises questions regarding the reason for the intensity of negotiations and why actors settled the differences only at the last minute. On the other hand, a closer look shifts the perspective. It becomes surprising that Parliament accepted the tight financial perspective of the Berlin summit at all, as well as a budget for 2000 that was very much in line with the Council's preferences. The EP had strong distributive incentives to reject the financial perspective, as well as the budget, because a return to the treaty provisions would have provided a higher rate of increase than the ceilings of the new financial perspective. Thus, the more challenging question is the following: Why didn't the tensions between the Council and the EP prevent the adoption of an uncontested budget?

The case study demonstrates that the 2000 budget does not stand in contrast to the theoretical propositions of Chapter 2. On the contrary, the propositions can account for the developments around the 2000 budget and the adoption of the interinstitutional agreement. Two variables played an important role: first and most important, the internal disunity and reluctance of the EP prevented an escalation of conflict with the Council and undermined support for a rejection of the interinstitutional agreement and the budget. MEPs were under pressure from their national governments and did not want to endanger budgetary peace. Second, conflict, nevertheless, dominated until the last minute because a failure of internal coordination within the Council prevented a settlement with Parliament at the second reading in the Council. The key forums of cooperation failed to facilitate a timely compromise and prolonged the negotiations right into the second reading of the EP. Table 4.2 gives an overview of the different steps of the adoption process of the 2000 budget.

Two issues dominated the adoption process of the 2000 budget: first, the negotiations over the interinstitutional agreement; and second, the dispute over financial aid to Kosovo.

The adoption of the interinstitutional agreement The negotiations between the Council and the European Parliament over the adoption of a new interinstitutional agreement were short but intense. Both sides cooperated closely to reach an agreement before the end of the German presidency and the European elections in June. Like the negotiations in 1988 and 1993, the EP gained institutional concessions for a general acceptance of the ceilings of the financial perspective (see Chapter 10). Yet, the acceptance of the ceilings in 1999 was harder for the EP than in previous

Table 4.2 Overview of the procedure for the 2000 budget

Annual budgetary procedure		Adoption process of the 2000 budget
Year: n–1	*First Reading in the Council:*	The Council provided aid for Kosovo through across the board cuts in heading 4
	First Reading in the EP:	EP rejected the cuts and financed the aid for Kosovo by a multi-annual revision of heading 4. The EP threatened to breach the interinstitutional agreement and to go beyond the ceiling by applying the maximum rate of increase if the Council refused to accept a revision.
	Second Reading in the Council:	As the conciliation meeting before the second reading failed to produce an agreement between the two arms of the budgetary authority, the Council reaffirmed its position from the first reading.
		Due to dwindling internal support for a breach of the interinstitutional agreement, the EP shifted towards a new strategy: the adoption of a budget with only a small sum for Kosovo, which would force the Council to consent to a revision during the financial year.
		Negotiations between the Council and the EP were complicated as the Council found it difficult to speak with one voice.
	Second Reading in the EP:	A compromise was found a day before the final vote: the aid for Kosovo was to be financed out of the flexibility instrument and Council and EP declared that they would return to the issue of revision once the Commission had drawn a multi-annual aid programme in spring 2000.

years, because of their tight character, in particular the ceilings for headings 3 (internal policies) and 4 (external policies). During the negotiations, the EP achieved a minor upwards-correction for heading 3. The heading 4 was left unaltered, although the Council accepted a joint declaration, which stated that, in view of the costs for the reconstruction of Kosovo, a revision of heading 4 would be undertaken in case the ceiling proved to be too tight.

The result of the negotiations, in which the EP was represented by a delegation headed by the chairman of the Committee on Budgets, was far from uncontested in the EP and gained parliamentary approval only through considerable pressure from national governments. In contrast to votes on previous interinstitutional agreements, the EP was polarised along national and political lines. While traditionalist circles in Parliament thought the financial perspective entailed ceilings that left insufficient space for Parliament's spending priorities (see the statements by

Mr Bourlanges and Mr Colom-I-Naval in the debate in the European Parliament from 6 May 1999), those MEPs whose national parties were in government found it difficult to elude the pressure on Parliament. The Spanish and the German governments were most active in lobbying 'their' MEPs, as they had a strong interest in a successful and expedient adoption of the interinstitutional agreement (interview with officials of the secretariat general of the EP and the Commission). The Spanish Prime Minister, Mr Aznar, sold the financial perspective at home as a personal success and did not want the MEPs of his party to contradict this by voting against it. Similarly, the German government, in the midst of devastating opinion polls, was eager to present the final adoption of the Agenda 2000 as a significant achievement of the German presidency. Consequently, the retiring German chairman of the Committee on Budgets, who was planning his return into national politics, presented plenary with a new interinstitutional agreement after only two months of negotiations and urged MEPs to endorse the compromise reached with the Council. In the vote, only a simple majority of MEPs (instead of the qualified majority usually required in budgetary matters) supported the agreement.[18] Yet, the EP president Mr Gil Robles, a Spanish member of Mr Aznar's *Partido Popular*, judged that the result of the vote was sufficiently high to declare the agreement as adopted.

The involvement of national party leaderships was considerably intensified by the run-up to the European elections, due to take place in June 1999. MEPs needed the support of their national party leadership for reselection onto the party list and the election campaign. At the same time, national party strategists sought to present their MEPs to national voters as being fully in line with positions of the national party. Without this national pressure, the EP would most likely have prolonged the negotiations over the interinstitutional agreement, as it had done in 1993 (interview with official from the secretariat general of the EP). Moreover, two other factors played a role: first, budgetary decision-making was no longer the central arena of conflict with the Council and, second, MEPs had just engaged in an intense conflict with Commission over the discharge, which had led to the collective resignation of the College of Commissioners. Thus, MEPs wanted to focus on the coming European election and were less interested in engaging in another conflict.

The narrow adoption of the interinstitutional agreement played an important role in subsequent budgetary procedures. Those members of the Committee on Budgets, in particular the rapporteur for the 2000 budget, Mr Bourlanges, who had opposed the interinstitutional agreement, saw the procedure for the 2000 budget as a chance to gain the multi-annual revision they had failed to achieve in the negotiations over the interinstitutional agreement – in particular as the developments in Kosovo presented Parliament with a strong argument for revision.

The first reading in Parliament MEPs tried to press the Council to consent to a revision, after the Council had refused to consent in its first reading of the budget. Parliament issued a threat: if the Council did not accept a revision, Parliament would leave the framework of the interinstitutional agreement and return to the treaty provisions, which would give Parliament the opportunity to exceed the ceiling of heading 4 (external policies).

The second reading in the Council The conciliation meeting before the second reading in the Council in late November marked a decisive point of failure. In previous budgetary procedures, the conciliation meeting had been key for resolving tensions between the two arms of the budgetary authority. This time, it had the opposite effect. It alienated the two sides and ended in a temporary breakdown of the negotiations. The breakdown resulted primarily from the inability or unwillingness of the Finish presidency to engage in an active compromise-finding exercise during the conciliation meeting. Instead, the presidency simply presented the Council's position and waited for the EP delegation to concede (interview with official from the secretariat general of the Council). This outraged MEPs. Moreover, the Commission failed to have significant moderating impact, as the new Budget Commissioner almost completely marginalised herself by insisting on the Commission proposal, which had long been rejected by both sides (interviews with Commission officials). Following the breakdown of the conciliation meeting, the Council largely reaffirmed its position of the first reading (Agence Europe 26.11.1999, No. 7601). Yet, as formal and informal trialogue negotiations between the presidency and Parliament resumed, the first contours of a possible compromise emerged: the use of the flexibility instrument and a declaration concerning the possibility of a revision in 2000.

Meanwhile, positions and majorities shifted within the Committee on Budgets. MEPs moved away from the original strategy of returning to the treaty provision. It had become clear to the rapporteur that there was no majority for his confrontational strategy. Among his own group, the EPP, support for a breach of the interinstitutional agreement was dwindling and many SPE members did not want to confront the mainly centre-left governments in the Council (Agence Europe 27.11.1999, No. 7602). Consequently, the majority of the Committee, including the rapporteur, settled on a new plan, the so-called 'Kosovo tomorrow' solution: the EP would adopt a budget that left only a limited amount for aid to Kosovo underneath ceiling of heading 4 and would, thus, force the Council to consent to a revision when money ran out during the first half of the financial year. A minority in the Committee, Dutch and Finish liberal members and German social democrats, were reluctant to follow even this, less confrontational strategy and wanted Parliament to agree with Council on the use of the flexibility instrument (see meeting of Committee on Budgets from 3 December 1999).

During subsequent talks between the two arms of the budgetary authority, the Finish presidency moved considerably towards the EP, thereby losing the support of the Council. Northern member states undermined the search for a compromise and rejected the results of the trialogue meetings. At this late stage of the procedure, they reintroduced an issue that had already seemed solved: they demanded that Parliament reduce a considerable amount of non-compulsory payment appropriations. It became clear that the Finish presidency was to pay dearly for failing to achieve a compromise at the conciliation meeting, where all delegations from the national capitals had been present, and where an agreement with the EP could have been achieved in direct negotiations between all actors involved. When this chance was missed and the issue had gained political significance, the Finish presidency found it nearly impossible to bring member states in line while trying to establish common ground with the EP. The internal split of the Council gave the EP the opportunity to exploit differences between the presidency and the Northern member states. Negotiations continued right into the second reading in the EP. Finally, it was the Commission that came back into the negotiations and played significant role in assisting the presidency and coordinating the positions of the member states (interviews with officials from the Commission and the secretariat general of the EP).

The second reading in the European Parliament The plenary debate in the Parliament took place although no final compromise had been achieved and informal and formal meetings continued until the day before the vote. The political groups had prepared two voting lists. One list entailed the 'Kosovo tomorrow' solution and the other related to the latest compromise proposal put forward by the Presidency. When the compromise was endorsed by the Coreper, the plenary agreed, with a large majority, to a reduction of payment appropriations, the use of the flexibility instrument, and to a declaration stating that the Council and EP 'take note of the fact that, if a sum requiring a financial effort significantly greater than that already programmed were to be agreed, this would entail exceeding the current for heading 4 of the financial perspective' (paragraph 2 in Annex of Colom-I-Naval report). Both sides, the Council and the EP, sold the compromise as a success. The Council emphasised that it had prevented a revision by financing the aid from a source that was already 'lost' to the EP. On the other side, the EP stressed that it had averted cuts in heading 4 and gained a declaration that increased the chance of a revision in spring 2000.

Summary: The importance of informal and formal dialogue

As in the previous section, the empirical material presented largely supports the propositions of Chapter 2. The introduction of the financial perspective and the interinstitutional agreement changed the incentive structure of budgetary actors and reduced the level of conflict. The treaty reforms of Maastricht and Amsterdam further strengthened this trend: on the one hand, the codecision procedure closed the asymmetry between the budgetary and legislative powers of the Parliament and reduced the institutional relevance of the budgetary powers; on the other hand, the EMU convergence criteria introduced an austerity pressure on national budgets from which actors on the European could not withdraw.

Prevailing distributive differences no longer led to opportunistic interpretation (due to the reduced scope of interpretation and the irrelevance of the maximum rate of increase), but resulted in 'revision games', in which the Parliament had to convince the Council of the need for a revision. In this respect, the case study of the 2000 budget revealed an interesting facet of interinstitutional relations under the financial perspective. The proposed strategy of 'Kosovo tomorrow' adopted by the Committee on Budgets in November 1999 was similar to a strategy used in the procedure for the 1992 budget. It constituted the only remaining strategic option (other than a rejection of the budget)[19] with which the EP could press the Council into a revision. In not serving the Council's distributive interests, the EP made the Council interested in a revision. Yet, the problems of this strategy are two-fold. First, threatening not to serve the Council's spending interests is often not credible. Most of the time, Parliament's spending interests include Council's ideal point and it is difficult for budget experts to convince their fellow MEPs that Parliament takes money away from important spending lines, only in order to gain more money in subsequent stages (through a revision). Second, the Council has a strong incentive not to give in to Parliament's blackmailing strategy, due to possible repercussions for future negotiations. The Council knows that Parliament would reuse this strategy if it worked on one occasion.

At the end of the analysis of the annual budgetary decision-making over three decades, it is useful to return to one of the early commentaries on problems of budgetary decision-making under the 1970 budget treaty, and to compare it with the budgetary procedure under the interinstitutional agreement. Chapter 3 quoted the rapporteur for the 1979 budget, Mr Bangemann, who gave a thoughtful account of the first significant conflict between the two arms of the budgetary authority. Mr Bangemann (1979: 176/177) argued that two deficiencies were fundamental to the failing of the budgetary procedure: first, the lack of an early agreement on the main political objectives and financial structure of the budget; and second, the lack of personal contacts and exchanges between the two arms of the budgetary authority, which helped to resolve tensions outside the exposed and separate forums of the readings in the Council and the EP.

The financial perspective and the interinstitutional agreement successfully addressed both deficiencies. The positive contribution is quite evident with regard to the first. Much of this chapter illustrated the clear structure and orientation that the ceilings of the financial perspective gave to annual decision-making. Regarding the second, the impact of the financial perspective and the interinstitutional agreement is not directly apparent, yet it is an important aspect of the reform.

After 1988, Parliament and Council gradually developed a routine of informal and formal dialogue at all levels and stages of the budgetary procedure. Close cooperation and regular exchanges became a dominant feature of interinstitutional relations. New forms of cooperation evolved and were subsequently codified in the interinstitutional agreements. For example, the *ad hoc* procedure introduced in the 1993 interinstitutional agreement strengthened the role of conciliation meetings. These meetings developed from a forum for the provision of information over agricultural expenditure, into an arena for wide-ranging debates over spending priorities, which the 1999 interinstitutional agreements extended to non-compulsory expenditure (see also Chapter 10). Another important forum for dialogue were the trialogue meetings at which the chairman of the Committee on Budgets, rapporteur of the Parliament, the Budget Commissioner, and the budget minister of the member state holding the presidency of the Council, closely negotiated all aspects of the annual budget. They tried to settle contentious issues as early as possible. While the trialogue became the joint steering committee of the budgetary procedure, the informal trialogue at the administrative level, which prepared the formal meetings at the political level, gave trialogue a strong administrative foundation.

These close contacts created a system of mutual reliance and coordination that prevented what Mr Bangemann identified as a dynamic of escalation, which tore the two arms of the budgetary authority in opposite directions. He argued that the later in the annual procedure that actors started to enter into talks, the more difficult it was to reach an agreement on a joint compromise. This occurred because institutions had already committed themselves in public, e.g. in press statements and debates during the readings, to their political objectives. Close contact and constant coordination from the beginning of the annual procedure minimised the possibility of escalation and contained the potentially damaging effects of differences over specific questions.

While many of the institutional channels that facilitated formal and informal dialogue evolved in the 1990s, some of them existed in the 1980s, such as the trialogue and conciliation meetings. They gained importance only as actors had started to respect each other and to cooperate as equal partners. Whether the EP was regarded as an 'equal partner' was a particularly sensitive issue for MEPS, which did not lose its relevance even though close cooperation was well established. MEPs still seemed to feel the need to prove themselves and reacted strongly against presidencies that did not display sufficient interest in cooperating with the EP. In contrast, presidencies that closely involved Parliament, such as the Luxembourg presidency in the procedure for the 1998 budget, achieved a particularly harmonious procedure (Discors 1998). Moreover, MEPs' urge to achieve symbolic victories also limited some of the conflict-reducing effect of dialogue on interinstitutional relations. As mentioned above, the Council regarded annual decision-making as a largely administrative act, while MEPs were eager to demonstrate the political relevance of their budgetary powers. This meant that the Committee on Budgets frequently entered intense debates with the Council and Commission over small sums or declarations, which had limited distributive importance, but were of symbolic value for publicity-seeking MEPs.

5 Blocking inter-governmental relations

Conflict between the UK and the other member states over British net-contributions (1974–1984)

In the previous two chapters, I concentrated on conflict between the EP and the Council within the annual budgetary procedure. I discussed tensions between member states, insofar as they had a significant impact on the Council's ability to participate in annual decision-making. I will now focus on conflict among member states outside the annual budgetary procedure, because much of the conflict between governments in budgetary politics took place in the intergovernmental setting. It concerned questions of financial reform and went beyond issues of annual budgeting. Conflict *outside* the annual budgetary procedure (in the intergovernmental setting) and conflict *within* the annual budgetary procedure are two complementary types of budgetary conflict at the European level. The following two chapters will assess the extent to which the impact of institutional change on the level of conflict *outside* the annual procedure was similar to the conflict-reducing effect of the 1988 reform on the level of conflict *within* the annual budgetary procedure. Thereby, this chapter centres on budgetary decision-making in the intergovernmental setting in the 1970s and the early 1980s, while the next chapter concentrates on the late 1980s and the 1990s.

Figure 5.1 reveals high levels of conflict in the intergovernmental setting between 1974 and 1988. It measures the number of European Council meetings per year that were dominated by disputes over budgetary issues. I have selected this indicator for two reasons. First, the involvement of the European Council on budgetary issues signifies the failure of other intergovernmental fora, namely the Agriculture Council, the Economics and Finances Council (Ecofin), or the Council of Foreign Affairs, to settle the budgetary disputes. Second, the dominance of budgetary debates at European summits reveals that (even) Heads of State or Government failed to resolve the differences among member states. The involvement of the European Council in disputes over budgetary issues is, by itself, an insufficient indicator of high levels of conflict. Only when the issue dominates the negotiations at the summit is it justified to assume that the intergovernmental setting is experiencing extreme difficulty in containing high levels of budgetary conflict. Behind this idea is the assumption that the European Council focuses usually on a wide range of issues, and concentration on one policy field is unusual. The data of Figure 5.1 is based on the thorough assessment of European Council meetings that Jan Werts (1992) presents

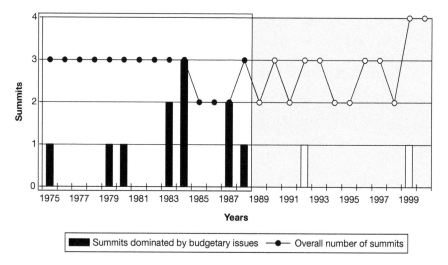

Dublin summit, March 1975: Disputes over British contributions that led to agreement on 'financial correction mechanism'.
Dublin summit, November 1979 and Luxembourg summit, April 1980: Disputes over British contributions that led to agreement on 'May Mandate'.
London summit, November 1981: Disputes over British contributions and CAP reform.
Stuttgart summit, June 1983, Athens summit, November 1983, Brussels summit, March 1984, and Fontainebleau summit, June 1984: Disputes over British contributions, the exhaustion of own-resources, and CAP reform that led to agreement on the introduction of the British rebate and an increase of the VAT ceiling.
Dublin summit, December 1984: Disputes over Greece's compensation demands for its consent to Iberian enlargement that led to introduction of the 'Integrated Mediterranean Programme' at the subsequent summit.
Brussels summit, June 1987, Copenhagen summit, November 1987, and Brussels summit, February 1988: Dispute over financial reform that led to the introduction of the financial perspective and the interinstitutional agreement.

Figure 5.1 Summits dominated by disputes over budgetary issues (1975–1988).

in his book *The European Council.* I have supplemented Werts' study with an analysis of the Presidency conclusions[1] and accounts in newspapers and official publications.

The chapter starts with an analysis of the potential for conflict created by the institutional settlement of the 1970 budget treaty. I argue that the settlement set strong incentives for new members, such as the United Kingdom and Southern member states, to challenge the distributive and institutional status quo. These challenges led to high levels of conflict, which dominated the 1970s and 1980s. Challenging member states were successful only when they gained the bargaining power to substantiate their demands. I will illustrate this argument in this chapter with one extensive case study. I have decided to concentrate on the most intensive budgetary conflict of the time: the battle between the British government and rest of the Community over Britain's net-contributions. Due to the extraordinary length and intensity of the conflict, ample empirical material is available, which allows me to analyse in detail how the conflict emerged, developed, and finally subsided. Although the dispute over British net-contributions is clearly a special case, it provides insights into the mechanisms and dynamics of conflict among member states that are relevant and even somewhat representative for other cases of intensive conflict, such as the dispute between the Community and Greece in the early 1980s, or the tensions after the accession of Spain and Portugal in the mid-1980s. In thoroughly analysing the British case, I seek to present sufficient evidence to substantiate my theoretical propositions on conflict in the intergovernmental setting.

This chapter is divided into three sections. First, I will briefly recapitulate my expectations with regard to the theoretical propositions that guide this work. I will then proceed to the case study, which focuses on the period between 1974 and 1984: 1974 has been taken as the starting point because the renegotiations of the British terms of entry took place that year. Yet, the section will cover some of the historical developments before 1974 that are necessary to understand subsequent disputes. The case study concludes with the Fontainebleau agreement in 1984, which introduced a permanent solution to the UK problem. The final section revisits the theoretical perspective and evaluates the extent to which the empirical evidence supports the propositions.

Theoretical perspective

Bargaining power and conflict incentives

We expect conflict between member states to be based largely on bargaining power and differences in distributive preferences (see Chapter 2). Member states will try to alter distributive outcomes in their favour. In the case of a stable majority with relatively homogeneous distributive interests, the demands of the minority will most likely be ignored in the annual budgetary procedure, where expenditure decisions are based on qualified majority voting. Transfering the debates over budgetary issues from the annual procedure to the intergovernmental setting is the only option left to the minority to gain voice for its distributive demands.

Generally, a member state can increase its bargaining power in three different ways. First, changes in bargaining power can result from the accession of new members. If the minority grows into the size of a blocking minority, then it can bring the decision-making process to a hold. Given the time pressure inherent in the budgetary procedure, a blocking minority can exercise considerable pressure on the majority. Second, the member state that opposes the distributive outcome can threaten to exit the Community. Yet, this threat is only effective and credible when the other member states want the member state to stay in the Community and when the member state would be willing to carry out the threat. Third, the member state can link the decision over the distribution of resources to a decision that has to be taken by unanimity. Three factors limit the application of these linkages: (1) the necessity to justify the linkage politically to other member states and to the domestic public; (2) the material loss that the blocking member state experiences from holding up the unanimous decision; (3) the difficulties of internal coordination within the national government, where the actors in different fields have to make the linkage successful. As a result of these three factors, linkages are most likely to occur in policy fields that are already politically or institutionally connected. Chapter 2 argued that the linkage of annual budgetary decisions to a field of unanimous decisions emerges automatically when expenditure hits the revenue limits. The member state that does not profit from the current distribution of resources then gains veto-power and makes its consent to an increase of the revenue dependent on distributive concessions.

Negotiations over an increase of the revenue and over exit threats take place within the intergovernmental realm and outside the annual budgetary decision-making procedure. A member state that has very little bargaining power will try to use the forum of the European Council to appeal to other member states for distributive change. Moreover, the intergovernmental realm becomes particularly relevant when discussions concern institutional issues, because governments have the exclusive power to enact institutional change. Chapter 2 contended that actors have an interest in challenging the institutional setting when rules strongly influence distributive outcomes. The more rules determine the distributive outcomes, the more conflict among actors will centre on institutional issues, in particular when actors are long-term oriented.

In the case of the 1970 treaty, the degree to which the distributive outcomes are predetermined by existing rules varies between expenditure and revenue sides of the EC budget. The distributive impact of the institutional setting is limited on the expenditure side. Qualified majority voting predetermines distributive outcomes only insofar as a majority makes the decisions. In contrast, on the revenue side, the distributive implications of the institutional setting are very high. The rules that determine the structure of the revenue side are far-reaching in their degree of detail and, although not part of the treaty, have quasi-treaty status (Strasser 1992: 28). Article 269 of the Treaty of the European Union (former: Article 201) demands that member states set these rules by unanimity and in consent with their national parliaments. Any changes in the structure of the revenue side are of institutional character.[2] Consequently, the distributive conflict over the sharing of costs almost immediately spills over to institutional conflict over the rules of the revenue side.[3]

The theoretical chapter also indicated that heterogeneity among member states and economic crises negatively affect the level of conflict. When benefits of integration are distributed unevenly and stark differences in economic prosperity exist, we expect to see strong demands for a change in the existing distributive pattern. Moreover, during times of crisis these demands will increase, but the resistance of other member states against demands for redistribution will also intensify.

Case study

Conflict over British net-contributions

This section presents a detailed analysis of the conflict over British net-contributions, which dominated EC politics for much of the 1970s and early 1980s. Table 5.1 gives an overview of the different attempts to settle the issue. Before examining these different decisions in detail, however, the first subsection introduces the economic and political background of the conflict.

The 'UK problem'

Central to the conflict between the UK and the other member states of the Community was a fundamental problem of equity. Given the pattern of trade and consumption of the UK on one hand, and the structure of the expenditure and revenue sides of the EC budget on the other hand, the UK had little to gain and much to pay (Taylor 1983). As the centre of a former worldwide empire, Britain's economy was still more oriented towards the Commonwealth than towards continental Europe. Britain was an importer of foodstuffs and products from non-EC countries. Not only did it have a small agricultural sector, but also a lower GDP than in many other member states, because Britain lacked a highly developed industry and service sector (Denton 1981, 1984; Godley 1980). Moreover, British society consumed more than it produced, resulting in disproportionately high VAT revenues (in comparison to a low level of GDP). This economic structure of Britain was pitted against an EC budget that was vastly dominated by expenditure for the CAP and, since the 1970 decision, financed by own-resources that were based on agricultural levies, custom duties, and a percentage of VAT. Thus, even before British entry to the EC it was clear for the British government that there would probably be a 'UK problem' concerning the EC budget (Laffan 1997: 51; Isaac 1984b).

Table 5.1 Overview of decisions on the issue of British net-contributions

Year	EC decision	Content of the decision	British Prime Minister (party in government) of the time
1973	Treaty of Accession	Seven year transition period for British contributions	Edward Heath (Conservative)
1975	Financial mechanism	Potential reductions of British contributions	Harold Wilson (Labour)
1980	May Mandate	Correction payments to Great Britain	Margaret Thatcher (Conservative)
1982	Renewal of May Mandate	*Ad hoc* prolongation of correction payments to Great Britain	Margaret Thatcher (Conservative)
1984	Fontainebleau agreement	British rebate that reduced British net-contributions	Margaret Thatcher (Conservative)

Yet, the existence and extent of the 'UK problem' was far from uncontested among member states. First, future predictions over budgetary expenditure and economic developments were very difficult, in particular as the effects of membership on the British economy were uncertain. Discussions over the UK problems always suffered from the lack of reliable figures and predictions that underlined the exact dimensions of the problem (Emerson and Scott 1977: 213). Second, the British government presented the problem as a static issue, while the other member states emphasised the necessity to take a dynamic perspective. They contended that it was up to Great Britain to rearrange its trading pattern from a commonwealth orientation towards a European outlook (Taylor 1983: 404–405). If British consumers redirected their consumption towards, for example, French, Irish or Danish foodstuffs, British payments into the budget would decrease, because it would not have to pay custom duties. Moreover, the high level of VAT was, so the argument of some member states, also Britain's own fault, as it did not live within its means.

Third, member states found it difficult to admit to the UK problem because they had, if not deliberately, at least knowingly constructed the financial *acquis communautaire* before UK accession and in a manner that ran counter to British interests (Dinan 1999: 63). In particular, France, which had rejected Great Britain's pleas for membership twice, had made its consent to British entry dependent on an agreement on the financing of the CAP among the six founding members of the Community. Fourth, the UK problem not only challenged the package deal among the original six member states, but was a threat to a fundamental assumption of European integration (Tonelli 1981; Møller 1982). This assumption was the implicit understanding that tensions over equity among nation states would be resolved almost automatically through the creation of new common spending policies, and an overall increase of prosperity through economic integration. The economic crises of the 1970s undermined this fundamental assumption as they demonstrated that member states were increasingly unwilling to adopt new spending policies. The occurrence of the UK problem meant that member states could no longer ignore questions of equity (Laffan 1997: 60). In her analysis of budgetary politics, Helene Wallace hit the spot. She wrote in 1983:

> the bargain struck amongst the founder member states did not explicitly include an agreement to tackle in common problems of resource distribution. Instead the Six sought a rough parity or equivalence of anticipated benefits from integration to be achieved through developing different strands of common policies. As the time passed the economic environment altered for the worse, policy sectors other than those directly specified in the Treaties generated pressing demands for action, and membership of the EC was enlarged. The consequences were *inter alia* that the debate over who got what, when, and how began during the 1970s to come into increasingly sharp focus, almost to the point of overshadowing discussion of other issues within the EC. Two particular criticisms of the Community's record were increasingly voiced: first, that the farming population consumed a disproportionately large share of the EC

budget; and second, that the raising and spending of Community produced a perverse pattern of burdens and benefits for individual members.

(Wallace 1983: 81–82)

From entry to 'renegotiation'

The issue of British contributions to the EC budget featured prominently in the accession negotiations and dominated the first years of Britain's membership. The Conservative government pursued a strategy of rapid accession and settled on a long transition period and a general recognition of the problem of large net-contributions. It hoped to alter the situation from inside the Community. The Labour government, which succeeded the Conservatives in 1974, rejected the original terms of accession and demanded renegotiations. It gained the introduction of a financial mechanism that would correct member states' contribution where strong imbalances between contributions to the budget and economic prosperity existed.

The British Prime Minister Edward Heath, who had been chief negotiator during Britain's failed bid for EC membership in the early 1960s, put British accession high on the political agenda of the Conservative government that took office in 1970. He attached much personal political capital to this mission and was determined to complete the negotiation rapidly. As Heath expected that Britain's bargaining position would be much improved once it became a full member, he was willing to accept temporary agreements and to defer problems to later negotiations (George 1998: 56; O'Neill 2000). At the same time, he knew that Britain's membership was far from uncontested within the political establishment and among the wider British public. The government had to achieve a negotiation outcome that could be sold as a success. In this respect, the dispute of preferential treatment for butter from New Zealand gained strong political prominence. The Heath government knew that it would only get the necessary endorsement of accession in Parliament when this issue was solved to the satisfaction of the New Zealand government. As France insisted on full compliance with the financial *acquis communautaire* and Britain could not expect much support from the other accession countries of which the agricultural exporters, Ireland and Denmark, were to benefit significantly from the EC budget, a link emerged between the Community's finances and New Zealand butter (O'Neill 2000: 186). Britain got a favourable agreement on New Zealand butter and settled upon a less favourable compromise on the financial terms of its entry (Kitzinger 1973: 97–100 and 136–138; O'Neill 2000). Articles 127 to 132 of the Treaty of Accession granted the UK a transition period of seven years, during which time British contributions would gradually converge towards the full amount. Moreover, the UK gained an assurance that future discussions should resolve 'unacceptable situations' if they occurred as the UK anticipated (Fugmann 1992: 281; Strasser 1992: 165).

Although this result was broadly in line with the British Prime Minister's demands, it had been clear from the outset that Britain would have to negotiate from a weak bargaining position. The Conservative government had committed itself so strongly to a rapid entry into the EC and Heath dearly needed the political success of achieving accession, that the British government had not expected major concessions. The mediocre terms of accessions reflected Heath's lack of bargaining power and his tactical decision not to question fundamentally the financial *acquis communautaire* but to hope for an improved bargaining position as a full member of the Community (O'Neill 2000: 356, 360).

Once the UK had joined the European Community, the British government again raised the problem of large net-contributions. Focusing on the expenditure side of the EC budget, Heath demanded the introduction of new common spending policies. In particular, he urged the other member states to consent to the creation of a European Regional Development Fund (ERDF) which, he hoped, would provide rapid and tangible benefits for Britain (George 1998: 57; Wallace 1977). The bargaining power of the British government was, however, still quite limited. Other member states, in particular West Germany, which would cover most of the bill for the ERDF, were willing to agree to its creation, only in exchange to British support for progress towards EMU. As Britain did not accept the link, negotiations proceeded slowly (George 1998: 63). It became clear that the fund would benefit Britain only if the size was considerable (Germany blocked this), or if the contribution would be geared almost exclusively towards the poorest regions of the Community (France blocked this). The British government insisted on a large amount and threatened to veto progress on other issues, including energy, unless the Germans would agree to pay more than they were offering. The British Prime Minister took a forthright approach similar to that of General De Gaulle in the 1960s, but 'Heath was not De Gaulle'[4]; it backfired and the position of Germany hardened (George 1998: 68; Wallace 1977). No agreement was reached before Heath left office in February 1974.[5]

The Labour Party, which had largely opposed entry into the European Community in 1971/72, won the general election in spring 1974 and immediately opened the 'renegotiation' of the terms of entry. Again domestic politics played an important role. For Prime Minister Harold Wilson renegotiation represented a unique opportunity to strengthen its political standing within the Labour Party and the country (George 1998: 174). In taking a tough line in the negotiations with the other member states, Wilson was able to steal the thunder of the vocal left of the Labour Party, which wanted Wilson to pull out of the Community. Moreover, his emphasis on Britain's national interests cut across the class divide in British society that dominated the political discourse over other policy issues. Finally, the planned referendum over the outcome of the renegotiations added a democratic claim to the government's policy towards EC membership and so excluded the issue of EC membership from the election campaign that followed in autumn 1974 (*Frankfurter Allgemeine Zeitung* 21 June 1974).[6]

The Prime Minister knew that the strong link of the renegotiations to domestic politics made the government's threat of an 'involuntary exit' (Schneider and Cederman 1994; Iida 1996) through a defeat in the referendum credible. Thus, the Wilson government entered negotiations with more bargaining power than the Heath government. At the same time, it was clear that the renegotiation and the referendum was motivated mainly by internal politics within the Labour Party and that Wilson's main objective was to gain a fast agreement that on paper sounded convincing (Denman 1996: 246). Moreover, it was far from clear that the threat of a British withdrawal from the Community – albeit being credible – was really regarded as much of a threat by the other member states.

With the budgetary contributions being one of the key items of renegotiation, the new government abandoned the strategy of the Conservative government to offset British large net-contributions by enacting new common spending policies. After the experience of the ERDF, it doubted whether such a strategy would bring immediate and tangible results for Britain. Instead, the Wilson government focused on the revenue side.[7] This was an important shift in the British strategy towards the UK problem.

The Foreign Secretary, James Callaghan, who led the negotiations, emphasised Britain's inability to make large contributions to the EC budget. This argument was based on calculations by the UK Treasury that demonstrated that Britain would pay 24 per cent of the EC budget in 1980 (once the transitional period of membership had been completed), compared to a 14 per share of the Community's GNP. Callaghan's focus on the gap between Britain's GNP and her contribution to the EC budget, i.e. the *gross*-contributions, instead of the gap between contributions and receipts from the budget, i.e. *net*-contributions, was an answer to the resolute refusal of other member states to accept the validity of the concept of *net*-contributions. Yet, even the definition of *gross* national contributions was contested. France argued that the contributions that came from import levies on agricultural produce and the application of the common external tariff on industrial goods were own-resources of the EC, and could not be counted as British contributions. Only the contributions that came from the VAT revenues could be classified as national contributions (George 1998: 84).

A complex compromise proposal by the Commission formed the basis for a final agreement at the Dublin summit in March 1975 (Dodsworth 1975). It introduced criteria of economic equity into the financing of the budget. On certain conditions, general-purpose grants would be automatically paid to economically weaker member states (Strasser 1992: 166).[8]

The Wilson government portrayed the 'financial mechanism' as a success and advised British voters to endorse the outcome in the referendum. France had made a concession by allowing contributions to include customs duties and import levies. Yet, it did so under the condition that the financial mechanism would be only provisional for a seven year trial period, and that the system would be gradually amended towards an exclusively VAT based definition of national contributions (George 1998: 188).

The end of the transition period – the May Mandate

Despite Wilson's claim of having succeeded, the financial mechanism failed to elevate the British problem of large contributions and small receipts. The mechanism was never applied as neither Britain, nor any other member states fulfilled the complex conditions.[9] This failure resulted from a British bargaining position that – although from the outset it seemed to be stronger than that of the Heath government – was actually weakened by the clear party political motivation of Wilson's bid for renegotiation. Moreover, it was also a consequence of a mistake of the British government that – relying in the negotiations mostly on the Foreign Office rather than the Treasury – signed up to a badly negotiated agreement.

Therefore, Britain became already during the transitional period second largest net-contributor after Germany. After mid-1978 the British government was certain that, once the full transitional period of membership came to an end in 1980, Britain would become the largest net-contributor to the budget. Thus, it became clear that the government would have to raise the issue again and focus on the British *net*-contributions (Jenkins 1980: 494).

James Callaghan, who had succeeded Wilson as Prime Minister in 1976, raised the issue and demanded a correction of the imbalance between high contribution and low benefits. With an eye on the up-coming general elections, Callaghan made a 15-minute statement against the expensive CAP at the Paris summit in March 1979, which met with strong resistance from the other member states (Werts 1992: 268). In his statement to the House of Commons after the summit, he stated that the UK would block the price setting in order to prevent a further increase of the budget (Thatcher database 79_076). Yet, the Labour government lost the general election before it could pursue this strategy further.[10]

When the leader of the Conservatives, Mrs Margaret Thatcher, came into power, European governments hoped the negotiations over the imbalances would lose their fierceness. The Conservative government was expected to be more pro-European than its predecessor. [11] Yet, when the new Prime Minister entered the scene, it became apparent that she put British interests on top of her European agenda and continued the strategy that Callaghan had initiated. Similar to her predecessors, Thatcher used the question of British contributions as an important instrument for improving her standing in domestic politics. It gave her the opportunity to present herself as a stern defender of national interests and a principled politician. She argued that British taxpayers' money should not be wasted on large European expenditure programmes and Britain should get its 'fair share' back from the EC, in particular at times when the British public had to accept unpopular cuts in domestic public spending (Thatcher 1993: 79 and 81).

At her first summit in Strasbourg, the Prime Minister achieved an agreement among member states in support of a Commission report on the UK problem. At the following summit in November 1979 in Dublin the Commission proposed – based on its report – to revise the 1975 rebate mechanism so as to give Britain a cash rebate of £350 million, in addition to a general increase of EC expenditure in Britain. Thatcher accepted the approach presented by the Commission, but insisted that the total return to Britain should amount to £1 billion and that a permanent solution had to be found. This caused a fierce debate among Heads of State or Government during which Thatcher (in)famously stated 'we want our money back' (George 1998: 148–149; Thatcher 1993: 79). The other governments regarded her statement as a direct attack on the concept of 'own-resources' and were unwilling to accept British demands. Yet, as the British government insisted on its position, negotiations continued for months and again failed to produce an agreement at the Luxembourg summit in April 1980.

The Prime Minister was able to keep the issue on the negotiation table because of her determination to disrupt Community business until a favourable solution was adopted (Thatcher 1993: 79). As she had strongly committed herself domestically to this strategy, her threats became credible. Key element of the strategy was the use of Britain's blocking power over the decisions on agricultural prices, proposed by Mr Callaghan in 1979 (Moravcsik 1998: 349).[12]

Price decisions in the Agricultural Council were always taken by consensus, although member states could adopt a decision by qualified majority if they followed the price recommendations of the Commission. As the Commission had proposed lower prices for 1980/81 than desired by most member stats, they needed Britain's consent to high prices. Britain strictly rejected high prices and made its support for price increases dependent on an agreement on British net-contributions (Butler 1986: 96). The connection between contributions and price-fixing was politically defensible, as higher prices for agricultural products meant an increase in British net-contributions. However, Britain did not have to enforce the linkage, because it was the French President who made the connection between a British consent to CAP decisions and some sort of compensation payments for British net-contributions to the budget. He was under strong domestic pressure from the agricultural lobby which, given the high rate of inflation, demanded significant price increases (Jenkins 1980: 498–499). Moreover, he wanted Britain to agree to a new sheep meat regime and the strengthening of the common fishery policy (Neville-Rolfe 1984: 415–417).[13] If the UK was to be compensated for its high contributions to the EC budget, the French president wanted to ensure that France would gain significant benefits from decisions on agriculture. Clear fronts emerged: the British insisted on reserving consent to a price decision until a settlement on British net-contributions, while France pushed for a price increase before 1 June 1980, threatening otherwise to pay French farmers out of the national budget.

Finally, Foreign ministers agreed on 30 May 1980 (a day before the deadline of the French ultimatum) on a formula for a reduction of British contributions in 1980 and 1981 in the form of *ad hoc* shadow spending programmes of 1.175 billion ECU for 1980 and 1.41 billion for 1981 (Strasser 1992: 369). This money reduced the British net-contribution by two-thirds; it was earmarked for special programmes in particular regions, inner cities, and energy projects. The scheme included the option of a one-year extension, which had to be decided in conjunction with a general reform of the EC finances.

The agreement, called the 'May Mandate', constituted a victory for the British government, although it did not entail the permanent solution that Thatcher had demanded.[14] Given the forecasts that the own-resources would be exhausted in 1982, member states were clearly reluctant to commit themselves to more than a two-year period (Jenkins 1980: 500). Moreover, they still had not accepted the need for a permanent correction mechanism, insisting that a solution could be found within the framework of spending policies. A permanent character, they feared, would set a precedent for future member states. The way the refunds of the May Mandate were set up, namely as *ad hoc* and temporary measures on the expenditure side, allowed member states to maintain the pretence that the Community was not trying to alter British net-contributions, but was instead taking special steps to help an individual member state with particular problems, such as neglected inner cities and marginalised regions.

Renewing the May Mandate and the settlement of Fontainebleau

Discussions over the future of EC financing and the UK problem emerged again in autumn 1981, when the Commission presented the demanded Mandate report on the reform of the EC finances and the British problem (Vanden Abeele 1982: 506–508). The Commission proposed a number of common spending policies, which would allocate significant benefits to Britain. The member states displayed little enthusiasm for the Commission proposals and were not inclined to accept British demands for a generally applicable rebate mechanism and CAP reform. Against this resistance, the British government tried to replicate its bargaining success from 1980 by linking again the settlement of the British problem to the decision on the agricultural prices for 1982/83.

However, in contrast to 1980, member states were unwilling to accept the link (Neville-Rolfe 1984: 442). At first, member states hoped that the British government would, after a while, give in, especially as member states had lent full and immediate support to Britain's war with Argentina over the Falkland Islands (George 1998: 150). Yet, as the British agricultural minister continued to block an agreement and vocal protest of the farm lobby put governments under mounting pressure,[15] the Belgian presidency broke with the tradition of consensual decision-making in the Agricultural Council and called for a majority vote on agricultural prices (De Bassompierre 1988: 27). The Commission facilitated this move by presenting price recommendations in line with the demands of the majority of member states (Neville-Rolfe 1984: 445).

The British government answered the call for a majority vote by invoking the 'Luxembourg compromise' of February 1966 in order to hold up a decision on agricultural prices. To the surprise of the British government, member states (after some internal discussions) disregarded Britain's veto and adopted the price increase with a majority. Only the Danes and Greeks voted against the increase on principled grounds. They wanted to ensure that the Luxembourg compromise would remain available as a political veto-option. The French government, which had always insisted on member states' blocking power when vital national interests were at stake, was in a difficult position. It had voted against the UK for distributive reasons, but wanted to keep the Luxembourg compromise intact as a veto-option. Hence, it argued that the Luxembourg compromise did not apply in this case, because no vital British interests were involved in the setting of agricultural prices. France emphasised that the Luxembourg compromise was therefore unimpaired. The UK government was extremely angry. Yet, it had no interest to dispute the French interpretation, because it wanted to keep what ever remained from the Luxembourg compromise for future decisions. Moreover, the UK government did not want to endanger the member states' support for the British actions in the Falkland war. The British permanent representative of the time, Sir Michael Butler, described the price-fixing episode of 1982 as 'our worst defeat. The lever we had used with the success to get the 30th May settlement in 1980 was knocked from our hands' (Butler 1986: 100). It was clear that the Foreign Office and Sir Michael Butler himself had miscalculated and underestimated the willingness of the other member states to override the British veto (Taylor 1983: 400).

Despite this defeat and the loss of bargaining power, foreign ministers agreed a week later on a sum for the 1982 British rebate. Butler (1986: 100) speculated that member governments felt slightly guilty (that they had overruled the British veto) and were therefore willing to cooperate. At the same time, the actual amount that the British government had to accept was considerably lower than what it had originally demanded.[16] By now member states recognised the UK problem but most of them were unwilling to settle on anything but a temporary arrangement for annual lump sum rebates. Realising that it had lost the 1980 lever, the British government let the budget problem rest for the moment.

A year later, the UK government regained bargaining power. More than ever before, it was able to substantiate its demands for a permanent solution with a strong veto threat. In the words of the British Foreign Secretary, Sir Geoffrey Howe:

> By 1983, however, we had a solid argument which would restore the strength of our bargaining position. Expenditure under the Community budget was now close to exhausting the total resources provided for under the Rome Treaty. The prescribed ceiling of expenditure (defined as equivalent to the yield of 1 per cent of VAT) could not be increased without the agreement of all member states, including ourselves. We could, and in due course did, make it plain that we were not willing to accept *any* increase in that ceiling (which almost all our partners desired) unless it was linked with an equally long-term reduction in the size of the British contribution.
>
> (Howe 1994: 306, emphasis in the original).[17]

The political link between the UK problem and the badly needed increase in revenue made an agreement inevitable. The Stuttgart summit in 1983 under German Presidency brought a major step towards such a settlement (Werts 1992: 275). It accepted that the solution to the British problem had to be a key element of an overall reform of the EC finances, which included preparations for enlargement and a restructuring of the CAP. In a 'Solemn Declaration on European Union by the Heads of State or Government', member states linked this financial reform with the plan to 'relaunch' integration and to provide 'a solid basis for the further dynamic development of the Community over the rest of the decade' (EC-Bull. 6–1983: 19). This was an attempt by the French-German axis (with the support of the Italian government) to extend member states' time-horizons and to facilitate a package deal by linking the redistributive questions to a new integration project that would be beneficial to all member states. For the British, the summit was a success. The British permanent representative, Sir Michael Butler, judged: 'It is clear in retrospect that the Stuttgart Declaration was the watershed in the whole five-year negotiation. Other members of the Community now had just as strong an incentive as the UK to want the post-Stuttgart negotiation to succeed' (Butler 1986: 103).

However, Britain's strong bargaining position and the Stuttgart declaration did not mean that a final decision was imminent. Two European summits (in Athens and Brussels) and numerous preparatory committee and Council meetings failed to produce a compromise. A settlement only emerged a year later at the Fontainebleau summit. Three reasons underlie the lengthy negotiation process that followed the Stuttgart summit.

The negotiation strategy of British government Margaret Thatcher had invested much political capital and was therefore not prepared to give in without a clear political victory. At the same time, she had to realise that her bargaining power was not unlimited. After the summit in Brussels in March 1984, where she had again refused to compromise, she recognised that she was about to overplay her hand (George 1998: 158; Denman 1996: 262). Within her own parliamentary party, MPs raised criticism against the stern position of the Prime Minister.[18] Moreover, French President Mitterrand and his Foreign minister suggested publicly that it might be better for all concerned if Britain ceased to be a full member of the Community (Moravcsik 1998: 351).

Collaboration between West Germany and France The close coordination between Bonn and Paris enabled the two governments to keep the British government at bay and to dominate the negotiations. The German chancellor had been willing to accept British demands early on, but he was persuaded by President Mitterrand not to settle too early (Attali 1995: 583, 641–642). Germany accepted the French expulsion threat against the British government and largely followed the strategy of the French. With German backing, Mitterrand blocked any agreement under Greek Presidency and prolonged negotiations into the French Presidency (George 1998: 153). Once the French government assumed the chairmanship, it displayed a strong interest in finding an agreement.

Pressure for an agreement on financial reform The Community had still some remaining revenue at the beginning of the negotiations. Thus, the pressure to settle was not sufficiently strong (Werts 1992: 275). Member states tried to prolong the negotiations as long as the existing resources allowed it. At the same time, member states slowly started to share the British interest in budgetary discipline (which was twinned with demands for a rebate). This was not only the case for West Germany, but also for the Netherlands and even France, which were to become net-contributors after an Iberian accession. Moreover, in contrast to previous summits West Germany, which would have to foot most of the bill for a UK rebate, came to Fontainebleau as a petitioning party. Not only was it eager to achieve a commitment to enlargement, it also sought to gain permission to compensate its farmers for the dismantling of the monetary compensation amounts that had been decided on as an early first step towards CAP reform (Werts 1992: 278).[19]

The Fontainebleau summit in June 1984 brought about a final settlement that lived up to the political commitments made in Stuttgart. Key elements were the introduction of a British rebate mechanism on the revenue side of the EC budget and an increase of the VAT ceiling to 1.4 per cent. Therewith, the British government finally achieved the reform of the revenue side that it had long demanded. The UK revenue share was to be reduced by 66 per cent of its net-contributions from 1985 and a one billion ECU refund was fixed for 1984. Incorporation of the rebate on the revenue side finally won the member states' support because it allowed them to sideline the budgetary powers of the European Parliament, which had repeatedly upheld *ad hoc* payments to the UK.

The agreement was designed in a manner that allowed the British government to claim that it had gained a *permanent* and *generally applicable* solution, while enabling the rest of the Community to maintain the opposite (Denton 1984: 124–126). The solution was permanent only in that it was linked with the duration applied for the 1.4 per cent VAT revenue ceiling. Although it was clear that this was introduced as a temporary solution, the fact that the VAT ceiling could be altered only through a unanimous decision gave Britain a veto-power over attempts to change or abolish the rebate mechanism. Moreover, the solution did apply only to the UK, but included a paragraph that underlined the general nature of the agreement: '. . . any other member state sustaining a budgetary burden which is excessive in relation to its relative prosperity may benefit from a correction at the appropriate time' (quoted in EC-Bull. 6–1984: 7). However, the Prime Minister had made one noteworthy concession. She accepted that only the (British) VAT contributions constituted the basis for the calculation of net-contributions, a principle that she had fiercely rejected before.[20] Although Fontainebleau did not end tensions between Great Britain and the other member states on issues like budgetary discipline and agricultural spending, it constituted the end point of the high levels of conflict that had arose over the UK problem.

Assessment and conclusions

This section assesses the extent to which the empirical evidence presented supports my theoretical arguments on the level of conflict in the intergovernmental setting. Overall, it is contended that the historical developments between the early 1970s and the Fontainebleau settlement 1984 reveal a story of a conflict-inciting institutional setting, much in line with the propositions formulated in Chapter 2.

Fundamental to the emergence of conflict was the increase in the heterogeneity among member states initiated with the accession of Great Britain, and a distribution of costs and benefits that (deliberately) disadvantaged Britain. Given its late entry to the Community, Britain had been excluded from the negotiations over the budget treaty and had to face the consequences of this exclusion. The high intensity of the distributive disadvantages led to strong British demands for change.

The economic crises of the 1970s made the other member states unwilling to elevate the UK problem by enacting new common spending policies. The British government was only able to gain concessions when it could substantiate its demands with the necessary bargaining power. Building on Table 5.1 from above, Table 5.2 illustrates the link between the bargaining power of the British government and the settlement of the UK problem. Prime Minister Wilson improved the conditions that Edward Heath had negotiated only marginally because British withdrawal was not regarded as a major threat by the other member states and the party political motivation of the call for renegotiation was too apparent. By contrast, Prime Minister Thatcher reached her final settlement only once she had the veto-power over increases in the own-resources. The distributive conflict on the policy level spilled over to conflict on the institutional level, because the British government realised that a solution on the expenditure side would not provide sufficiently tangible benefits to elevate the UK problem and that the reform of the highly institutionalised revenue had to come as a change in the rules.

Table 5.2 Overview of the effect of bargaining power on decisions on the issue of British net-contributions

Year	EC decision	Content of the decision	Bargaining power
1973	Treaty of Accession	Seven year transition period for British contributions	*Weak bargaining power* Heath government was committed to British membership.
1975	Financial mechanism	Potential reductions of British contributions	*Weak bargaining power* Wilson government threatened 'involuntary exit' through national referendum. Member states regarded British withdrawal not as a major threat and the party political motivation of the call for renegotiation was too apparent.
1980	May Mandate	Correction payments to Great Britain	*Medium bargaining power* Thatcher government linked UK problem to a veto on agricultural price setting.
1982	Renewal of May Mandate	*Ad hoc* prolongation of correction payments to Great Britain	*Weak bargaining power* Link to agricultural price-setting broke down, as member states did not accept British veto.
1984	Fontainebleau agreement	British rebate that reduced British net-contributions	*Strong bargaining power* Thatcher government linked UK problem to increase of VAT ceiling *But:* Britain encountered expulsion threat from France and Germany.

Overall, the institutional structure provoked high levels of conflict in two respects. First, the existing setting clearly disfavoured Great Britain, which led to demands for change. Second, the institutional framework lacked procedures that would have allowed the British government to achieve distributive adaptations without having to resort to exit threats (in the case of the Wilson government), or to blocking intergovernmental affairs (in the case of Thatcher government).

In addition to the institutional setting on the European level, the interaction with *domestic politics* played an important role in prolonging and exacerbating the conflict among member states, in particular with regard to British domestic politics. Given the political divide over British membership, consecutive British governments used the question of net-contribution as a tool to establish themselves as strong advocates of British national interests. Focusing attention to the 'common enemy' helped to unite voters in an otherwise divided society, as well as to bridge the divide over Europe within the party membership of both parties, the Conservatives and Labour. It also allowed governments to pursue the double strategy of staying within the EC, which served the economic interests of the British economy, while stealing the thunder of populist attacks against British membership from the right and the left wings of the political spectrum. Therefore, net-contributions gained a political importance and symbolic value that exceeded their actual financial relevance.[21]

In channelling the discussion over pros and cons of British membership into the question of net-contributions, the British government increased its bargaining power at the European table. In line with Robert Putnam's two-level game (Putnam 1988), strong political commitment at home signalled to the other member states that the British government was determined to achieve major financial concessions and that its threats were credible (Iida 1993, 1996; Carrubba 1997). The limits of this strategy were set by the degree to which member states were interested to keep the UK in the Community, as well as the internal unity of the government on the confrontational strategy, i.e. additional 'nested games' (Tsebelis 1990) within the respective governing party.

The downside of this strategy was the fact that it made it almost impossible for the British government to accept a political compromise significantly below its original demands. The *politicisation* of the issue foreclosed the possibility of arranging a 'quiet' technical solution in which both sides could save face and the issue would be dropped. Politicisation also entailed *escalation*. The performance of the British Prime Ministers on the European stage influenced not only British domestic politics, but also forced other national governments to commit themselves to their political positions and to introduce the issue into their national political arenas. Consequently, all member states were increasingly unwilling (and, given domestic pressure, unable) to settle upon a compromise.

This escalation of conflict had the negative side effect that the *Commission* was almost completely marginalised as a resolver of conflict among member states. The Commission had originally played an important role in the discussion, as the high uncertainty and complexity of the UK problem made reliable figures an essential feature of the debate. It was clear that the Commission's proposal during the renegotiation in 1974/75 was the key focal point on which member states settled

(Emerson and Scott 1977). Even in the protracted negotiations over the May Mandate, the Commission managed to provide the framework for the final solution (Jenkins 1980: 499–500). Yet, after 1980, the Commission increasingly lost credibility and importance, which was worsened by inflationary high numbers of reform proposals that the Commission presented. From the Stuttgart summit in 1983, negotiations were almost exclusively run without significant impact from the Commission. The *Financial Times* (2 December 1983: 18) wrote: 'The European Commission's steady loss of authority and influence has been confirmed by its inability to retain the initiative and to hold many of its proposals at the centre of the discussion.'

The Budget Commissioner of the time, Christopher Tugendhat, explains from the Commission perspective why it was difficult for the Commission to continue playing a significant role in the dispute over the UK problem:

> The Commission is at its best when there is a wide measure of agreement between the member states over ends and differences only on means. It can also be very good at reconciling two or more camps of roughly equal weight. But it has great difficulty in composing its internal differences to the point where it can act decisively in bringing together a large majority and a small minority. That is why the final stages of the British budget problem, after the Commission had done all the preparatory work and pointed the way to a settlement, could be successfully concluded only by the big three – President Mitterrand in the chair, Chancellor Kohl and Mrs Thatcher – acting together behind the scene.
>
> (Tugendhat 1986: 144)

In other words, once the dispute was politicised and established on the inter-governmental level of European summitry, the Commission had little space for intervening in the negotiations. Yet, the comparison with the negotiations in 1987 and 1988 over the establishment of the financial perspective suggest that the Thorn Commission of the early- and mid-1980s was a particularly weak Commission. Many of its proposals lost status as sources of credible forecasts and far-reaching institutional reforms (interview with Commission official).

In popular accounts of the conflict over British net-contributions, the intensity of the conflict and the high degree of politicisation are almost exclusively attributed to the *personality of Margaret Thatcher*. Yet, the empirical evidence in support of this view is limited. Although her assertive bargaining style and her strong involvement in the negotiations played a significant role, Thatcher followed a trail that had already been established by her predecessors. It seems safe to say that other British prime ministers would probably have pursued a quite similar strategy. The intensity of the UK problem (in particular after the end of the transition period) and its role in domestic politics made a confrontational strategy almost inevitable for the British government.

However, as much as the empirical evidence supports the propositions introduced in Chapter 2, an interesting additional factor needs to be mentioned: normative and ideological justifications of political actions also complicated negotiations and increased the level of conflict.

The UK demand for corrections was a fundamental attack on the foundations of the EC. It introduced the question of equity. This was not only a danger to the existing pattern of distribution and benefits of member states, but it was also perceived as an overall attack on the supranational normative framework of the Community. Thatcher's 'we want our money back' shocked the other governments because it broke with the common understanding that the EC had (at least nominally) its 'own-resources'. In ostracising the British demands as requests for *just retour*, the other member states legitimised the defence of their distributive interests as an exercise for the protection of the Community spirit. At least partly, this argument was a justification that actually carried normative weight for member states and enforced politicians' determination. Similarly, Britain defended its political position with normative arguments. The UK problem was presented as a question of fairness and of efficiency. The British government argued that it was unfair that a relatively poor country, such as Britain, was paying for relatively rich member states, such as Denmark or France. And it was inefficient to subsidise European farmers instead of importing agricultural products from the world market. British politicians seemed united in this justification, which strengthened their conviction that it was justified to fight their point (Thatcher 1993: 82). The strength of these two justifications complicated the negotiations and gained force as the conflict escalated.

The discrepancy between the two normative justifications reveals an interesting additional point: the exclusion of Britain from the enactment of the 1970 budget treaty, which laid the foundation of the budgetary politics in the 1970s and 1980s, had a normative impact. Great Britain did not feel bound by the treaty, never having consented to it (except implicitly through the accession treaty). It seems that British participation in the negotiations and the enactment of the treaty would not only have altered the institutional outcome, but also increased the normative acceptance of the distributive order that resulted from it. Chapter 7 will come back to this point.

6 Accepting inter-governmental burden sharing

Negotiations between Germany and the other member states over German net-contributions within the framework of the financial perspective (1992–1999)

Similar to the shift described in Chapter 4 for conflict between Parliament and Council in the annual budgetary procedure, this chapter reveals the strong conflict-reducing effect of the introduction of the financial perspective on intergovernmental relations outside annual budgetary decision-making in the 1990s. As Figure 6.1 illustrates, the financial perspective channelled potential conflict into designated renegotiation points.

I will present a case study to aid in the detailed analysis of the conflict-reducing effect of the financial perspective. Although the descriptive statistics of Figure 6.1

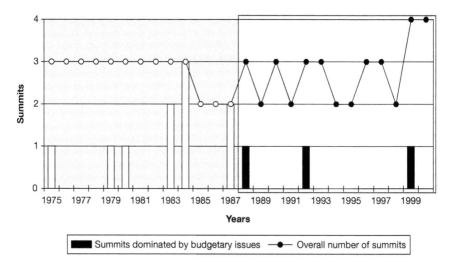

Brussels summit, February 1988: Introduction of the financial perspective.
Edinburgh summit, December 1992: Renewal of the financial perspective.
Berlin summit, March 1999: Renewal of the financial perspective.

Figure 6.1 Summits dominated by disputes over budgetary issues (1988–2000).

already indicate that a correlation exists between new institutional settlements and the level of conflict, I do not know the exact manner in which the institutional change reduced the level of conflict. As in the previous chapter, I, therefore, apply a process-tracing approach to a single case study, which enables me to analyse in detail the effects of the new institutional setting on the ability of actors to contain conflict. I have selected a situation of a major potential conflict as a case in point: the discrepancy between Germany's position as largest net-contributor to the EU budget and the huge financial and economic burden it had to shoulder through unification. This 'German problem' (Laffan 1997: 54–56) could have dominated and blocked EU politics in the 1990s to the same degree, as did the British problem in the 1980s. Instead, Germany respected the existing financial framework, worked together with other net-contributors in gaining austere annual budgets and put forward its demands for a reduction of net-contributions when the financial perspective was renegotiated.

The German problem provides an ideal case for the analysis of conflict in the intergovernmental setting for three reasons. First, similarities in intensity and nature make the German problem comparable to the UK problem. In limiting the variation of non-institutional factors, I can concentrate fully on the impact of institutions and assess how the change in the institutional setting (independent variable) reduced the level of conflict (dependent variable). Second, the German problem is a 'hard case' for my theory of conflict, because the large scope and intensity of German net-contributions make it surprising that the levels of conflict remained low. Confidence in my theoretical propositions increases if they are (even) able to account for these surprisingly low levels of conflict. Third, although the German problem remains a special case, it reveals relevant mechanisms and dynamics of conflict-containment. In this respect, it is somewhat representative for other potential conflicts that evolved in the 1990s around the net-contributions of other member states, such as the Netherlands (see the 'Dutch problem', Laffan 1997: 56–59).

Similar to Chapter 5, this chapter is divided into three sections. First, I will briefly recapitulate what I expect to find following my theoretical propositions. In the following section, I will present the case study. The starting point of the case study is the round of negotiations over the new financial perspective in 1992, when the German problem materialised. The case study concludes with the negotiations over the Agenda 2000, in the course of which Germany accepted a settlement for the coming seven years. The final section links back to the theoretical perspective and evaluates the extent to which the empirical evidence supports my original propositions.

Theoretical perspective

Channelling discontent

We expect that potential conflict occurs when countries experience economic crises and when the gap between their contributions into the budget and the benefits from it widens, without their compensation through non-budgetary gains from integration. The accession of less prosperous countries is likely to increase budgetary tensions, as they bring in new demands for redistribution. As argued in Chapter 2, the institutional setting of the decision-making process is likely to be a decisive variable that influences whether potential conflict translates into a high level of actual conflict, or can be settled within the boundaries of the existing procedures. The institutional setting impacts on the distribution of bargaining power. In general, a member state that is unsatisfied with the distributive order and does not have the bargaining power to initiate budgetary change will try to obstruct intergovernmental relations in order to increase its bargaining power. In the case of the financial perspective, we assume that the new institutional framework prevents member states from obstructing intergovernmental relations. It channels discontent into designated renegotiation points at which member states can substantiate their distributive demands with full veto-power.

Hence, a member state that seeks to change the existing distributive order has an incentive to stay within the financial perspective and to articulate its demands when the multi-annual budget plan is up for renewal. Three factors contribute to the incentive for compliance. First, it is unlikely that the member state has the bargaining power to force other member states to change the existing financial perspective before a renegotiation is scheduled. Second, a revision of the financial perspective entails high costs. The reopening of a package could lead to various distributive demands from other member states and would include negotiations with the EP. Third, the framework of the financial perspective ensures that each member state will have the institutional bargaining power of a veto player at the end of the multi-annual budget. At the point of renegotiation, a government is guaranteed that it can prevent the drawing up of a new financial perspective until a satisfying agreement is reached.

Clashes at the designated points of renegotiation are contained by the fact that the European Council adopts the financial perspective as part of a large package deal. This allows for linkages between different issues of the budget and across policy fields. Purely zero-sum distributive conflict turns into positive-sum games where maintaining political stability becomes an important additional objective. Following Moravcsik (1998), it seems likely that the outcomes of these intergovernmental summits represent *en gros* the interests and bargaining power of the different member states.[1] Institutional actors, such as the Commission and the presidency, play a positive role in setting the agenda and moderating the negotiation process.

Case study

Conflict over German net-contributions

This section presents a detailed analysis of the conflict over German net-contributions. The issue of large net-contributions became financially relevant after unification and entered German domestic politics in 1994, as Table 6.1 illustrates. Yet, it had minimal effect on intergovernmental relations and was settled at the negotiations over a new financial perspective in 1999.

Table 6.1 Overview of political developments on the national and European level concerning German net-contributions

Year	National level	European level
1992		Adoption of a *new financial perspective* (Delors II) at the Edinburgh summit.
1993	Bundesbank-Report on German net-contributions and approaching	
1994	national and European elections provoked national debate.	
1995	Bundestag endorsed own-resources ceiling in full compliance with existing financial perspective.	Kohl government pushed for budgetary discipline in annual budgetary decision-making.
1996	German Länder and the national ministry of finance issued reform proposals.	
1997	Kohl government started to make firm statements against the current system of burden sharing.	Kohl government criticised Commission proposals for the new financial perspective (Agenda 2000).
1998	National elections further intensified government statements.	Kohl government demanded from European Council a strong commitment to addressing the German problem in the new financial perspective (Agenda 2000).
1999		Adoption of a *new financial perspective* (Agenda 2000) at the Berlin summit.

The German problem

The core of the German problem was a significant discrepancy between Germany's increasingly large net-contributions to the Community's budget and the decline of its economic prosperity in the aftermath of unification. This discrepancy emerged in the early 1990s and inserted a potential for conflict into budgetary politics that was quite similar to that of the UK problem of the 1970s and 80s.

As a highly industrialised economy with a relatively small agricultural sector, West Germany had always been the biggest net-contributor to the Community's budget. This position was justified by Germany's economic strength and the benefits that market liberalisation brought to the German economy. Politically, European integration gave West Germany the unique opportunity to regain acceptance on the international stage. German net-contributions were regarded as a relatively small price for its diplomatic comeback after the lost war. Nevertheless, Germany's role as biggest net-contributor was not completely uncontested. Economic crises in the 1970s sparked calls for a reduction of Germany's net-contributions. Under the chancellorship of Helmut Schmidt, the West German government coined the term 'paymaster of the Community', hinting that Germany's willingness to pay for an ever-expanding EC budget was not unlimited (Bulmer and Paterson 1987: 67–68). Yet, West Germany never strongly argued its case.[2] In contrast, it played an instrumental role in relaunching European integration in the 1980s, providing the political and financial means with which to embark on the single market project and the budgetary framework of the financial perspective (Shackleton 1990).

With the fall of the Berlin Wall, Germany shifted its political focus east-wards and assumed responsibility as key financier of the economic and political (re-)construction of East Germany and the new democracies of the former Soviet bloc. This induced a significant financial burden on the German taxpayer's purse. At the same time, Germany's contributions to the EC budget increased following its commitment to a redistributive financial perspective in 1988. Moreover, unification changed the shape of Germany. Not only had it become a bigger country, the accession of 18 million East Germans also considerably reduced the prosperity per capita. By 1992, Germany had dropped back from second to sixth place in terms of member states' purchasing power standards and faced an annual net-contribution of DEM 22 billion (Deutsche Bundesbank 1993: 64–65; see Figure 6.2).

As the contours of the German problem became fully apparent, Germany found itself in a relatively similar situation to that of Great Britain in the 1970s and 1980s. Its farming sector was too small to receive significant benefits from the EC budget and its regions did not qualify for large-scale structural aid. At the same time, its contributions to the budget did not reflect its relative decline in economic prosperity and the existing pressure on national public spending.[3] Like the UK problem, the German problem raised the question of 'fairness' of the existing Community's system of burden sharing, in particular as other rich member states, such as Denmark, were still net-beneficiaries. It seemed that EC budgetary politics had to

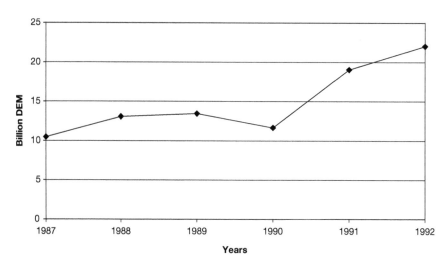

Figure 6.2 Germany's net-contributions to the EC budget (1987–1992).
Source: Deutsche Bundesbank 1993: 65.

address the issue in order to prevent a replay of the budgetary battle of the previous decades.

However, although member states had accepted the link between prosperity and net-contribution when granting the UK a budgetary rebate, many questioned its appropriateness in the German case. First, 'net-contributions' were still a contested concept, not only with regard to their actual calculation, but also in relation to their political significance (see Appendix No. 3; Deffaa 1997). Although Germany was undoubtedly paying more into the EC budget than it received, German net-contributions were regarded as membership fee for a club whose amenities, e.g. full market access for German goods, still profited Germany greatly. Second, the new unified Germany had become a key regional power whose responsibility, in the eyes of other member states, entailed paying the lion's share of upholding political stability in Europe (W. Wallace 1995), in particular as the price was still relatively low in comparison to the German GNP. Third, in contrast to the UK problem, the German problem could not be addressed in isolation from vital, financial interests of the other member states. On the one hand, German net-contributions had always been a constitutive element of European budgetary politics, if not of European integration. Hence, change would challenge the existing system of financial and political relations among member states as a whole. On the other hand, the German problem was not unique. With the increase of the redistributive nature of the EC budget, other countries, such as the Netherlands and (after their accession in 1995) Austria and Sweden had become large net-contributors. Although these member states supported Germany's demands for solution of the German problem, the link between the German problem and their own demands made an isolated solution for Germany impossible.

Delors II and the Edinburgh summit

The emergence of the German problem coincided with the negotiations over the renewal of the financial perspective in 1992. Governments had just signed the Maastricht Treaty and faced what newspapers had branded the 'bill of Maastricht' (*Liberation* 10 February 1992). Yet, despite intensive distributive demands from the different member states, governments managed to settle their differences and came to an agreement at the Edinburgh summit in December 1992 (see Appendix No. 3). The new financial perspective slightly reduced the rate of budgetary increase, but failed to address the German problem. Restraining itself from pushing for distributive change, Germany had facilitated a compromise by again accepting the role as the largest net-contributor (Laffan and Shackleton 1996: 87). Key reasons for Germany's behaviour lay in the package deal character of the financial perspective and the link to German unification (Wagner 2001: 216).

An important characteristic of Edinburgh agreement was its link to the Maastricht Treaty. Governments had just adopted the treaty, which laid the foundations for political and monetary union. During the treaty negotiations, the less prosperous member states, led by Spain, had made their support for monetary union dependent on a guarantee for further financial transfers from the EC budget (*Financial Times*

19 November 1991). Given that unanimity among member states was necessary for treaty decisions, the bargaining power of Spain had been very strong.[4] Thus, the member states had to accept Spanish demands for side-payments. They had added a protocol to the Maastricht Treaty that guaranteed Spain, Portugal, Greece and Ireland the establishment of a cohesion fund.

Shortly after the new treaty was signed, the Commission presented its proposals for a new financial perspective, the 'Delors II package' (Baché and Jouret 1992).[5] Similar to the first financial perspective, it proposed a doubling of the spending for regional and structural policy for a five-year period, resulting in an increase of the own-resource ceiling from 1.20 to 1.37 percentage of GNP. Member states reacted to these proposals differently (*Financial Times* 12 May 1992). While the 'Southern' member states, Greece, Spain, Portugal, and Ireland, welcomed 'Delors II', 'Northern' member states strongly criticised the proposed budget increases. The German government did not raise the German problem as a separate issue, but acted in coalition with the British and other net-contributors. Germany made clear that it preferred to leave the own-resources ceiling unchanged.[6] Yet, the Northern coalition was not without internal tensions. The British government insisted in keeping the rebate, while Germany and other member states questioned the justification for continuing this privilege – although Germany was not interested in letting negotiations collapse over this issue (*Süddeutsche Zeitung* 25 November 1992; *The Independent* 18 November 1992).

The Maastricht Treaty affected the negotiations, not only in form of the above-mentioned cohesion fund protocol, but also through the ratification process that took place at the same time as the negotiations over the financial perspective. Ratification had two effects: on the one hand, it gave member states, such as Spain (and to some degree Great Britain),[7] the opportunity to threaten other member states with withholding ratification of the Maastricht Treaty in the national parliament, if there was an unfavourable outcome to the negotiations. On the other hand (and this intensified the effect of the first) the rejection of the treaty in the Danish ratification referendum in June 1992 and the near rejection in the French referendum in September caused significant political turmoil. All over Europe, public opinion on European integration experienced a considerable setback. The ratification debate over the Maastricht Treaty made citizens realise the extent to which the EC was already affecting their lives, taking many unaware (Wolf 1992: 313). Moreover, the European Monetary System underwent a major crisis in 1992, during which Britain left the system (*Süddeutsche Zeitung* 14 December 1992). Against this background, the pressure on European governments to settle upon a new financial perspective was high; a failure of the negotiations would have entailed considerable political costs for the Community and would have called the Maastricht project into question (Schmuck 1993).

During the final negotiations at the Edinburgh summit, the British presidency combined an agreement on the financial perspective with several other political decisions (Shackleton 1993b; Jouret 1993). Heads of State or Government agreed on special exemption clauses in the Maastricht Treaty for Denmark and Britain, the application of the new subsidiarity principle, a decision on the number of German

MEPs (taking account of unification), the start of the accession negotiations with Austria, Sweden, Norway and Finland, a European initiative for economic growth and declarations concerning the European political cooperation. Within the complexity of these issues, a compromise was found that did little to reduce Germany's large net-contributions (except for a minor shift in the structure of the own-resource and an increase in structural spending for the new Länder), but it satisfied German interests in other areas. The increase in the number of MEPs and the start of accession talks with new applicant countries (originally blocked by Spain) had been key objectives of the German government (Schmuck 1993).

Overall, two features characterised the Edinburgh agreement (Shackleton 1993a). First, the linkage to the Maastricht Treaty and other political decisions facilitated a compromise. It gave the cohesion countries the bargaining power to claim side-payments for their consent to EMU and generally increased member states' interest in finding an agreement. Shackleton (1993a: 387) writes: 'Despite all differences of view, there remained a strong sense of obligation to find a joint solution. This need not be attributed to any sense of idealism but should be seen in the context of a Community where there is a significant linkage between issues.' Second, given the preferences of the governments and the unanimity rule for decisions on the financial perspective, the scope for major change was extremely limited. The old and the new financial perspective did not differ much. Net-contributors had prevented major increases, while cohesion countries achieved the selective increase of the redistributive regional policy. 'The *acquis communautaire* weighted heavily in the calculations of everybody' (ibid.). Incrementalism dominated as a problem-solving strategy and prevented far-reaching changes.

Germany had a strong interest in gaining a consensus on a new financial agreement and was therefore willing to shoulder the largest financial burden. Although the German government would have had the institutional bargaining power to veto the final outcome, it did not regard the German problem as sufficiently salient to justify a major row over the issue. This was related to the government's strong political attachment to the Maastricht Treaty and a commitment, made in 1990 during the unification process, that Germany unification would not take place at the expense of the less prosperous member states (Weidenfeld 1998: 412).[8] Chancellor Kohl honoured this promise and ensured that a budget battle did not endanger the success of the Maastricht project. Much of his political standing and personal credibility was associated with German unification and the Maastricht Treaty. In general, German politicians regarded the completion of the Maastricht Treaty and an agreement on the financial perspective as an important element in ensuring their European partners that the unified Germany would not constitute a threat to European integration.

Respecting the financial perspective: between Delors II and Agenda 2000

While the German government had accepted a new financial perspective that did not address the German problem, domestic politics was slow to pick up the issue.

The government was not interested in questioning the results of the Edinburgh summit. Moreover, the political establishment in Germany regarded the 'paymaster' argument as largely unacceptable, anti-European populism. The publication of an article in the monthly report of the German Bundesbank in November 1993 marked a key turning point. Although very tame in its tone, it drew attention to the German problem. The article observed that the German net-contribution 'has increased sharply, and can be expected to go on rising in the next few years' although 'Germany as a whole has dropped back to sixth place (in terms of purchasing power standards)' (*Deutsche Bundesbank* 1993: 61 and 64). The Bundesbank did not request immediate institutional or political reforms, but recommended an approach of strict budgetary discipline at the EU level (ibid.: 75).

The fact that the well-respected Bundesbank took up the issue of rising net-contributions was sufficient for the implicit consensus on the 'paymaster' argument to deteriorate (*Financial Times* 18 November 1993; *Frankfurter Allgemeine Zeitung* 18 November 1993; *Süddeutsche Zeitung* 20 November 1993; *Die Zeit* 26 November 1993; *Handelsblatt* 26/27 November 1993). A political debate began that spread into all areas of the political spectrum as European and national elections approached in 1994. Trying to benefit from scepticism against EMU and the Maastricht Treaty, the Bavarian CSU, as well as right-wing MPs from the CDU, called for a reduction of the German net-contributions (*Süddeutsche Zeitung* 25 February 1994; *Frankfurter Allgemeine Zeitung* 2 February 1994). Although partly responsible for the Edinburgh agreement, the party leader of the CSU, the German finance minister Theo Waigel, responded to party internal pressure and spoke out against the 'flagrant injustice of the German contributions' (*Le Figaro* 24 January and 29 January 1994). The opposition joined the chorus, criticising the government for having failed to address the issue. Finally, low public support for the government and approaching European and national elections (June and October 1994) made a reluctant Chancellor Kohl enter the debate. In a major confrontation with the opposition in the Bundestag, Kohl made it clear that Germany had reached the limit of its financial contributions to the EU (*Financial Times* 28 May 1994).

Although the German problem had suddenly become a relevant issue in German domestic politics, the scope and effect of its politicisation were still limited and vague. Voters did not seem to regard the issue as decisive for their political choice and the debate did not translate into clear political proposals (Janning 1994: 306–307). The government made no particular effort to raise the issue with its European partners.

The government's approach to the German problem gained shape after the national elections. The government specified its stance on the question of Germany's large net-contributions in February 1995, during the ratification debate in the German parliament on the Council decision to raise the own-resource ceiling (as envisaged by the financial perspective).[9] It made clear that it did not question the existing financial perspective and that it would fully obey the agreement for the complete period until 1999 (*Deutscher Bundestag* 16 February 1995: 1413–1414).[10] In the meantime, the ministry of finance would try to contain German contributions by pressing for an austerity approach in annual budgetary decision-making. Annual budgets that remained significantly below the ceilings of the financial perspective would automatically reduce the scope of German net-contributions.

Overall, the government opted for a strategy that did not question the fundamentals of the financial perspective, but tried to accommodate the problem within the existing framework. The strategy seemed promising as the accession of two new net-contributors, namely Sweden and Austria, strengthened the camp of net-contributors.[11] In addition to these concrete steps, the German finance minister repeatedly raised the issue of Germany's net-contributions in meetings with his European colleagues, stating that a reform was 'urgently necessary' (*Financial Times* 6 April 1995). He brought the issue onto the European agenda for mainly domestic reasons, knowing full well that a reform was not planned before the end of the current financial perspective. At the same time, raising the issue repeatedly also served the purpose of creating awareness among member states and of gradually establishing the claim that the new financial perspective would need to provide a solution to the German problem.

With increasing pressure on German public expenditure (induced by the EMU convergence criteria and persistently high costs of reconstructing Eastern Germany), the German problem became a permanent reference point in the political debates over Germany's role in the EU. It was therefore no surprise that the German Länder, which since the early 1990s had felt that they were the main political losers of European integration, addressed the issue of German net-contribution, and demanded reform.[12] The German second chamber, the Bundesrat, issued several statements in 1995 (*Süddeutsche Zeitung* 13 May 1995), and presented a far-reaching reform proposal early 1997 (*Länder* 1997). Oriented towards the German *Länderfinanzausgleich*, it devised a system of redistribution quotas for member states (based on their respective purchasing power per capita), which would significantly reduce Germany's net-contributions.

The federal government reacted to the reform discussions among the Länder by introducing its own reform initiative. The permanent secretary in the federal ministry of finance presented a proposal that combined a concentration of structural spending and the abolishment of the UK rebate, with the introduction of a general capping system that would limit countries' net-contributions (Stark 1996).[13] As the domestic debate on the German problem flourished, even the Commission president Santher felt obliged to admit in an interview with a German newspaper in July 1996 that the Community's financing system should be more equitable. Yet, he made clear that reform would not take place before 1999, when the financial perspective was to be renewed (interview quoted in *Agence Europe* 31 July 1996).

Agenda 2000 and the Berlin summit

In presenting its proposals for a new financial perspective ('Agenda 2000') in July 1997, the Commission initiated the negotiations over financial reform well before the end of the old financial perspective. The Commission proposed reforms of the CAP and the structural funds in order to finance EU enlargement within the existing own-resource ceiling. The German government quickly responded to the proposals, emphasising its interest in a significant reduction of the German net-contributions. However, Chancellor Kohl did not have a clear line on the overall reform package (Janning 1997: 299). His government found it difficult to combine its stance on the German problem with its position on CAP reform and enlargement. On the one hand, it demanded a significant reduction of German contributions to EU budget, which was only feasible through considerable cuts in the main expenditure policies. On other hand, the government rejected a far-reaching reform of the CAP, as this was strongly opposed by the well-organised German farmers' lobby.[14] Similarly, it strongly supported the accession of Central and East European countries, but it knew that enlargement entailed considerable costs and was not feasible without CAP reform (Janning 1998: 313–315).

The German finance minister Waigel tried to square the circle of CAP reform and the German problem by demanding the introduction of a general rebate system for large net-contributors. Drawing on the proposal presented by his permanent secretary the previous year, Waigel insisted on the abolishment of the UK rebate and proposed a capping model that limited the net-contribution to a specific percentage of GNP. The rationale behind this proposal was very similar to that of Margaret Thatcher in the 1980s. Waigel recognised that a rebate system would elevate the German problem without incurring the costs of fighting for major spending reform and openly agonising the agricultural lobby on which his CSU strongly depended. As had been the case for Thatcher, Waigel's approach constituted a clear breach of the still dominating, implicit agreement among member states that corrections of a country's net-contributions should be achieved through the expenditure side (either through overall savings or new spending policies directly benefiting the country). Germany's demands for a rebate were, therefore, widely criticised as '*non-communautaire*' (Wagner 2001: 217). In particular, the unity and vehemence of the German government on the issue surprised other member states. Not only the finance minister, but also the foreign minister and the Chancellor emphasised the importance of solving the German problem (*Agence Europe* 3 September 1997).[15] In this respect, the ministry of finance had gradually won the argument within the government; the chancellery and the ministry of foreign affairs had put their reservations against a confrontational strategy aside.

The government was under strong domestic pressure: 1997 was the reference year for the fulfilment of the convergence criteria, which posed major strains on German public spending. Chancellor Kohl was determined to achieve the introduction of the Euro even against a sceptical (if not hostile) German public. In order to realise this objective, he was willing to emphasise German national interests on other issues, such as budgetary reform. Similar to the tactics of Margaret Thatcher (although less forcefully), the government tried to cover domestic tensions over public spending by demonstrating its determination to safeguard taxpayers' money on the European level.

In 1998, with national elections due in the autumn and devastating results in opinion polls, the political actions of the government gained a formerly unknown assertiveness. At a meeting of the Council of Economic and Finance Ministers (Ecofin) in March 1998, Waigel threatened his colleagues to veto decisions on other policies if they did not commit themselves to the introduction of a correction mechanism (Wagner 2001: 217). And at the Cardiff summit in June 1998, which set the timetable for the subsequent reform negotiations, Chancellor Kohl demanded that the conclusions of the presidency entailed reference to Germany's demands for a solution of the German problem (*Süddeutsche Zeitung* 13 July 1998; presidency conclusions of the Cardiff summit: paragraph 54, EU-Bull. 6–1998). The reform negotiations came to a virtual standstill in the summer of 1998, as the EU was waiting for the end of the German election campaign (*Financial Times* 29 September 1998).

With the introduction of a new German government, negotiations at working group, Coreper and Council level regained momentum (Laffan 2000a: 7–8). The new government was immediately plunged into intensive discussions and faced the prospect of having to conclude the negotiations under German presidency in the first half of 1999. The new Chancellor Gerhard Schröder and his foreign minister, Joschka Fischer, applied a strategy that combined national interest with pragmatism.

From the start, they made it clear that they would continue with the Kohl government's approach and push for solution to the German problem (Maurer 2000: 46). In numerous statements, the government tried to fight off expectations that Germany would facilitate an agreement on the financing of enlargement and a successful presidency by bearing the lion's share of the costs (*Frankfurter Allgemeine Zeitung* 6 January 1999; Janning 1998: 327). The German public had high expectations, in particular as Schröder had positioned himself in the preceding election campaigns as a defender of the national interest.[16] Once in the chair, Schröder used the presidency as an instrument for direct and intense exchanges with the different member states, which even led to clashes with Germany's traditionally strongest ally France over CAP reform (*Frankfurter Allgemeine Zeitung* 20 March 1999; Laffan 2000a: 11). Part of the government's force stemmed from the fact the new Red-Green coalition in Bonn was less dependent on the agricultural constituency than the previous government had been, and could take up a new reform proposal presented by the Commission in a controversial report on the own-resource system in October 1998 (Commission 1998). In this report, the Commission had breached with the tradition of contesting the concept of net-contribution and had instead substantiated the demands of the large net-contributors, in particular Germany. As a solution to the German problem, the Commission had favoured a system of co-financing, by virtue of which a quarter of European agricultural expenditure would be paid out of national budgets.

This emphasis on national interest in Schröder's strategy was accompanied by a good bit of pragmatism. From the start, the new government knew that a radical solution to the German problem was almost impossible to achieve. The coalition agreement between the social democrats and the Green Party was quite frank in stating that the objective of a fairer system of contribution to the EU budget should be pursued mainly through the expenditure side (in line with the implicit agreement among member states) and not, as the previous government had demanded, through a reform of the revenue side in the form of a capping model (quoted in Wagner 1999:

38). In the course of negotiations, Germany's role as a key European power with a strong interest in political stability and Eastern enlargement, as well as its position in the presidency of the Council, created an increasingly heavier counterweight against a strategy of national interest.

Much of the final negotiations resembled the developments around the Delors II package. Again, the key cleavages centred on the level of structural expenditure (dividing the North from the South), the UK rebate (separating the UK from the rest of the member states) and, to a larger extent than in 1992, CAP reform (with France as the key opponent of co-financing) (Laffan 1999: 6). Moreover, negotiations over the financial perspective were once more linked to other non-budgetary issues. Impacting directly on the debates at the final summit in March 1999 in Berlin, the collective resignation of the Commission created an institutional crisis that demanded immediate political actions by the European Council. Furthermore, the outbreak of war in Kosovo shifted political attention to Europe's capacity to act collectively on foreign policy matters. A linkage to previous treaty decisions also existed, in form of the Amsterdam Treaty, although it was less prominent and did not precommit side-payments, as had been the case with the cohesion fund protocol at Maastricht. Similar to the British presidency in 1992, the German presidency had a strong interest in gaining credit for a successful conclusion of the negotiations. Schröder was in dire need of a political success. His government had just lost the regional election in Hesse, was facing European elections in June, and had experienced the spectacular resignation of the prominent finance minister and party chairman, Oscar Lafontaine, only a fortnight before the Berlin summit (*Frankfurter Allgemeine Zeitung* 12 March 1999).

Similar to Edinburgh, Berlin brought about a heavily incremental agreement that postponed major reform decisions. Member states concentrated on defending their core distributive interests (Begg 1999a,b; Laffan 1999; Galloway 1999; see also Appendix No. 2):

- France and Denmark prevented co-financing and were thus willing to concede an increase of their net-contributions.
- Spain and the other cohesion countries accepted a reduction in budgetary expenditure in return for an extension of the cohesion fund until 2006.
- All member states endorsed the setting aside of resources for accession countries (through the creation of a separate heading), but essentially postponed the decision of how the expenditure programmes for the EU 15 would be financed once the new member states became fully eligible.
- The large net-contributors, i.e. Sweden, Austria, the Netherlands and Germany, gave up their demands for a capping model and gained a strengthened GNP link between the own-resources system, annual ceilings that stayed significantly below the revenue ceiling of 1.27 per cent of GNP and a slight reduction of their contribution to the financing of the UK rebate.
- The UK defended its rebate and accepted in return that pre-accession expenditure would not fall under the UK rebate and that the UK would forgo any benefits it would have received from changes in the structure of the revenue side.

• Italy got an Italian Commission president and thus had to agree to the changes in the revenue structure, which increased Italian contributions to the budget.

A list of 13 last-minute side-payments for specific distributive projects 'sweetened' the financial compromise and facilitated an agreement that governments could sell to their voters back home (*Financial Times* 27 March 1997).

Overall, Germany was regarded as the 'loser' of the agreement (Laffan 2000a: 17). Although German net-contributions were to go down over the following seven years (Jessen 1999), the government had failed to achieve a significant reduction of its net-contributions. The opposition strongly criticised the Schröder government for failing to get a better deal (Das Parlament 2./9. April 1999: 6–7). Yet, Chancellor Schröder and minister Fischer had opted for political stability and a successful presidency. They presented the Berlin summit as part of a sequence of political summits during their presidency in which the government strengthened Germany's role as a key player on the international stage.[17] Schröder speculated that once the outcries from the opposition benches had faded, the German problem would disappear from the domestic agenda. Coincidently, an article in the monthly report of the Bundesbank from June 1999, a follow-up to the article that had initiated the debate in 1993, bolstered their strategy (*Deutsche Bundesbank* 1999). It showed that the German problem had been a particularly pressing problem in the mid-1990s; although it still existed, the German problem had now lost some of its significance (Figure 6.3). The Bundesbank gave the following reasons for this development: the accession of other net-contributors in 1995, the shift in the structure of the own-resource system towards the GNP resource, a below average rate increase of the German GNP, and augmented structural payments from the EU budget to the new Länder.

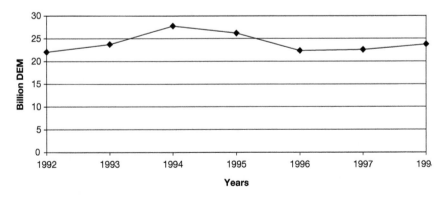

Figure 6.3 Germany's net-contributions to the EU budget (1992–1998).
Source: Deutsche Bundesbank (1999: 60)

Assessment and conclusions

This concluding section assesses the extent to which the empirical evidence presented supports the theoretical arguments. Overall, it contends that the case study largely backs the propositions developed in Chapter 2. Although the 'German problem' resembled the 'UK problem' of the 1970s and 1980s in scope, the institutional setting of the financial perspective channelled the German demands for distributive change into designated renegotiation points. It prevented the outbreak and escalation of conflict. Due to the package deal character of agreements on financial perspectives, member states' distributive demands were generally accommodated. Once unanimously adopted, governments respected the outcomes.

As in the previous chapter, the case study illustrated the role of *domestic politics* for the transformation of potential into actual conflict and for the escalation towards high levels of conflict (Carrubba 1997). When a member state experiences an economic crisis and a decline in economic prosperity relative to other member states, while it continues to pay a large share into the EU budget, potential conflict emerges. This potential conflict develops into actual conflict, when a government takes up the issue and raises it at the European level. Following the assumption that politicians' preferences are determined by their interest in re-election (see Chapter 2), politicians raise the issue of net-contributions for two reasons. First, they assume that they can gain a reduction of the large budgetary burden and use the recuperated money for domestic purposes. Second, they want to demonstrate to their voters that they defend national interests. In this case, the symbolic importance of the net-contributions exceeds the financial relevance of the actual amount.[18]

The motivation of German politicians to raise the problem of net-contributions in the mid-1990s combined these two reasons – with the second clearly dominating the first. The government sought to ease the financial pressure inflicted by contributions to the EU budget on the national budget, but more importantly it wanted the German public to see that it was actively pursuing this point at the European level. This explains why the issue conquered the domestic political agenda, especially during election campaigns, although the government never actually intended to press for a solution to the German problem before 1999. In this respect, Laffan's assessment of Agenda 2000 negotiations is telling. She argues that:

> [I]ts [Germany's, J.L.] ntional preference for a significant reduction in its net-contributions was unrealistic from the outset because of the need for the leading power to pay for the maintenance of the system. Moreover, the German national preference for budgetary cuts is in conflict with its stated preferences for enlargement, a process in which it has the greatest geopolitical stake. The actual budgetary costs borne by Germany remain modest and Germany together with the other members of the net-contributors' club succeeded with Agenda 2000 in halting the budgetary increase, a feature of the last two budgetary deals.
>
> (Laffan 2000a: 20)

If German demands were unrealistic and exorbitant, it seems likely that German politicians must have known it all along and used the issue mainly for domestic reasons.

Domestic factors, such as (1) the popularity of the government, (2) public mood towards the European Union, and (3) the general approach of the government towards the EU, play an important role in determining whether politicians take up the issue of net-contributions. They also influence the determination with which a politician pursues the issue. An unpopular government will readily take up the issue, particularly during election campaigns. The German case illustrated that, as the public opinion towards the EU swung and general scepticism against the Euro spread, the problem of large net-contributions offered a welcome opportunity for the government to accommodate public demands for a stronger focus on national interests. Yet, as the German government's position on other EU related political issues was largely pro-integrationist, the political space for politicising the issue of net-contributions was restricted. The German government never wanted to undermine its role as a key actor in European integration and did, in the end, compromise in order to preserve stability. In contrast, the British government in the 1980s had a different political understanding of its role in Europe and granted the budgetary conflict almost unlimited political space. This is an important difference between the German and the British case.[19]

The financial perspective played a decisive role in channelling the German problem into forms of interaction that prevented escalation. At no point in the 1990s did the German government seriously consider the option of demanding a complete change of the financial perspective. It fully accepted the formal procedure of renewal. The political costs of mobilising the member states to agree to a reform halfway through a financial perspective were too high. The German government obeyed the obligations of the financial perspective even when its MPs could have voted against the own-resource decisions in 1995 (see above). In contrast to the British government two decade earlier, the German government was unable to blame other member states for the emergence of the German problem. Germany's consent to the 1992 financial perspective made it difficult for the government to fundamentally question the existing distributive order (*membership in the enacting coalition*). Moreover, the commitment to a complete review in 1999 assured the German government that the German problem would be on the political agenda, once the negotiations over a new multi-annual budget plan began (*scheduled discussion*). Thus, it did not have to establish the German problem as a pressing issue on the European agenda, as did the British government.

The financial perspective, with its long-term commitment, had another important conflict-reducing effect. It allowed German politicians to raise the German problem for domestic purposes without politicising it to a point of no return (*limited effect of politicisation*). They did not trap themselves in a position from which they could not back down anymore, as had been the case for Margaret Thatcher. The prime minister's strong statements concerning British net-contributions and the constant negotiations on the European level increased domestic expectation of a large political success. With increasing politicisation of the issue in Britain and abroad,

Thatcher almost completely lost space for political manoeuvres and a satisfactory compromise. In contrast, the German finance minister Waigel was able to raise the issue repeatedly in the German media, knowing full well that a reform was not due before 1999.[20]

At the renegotiation points, the *package deal character* allowed Germany to establish an agreement that, although not fulfilling all its distributive demands, could still be sold as beneficial to the German public. The institutional embeddedness of the financial perspective in a huge intergovernmental event under the direction of the Heads of State or Government allowed a process of logrolling in which every member state had a veto power and could demand budgetary or non-budgetary compensation for consenting to a final agreement. This turned the zero-sum negotiations into a positive-sum game in which member states only settled when each one had achieved some gains.

The case study also revealed that a strong status quo bias arose from this system of large bargaining events. Incrementalism dominates as the key instrument of problem solving. Both financial perspectives (Delors II and Agenda 2000) displayed a high degree of continuity and a lack of radical reform decisions. Member states focused on preserving their key distributive benefits and showed little willingness to approach political change.[21]

The status quo bias of the financial perspective relates to question of whether a *norm of compliance* and a new logic of appropriateness increased the conflict reducing effect of the financial perspective and its multi-annual framework, as Laffan (2000b) argues. It is difficult to assess the exact effect of a norm, because such a logic of appropriateness would have only strengthened the existing logic of consequentialism in the presented case study, and would not have stood in contrast to it.[22] Comparing the UK case with the German problem, it seems that the evolution of norms is linked to normative and ideological justifications of political actions and a high degree of politicisation and escalation. Justifications become most prominent when conflict has reached already a considerable level and the politicisation of the problem induces the need for a member state to legitimise its position. Escalation entrenches these justifications and creates a norm of conflict. Yet, as long as conflict is low, the need for a member state to legitimise its actions is not strong. Hence, a norm does not emerge and does not induce a separate impact on the member states' behaviour. The next chapter will return to this point.

Finally, two actors play a significant role at different stages of the negotiation process: the *Commission* in the preparatory phase, and the presidency in the final negotiation phase. The Commission set the agenda with its long-term proposals in 1992 and 1997/98 and thus, impacted on the final outcome of the negotiations. Yet, its influence on the level of conflict during the negotiation phase was marginal. In addition to institutional reasons, this resulted partly from the fact that, in contrast to 1988, the Commission was weakened in 1992 and especially in 1998/99. While Delors had gambled away the Commission's reputation as honest broker (in 1992), Santher and his team were caught in fraud allegations (in 1998/99), which culminated in their resignation shortly before the Berlin summit.

In the run-up to the 1992- and 1999-agreements, the *presidency* coordinated the negotiation and tabled compromise proposals (see on the German presidency, Laffan 2000a). In bilateral negotiations, it made out the political positions of the different member states and offered side-payments. It is no coincidence, that all three financial perspectives were brokered under the presidency of big member states.[23] Presidencies need to have the political and financial weight to force other member states to compromise, and to allow it to make concessions, if necessary from its own purse (as in the case of Germany in 1999), in order to facilitate a final agreement. This is an interest contrast to treaty negotiations, where a small, skilful (almost neutral) member state seems to be the preferred presidency, which keeps the level of conflict low and leads member states to acceptable outcomes.[24]

7 Summary of the findings and update of the theoretical explanation

Concluding Part I of the book, this chapter summarises the main findings and updates the theoretical explanation introduced in Chapter 2. The key objective of Part I was to answer the following question: What determines variation in the level of conflict in EU budgetary politics? Chapter 2 put forward the argument that the institutional design of the decision-making procedure is a decisive variable in influencing the level of conflict. The empirical chapters revealed the high explanatory value of this argument and the detailed propositions that followed from it.

In this chapter, I go beyond the original propositions. Building on the issues raised in the concluding sections of the empirical chapters, I want to develop the theoretical explanation further. The original rational choice-propositions built on three assumptions: (1) a logic of expected consequences and bounded rationality; (2) material self-interest; and (3) explicit and codified institutions. The empirical chapters revealed that the first two assumptions worked fairly well as proxies for actors' preferences and orientations. Budgetary actors pursued their objectives rationally and were largely motivated by distributive interests. However, the third assumption failed to reflect the full scope of the resources available to, and constraints faced by different actors. Institutions impacted on actors' strategies not only as codified and explicit rules, but also as norms and trust. Actors justified their actions with normative arguments that, over time, exerted independent influence on actors' behaviour. Close contacts between actors and a reliable reputational mechanism led to trust among actors, which facilitated cooperative outcomes. Both aspects of non-codified institutions do not stand in contrast to the rational choice explanation, but add an important element that is not captured with a restriction to explicit institutions.

For the purpose of summary and update, I break up the institutionalist argument of Chapter 2 into two parts. First, the *inception argument* states that institutional settings influence the level of conflict by creating a large potential of conflict. The exclusion of relevant actors and their interests in the process of enacting the institutional setting plays a decisive role in determining whether an institutional setting induces potential conflict. Second, the *management argument* asserts that institutional settings affect the level of conflict by providing means to overcome conflict or by setting incentives that intensify existing rivalry between actors (Figure 7.1 illustrates the main elements of these two arguments).

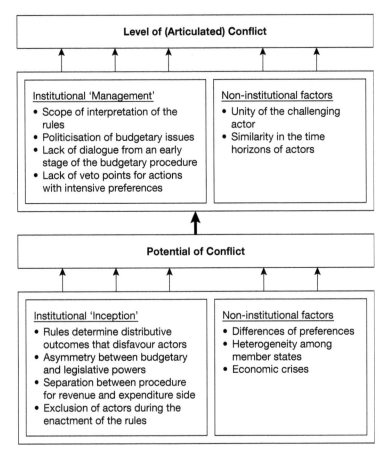

Figure 7.1 Institutionalist explanation of the level of conflict.

The inception argument

Institutional settings that induce conflict

Chapters 3 and 5 demonstrated that the institutional setting of the 1970 treaty was responsible for the scope and intensity of what can be called the 'UK problem' and the 'EP problem'.[1] When the United Kingdom entered the Community in 1973, it faced a highly institutionalised distributive order. It left the British government not much choice other than to demand changes in the distributive outcomes and to challenge the institutional setting. Similarly, the EP became the second arm of the budgetary authority in a decision-making procedure, which failed to take into account the Parliament's demands for a more far-reaching transfer of decision-making powers. The procedure also introduced an asymmetry between legislative and budgetary procedures that was bound to produce clashes between the two realms. The attempt to reconcile the two procedures through the distinction between compulsory and non-compulsory expenditure did not help.[2] Hence, the institutional setting created a potential for conflict between the Council and the EP that overshadowed the annual budgetary procedure from the start.

The exclusion of the United Kingdom and Parliament in the original treaty negotiations were key factors in the genesis of conflict (Lindner and Rittberger 2003). In the case of the UK, member states adopted the institutional setting, if not deliberately, at least knowingly against British interests. The inclusion of Britain in the treaty negotiations would have prevented the enactment of such an institutional setting. In the case of the EP problem, Parliament tried to influence treaty negotiations but failed to have a significant impact on the institutional outcome.[3] Like the British case, the EP's inclusion in the treaty negotiations would have allowed the EP to coordinate its interest with those of the member states at an earlier stage.

The exclusion from the enacting coalition conditioned actors' willingness to accept the outcome of the treaty negotiations. Actors that have adopted an institutional setting as part of the enacting coalition are likely to feel bound by the agreement. They accept the institutional setting because they realise that it resulted from negotiations in which a more favourable outcome was impossible. They may feel that their interests have been recognised and included in a mutual compromise. Moreover, a reputational mechanism and an extended time-horizon set incentives for compliance: non-compliance damages a reputation as a reliable partner in future treaty negotiations.

The comparison with the financial perspective illustrates the difference made by inclusion in the enacting coalition. Germany was part of the European Council that adopted the 1992 and the 1999 financial perspectives. Although it did not achieve institutional outcomes that elevated the German problem, it gained relevant concessions and benefits: on budgetary issues, the grant of regional support for East Germany in 1992 and a consensus on austerity in 1999; and, more importantly, on non-budgetary issues, an increase in the number of German MEPs in 1992 and a success of the German presidency in 1999. The role as one of the key member states that enacted the financial perspective committed Germany to compliance. Germany felt bound by the distributive and institutional framework. Non-compliance would have not only endangered the existence of the financial perspective, but also damaged Germany's stance in the following negotiation round. Similarly, the EP became part of the institutional triangle that enacted and subsequently renewed the interinstitutional agreement. It gained significant institutional concessions from the Council and achieved an institutional setting that was much more in line with the EP's interest than the treaty and that the EP regarded as an adequate reflection of the EP's bargaining power. Once adopted, the EP felt bound by the agreement.

In addition to the impact of exclusion, the 1970 institutional setting induced conflict by separating the expenditure from the revenue side and by splitting the expenditure side in autonomous subfields. Spending decisions committed increasingly more money while the revenue of the Community declined. The resulting distributive pressure intensified existing tensions between the EP and the

Council and among member states. Yet, budgetary actors were limited in their ability to contain expenditure that resulted from the legislative commitments and the prices set by the Agricultural Council.

Finally, institutional change brought about by the Single European Act and Maastricht Treaty gradually closed the asymmetry between legislative and budgetary procedure, and thus eliminated an additional source of interinstitutional conflict. The Parliament's participation in the legislative procedure ended the exclusive role that the budgetary procedure had played for MEPs.

The management argument

Institutional settings that fail to provide means to overcome conflict

Institutional settings affect the actors' ability to deal with potential conflict. Limited scope of interpretation, fora for dialogue and for renegotiations of distributive fundamentals and a normative consensus on the dominant concept of governance keep the level of conflict low.

Large scope of interpretation gives actors a high degree of autonomy when applying rules. In presenting an alternative interpretation, actors can achieve more favourable distributive outcomes and alter the institutional setting. Consequently, the regulating force of rules deteriorates. Distributive conflict spills over onto the institutional level and becomes conflict over rules. Moreover, the scope of interpretation allows both sides to claim that they are in compliance with the rules. The more the preferences of actors and their normative backgrounds differ, the more conflict intensifies. In the case of the interinstitutional conflict between the EP and the Council, the large scope of interpretation coincided with the contrasting concepts of governance: the supranational concept put forward by the EP and the intergovernmental one emphasised in Council (see below). The complicated and vague compromise between supranational and intergovernmental elements in the budgetary procedure of the 1970 treaty and the lack of a consensus on the long-term objective of European integration (*finalité*) gave both sides the opportunity to insist on their respective position and led to intensive clashes.

In these clashes, the emphasis of the institutional dimension played an important role in uniting the EP behind the Budgets Committee. The more the Committee stressed the institutional importance of a decision, the more MEPs were willing to follow the Committee's recommendations. Therefore, budgetary strategists in the EP had a strong incentive to fuel institutional conflict in order to strengthen their internal position. The financial perspective made it difficult for the Budgets Committee to continue this strategy. It reduced the scope of interpretation; it also limited the distributive impact of institutional struggles, because it guaranteed spending committees levels of non-compulsory expenditure above the maximum rate of increase.

Although the *politicisation of budgetary issues*, i.e. the involvement of politicians and the media, often leads directly to an escalation of conflict, the institutional setting mediates the link between politicisation and conflict and can, under certain circumstances, contain the negative effects of politicisation. In the case of net-contributions in EU budgetary politics, the motivation for politicians to politicise issues stems largely from the symbolic and political relevance of net-contributions. Politicians decide to use net-contributions as an argument in the domestic political arena when the popularity of the government and public mood towards the European Union are low and the general approach of the government towards the EU is already relatively hostile. The comparative analysis between the UK problem and the German problem illustrated that the institutional setting plays an important role in determining whether the politicisation of the issue on the domestic level leads to high levels of conflict on the European level. In the UK case, the politicisation led to escalation, because the British demands induced a politicisation of the question of British net-contributions on the European level and subsequently, also at the domestic level in the other member states. This pushed both sides towards extreme positions and made compromise impossible. In contrast, in the German case the government could politicise the issue for domestic reasons, but did not trigger escalation on the European level. It was clear that the German government would wait until the financial perspective was due to be renegotiated. Other member states knew that Germany's demands fulfilled mainly domestic purposes. At the same time, Germany was guaranteed that the German problem would be discussed in the renegotiations over the financial perspective. It did not have to establish the German problem on the political agenda, as had been the case for Britain in the 1980s. The packaged deal character of the financial perspective finally allowed the German government to sell the result of renegotiations, even though its demands were not met.

The financial perspective not only limited the *effect* of domestic politicisation, but also reduced the *degree* of politicisation. It separated large budgetary bargains from minor budgetary decisions. At the level of large budgetary bargains, the incrementalism of the financial perspective reduced the degree of politicisation. Due to the unanimity rule, member states developed core distributive territories, which they regarded as untouchable and compromised only on issues outside these territories. For example, Britain was unwilling to compromise on the rebate and Spain would not allow significant cuts in regional expenditure. Member states accepted each other's core interests, which reduced the space for distributive change and minimised conflict. At the level of annual budgetary procedure, decision-making became largely the domain of experts (Nicoll 1995). The financial boundaries set on budgetary decision-making through the headings and ceilings of the financial perspective limits the options available to budgetary actors to question and challenge annually the budget in its entirety. Boundaries and the rule of experts also minimise the extent to which conflict included issues from fields outside budgetary politics.

Close *contact between actors* interrupts the spiral of escalation at an early stage because it prevents the two sides from committing to extreme positions. Instead, actors are in constant negotiations from an early stage of the budgetary procedure. Actors start to approach the procedure as a joint exercise rather than as separate tasks that clash at the end of the procedure. In the case of interinstitutional conflict, the existence of fora for dialogue, such as the trialogue and the conciliation procedure, intensifies contact between the institutions and limits the reliance on political agreements at a late stage of the procedure.

One important aspect of contact is its personal side. It facilitates the evolution of trust and mutual cooperation. This is particularly the case when the social and professional positions of actors are similar. Mutual cooperation was strongest among finance attachés in the Council. Finance attachés used the autonomy that they had gained from the financial perspective and developed a strong ambition to settle as many disputes as possible at the committee level. They relied on each other's willingness to facilitate compromises and to settle differences. This also occurred in the contacts on the administrative level among the three institutions. Officials from the directorate-general budget (of the Commission) and the secretariat generals of the Council and of the EP gradually developed close personal links, which helped to prevent escalations at an early stage. On the political level, these contacts gave Parliament a sense of being treated as an equal partner. The emergence of the second reading in the Council (and the preceding conciliation meeting) as the forum of the final budgetary debate between Parliament and Council established personal negotiations between MEPs and ministers as a means of settling remaining differences.

Overall, budgetary politics under the institutional setting of the financial perspective resembles what Richardson and Jordan (1979: 101–103) describe as 'negotiated order' – a common way of structuring political processes in national and European politics (Richardson 1996, 2000). 'Negotiated orders' are constituted by three characteristics: the compartmentalisation of policy problems; the evolution of a relatively stable community of experts; and incremental policy change.[4] In the words of Richardson and Jordan:

> 'Parties to the dispute have to weigh up risk of damaging long-term relationships if they adapt intransigent positions' (p. 101). 'Uncertainty and risk, as well as conflict and competition, are avoided through the formation of stable relationships' (p. 103). 'A further dimension of negotiated order (. . .) is a tendency to concentrate on small manageable problems. Part of the mode of negotiation is to translate large unbargainable conflicts into smaller negotiatable items. (. . .) [T]he agreement reached in this complexity do not occur by chance: they are "patterned". The outcome becomes, to a certain extent, predictable. The re-constitution of this order can be conceived in terms of a complex relationship between the *daily negotiative process and a periodic appraisal process*' (p. 102, emphasis in original).
>
> (Richardson and Jordan 1979)

This does not mean that the different actors do not pursue their self-interest or act irrationally. It simply states that political actors, such as the member states, the Council or the EP, are represented in the decision-making process more by their budgetary experts than by senior politicians. Although these experts are still oriented towards the distributive and institutional interests of their respective institutions, they have an incentive to settle conflict at the expert level. Close and repeated contacts force them to take into account the reputational costs that an exclusive orientation towards short-term benefit-maximisation would entail.

As much as the institutionalisation of conflict in the 1980s resulted from the lack of dialogue and the scope of interpretation, it was also fuelled by strong *norm-based* arguments with which actors backed up their distributive interests. Parliament and Council regarded their unwillingness to compromise as legitimate. The necessity to justify the confrontational strategy stemmed from the general norm of cooperation among institutions embedded in the treaty. During the first years of the application of the treaty provisions in the 1970s, the EP followed the treaty's norm of cooperation and searched for compromises with the Council. As MEPs realised that their expectations would be disappointed, they moved towards confrontational strategies. Encouraged by the direct elections, they developed a 'democracy argument' (linked to their supranational 'concept of governance'), which justified the shift towards confrontation. Parliament's drive for more power was presented as a measure for democratising the Community. The Council opposed Parliament's position with its own norm-based argument, which was linked to the Council's intergovernmental 'concept of governance'. Council presented itself as the representative of European taxpayers' interests. The coexistence of two rivalling normative arguments made a settlement on compromises very difficult. Moreover, the escalation of conflict entrenched these normative arguments, which consequently surpassed their function as justifying behaviour. In the case of the Parliament, entrenched norms developed an independent effect on MEPs' approach to conflict. MEPs were trapped in their 'democracy argument' and lost the flexibility to move towards the Council's positions.

Cooperation in the 1990s did not develop norm-based arguments. Cooperation did not stand in contrast to the norm of cooperation embodied by the treaty and the interinstitutional agreement. Hence, cooperative strategies that followed from the favourable incentive structure of the new institutional setting did not need to be justified. The low levels of conflict kept negotiations within the boundaries of interest-based discussions.

The role of norm-based arguments in EU budgetary politics is much in line with Schimmelfennig's theory of 'rhetorical action' (Schimmelfennig 2001). Schimmelfennig describes norms and standards of legitimacy as constraints and resources that affect actors' bargaining power and influence policy outcomes:

> Actors who can justify their interests on the grounds of the community's standard of legitimacy are therefore able to shame their opponents into norm-conforming behaviour and to modify the collective outcome that would have resulted from constellations of interest and power alone.
>
> (2001: 48)

Actors use norm-based arguments strategically in pursuit of their self-interest. Through the membership in a community with a dominant standard of legitimacy, actors are 'rhetorically entrapped' (ibid.), and considerably limited in their ability to pursue their self-interest. British demands for a rebate illustrate the impact of standards of legitimacy. For a long period, member states managed to ostracise Britain's demands as *just retour* and 'anti-communitarian'. In interinstitutional conflict, actors did not rely on one dominant standard of legitimacy, but tried to establish their variant as the dominant one. Strong rhetorical commitment to these norm-based arguments trapped actors into maintaining them, even if distributive interests might have made actors willing to compromise. Although Schimmelfennig borrows the emphasis on norms from sociological institutionalism, his theory is based fully on the assumptions of self-interest and the logic of expected consequences. Actors follow norms not because of a logic of appropriateness, but as the result of a shaming mechanism or as they enhance their bargaining power.

At the end of this chapter, we can conclude that the rational choice explanation presented in Chapter 2 is able to account for much of the empirical developments behind the variation in the level of conflict between 1974 and 2000. An update of the explanation is only necessary with regard to informal institutions. The strategic use of norm-based arguments and the evolution of trust influenced the actors' ability to effectively deal with conflict.

Part II[1]

Institutional change in EU budgetary politics

8   A rational choice-institutionalist explanation of institutional change in EU budgetary politics

In the previous part, I focused on conflict in EU budgetary politics and argued that the reform of the institutional structure of the decision-making procedure in 1988 was the main reason for a significant reduction in the level of conflict. The institutional setting provided the explanatory (independent) variable that accounted for variation in the level of conflict (dependent variable). In this part, I take a different perspective and try to explain the institutional change of 1988. The institutional setting itself will, therefore, become the dependent variable. On the basis of theories of institutional change and path dependence, I will identify a set of explanatory (independent) variables that account for the variation in the stability of institutional settings (dependent variable). I seek to provide an explanation for the mechanisms that ensure institutional stability and the processes that lead to far-reaching changes. For the empirical assessment of my explanation, EU budgetary politics provides two cases of institutional settings that experienced a long period of stability. After years of stability, each case developed differently, the 1970 institutional setting was radically changed by the 1988 reform, while the 1988 institutional setting has remained stable. I will be able to compare the two periods of stability and to detect the differences that eventually split the two cases of stability, resulting in change in the 1970 case and continuous stability in the 1988 case.

This chapter is divided into three sections. First, I will define institutional change and distinguish between different forms of change. Second, I will combine these forms of change with the theory of path dependence that sheds light on the timing of change. Finally, the last section of this chapter applies the theoretical arguments to EU budgetary politics and derives rational choice propositions for the subsequent empirical chapters.

Forms of institutional change

What is change and how does it occur?

Over the last several years, institutional change has risen to the top of the institutionalist research agenda. This is not surprising. Given the importance that institutionalists ascribe to institutions, the question of why and how institutions change follows logically from an institutionalist focus. In this first section, I briefly introduce a definition of change and present the different sources and forms of institutional change.

Institutions[2] face pressure for *change*. I define change as: *the introduction of new rules or interpretations that supplement or replace existing rules and interpretations.* Pressure from change can come from three sources:

- the necessity to interpret and to complete imprecise rules of an institutional setting (*concretisation*);
- the necessity to alter the institutional setting to unforeseen events or to new insights (*adaptation*); and
- individual actors' self-interest in changing the existing rules in order to secure the most beneficial distributive outcomes (*alteration*).

The first two sources of change follow a 'functionalist logic' where actors are mainly efficiency driven. For example, actors realise that a rule is difficult to apply, as it is not appropriately specified; they decide to 'repair' that deficiency and further specify the rule. The last source of change is based on a 'power-seeking logic'. The three sources are not mutually exclusive. Concretisation, for example, often comes as an opportunity for actors to press for alteration (Stacey 2001). Frequently, specific institutional settings are linked with certain sources of change.

Change can take different forms depending on the actors involved and their actions. I distinguish between two sets of actions: those changes that leave the existing set of formal rules unchanged (*informal changes*), and those that alter them (*formal changes*). This distinction is based on two assumptions. First, actors interact within a set of highly formalised and binding rules (like those of a constitution). They can either change these rules (which is very costly) or supplement them with new rules or rule interpretations of less binding nature, although these rules may still be legally codified and explicitly stated. Second, the group of actors that introduced highly formalised and binding rules in the enacting phase is often not identical to the group that implements the rules in the execution phase (see Lindner and Rittberger 2003: 447–455).

There are three forms of *informal changes*:

- *unilateral interpretation:* an actor (or a group of actors) reinterprets rules and thus, specifies the rules without consulting the other actors involved;
- *joint interpretation:* actors come to an implicit or explicit agreement on how a rule should be applied; it is less binding, in that it only supplements, but does not replace the extant, highly formalised institutional structure; and
- *third party interpretation:* a third party interprets and specifies the existing rules.

And there is *formal change*:

- *explicit rule change*: actors that enacted the original set of rules decide to change or amend them.

The remaining part of this section explores the factors that influence the emergence of these different forms of change.

Unilateral interpretation seems most likely to occur when the degree of rule imprecision is high and the scope for applying rules to one's favour, without being sanctioned, is considerable. Actors that are excluded from other options, or that see these other options as too costly will undertake unilateral interpretation. As unilateral interpretation is limited by the binding nature of existing rules and by the possibility of negative sanctions from other actors, its impact on the institutional setting is not far-reaching, and the rationale behind its use is based primarily on a strategy of small-steps.[3]

Joint interpretation is likely to occur when dispute over rule interpretation seems resolvable and actors want to prevent the occurrence of rivalling unilateral interpretations that undermine the effectiveness of existing rules. Joint agreements on interpretation are often preferred to formal rule changes because the less binding nature of joint interpretation inflicts lower sovereignty costs, and allows actors to change the agreements more easily (Abbott and Snidal 2000). Moreover, actors of the executing phase who are not involved in the enactment of formal rules have an incentive to establish a joint interpretation rather than allowing gaps to be filled without them.[4]

Third party interpretation is likely to occur when the formal rules entail a high degree of delegation, and when actors assume that they can gain a favourable interpretation from the third party (Stone Sweet *et al.* 2001). Unilateral interpretation often precedes a third party interpretation. If the involvement of the third party is not automatic, actors must decide, in reaction to unilateral interpretation, whether they want to include a dispute resolution mechanism. Their decision will depend on their expectations regarding the decision of the third party. Thus, the reputation of the third party and the degree of uncertainty over the outcome are decisive for actors' considerations over the inclusion of a third party. Moreover, the third party's ruling carries a strong binding force in most formal rule settings. Once a ruling is made, actors therefore lose the opportunity to pursue other options (except for formal change). Given the uncertainty over the outcome of third party dispute resolution, the binding nature of the ruling, and the direct costs of involving the third party (e.g. costs of lawyers and length of the court suit), third-part interpretation is often more costly than joint interpretation (see Figure 8.1).

Formal change[5] is the most costly of the four options (see Figure 8.1) and only occurs when actors seek to enshrine a rule specification or modification in the existing set of highly formalised rules. Contracting costs and uncertainty over outcomes are high. A formal change entails the risk that the whole package of formal rules is renegotiated, including previously accepted rules. On the other hand, actors that have the exclusive right of formal change will guard their power against the substitution of formal rules by a set of less formal rules resulting from joint interpretations, and thus opt for formal changes.

The four forms of change are not mutually exclusive. They often occur in combination and sequence with each other. Unilateral interpretation may, for example, precede joint interpretation and third party involvement; or third party

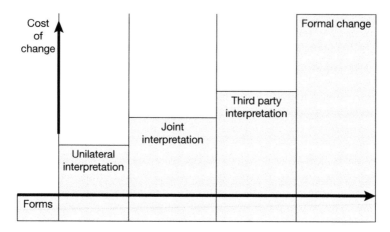

Figure 8.1 Cost of the forms of change.

involvement may be used as a threat, in order to facilitate joint interpretation. Yet, this typology of change does not assume that there is a quasi-automatic transformation process by which, over time, joint interpretations transform from an implicit informal understanding via a semi-formal agreement into new formal rules. The advantages of informal agreements can be stable over time.

The timing of stability and change

When does change occur?

In this section, I seek to shed light on the temporal dimension of institutional change. Drawing on the theory of path dependence (North 1990; Thelen 1999; Pierson 2000a, 2004), I will show that actors are significantly constrained in their ability to initiate institutional change and that political institutions tend to remain stable over time. I contend that it is necessary to comprehend the foundations of institutional stability in order to understand institutional change. In the first part of the section, I introduce the theory of path dependence and discuss the causes of institutional inertia in politics. I subsequently seek to explain the timing of change.

Explaining stability

Margaret Levi's definition informs my understanding of path dependence (1997: 28, quoted in Pierson 2000a):

> Path dependence has to mean, if it is to mean anything, that once a country or region has started down a track, the costs of reversal are high, there will be other choice points, but the entrenchments of certain institutional arrangements

obstruct an easy reversal of the initial choice. Perhaps the better metaphor is a tree, rather than a path. From the same trunk, there are many different branches and smaller branches. Although it is possible to turn around or to clamber from one to the other – and essential if the branch dies – the branch on which a climber begins is the one she tends to follow.

For the institutionalist analysis, this definition of path dependence means that institutional settings tend to be stable and develop incrementally in the form of small on-path changes. However, 'if the branch dies' the institutional setting changes radically and experiences a large off-path change.

Paul Pierson (2000a) relates this view on path dependence closely to the concept of increasing returns, which Paul David and Brian W. Arthur developed from their research on technologies in a market setting (David 1985; Arthur 1994). Increasing returns stabilise an existing path by decreasing the attractiveness of switching to an alternative. Applying this concept to the political analysis, he contends that increasing returns are a ubiquitous feature of politics because of four key characteristics, namely *the collective nature of politics*, *the institutional density of politics*, *political authority and power asymmetries*, and *the complexity and opacity of politics*, which promote the emergence of increasing returns. The following paragraphs examine these four characteristics more closely and summarise Pierson's argument. Yet, as Pierson runs the risk of overemphasising the relevance of increasing returns for institutional inertia, the paragraphs add, where necessary, further explanations of institutional stability in politics.

The collective nature of politics Political initiatives are mostly collective actions and, as such, face the problem of free riding (Olson 1971). As institutional change is a public good, actors have an incentive not to involve themselves in its provision. Costs of initiating and organising change are high. If at all, actors seek to support the initiative that is most likely to generate a promised change, orienting their behaviour according to expectations about the behaviour of others. Therefore, a new initiative has to be able to mobilise a critical mass to be potentially successful ('network externalities'). Institutional stability is likely to result in this case.

The institutional density of politics Political interaction takes place in institutionalised settings that put extensive, legally binding constraints on behaviour. In contrast to the market setting, exit is often prohibitively costly. North (1990: 95) points out that institutions develop into an 'interdependent web of an institutional matrix', in which different institutions are entangled and intertwined (on interdependence, see also Aggarwal 1998). Independent change of one institution becomes almost impossible, as it would demand simultaneous change of the other elements of the institutional matrix. Even in the situation where the institutional setting does not necessarily generate increasing returns, switching costs are very high.

True *et al.* (1999), however, extend North's notion of the 'interdependent web of an institutional matrix'. They argue that politics is divided into different policy subfields, each with its own policy community of specialists and experts. A dominant coalition of actors is likely to control the process of political and institutional change within each of these communities ('policy monopoly'). Institutional inertia becomes deeply entrenched, as each of these dominant actors coalitions will block changes in order to maintain a dominant position (see the following point on power). In contrast to Pierson's positive feedback processes that reinforce the path through increasing returns, True *et al.* emphasise that negative feedback processes stabilise the local 'policy monopolies'. Any attempt to initiate institutional or political change is prevented by the dominant actor coalition and hindered by the interdependent character of the institutional matrix.

Political authority and power asymmetries Institutional settings have distributive implications and determine the decision-making power of the actors involved. Small power asymmetries that were manifest at the creation of an institutional setting can subsequently widen as they are built into the institutional setting. This generates a positive feedback mechanism, as it strengthens the actors that have the highest interest in preventing change (Genschel 1997).

Knight (1992, 1995) shares the notion of power, but portrays it, in contrast to the path dependence literature, as *the* key for explaining institutional stability and change. For Knight, actors are constantly interacting in a coordination game over rules. The actors that possess the most bargaining power (i.e. the power to initiate or prevent change) dictate the interpretation and adaptation of rules. As mentioned in Part I, actors with a long time-horizon and strong preference for institutional change are likely to challenge the existing rules. The success of these challenges is determined by actors' bargaining power, which in turn is influenced by the rules that govern the process of interpretation and adaptation of rules (i.e. the meta-rules), and the ability of actors to issue credible threats. Overall, Knight portrays inertia as the product of the dominance of a group of actors that have the interest in keeping the institutional setting stable and the power to do so.

The complexity and opacity of politics In contrast to economic interaction on markets, goals and objectives in politics are very complex. This makes it difficult to link actions and outcomes, to measure results, and to assess institutional settings. On markets, an important correction mechanism reassures efficiency: competition. Competition forces less efficient organisations out of the market. Prices and profits offer clear indicators for the efficacy of a production mechanism. Competition generates innovations and companies learn from the success of others by copying their methods and strategies. A political environment is typically more permissive. Pressure from other competing institutions is less pronounced and improvement through trial-and-error is far from automatic. Large political institutions are often very inflexible and change-resistant.[6]

In demonstrating the potential inefficiency of a stable path, the path dependence literature seeks to rebuff functionalist explanations of institutional stability (Pierson 2000b, 2004). It denounces the tendencies of functionalists to justify *post hoc* the stable solution as beneficial for actors. Functionalists often assume that stable institutions fulfil certain functions because otherwise they would not be stable.

Although the path dependence literature crushes such arguments convincingly and with force, it runs the risk of ignoring negative feedback processes stemming from the (under-)performance of an institutional setting. Decreasing returns of institutions and mounting running costs undermine the stability of a setting. As I will discuss in the next section, they can create significant pressure for change, because actors may need resources elsewhere, or because politicians, facing reelection, find it difficult to justify the persistence of an institutional setting that produces inferior results. Overall, a focus on the performance does not stand in contradiction to path dependence. While the path dependence literature correctly cautions against automatically equating stability with efficiency, we cannot fully exclude the positive impact that the smooth functioning of an institutional setting has on its stability.

Explaining change

The literature on path dependence presents compelling explanations of stability. Yet, its accounts of change often seem less convincing. Analysts of path dependence have the tendency to fall into one of the following three traps:

1 *Ignorance.* They ignore institutional change altogether and see the institutional setting as completely stable. In doing so, they fail to realise that in order for the path metaphor to make sense, a certain element of movement along the path is necessary. Path dependence shows that the scope of actors' choices narrows, rather than reaching a point of inertia.
2 *Tautology.* Douglas C. North (1981, 1990), one of the great pioneers of path dependence, emphasised the need to account for change at a very early stage in the development of this field. According to North (almost) all change is incremental and evolves from the existing institutional setting. As much as he is correct in pointing out the historical heritage of institutions, North nevertheless runs the risk of turning the path metaphor into a tautology (Deeg 2001). If all movements and choices of actors are part of the same path, what exactly does path dependence teach us? The definition becomes too all-encompassing to retain its analytical force. Moreover, the analyst faces the problem of infinitive regress. Where should the analysis begin, if all institutions are historically conditioned? For Pierson's concept of increasing returns to make sense, the beginning of the path, where small and contingent events have a significant impact in determining the subsequent course of the path, must be located.
3 *Exogenousation.* In order to square the circle of accounting for change, analysts assume that exogenous shocks induce sudden breakdowns of the paths, as actors jump to a new path. Such explanations remain unsatisfactory, however, as they rarely indicate when paths are vulnerable to exogenous shocks. Moreover, empirical analyses show that radical destruction seldom occurs and that the experience of the current path impacts on the likelihood that a new path is created.

Thelen (1999) presents a convincing attempt to sideline these traps and to advance the path dependence literature into a unitary framework that explains how and in which form change occurs. She argues that:

> Institutions rest on a set of ideational and material foundations that, if shaken, open possibilities for change. But different institutions rest on different foundations, and so the processes that are likely to disrupt them will also be different, though predictable.

> (Thelen 1999: 397)

Ideational and material foundations constitute the *mechanism of reproduction* that stabilises an institutional setting. Thelen concludes that 'the key to understanding institutional evolution and change lies in specifying more precisely the reproduction and feedback mechanisms on which particular institutions rest' (1999: 400). Although she does not offer exact predictions of when changes occur, her approach offers a useful definition of the two forms of change mentioned above, i.e. on-path and off-path changes.

- *On-path changes* can be described as adaptations of the existing path that are in line with the current mechanism of reproduction.
- *Off-path changes*, on the other hand, replace the existing mechanism of reproduction and introduce a new one.

Thelen suggests that a path is vulnerable to jumps when it experiences 'collusions' or 'intersections' with political processes that undermine its mechanism of reproduction (1999: 396). On-path and off-path changes vary in the degree to which the reproduction mechanism is able to resist or accommodate the pressure for change. Different reproduction mechanisms have vulnerabilities to different 'collusions' or 'intersections'. Understanding which reproduction mechanism stabilises the existing institutional design (*logic of stability*) allows the researcher to identify the factors that weaken the mechanism and lead to change (*logic of change*).

Overall, Thelen's analysis provides the following helpful instructions for the research on institutional change: first, one needs to identify the reproduction mechanism that stabilises the institutional setting; second, one can deduce specific vulnerabilities in the institutional setting from the reproduction mechanism; and third, one has to analyse when and how the incidences ('collusions' or 'intersections') occur that hit the vulnerable points of institutional setting. Hence, change becomes predictable because it is linked with the occurrence of specific incidences.

Unfortunately, Thelen fails to give details on the nature of different reproduction mechanisms. It is, therefore, necessary to develop Thelen's approach further. From Pierson's analysis of path dependence in politics, I would identify three reproduction mechanisms: *the power of the dominant actor coalition*; *the interdependence within an institutional matrix*; and *large switching costs*. A possible fourth reproduction mechanism could be the capacity of an institutional setting to accommodate pressure for change in *small on-path changes.* The following paragraphs portray these four reproduction mechanisms focusing, in particular, on their in-built vulnerabilities.

1   *Reproduction mechanism: power of the dominant actor coalition.* Institutional changes coincide with an increase in the relative bargaining power of the coalition of actors interested in institutional change (see the above-mentioned work of Jack Knight, 1992, 1995). The source of increase in bargaining power can be endogenous and exogenous. Actors can build up bargaining power by gaining a strong reputation and by learning to interact skilfully within the existing rules (*endogenous factors*). Alternatively, actors may gain bargaining power through external changes, such as an alteration in the membership that leads to an increase of the size of the change coalition or the occurrence of linkages with other fields of interaction where the bargaining power of this field can be transferred to the negotiation over institutional change (*exogenous factors*). Many of the exogenous factors lead to a sudden empowerment of the change coalition, while endogenous factors tend to function in a more gradual manner, as bargaining power has to be built up and communicated to the dominant actors' coalition. Most important, the ways in which changes in bargaining power translate into institutional change depends on the sources of dominant actors' bargaining power.

2   *Reproduction mechanism: the interdependence within an institutional matrix.* When stability is based on the interdependence of policy subfields, it is overcome only if a higher-level authority takes up the issues at stake in the policy subfield (necessary condition), and combines it with the issues in the other subfields (sufficient condition) (see True *et al.*'s 1999 argument on 'punctuated equilibrium').[7] Its hierarchically superior position allows the higher-level authority to overrule entrenched interests in the subfields, to de-block the countervailing forces that result from the linkage between the different subfields, and, finally, to initiate institutional change. Although this explains a breakdown in an institutional setting that is stable due to its interdependent character, it leaves unanswered questions regarding the involvement of a higher-level authority and the establishment of the link between subfields. With True *et al.* (1999), three main factors can be identified. First, if a change coalition is able to block the political process in one field then it can press the higher-level authority to take up the issue. The linkage with other fields might be created through self-organised alliances among different change coalitions. This leads to the second point. The higher-level authority has a political responsibility over the subfields. It is judged against its ability to manage the subfields well. If the costs of continuing a certain inferior institutional design significantly increase and institutional reform become a salient political issue, then the high-level authority gains an interest in searching for a solution; in this case a third factor comes into play. An entrepreneur may lobby the higher level for change and, most importantly, present institutional proposals that link the interdependent issues.

3   *Reproduction mechanism: large switching costs.* Stability that builds on large switching costs erodes when (a) uncertainty over the distributive impact of institutional

choices and the outcomes of negotiations is low, (b) the compatibility between the existing institutional setting and a new reformed design is high, and (c) the opportunity costs increase significantly. If an alternative institutional setting is compatible with the existing design then switching costs are low, because interaction with 'users' of other settings is not endangered (network effects), and the existing knowledge can be transferred. Similarly, if the distributive implications of an alternative institutional setting can be clearly assessed, then even risk decreases actors' willingness to consider a switch. This is mostly the case when an institutional reform is linked to a specified distributive framework. Opportunity costs entail the benefits that actors forgo when continuing to follow the existing path. They can rise with a decline in the distributive benefits of an existing institutional setting. Such decreasing returns (Deeg 2001) might have exogenous reasons, e.g. an increase in group membership and worsening of an economic environment, or endogenous ones, e.g. the existing setting is worn out. Opportunity costs often rise due to shifts of political priorities: the political capital and resources spent on continuing an inferior system is needed in other areas, so that actors are willing to invest in reform in order to focus on a different issue. However, the overall amount of switching costs (relative to opportunity costs) is misleading because individual actors will follow personal, rather than collective costs-benefit analyses. Combined with the power approach, this means that institutional change is likely only when the coalition that is able to initiate change (necessary condition) perceives its individual switching-costs as lower than the opportunity costs (sufficient condition).[8]

4   *Reproduction mechanism: Small on-path changes.* Institutional stability that builds on the accommodation of pressure for change through small on-path changes is likely to deteriorate when the preferences of the change coalition are very strong, and when the scope and nature of the demanded change prohibits its realisation through successful on-path change. So far, I have argued that mechanisms of reproduction have their specific points of vulnerability. When events occur that touch these points, the reproduction mechanism loses force. Yet, when pressure on the points of vulnerability mounts, the reproduction mechanism loses force and finally breaks down. Off-path change takes place: the departure from the old path results in the establishment of a new path with a new reproduction mechanism.

However, three elements of off-path change slightly complicate the distinction between off- and on-path changes. First, the *new reproduction mechanism* does not have to be very different from the previous one. It can be based on the *same principle*. For example, a power-based reproduction mechanism of a certain dominant coalition is replaced by one supporting a different coalition. Second, an institutional setting can have *more than one reproduction mechanism*. For example, the switching costs mechanism is often also backed by the interests of the dominant actor coalition. Third, the combination of two or more reproduction mechanisms can mean that (a) *off-path changes* occur in a *step-wise, almost incremental, process* where reproduction mechanisms do not break down simultaneously, and (b) *hybrid forms* of institutional settings evolve where new

Table 8.1 Factors that influence the emergence of off-path change

Independent variables	Dependent variables *Off-path change comes about when:*
The *bargaining power* of the dominant actor coalition (BPda) relative to that of the change coalition (BPcc)	BPda<BPcc
Interdependence of subfields in the relevant policy area	Independence is overcome
Opportunity costs (Ocda) relative to the *switching costs* (SWda) of the dominant actor coalition	OCda > SWda
Availability of venues of *small institutional adaptations*	Small changes fail to ease pressure for change

reproduction mechanisms coexist with a heritage of previous institutions (Deeg 2001). Although these features may make a new reproduction mechanism look like the adaptation of an old one, the notion of path dependence only makes sense when a distinction is drawn between on-path and off-path changes.

The main argument concerning these two forms of change is one of strength (see Table 8.1). It builds on the dynamic described in the fourth reproduction mechanism. When the reproduction mechanism is under pressure it will try to ease the pressure through modifications of the existing institutional setting in an incremental manner. Genschel (1997) describes this very convincingly in his account of 'patching-up' and 'transposition' in the health-care and the telecommunications sectors in Germany. The main elements of the institutional setting remain unaltered but some elements or functions are altered in order to accommodate the growing pressure for change. Yet, when the pressure against the mechanism of reproduction exceeds a level that can be accommodated within the existing institutional setting, an off-path change occurs. [9]

Propositions on institutional change and stability in EU budgetary politics

Following this theoretical discussion of institutional stability and change, I develop propositions about the likelihood of off-path change in EU budgetary politics in the section that follows. These propositions will be empirically tested in subsequent chapters. I regard the 1970 and 1988 institutional settings as two distinct institutional paths, with individual reproduction mechanisms. Both paths have experienced long periods of stability, which ended for the 1970 institutional setting with the far-reaching reform of 1988.

As I have argued above, key to understanding the timing of stability and change is an analysis of the reproduction mechanisms that stabilise an institutional setting. The characteristics of budgetary politics provide an indication of which reproduction mechanisms are most likely to be at work.

First, budgetary politics is mainly about distribution. Actors in budgetary politics seem to be motivated by distributive interests and choose institutional settings in order to secure individual benefits. Therefore, I expect that the most prevalent reproduction mechanism stabilising institutional settings in budgetary politics is the bargaining power of the dominant actor coalition. Change occurs when the dominant actor coalition loses bargaining power to a change coalition.

In the case of the 1970 institutional setting, the dominant actor coalition is most likely the group of six founding member states that enacted the treaty, while the change coalition entails new member states and the EP. Stability is ensured as long as the change coalition lacks the bargaining power to substantiate its demands for change. It deteriorates as the change coalition gains veto- and blocking power. In the case of 1988 institutional setting, bargaining power is spread more equally among actors. Every member state and each institution has the veto-power to prevent the renewal of the financial perspective, but needs the consent of the other actors to initiate change.

Second, similar to what Hemerijck and van Kerbergen (1999) argue for welfare policies, budgetary politics is likely to be dominated by different subfields and clusters. EU budgetary politics seems particularly prone to such divisions, as the EU Budget Council has little authority over spending Councils and shares budgetary powers with the EP (in contrast to national budgetary politics, in which the finance minister often dominates the spending departments and can rely on a stable majority in Parliament). Major subfields in EU budgetary politics seem to be: (1) the revenue side that is institutionally detached from the expenditure side, (2) the interaction between Council and EP over (mainly non-compulsory) expenditure, and (3) the CAP, which follows a decision-making system outside the budgetary process. Therefore, I assume that the stability of the system is, to a significant extent, based on the interdependence of the different subfields. Attempts to create changes within the individual subfields fail or have only modest effects. Effective change will only occur when the higher-level authority, the European Council, takes up the demand for institutional change (necessary condition) and treats institutional reform of the subfields as a connected issue (sufficient condition).

The questions of why the European Council takes up demands for institutional change and how the issue linkage is to be created have to be answered empirically. I mentioned three possibilities above: an increase in bargaining power of a change coalition that coordinates itself with the demands for change in other subfields; rising opportunity costs that increase the political pressure on the European Council to become involved; and the activities of the European Commission, which aims to initiate a change discussion on the European Council level, and presents a proposal that establishes the linkage between the different subfields. In the case of the 1988 setting, interdependence between the subfields and the involvement of the European Council have been institutionalised. Renegotiation points provide fora for simultaneous change of the different subfields, making small changes likely.

Third, other reproduction mechanisms may also play a role, but their relevance cannot be predicted from the characteristics of EU budgetary politics. I assume that the dominant actor coalition feels a pressure to change when the opportunity costs of continuing with the current design exceed the switching costs. While the switching costs are influenced by the form and feature of the proposed new design, opportunity costs rise when actors perceive the current situation as a crisis. This is often the case when high levels of conflict dominate the political process and policies persistently fail to achieve their objectives. National governments start to experience domestic pressure from the public and the media, which expects politicians to initiate reform. Opportunity costs also increase when actors want to use the political capital that is absorbed in continuing the current institutional setting in other policy fields. Reform becomes likely when, for example, budgetary politics loses its status as a key policy field, and politicians want to divert political attention to another field of European integration.

Reform pressure is low when the existing institutional setting is not rivalled by an attractive institutional alternative. In this respect, functionalist explanations may have a certain relevance. The above-mentioned reproduction mechanisms indicated that changes seem likely in the 1988 institutional setting, as bargaining power was more equally spread and interdependence was institutionalised. If we, nevertheless, encounter stability in the 1988 institutional setting, this may be explained by the lack of better alternatives and the high degree of satisfaction of the participating actors. This links the fourth reproduction mechanism: the accommodation of demands for change through small changes.

Fourth, pressure for change may build up gradually (e.g. from bargaining power of the change coalition or rising opportunity costs). Stability is ensured when this pressure is eased through small alterations of the institutional setting. However, when demands for change are far-reaching, and cannot be accommodated through small changes, the pressure for change increases further, and leads to off-path change. Hence, the 1970 institutional setting may have been stabilised by small changes for a short period, but it is likely that in the time preceding the 1988 reform, small changes either did not occur or failed to accommodate the pressure. From the institutional design of the 1988 setting, we can infer that accommodation of pressure through small changes seems to have been a relevant reproduction mechanism. The veto-power for member states and EU institutions and designated renegotiation points, at which updates of the financial perspective and interinstitutional agreement were institutionalised, are likely to have made small changes a prominent feature of the 1988 institutional setting.

Given the costs attached to the different forms of change, the fact that the 1988 institutional setting was not codified as formal treaty provisions will have contributed to lowering the switching costs. It will also have made it easier for the EP, who is not involved in treaty changes, to act as an engine for change.

The following propositions summarise the main results of the chapter (Box 8.1). They focus on the emergence of off-path change and are based on three assumptions. First, as long as no off-path change takes place, an institutional setting is regarded as stable. Second, an institutional setting can be built on a combination of reproduction mechanisms. Third, there may be similarities between the types of reproduction mechanisms that stabilised the 1970 and the 1988 institutional settings.

Box 8.1 Propositions on institutional stability and change

1   Institutional stability is based on or a combination of the following reproduction mechanisms: *relative bargaining power of the dominant actor coalition*; *interdependence of policy subfields*; *high switching costs*; and *small institutional adaptations (on-path change)*.

2   Major institutional change (*off-path change*) occurs when the reproductions mechanisms that stabilise an institution break down.

3   The form, which off-path change takes, is influenced by the willingness of actors to bear high *costs of change* informal change is less costly than formal change and by the *distribution of the power to enact formal change*.

4   Certain reproduction mechanisms are more likely to *collapse through informal off-path changes* than others: (a) informal institutions reduce the power differences between actors that do not have the power to enact formal change and those that have; (b) the introduction of informal institutions incurs lower switching costs than the enactment of formal change.

Overall, I expect off-path change takes place in EU budgetary politics: (1) when a significant increase in the *bargaining power* of the change coalition takes place; (2) when the *European Council* takes up the question of reform and connects the *different subfields* of the budget; (3) when the *opportunity costs* of continuing the existing institutional setting exceed the switching cost for the dominant actor coalition; and (4) when *smaller reform attempts* fail to ease reform pressure.

9 Resisting reform

The stability of the institutional path of the 1970 treaty and its final breakdown (1974–1988)

Why did it take so long until a successful reform changed the institutional setting of budgetary politics and reduced the level of conflict? In this chapter, I will analyse the stability of the institutional path initiated by the 1970 treaty, and identify the factors that triggered institutional change 15 years later.[1] In line with the propositions introduced in Chapter 8, I contend that a combination of reproduction mechanisms cemented the original institutional setting. The bargaining power of the enacting coalition, the interdependence of different subfields of budgetary politics and high switching costs contained pressure for change and prevented major reforms for a long period. Only as the change coalition gained bargaining power, linkages between the subfields were drawn and the opportunity costs of continuing with the existing setting significantly increased, the reproduction mechanisms lost force and institutional change occurred. Moreover, pressure for change had accumulated because the institutional setting failed to accommodate demands for change in small on-path changes.

The institutional path of the 1970 treaty was characterised by three key features:

- A revenue system that replaced national contributions from member states with European 'own-resources', based on a fixed percentage of VAT revenue, customs duties and agriculture levies.
- A distinction between compulsory and non-compulsory expenditure, which gave each of the two arms of the budgetary exclusive authority over one of the two groups and (at least *de jure*) excluded the Commission from the second half of the budgetary procedure.
- A separation of the expenditure and revenue sides, which allowed for the adoption of spending decisions regardless of revenue constraints, and denied a link between national contributions and budgetary returns.

The chapter is divided into four sections. The first three assess the impact of three reproduction mechanisms in turn. The reproduction mechanism of small on-path changes is not presented in a separate section, as it did not play a significant role in stabilising the institutional setting. The final section analyses the extent to which additional factors contributed to the occurrence of the 1988 reform.

Bargaining power

Bargaining power is a reproduction mechanism that builds on the ability of the dominating actor coalition to maintain the existing institutional setting. Following this mechanism, change can only occur when a new group of actors gains sufficient bargaining power to succeed the currently dominating coalition. In the case of the 1970 setting, two actors had a strong interest in institutional change: the European Parliament and the United Kingdom. Both institutions were dissatisfied with the distributive outcomes of the existing procedure and regarded institutional reform as the key to achieving distributive change. However, despite the mutual interest in institutional reform, their institutional preferences were very different. This section portrays both actors and their attempts to achieve institutional change.

The European Parliament

As illustrated in Part I, the European Parliament was eager to strengthen its role in budgetary decision-making. Unsatisfied with the outcome of the treaty negotiations in 1970, it pressed for institutional change whenever possible. The scope of interpretation helped Parliament. First, the EP could justify its claim that the current institutional setting needed 'concretisation' and 'adaptation'. Second, the scope of interpretation offered the EP the possibility to achieve small changes ('alteration'), by putting forward 'unilateral interpretations' (for the terminology, see first section of previous chapter) (Läufer 1979; Glaesner 1982).

Not only did unilateral interpretation offer a promising strategy for change, it was effectively the only option open to the EP. 'Formal change' of the treaty provisions, the EP's ultimate goal, was within the exclusive decision-making realm of member states and the EP did not have the bargaining power to force member states into enacting a new budget treaty. Similarly, 'third party interpretation' of treaty provisions seemed a difficult and uncertain option for the EP. On a procedural level, there were originally some doubts whether the EP had the right to take action before the European Court of Justice (ECJ) and what the object of a possible lawsuit against the Council could be (Bradley 1987). Strictly speaking, Council decisions in the budgetary process did not constitute legal acts and could, therefore, not be easily challenged (Skiadas 2000: 8). On the political level, an involvement of the ECJ entailed the risk that the ruling might favour the Council.

In the first years of the new treaty, an agreement between Council and Parliament on a 'joint interpretation' of the treaty provisions was made impossible by Council's unwillingness to accept the need for a 'concretisation' or 'adaptation' of the treaty.[2] Only slowly did the Council realise that the application of vague and inconsistent treaty provisions was not only complicating the decision-making process, but also weakening the Council. However, instead of consenting to a 'joint interpretation', the Council opted for a 'unilateral interpretation'. Member states adopted an internal agreement that tried to prevent the occurrence of disputes over treaty provisions by assuring unity among member states (see case study of the 1979 budget in Chapter 3, p. 51–56).

Against strong criticism from Parliament and demands for a 'joint interpretation', Council insisted that the treaty offered a workable basis for the budgetary decision-making process. In line with this maxim, the Council reproached the EP's 'unilateral interpretations' by taking Parliament to Court ('third party interpretation'). However, the third-party did not get involved. The Council used the ECJ as a threat, but was eager to settle with the EP the specific budgetary issues in question (but not the general institutional differences!) before the ECJ issued its ruling. The Council always withdrew its lawsuits once a compromise had been found. The Council seemed to regard the risk as high that the ECJ would adopt a ruling in favour of the EP.

In 1981/82 the Council temporarily shifted its strategy and accepted the need for 'joint interpretation'.[3] Successive clashes with the EP over institutional questions had raised the political costs of continuing with the current budgetary procedure (see the section on switching and opportunity costs below). Following the dispute over the 1982 budget, the presidents of Parliament, Council and the Commission started negotiations on a 'joint interpretation' of the treaty provisions (see case study of the 1982 budget in Chapter 3, p. 00).[4] Negotiations centred on questions related to expenditure classification, the application of the maximum rate of increase of non-compulsory expenditure and the separation between budgetary and legislative decision-making. The atmosphere was cooperative and friendly (see verbatim of the meeting on 28 May 1982). The three presidents wanted the negotiations to succeed. Within months, the institutions had settled upon an agreement and adopted a 'Joint Declaration on various measures to improve the budgetary procedure' (OJ C 194/1–35, 28 July 1982).

This joint declaration constituted a compromise for both sides. The Parliament gave up important aspects of its interpretation of the maximum rate of increase and agreed on a comprehensive list of classifications, based on the headings and lines in the 1982 budget. In exchange, the Council moved towards the Parliament stance on the delineation between budgetary and legislative powers. It promised to abstain from setting financial amounts in its regulations and agreed with EP that appropriations in the budget entered for 'significant new Community action' required a regulation. In order to ensure the successful application of the joint declaration, a new procedural element was introduced: the presidents of the three institutions would convene at 'trialogue' meetings when budgetary disputes re-emerged.

Although introduced as a major interinstitutional achievement, the joint declaration did not significantly alter the institutional setting. What were the reasons for this failure? First, the adopted clarifications left, in fact, considerable scope of interpretation. In the case of classification, the joint declaration did not do much to make already vague treaty provisions more specific. The list of classifications soon lost validity. New budget lines emerged and gave rise to tensions, e.g. in the dispute over the classification of UK compensation payments (Dankert 1983: 710). Similarly, the provisions for a clarified separation between legislative and budgetary powers induced discussions over what constituted 'significant new community actions'. Parliament continued to adopt budget lines without legal bases and the Council fixed spending amounts in its legislative decisions.

Second, the procedural innovation of the joint declaration, the 'trialogue' meetings, soon revealed a key weakness. The meetings did not commit the institutions to finding a solution. If the presidents of the three institutions did not resolve their differences, the conflict remained. The trialogue procedure did not provide a viable default option (Commentaire J. Megret 1999: 66–68; interview with Commission official).

Third, budgetary actors simply disobeyed the rules of the joint declaration, as they did not feel bound by the new agreement.[5] The compromise that the three presidents had adopted did not have the needed political backing in the Council and Parliament to make the agreement work. On the side of the Council, the Belgian presidency had, in the negotiations, gone beyond the unanimous position of the Council. The pro-European Belgian government under its foreign minister, Leo Tindemans, himself a former MEP, settled upon a compromise that largely ignored the deep scepticism of a number of member states in the Council. In the discussions over the results of the negotiations, German, Danish and British representatives voiced criticism. They feared that the agreement would strengthen Parliament's role in budgetary decision-making (see 'extracts of discussion' of the meeting between the Council, a delegation of Parliament and the Commission on 22 June 1982; and draft minutes of the same meeting). Against this resistance, a consensus in the Council was achieved only because the Belgian Presidency, supported by the Commission and senior representatives of the EP, stressed that these worries were unfounded. As soon as the presidency changed, the downside of the Belgian strategy emerged. Most member states had little interest in making the joint declaration work. The internal agreement on budgetary discipline in 1984 confirmed that the majority of the Council had reverted to the strategy of 'unilateral interpretations', relying exclusively on the bargaining power of the Council.

The situation was similar on the side of the EP. Signs of reluctance to comply with the new rules became visible as soon as Parliament adopted the joint declaration together with a resolution. In this resolution, the EP emphasised that, if any of the other institutions would not comply with the joint declaration, the EP would reserve itself the right to revert to the treaty provisions. Parliament also underlined that it regarded the classifications agreed upon in the joint declaration as solely provisional (see Läufer and Siebert 1988: 197; Strasser 1983).

As the Council did not display much willingness to make the joint declaration work, Parliament justified its return to a confrontational strategy by alleging that the Council was breaching the agreement. Moreover, the inability of member states to solve the interrelated issues of exploding CAP costs, the UK problem and the exhaustion of own-resources motivated the EP to continue challenging the institutional setting (see below the section on interdependence). The EP assumed that, given the Council's internal division, the joint declaration did not sufficiently reflect the Parliament's bargaining power.

As tensions over the institutional setting increased, budgetary actors sought clarification from 'third party interpretation'. In 1986, the Council went to the Court following the adoption of the disputed 1986 budget (case 34/86; Bieber 1986; Glaesner 1987). In contrast to previous occasions, Parliament and Council did not pre-empt a Court ruling through a political solution, but waited for the Court to settle the dispute over classification. As mentioned in Chapter 3, the ECJ decided on the specific budgetary issue in question but refrained from giving an authoritative interpretation of the provisions on classification. Instead, it urged Parliament and Council to solve the question by way of 'joint interpretation'. The institutions did not follow the Court's advice.

Parliament gained the necessary bargaining power to demand institutional concessions only as the opportunity costs increased, and as the Council realised that a solution to the Community's financial problems would only be possible through a major reform that linked the different subfields of budgetary politics (see below). Table 9.1 summarises the failed attempts to ease pressure through minor adjustments of the institutional setting in annual procedures between 1974 and 1988.

The United Kingdom

Like the European Parliament, the United Kingdom had a strong interest in institutional change. Two institutional objectives dominated the British agenda: first and most important, a reform of the revenue side that would take into account Britain's large contributions to the EC budget; and second, the introduction of institutional measures that ensured budgetary discipline.

Reform of the revenue side

As illustrated in Chapter 5, the British government regarded the distributive framework of the Community as highly disadvantageous. Soon after accession, it came to the conclusion that only a rebate on the revenue side rather than the enacting of new expenditure policies could significantly alter the financial burden of British EC membership. Given the high degree of institutionalisation of the revenue side, this meant that Britain had to lobby for change in the rules of the revenue side.

The struggle over British demands for institutional reform dominated European affairs in the late 1970s and early 1980s. Over years, member states either completely resisted or tried to accommodate British demands through minor adjustments. The breakthrough came at the Fontainebleau summit in 1984 when member states finally settled on a British rebate (see Chapter 5). The British government was successful only because it had suddenly acquired the necessary bargaining power for substantiating its demands. Due to the exhaustion of own-resources, Britain was able to link the question of the rebate with the increase of own-resources. Facing British veto-power, member states gave in and altered the rules of the revenue side.

The resulting institutional change was considerable. It cut off an important element of the institutional path introduced in the 1970 treaty: the concept of own-resources. Own-resources had been designed to make the Community independent from national budgets and to provide an exclusive source of revenue. The rebate broke with this vision and essentially returned to the concept of national contributions. Although duties and levies were excluded from the rebate, Fontainebleau

Table 9.1 Overview of adjustments of the institutional setting until the 1988 reform

Year	Unilateral interpretations		Joint interpretations	Third-party interpretations
	EP	*Council*		
1974				
1975			Joint declaration on the conciliation procedure	
1976				
1977				
1978				
1979		Internal agreement in the Council concerning the maximum rate of increase		
1980	The EP pursued strategy of 'opportunistic interpretation'			
1981				
1982			Joint declaration on various measures to improve the budgetary procedure	
1983				
1984		Internal agreement of the Council on budgetary discipline		
1985				
1986				Ruling of the European Court of Justice
1987			*1988 reform:* Interinstitutional agreement on budgetary discipline and improvement of the budgetary procedure	
1988				

accepted that, not European taxpayers, but national governments provided the own-resources for the Community. Moreover, the rebate agreement also brought in the national level as a reference point for the expenditure side. In accepting net-contributions as the basis for British claims, member states loosened the concept of European spending policies that benefited European citizens and farmers, and not national economies.

Measures for budgetary discipline

Although the rebate was Britain's key institutional objective, the British prime minister, Margaret Thatcher, also insisted on containing the EC budget. This political objective, which was directed mainly against agricultural expenditure, became known as 'budgetary discipline'. Originally a purely distributive argument, the objective gained an institutional dimension as it became increasingly clear that spending containment (in particular for the CAP) could only be achieved through an institutional commitment device that set explicit limits on expenditure. In contrast to the demand for a rebate, the UK was not completely isolated in its call for budgetary discipline. Germany, the largest net-contributor, generally supported a commitment to prudent budgeting.[6]

With the exhaustion of own-resources and the massive increase in agricultural expenditure, the bargaining power of the UK increased (see below section on switching and opportunity costs). In the wake of the Fontainebleau summit, the Council adopted an internal agreement that accepted the need for budgetary discipline, not only for non-compulsory expenditure, but also for agricultural spending. The agreement entailed concrete provisions that prohibited (1) CAP spending to increase above the rate of increase of the own-resources, and (2) non-compulsory expenditure to rise above the maximum rate of increase (Rev. CM 1985). Yet, the nature of the agreement remained informal and was binding only in a political sense.[7] The bargaining power of the United Kingdom and the member states supporting budgetary discipline was insufficient to ensure compliance with the agreement. The EP torpedoed the internal agreement of Council, which it regarded as a breach of the 1982 joint declaration, and member states put specific distributive interests above their political commitment to budgetary discipline. As the following subsection on interdependence will illustrate, finance ministers soon realised that, without the involvement of the EP and agricultural ministers, an isolated approach on budgetary discipline was deficient.

A lasting institutional agreement on budgetary discipline was finally achieved as part of the 1988 reform. As in the case of the rebate decision at Fontainebleau four years earlier, the link to an increase of own-resources gave the British government a veto-power and the ability to press for an agreement on budgetary discipline. However, very important for the breakthrough was also the fact that an increasing number of member states started to endorse budgetary discipline. As the section on switching and opportunity costs will demonstrate, member states began to see the need for an institutional link between the expenditure and revenue side, because the political and financial costs of continuing the current system had risen drastically despite the limited revenue. Moreover, they sought to commit the Community to budgetary discipline in order to limit the distributive demands from poorer member states.

Concluding this section, it is clear that bargaining power was a key reproduction mechanism that enforced the existing institutional path and eventually affected its change. The EP did not have the bargaining power to achieve a significant institutional change and the UK gained institutional change only when it was able to build on its bargaining power in the decision over an increase of the VAT ceiling. Nevertheless, bargaining power alone paints an incomplete picture of the stability and change of the original institutional path. The reproduction mechanisms of interdependence and switching costs also played a significant role.

Interdependence

The interdependence between different subfields of budgetary politics made a successful reform dependent on actors' ability to combine change efforts in the different subfields. Attempts to achieve change in one subfield were destined to fail if they were not coordinated with change in the other subfields. The involvement of a higher political level enabled institutional change by establishing and enforcing links between the subfields. While Figure 9.1 gives an overview of all inter-linkages among the different subfields of budgetary politics, this section illustrates the stabilising effect of interdependence and its final breakdown with two brief case studies: (1) the linkage of interinstitutional relations to budgetary discipline, the UK problem and the CAP; (2) the linkage between CAP reform and budgetary discipline.

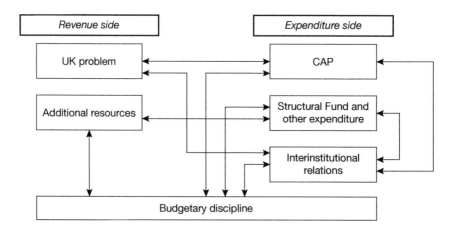

Figure 9.1 Subfields and interdependence in EC budgetary politics.

The linkage of interinstitutional relations to budgetary discipline, the UK problem and the CAP

Parliament's efforts to achieve institutional change were interlinked with the Council's attempt to move towards budgetary discipline and to solve the UK problem. Institutional change within the different subfields proved unattainable, as long as change efforts were not combined and coordinated. In the case presented, interdependence was particularly strong because the reforms demanded by the change coalitions in the different subfields stood in partial opposition. Parliament wanted to abolish the distinction between compulsory and non-compulsory expenditure, while the UK demanded rules that strengthened the maximum rate of increase of non-compulsory expenditure (in addition to CAP reform). The antagonism of these two change coalitions further strengthened the stability of the existing design. Small changes in one subfield intensified demands for change in another and made coordination between the reform efforts unlikely.

As mentioned above, increased bargaining power and a rise in the political costs of the existing institutional setting facilitated an internal agreement in the Council on budgetary discipline in 1984. The agreement failed to achieve its objectives, despite a relatively clear political commitment to prudent spending policies. A key reason for the failure was the EP's unwillingness to endorse any institutional innovation adopted by the member states without previously consulting the EP. The EP torpedoed the implementation of the internal agreement and made parliamentary support for budgetary discipline dependent on an increase in the EP's political involvement in budgetary decision-making. The Council vehemently opposed the institutional demands of the EP. For the Council, an increase in the political involvement of the EP was only acceptable if EP ensured that this would not lead to a sharp rise in non-compulsory expenditure. As long as both countervailing interests were not coordinated, change in the two subfields did not succeed.

Moreover, the Council's inability to settle the UK problem, to bring the CAP expenditure under control and to provide sufficient resources for the running of the Community made the EP unwilling to settle within the existing rules of the budgetary procedure. This occurred, not only because the EP sensed its chance of capitalising on the internal weaknesses of the Council, but also because the rise in agricultural expenditure pushed the budget towards the limits of the existing own-resources. This development seriously limited EP's ability to set non-compulsory expenditure and intensified institutional demands of the EP. This, in turn, infuriated the Council and made constructive negotiations over institutional reform (even in the form of minor on-path changes) almost impossible. The escalation of institutional demands *de facto* stabilised the existing institutional setting.

Only as the Council was about to overcome the problems of CAP expenditure, of the UK rebate and of the limited own-resources in the 1988 reform, did the Council and EP enter into serious negotiations over a new institutional setting for their relationship. A key factor in overcoming the interdependence was the involvement of the higher level, namely European Council and the EP president (in fulfilment of the 'necessary condition', see for terminology the preceding chapter)[8] and, as 'sufficient condition', the presentation of the different problems of budgetary politics as a package, which the Commission President Jacques Delors had done in a far-reaching negotiation proposal in February 1987 (Com (87)100).

The linkage between budgetary discipline and CAP reform

From the late 1970s, the Commission, the UK and other member states tried to initiate distributive and institutional changes in the framework of the CAP. These attempts failed repeatedly. The CAP community was a tied network of politicians, bureaucrats and lobbyists that strongly resisted change. Every year, the Agriculture Council adopted price decisions and preserved the existing system of subsidies in complete ignorance of the budgetary repercussions of these decisions. Moreover, the Budget Council, which had to cope with the financial effects of the policy of high prices, did not seriously challenge the autonomy of the Agriculture Council. Demands for budgetary discipline within the Budget Council were either rejected or channelled towards non-compulsory expenditure. Over time, it became clear that isolated reform in one field was impossible: the change coalition in the Agriculture Council needed support from the budget experts and budgetary discipline was unfeasible without reform in the agricultural sector (Ungerer 1988).

Although the Commission had tried to present changes in the CAP as an essential and necessary part of budgetary reform, linkages between the CAP and the budget were only established as the budget reached the limits of the own-resources in 1983/84. As mentioned above, in the ensuing negotiations in the European Council, the British government consented to an increase in own-resources dependent on a final solution for the UK problem, a decision on budgetary discipline and on CAP reform. Although the UK gained minor concessions on CAP reform and a political agreement on budgetary discipline, the British rebate essentially bought off Britain's insistence on institutional reform. The resulting agreements on CAP reform and budgetary discipline were limited in effect; expenditure continued to rise at a much higher rate (Hendriks 1991: 70; Patterson 1997: 137). The link between the Agricultural Council and Budget Council, established in the agreement, was ultimately never enforced. Only a year after the agreement had been adopted, Germany, although a key proponent of budgetary discipline, caused the most serious blow to the 1984 reform. The German agriculture minister, Ignatz Kiechle, pushed the Agriculture Council towards a decision on prices for 1985/86 that went far beyond the commitment on budgetary discipline (Fennell 1997: 167).[9]

The episode demonstrated that the involvement of the European Council, and a formal linkage between CAP and budget reform alone, would not suffice. It became clear that the 'sufficient condition', mentioned in Chapter 8, was only fulfilled when backed by strong political force. Although the exhaustion of the own-resources created pressure to establish the linkage, the European Council did not enforce it. Agricultural reform was *de facto* left to the Agricultural Council, which simply continued with its high price policy, while the Budgetary Council failed to achieve budgetary discipline, as long as the agriculture expenditure kept rising.

This changed with the Commission's proposal for a far-reaching budget reform in 1987 (Pinder 1988).[10] The Commission presented its proposal as a package of tightly interlinked reforms and ensured that none of the subfields was exempted from the reform negotiations. This meant that agriculture was fully included. After intense debates, Heads of government settled upon an agreement that combined CAP reform with the introduction of a framework for budgetary discipline. It established the authority of the Budget Council over agricultural expenditure and, as part of financial perspective, devised annual ceilings for the CAP. The package character of the proposal and the final agreement not only enabled reform, but also facilitated compliance in the following. In contrast to previous years, agricultural ministers could not afford to disobey, as this would have endangered the whole package (see Chapter 10).

Switching costs and opportunity costs

In addition to bargaining power and interdependence, the political costs of institutional reform (switching costs) played an important role in stabilising the existing institutional path. Even though actors accepted that reform was necessary, the switching costs and the uncertainty over the gains from a new system (opportunity costs) prevented change. Nevertheless, the institutional path entailed characteristics, such as the disconnection of spending decisions and revenue developments, which gradually built up reform pressure, and played into the hands of the actors demanding institutional change. As the cost of continuing the current system started to exceed the sum of switching costs and the costs of running a reformed system, the reproduction mechanism lost force and no longer prevented change.

Interinstitutional relations and the expenditure side

Even though member states started to accept that the existing treaty provisions warranted clarification, the costs of reforming the treaty and the risks that new negotiations entailed were regarded as too high.[11] Instead, the Council entered into negotiations with the EP over 'joint interpretation' and tried to reduce the political costs incurred by a continuation of the conflict.[12] The resulting joint declaration of 1982 was close enough to the treaty and sufficiently informal as to minimise switching costs. When this on-path change failed, the Council unsuccessfully sought to address the problem through the internal agreement on budgetary discipline in 1984 and third-party interpretation in 1986 (see above). In the run-up to the 1988 reform, the rising political costs of continuing conflict affected Council and EP alike. Both institutions regarded a system without conflict as beneficial.[13] Moreover, the form of an interinstitutional agreement ('joint interpretation') as the framework of the reform kept switching costs limited and a return to the treaty provision as a back-up option.

Established spending patterns and vested interests made reform of the expenditure side difficult. Despite rising expenditure for the CAP, member states were reluctant to incur the political costs of switching to a new regime. Distributive demands of new member states were granted in the form of additional expenditure, rather than through reallocation of existing spending policies. As the political costs of establishing a link between expenditure and revenue sides were regarded as very high, expenditure escalated and gradually induced significant reform pressures. In particular, agricultural spending exploded due to market developments and an incentives structure that fostered overproduction. After the Iberian accession in 1986, the strengthened coalition of poorer member states demanded significant increases of the budget, which added to the pressure and made institutional reform almost inevitable.

Revenue side and rising opportunity costs

Significant changes in the structure and scope of own-resources were resisted, because the revenue side was highly institutionalised. Distributive and institutional change demanded formal ratification by national parliaments, which entailed high political costs. Moreover, uncertainty over actual distributive consequences of a new system made member states reluctant to enact changes. The negotiations over British demands for a rebate were, for example, accompanied by long discussions over speculations regarding the costs of existing and alternative revenue settings. Finally, even small change in the rules of the revenue side entailed the risk that they would damage the idea of 'own' resources and induce a chain of claims by other member states. This was certainly the fear around the demands of the British government for a rebate mechanism.

Nevertheless, member states adopted an on-path change of the revenue side in the form of the correction mechanism in 1975, and off-path changes in form of the rebate decision in 1984 and the introduction of a new revenue source in 1988. Although these decisions largely related to the bargaining power of the change coalition, mounting pressure on the existing institutional setting paved the way for member states' willingness to enact a new one that promised to secure an ordered development of own-resources and expenditure. This process came to a head in 1988: expenditure and revenue sides clashed constantly and negotiations over increases of the own-resources led only to *ad hoc* measures, such as repayable intergovernmental advances. Moreover, the framework of a multi-annual budget plan, introduced in the 1988 reform, clearly indicated the distributive effects of the reform, and thus reduced the uncertainties and switching costs of the reform.

In addition to rising costs of the existing institutional system, the alternative of a budgetary procedure without major conflict became increasingly attractive, because the political capital vested in budgetary politics was needed for the completion of the single market. With the adoption of the Single European Act, European integration had regained momentum and reduced the relevance of short-term budgetary gains. The joint objective of a single market created the willingness among member states and the EP to facilitate the transition towards a single market by settling upon a long-term budgetary reform.

Conclusion

Bargaining over institutional change

This chapter demonstrated that the empirical evidence of the 1970s and 1980s largely supports the propositions introduced in Chapter 8. Three reproduction mechanisms stabilised the institutional path of the 1970 treaty. A powerful enacting coalition fought off demands for institutional change, the interdependence between subfields undermined isolated reform efforts within the subfields and high political costs of switching to a new regime prevented reform, even when budgetary actors recognised the need for reform. Over time, the reproduction mechanisms lost force and off-path change occurred. The first element of the off-path change was the introduction of the British rebate, which initiated the end of the concept of own-resources. The main shift occurred when the bargaining power of the dominant actor coalition deteriorated, opportunity costs considerably increased and reform efforts in the subfields were combined to one major reform in 1988. Table 9.2 illustrates the large extent to which the new path broke with the characteristics of the old institutional setting. The following chapter will closely analyse the different elements of the new path and assess their institutional stability.

However, before turning to the next chapter, I wish to extend this explanation of the stability and final breakdown of the 1970 institutional path. The analysis of the developments of the 1970s and 1980s through the lenses of the three reproduction mechanisms runs the risk of portraying stability and change as processes of an almost

Table 9.2 Characteristics of the institutional settings of 1970 (old path) and of 1988 (new path)

Old institutional path	New institutional path
A revenue system that replaced national contributions from member states with European own-resources, based on a fixed percentage of VAT revenue, customs duties and agriculture levies.	A revenue system that was linked to GNP, which constituted a return to national contributions; and an exception for the UK, which accepted the concept of net-contributions.
A distinction between compulsory and non-compulsory expenditure, which gave each of the two arms of the budgetary exclusive authority over one of the two groups and (at least *de jure*) excluded the Commission from the second half of the budgetary procedure.	The fusion of compulsory and non-compulsory expenditure into one large multi-annual budget plan, which all three institutions adopted and revised jointly.
A separation between expenditure and revenue sides, which allowed for the adoption of spending decisions regardless of revenue constrains and denied the link between national contributions and budgetary returns.	Annual ceilings for all areas of spending that limited spending decisions; and decisions by spending Councils that exceed the ceilings were prohibited and only possible after a revision of the financial perspective.

mechanical nature. This would give an incomplete account. The dynamics of the bargaining processes, in particular in the run-up to the 1988 reform, and the specific constellation of (individual) actors, chiefly contributed to the impact of the reproduction mechanisms. In 1987/88, a successful conclusion of the negotiations over the Commission proposals was far from certain. Discussions were repeatedly on the brink of complete collapse (Johnston 1994: 90–97). The impact of two (f)actors seemed to have been decisive to bring about a final agreement in February 1988: the skilful Commission president Jacques Delors and the German presidency under Chancellor Helmut Kohl.

The Commission under president Jacques Delors

The influence of the Commission in establishing the linkage between the different reform efforts and the creation of momentum for change, stemmed largely from the central role played by its president, Jacques Delors (Laffan 2000b: 58–61). Although it is difficult to assess the exact impact of individuals in a highly institutionalised political process, Jacques Delors and his effective cabinet transformed the Commission and made it the vanguard of reform.

Appointed as Commission president in 1985, Delors put the financial problems of the EC on top of his political agenda. He approached the problems with a reform strategy that was characteristic of his political style: the solution was presented as a large package and linked to a political project that enjoyed unanimous support among member states. The Delors biographer George Ross describes this approach as the 'Russian doll'-strategy. The 1988 reform was to become Delors' most significant Russian doll (Ross 1995: 49).[14] Delors initiated the debate on institutional change by portraying budgetary reform as a direct follow-up to the adoption of the Single European Act.[15] The single market became the large outer doll, in which all of the different subfields of budgetary politics were housed. Delors transferred the commitment to the single market over to budgetary reform and suggested that one was unfeasible without the other. Once member states accepted this link, it was difficult for them to withdraw from the reform negotiations. Moreover, the package character of the reform proposals of the Commission left member states little space to dispute individual elements of the reform (Delors 2004; Ross 1995: 41; Ehlermann 1988; Biehl 1988).

Delors' close ties to the European Council and his personal involvement were decisive for the success of his strategy. He had earned the respect of the European Council in the negotiations of Single European Act and used it strategically for the 1988 reform (Endo 1999: 59). He ensured that the main reform negotiations took place in the European Council and that Heads of State or Government continued to accept his role as equal partner and key agenda-setter. During the final negotiations of the Brussels summits, Delors moved inexhaustibly between the different delegations and tried, in close cooperation with the German presidency, to broker a viable compromise. At the same time, the Commission president kept close links to MEPs who saw in him their former colleague and a European visionary (interview with former MEP). On the administrative level, Delors had exchanged some of the personnel and much of the approach of the DG Budget. In close cooperation with the president and the cabinet, the budget experts of the Commission regained the credibility that they had lost under the Thorn Commission. Commission figures and calculations were now accurate and became the reference point for the discussions among member states (interview with Commission official).

The German presidency under Chancellor Helmut Kohl

Although all three presidencies involved in the negotiations over the 1988 reform affected the negotiation process positively, the German presidency was of particular significance (Delors 2004; Johnston 1994: 90–97; Ehlermann 1988). As so often in budgetary politics, negotiations for the final budgetary agreement fell under the presidency of a large member state (see Chapters 5 and 6). This had not been intended. Originally, the summit of Copenhagen in December was supposed to bring the negotiations to a successful end. However, as Copenhagen failed, the final negotiations were postponed to an extraordinary summit under the German presidency in February 1988. The German government had a strong interest in completing the negotiations not only because Chancellor Kohl wanted to receive the political credit for a successful agreement, but also because Germany sought to clear any obstacles for the completion of the single market, from which it expected to benefit. At the same time, Germany was eager to prevent a far-reaching CAP reform on which the Commission, Great Britain and the Netherlands insisted (Patterson 1997: 147). Here, the German government was in line with the French, who adamantly opposed spending cuts for farmers. Chancellor Kohl used his bargaining power and Germany's financial means to achieve these different objectives. He settled the conflict among member states by assuming the lion's share of the costs incurred in a doubling of the structural funds and a limited CAP reform. Moreover, he coordinated closely with the French government and Commission president Delors in forcing Britain to consent to the agreement.

10 Initiating a new institutional path

Stability of the financial perspective
and the interinstitutional agreement
(1988–2000)

The 1988 reform initiated a new institutional path that introduced enduring stability; in this chapter, I seek to explain the foundations of this institutional stability. In line with the propositions of Chapter 8, I contend that the same reproduction mechanisms, i.e. the bargaining power of the enacting coalition, interdependence between different subfields and high switching and low opportunity costs, that prevented changes in the 1970 institutional setting also stabilised the financial perspective and the interinstitutional agreement in this period. Moreover, general satisfaction over existing path, in combination with specified venues for negotiating on-path alterations reduced the pressure for change.

Similar to the preceding chapter, this chapter is divided into four sections. The first three assess the impact of the three reproduction mechanisms in turn. Empirical evidence on a fourth reproduction mechanism, namely small on-path changes, is not presented separately but integrated in these three sections. In contrast to the 1970 institutional setting, the 1988 institutional setting relied to a considerable degree on this (fourth) reproduction mechanism. The final section analyses the extent to which additional factors contributed to the stability of the 1988 reform.

Bargaining power

A large coalition of actors backed the new institutional setting. All member states in the Council, the Commission and the EP jointly enacted the financial perspective and the interinstitutional agreement. Revision and renewal were only possible when all actors agreed. This gave each participant the blocking power against revisions and modifications of the agreement during its application period and against its renewal at the end of the application period. Moreover, withdrawal from the agreement was possible at any time, as the binding force of the agreement was of a political, rather than a legal nature (see Monar 1994 and Snyder 1995 on 'soft law' status of the interinstitutional agreement). The voluntary and temporal nature of the new institutional setting distributed the potential blocking power equally among the actors and made the functioning of the agreement dependent on the relative satisfaction of all participating actors. Consequently, actors' actual bargaining power was linked to the intensity of their preferences. The more actors wanted change and regarded an alternative institutional setting as beneficial, the more they would be willing to use blocking power at renewal points or simply withdraw from the agreement.

Between 1988 and 2000, pressure for institutional change came essentially from the EP and the group of net-contributors. The following two subsections will illustrate their attempts to achieve change. The main focus will lie on the EP, as it pursued its quest for change considerably more intensively, although it never breached the rules of the interinstitutional agreement (IIA).

The European Parliament

Although the EP regarded the interinstitutional agreement as a significant improvement, a strong interest in institutional change still guided Parliament's stance in budgetary politics. As Chapter 4 illustrated, two developments dominated EP budgetary affairs in the late 1980s and the 1990s. First, budget experts were able, at least temporarily, to increase their internal grip over budgetary matters. They gradually moved towards the distributive position of the Council accepting, within limits, the necessity for budgetary prudence and focused mainly on the institutional dimension. Second, the relevance of budgetary politics within the EP decreased and MEPs in the spending committees were less willing to invest much political capital in budgetary matters. They did not want to risk a possible breakdown of the financial perspective, which guaranteed high levels of expenditure. Moreover, with the increase of legislative powers, the EP was no longer dependent on its budgetary powers as a means of seeking power and publicity. Overall, these two developments prompted the EP to continue to pursue its objective of rule change (possibly even more than before), even while its bargaining power was somewhat limited by internal disunity and a lack of determination.

Despite these internal limits on Parliament's bargaining position, the EP achieved a series of agreements with the Council and the Commission on 'joint interpretations'. The EP was able, in successive renegotiations, to move the IIA towards Parliament's ideal point. Table 10.1 gives an overview over the institutional adjustments that occurred between 1988 and 2000. The following two subsections focus on (1) the application of the first IIA from 1988 to 1993, and (2) on the application of the second IIA (1994–1999), and on the first experiences with the third IIA (1999/2000).

Developments between 1988 and 1993

The EP pursued its institutional objectives within the framework of the interinstitutional agreement and did not want to endanger the new interinstitutional setting. Nevertheless, the application of the interinstitutional agreement revealed a number of issues where EP and Council disagreed:

- *The distinction between privileged and non-privileged non-compulsory expenditure.* The European Council had introduced the distinction between two forms of non-compulsory expenditures at the Brussels summit in February 1988. Where the

Table 10.1 Overview of adjustments of the institutional setting between 1988 and 2000

| Year | Unilateral interpretations | | Joint interpretations | Third-party interpretations |
	EP	Council		
1988		Insisted on distinction between privileged and non-privileged non-compulsory expenditure	*1988 reform:* Interinstitutional agreement on budgetary discipline and improvement of the budgetary procedure	
1989				
1990	Challenged revenue side treaty provisions			
1991				
1992				Ruling of the European Court of Justice on revenue side
1993			New interinstitutional agreement on budgetary discipline and improvement of the budgetary procedure	
1994	Challenged the treaty provisions on classification			
1995	Challenged the treaty provisions on classification	Joint declaration on the incorporation of financial provisions into legislative acts		Ruling of the European Court of Justice on classification
1996		Joint statement on improving the provision of information to the Budget Authority on fisheries agreements		
1997	Challenged agricultural forecast of the Commission	Interinstitutional agreement on provisions regarding financing of the Common and Security Policy; 'Memorandum of Understanding' on annual revisions of the agricultural forecasts		
1998	Challenged binding nature of the financial perspective		Interinstitutional agreement on legal bases and implementation of the budget	Ruling of the European Court of Justice on budgetary appropriations without legal bases
1999			New interinstitutional agreement on budgetary discipline and improvement of the budgetary procedure	
2000				

ceiling of the heading constituted spending objectives, this was 'privileged non-compulsory expenditure'; 'non-privileged non-compulsory expenditure' resulted where the ceiling fulfilled the function of an upper limit (EC-Bull. 2–1988: 10). While the first fell outside of discussions regarding the maximum rate of increase, the second had to stay within the rate. The EP rejected this distinction immediately, stressing that the maximum rate of increase had lost its relevance with the introduction of the financial perspective, and that the Council had to accept any increase of non-compulsory expenditure as long as it remained below the ceiling. The EP saw its position strengthened by the interinstitutional agreement, which treated non-compulsory expenditure as a unitary entity (Article 15 of the interinstitutional agreement). With both institutions insisting on their position, the issue became entangled in the more general discussion over the status of the interinstitutional agreement relative to the treaty (Cammarata 1995: 31–34). Finally, the Council accepted *de facto* the EP's interpretation, although it upheld the ritual of agreeing to an 'exceptional' increase of the maximum rate (Isaac 1994: 28).

•   *The flexibility of headings and ceilings.* While the Council insisted on strict compliance with the expenditure ceilings under different headings, the EP complained about the rigidity of the financial perspective. It was difficult for the EP to accept that it could not increase expenditure for new policy projects, despite the fact that the positive economic climate generated significant surplus of own-resources and the development of market prices kept agricultural expenditure considerably below its ceiling (Timmann 1989: 19). The EP tried to circumvent a strict application of headings and ceilings through revisions of the financial perspective. With regard to external expenditure, the Council willingly accepted this seven times in the first years of the IIA (see Chapter 4).

As the interinstitutional agreement had reduced the relevance of treaty provisions, the EP did not focus much attention on challenging the treaty. Nevertheless, it undertook attempts to increase its powers where the possibility of opportunistic interpretations of the treaty provisions still existed:

•   *Own-resources.* A minor incidence of rule contestation occurred when the EP challenged its exclusion from decision-making on own-resources and reinstated a small correction of the revenue side in the supplementary and amending budget No. 2 for the 1990 budget, which the Commission had proposed and to which the Council objected (EC Bull. 7/8–1990: 125). The Council challenged the action before the Court of Justice and won the case in March 1992 (Case C-284/90). The EP had not attached much importance to the matter, but could not resist the opportunity to emphasise its demands for parliamentary involvement in decisions over own-resources (Timmann 1991b: 138).

•   *Classification.* Having realised that the Maastricht Treaty would not alter the treaty provisions on the budgetary procedure, the EP stated in September 1991 that it planned to challenge the distinction between compulsory and non-compulsory expenditure (Régnier-Heldmaier 1994: 98). MEPs did not pursue the issue until the procedure over the 1994 budget, which began as the negotiations over the renewal of the interinstitutional agreement were fully under way, when the EP contested the classification of a number of agricultural budget lines as compulsory. Thus, it created a pressure on the negotiations to find a solution on the issue of classification.

Overall, rule contestation of the EP was relatively limited. The EP challenged specific rules of the interinstitutional agreement during their application without threatening non-compliance and contested treaty provisions only on a low scale. The EP possessed neither sufficient bargaining power, nor the preference intensity to undertake major challenges. The positive economic climate and a consensus on an increase in external expenditure reduced the distributive pressure that would, otherwise, have fuelled institutional demands.

Major institutional negotiations took place as part of the renewal of the interinstitutional agreement. After the Edinburgh summit in December 1992 had (just about) achieved an agreement among member states on a new financial perspective, the Council was unwilling to reopen the multi-annual budget plan. As a result, negotiations with the EP centred on institutional issues, and the EP gained the bargaining power to demand large concessions in exchange for accepting the distributive framework of the financial perspective.[1] Negotiations took considerably longer than the ones for the 1988 interinstitutional agreement, resulting in a more detailed and complex agreement (Isaac 1994: 34–37). It included many of the institutional demands voiced by the EP during the application of the 1988 agreement and extended the scope of the agreement towards existing treaty provisions:

- The distinction between non-privileged and privileged expenditure was ruled out (Paragraph 17 of the new IIA).
- In order to ensure more flexibility, the interinstitutional agreement introduced two new reserves – an emergency reserve and one that guaranteed loans to non-member countries – that were installed under a separate heading in the financial perspective. In a procedure of negative codecision, the reserves could be activated on a Commission initiative, even if Council and EP failed to secure an agreement (Paragraph 15).
- The interinstitutional agreement addressed the issue of own-resources, stating that the Commission should present a report on possible changes to own-resources. The institutions were also to participate in a conference on the future developments of the own-resources system in anticipation of the inter-governmental conference scheduled for 1996 (Statement of the own-resources system).
- The distinction between compulsory and non-compulsory expenditure was addressed: (1) a new *ad hoc* conciliation procedure was set up, which intensified the cooperation on compulsory expenditure (Annex II); (2) headings 2 and 3 were classified as non-compulsory expenditure (Paragraph 16); and (3) the institutions committed themselves to reviewing the treaty provisions on the budgetary procedure, including the distinction between compulsory and

non-compulsory expenditure, at the intergovernmental conference in 1996 (Statement on the budgetary procedure provisions of the Treaty).

The new IIA constituted significant on-path change, even though it left the key principles of 1988 path unaltered. Backed by its veto-power and the Council's willingness to trade distributive concessions against institutional ones, EP gained a settlement that somewhat altered the rules in favour of the institutional position of the EP (Cammarata 1995: 48).

Developments between 1994 and 2000

Similar to budgetary politics under the 1988 IIA, the EP did not openly challenge the rules of the 1993 IIA, the application of which proceeded relatively smoothly. Only once, in 1998, did the EP challenge the binding nature of the ceilings of the financial perspective. In view of the approaching renewal of the interinstitutional agreement, the EP sought to gain a commitment from the Council regarding the introduction of a new flexibility reserve that would reduce the rigidity of the financial perspective. Armed with the threat that it would return to the application of maximum rate of increase, the EP gained the demanded commitment (Guth 1999: 174–175). [2]

However, the EP did carry out a serious institutional attack in relation to the treaty provisions: during the 1995 budget procedure, it challenged the classification of agricultural expenditure as compulsory (see detailed case study in Chapter 4). The EP did not want to endanger the institutional framework of the interinstitutional agreement, but sought to achieve institutional change by pressing its 'unilateral interpretation' of the treaty upon the Council. The Council responded by taking the EP to Court. The EP accepted this 'third-party' involvement. Although the ECJ sided with the Council and annulled the adoption of the 1995 budget, it did not decide on the general question of the expenditure classification (Case C-41/95). Similar to its 1986 ruling, the ECJ returned the issue to the budgetary authority and encouraged Parliament and Council to find a permanent political solution to the problem (Fouletier 2001). For the EP, the ruling of the ECJ limited the possibility of further challenges to the classification of agricultural expenditure. Hence, Parliament hoped for a treaty change at the intergovernmental conference in 1996. Although the 1993 IIA committed member states to review the distinction between compulsory and non-compulsory expenditure, it did not alter the treaty provisions on the budgetary procedure. Parliament's bargaining power had been too weak to press the issue, in particular as budgetary politics no longer enjoyed high priority among MEPs and, institutionally, the EP played a limited role in treaty revisions.

The failed attack on classification did not mean that the budgetary experts in the EP were completely unsuccessful in their attempts to extend budgetary powers in the area of compulsory expenditure. In December 1996, the EP gained the adoption of the 'joint statement of improving the provisions of the information to the budgetary authority on fishery agreements'. Although the Council regarded fishery agreements as compulsory, it accepted that the EP and Council would make decisions on these budget lines jointly in the *ad hoc* procedure (Commentaire J. Megret 1999: 27). Moreover, the EP succeeded in challenging the Commission forecasts of the agricultural expenditure. The Council accepted a 'Memorandum of Understanding' on annual revisions of the agricultural forecasts (in autumn), which effectively reduced the ability of the Commission and the Council to adopt unrealistically high CAP budgets (Guth 1998: 157; Godet 2000: 279).[3]

The budget experts of the EP also became involved in renewed discussions over the interpretation of treaty provisions on two other issues. The EP had not, or had only indirectly initiated discussion on these issues, both of which were related to the separation between legislative and budgetary powers:

- *Legislative acts with financial implications.* In defence of Parliament's budgetary powers, the Committee on Budgets had always insisted that legislative acts, adopted by the Council through its exclusive legislative powers, should not precommit the decisions of the budgetary authority. The introduction of the codecision procedure in the Maastricht Treaty, which granted MEPs full legislative powers over certain policy areas, changed the situation. The Committee on Budgets came under internal pressure from Parliament's legislative committees, which challenged the prerogative of the budgetary authority in areas in which the EP was an equal partner in the legislative procedure. The Commission, Parliament and Council finally agreed upon a 'Joint declaration on the incorporation of financial provisions into legislative acts' in March 1995 (EC. Bull. 3–1995: 88). The declaration granted legislative decisions adopted under codecision the right to set financial amounts that the budgetary authority had to accept. For all other legislative acts, the budgetary authority would still determine the expenditure and the Council promised to abandon its practice of setting 'amounts deemed necessary' (Commentaire J. Megret 1999: 27).
- The second issue concerned the adoption and execution of budget lines without legislative bases. Over the years, the EP had swiftly extended its powers to initiate new policies through unilateral interpretations. Against the Council's resistance, it introduced new spending programmes in areas devoid of legal bases for such action. (Theato and Graf 1994: 91–104). Although there were several earlier attempts to settle the dispute, an agreement on 'joint interpretation' only emerged after an ECJ ruling in May 1998 that strengthened the position of the Council (Case C 106/96). Within a few months after the ruling, institutions adopted an 'Interinstitutional agreement on legal bases and implementation of the budget' (Deffaa 2000: 173–174; EC Bull. 10–1998: 92). The agreement specified and significantly limited the ability of Parliament to adopt budget lines without legal bases (Commentaire J. Megret 1999: 29–30).

Overall, the six years under the 1993 interinstitutional agreement had brought several on-path changes. These innovations had only partially resulted from challenges by the EP and were largely clarifications that had become necessary due to circumstances independent of the activities of the budget experts in the EP.

The negotiations over the renewal of the interinstitutional agreement in 1999 offered the EP the opportunity to underpin its institutional demands with more bargaining power. Like the negotiations over the 1993 IIA, these negotiations centred mainly on the institutional domain (Baché 1999: 377–378; Chevalier 2000a,b).

- The agreement subsumed all institutional innovations generated in previous years, as well as the 1982 joint declaration (Paragraphs 7 and 33–39).
- A new flexibility instrument was introduced as additional reserve (Paragraph 24).
- The EP gained concessions from the Council in the area of classification (Paragraph 31 and Annex IV).
- Based on the positive experience of cooperation that the new *ad hoc* procedure had generated, conciliation was extended (Paragraph 27 and Annex III).

On the distributive dimension, negotiations faced a major problem. Although the EP had moved towards the Council's austerity approach over the years, it regarded the financial perspective that the European Council had adopted in Berlin in March 1999 as far too tight. With its narrow ceiling, the financial perspective violated an important (implicit) principle, on which the interinstitutional agreement was based: ceilings of the financial perspective would lie above the amount that the application of the maximum rate of increase would offer. In the past, this distributive advantage had been an important factor that ensured compliance with the financial perspective. The EP strongly criticised the European Council and was, at first, not willing to accept the distributive framework in exchange for an institutional concession, as it had done in 1993. Yet, internal disunity and lack of determination significantly weakened Parliament's bargaining position and made Parliament accept the tight distributive framework of the financial perspective (see Chapter 4).

The first two years of the application of the 1999 interinstitutional agreement demonstrated that tight ceilings intensified the distributive conflict. They sparked discussions, not only about breaking the interinstitutional agreements, but also over new rules that would increase the flexibility of the financial perspective (Godet 2000: 291–293). Nevertheless, the bargaining power and determination of the EP was insufficient to transform the feeling of annoyance into a focused challenge to the institutional setting.[4] Parliament accepted the new distributive and institutional framework and did not endanger the stability of the institutional path introduced in the 1988 reform.

Net-contributors

Demands for institutional change were less pronounced among the member states. The existing institutional setting largely reflected the institutional preferences and bargaining power of member states in the Council. In addition, changes in the rules would not have had immediate distributive effects, as distributive outcomes were largely determined by the negotiations over the financial perspective.

The main exception to the general consensus over the institutional setting was the interest of the new 'net-contributors club' in changing the rules that governed the revenue side (Laffan 1997: 54–60; Laffan and Shackleton 2000).[5] Germany, the Netherlands and, after 1995, Sweden and Austria voiced their interest in the introduction of a rebate mechanism that would reduce their large net-contributions to the EU budget. As Chapter 6 illustrated for the case of Germany, these demands were made forcefully, but did not seriously challenge the institutional setting. Net-contributors obeyed the existing rules and waited until the renegotiations over the financial perspective gave them the blocking power to underscore their demands. However, the Berlin summit did not result in the demanded institutional change. It had become clear that the bargaining power of the four member states and the intensity of their preferences were not strong enough to achieve a more far-reaching reform. Instead, they accepted minor on-path changes, such as the reduction of the contributions to the financing of the UK rebate for the four net-contributors and an adjustment in the balance between the different revenue sources, that secured the necessary unanimous support among member states.[6]

Interdependence

Interdependence was an important part of the stability of the institutional path initiated in the 1988 reform. The new setting made the interdependence of subfields an explicit element of its design. Changes in the subfields were institutionalised as part of regular overall reviews, which took place when the financial perspective and the interinstitutional agreement were renewed. This enforced interdependence prevented institutional change outside the reform cycle, because far-reaching changes in an individual subfield would have been regarded as disobedience with the overall framework. Such change was, therefore, only possible as part of a complete reform enacted by all three signatory institutions. The subfield of interinstitutional relations (between the EP and the Council) was a slight exception in this respect, because it saw small changes between the renegotiation points. However, it did adhere to the overall pattern: the key adaptation took place as part of the renegotiations of the financial perspective and the interinstitutional agreement.

Overall, institutionalised review at the renegotiation points made minor on-path changes a central feature of the institutional path. Institutional demands, when backed by the willingness to use blocking power, were usually accommodated. As a result, frustration over institutional demands did not build up, but was channelled towards renegotiation points. Reforms of the structural funds and the CAP, for example, were central elements of all three financial perspectives. Demands for reform were channelled towards the reform venues and resistance was (at least partly) overcome through the integration of the reform proposals into a package of various distributive and institutional changes.[7] Similarly, net-contributors restrained from openly challenging the existing institutional setting before the end of the application period of the financial perspective. They knew that an isolated change of the revenue side was impossible without opening-up the whole package.

Switching costs and opportunity costs

High switching costs contributed to the stability of the institutional path. In particular, it preserved the path's status as soft law outside the treaty. Despite pressure from the EP and the Commission to incorporate the IIA into the treaty, Council always resisted the constitutionalisation of the new path. The costs and the risk associated with treaty negotiations were regarded as too high.

In the negotiations for the Maastricht Treaty, the Commission proposed to incorporate the notion of budgetary discipline and multi-annual programming into the new treaty (EC Bull. Suppl. 2/91). It also presented detailed ideas for a reform of the budgetary procedure. Member states largely ignored these proposals, leaving the budgetary provisions of the treaty unchanged, except for an allusive remark to budgetary discipline (Isaac 1994: 29; Magiera 1995). Negotiations for Amsterdam Treaty repeated this scenario. Based on a declaration in the 1993 interinstitutional agreement that committed member states to reviewing the distinction between compulsory and non-compulsory expenditure and the system of own-resources, the Commission and the EP proposed changes in the treaty provisions (interview with Commission official). Despite support from Belgium and Spain for the treaty change, discussions among member states did not lead to a reform of the budgetary *acquis* (Brinkhorst 1997: 24; Laffan 2000b: 69). Finally, in the run-up to the negotiations for the Nice Treaty the Commission decided not to present reform proposals again. Instead, Commission officials participated in a reflection group organised by the secretariat general of the European Parliament. Some of the results of the group's deliberation were incorporated in the reform proposals presented by the Committee on Budgets in a report for the intergovernmental conference. Needless to say, the Nice Treaty did not entail changes in the budgetary provisions.

The lack of constitutionalisation of the new path illustrates the impact of switching costs and stands in contrast to the thrust of the institutionalisation literature. Obviously, much of the stability of the institutional setting relates to the bargaining power of member states that did not want a shift in the balance of power between Parliament and Council. However, Hix (2002) argues that member states generally have an interest in consenting to the incorporation of successful 'soft law' agreements. Such a constitutionalisation, so Hix's argument, has efficiency-enhancing effects and does not alter the existing power distribution, as it simply formalises existing informal arrangements. That constitutionalisation did not take place (against Hix's prediction) demonstrates that member states feared the costs and risks that the reopening of the treaty provisions would have entailed. Negotiations over the treaty provisions on the budgetary procedure could have induced a series of new institutional demands (interview with representative of national delegation). Moreover, the existing dualism of soft-law agreements and treaty provisions seemed to work well. The political nature of the agreement forced institutions to cooperate if they wanted to keep the institutional setting intact; the fallback option of the treaty served as a useful threat for ensuring compliance with the IIA (interview with Commission official). Hence, the opportunity costs resulting from a (possibly) more efficient setting were low. Furthermore, it would have been difficult to introduce the soft-law agreements into the treaty while simultaneously preserving the flexibility that the dualism entailed.[8]

Conclusion

Functional superiority

The stability of the new institutional design stemmed from a combination of a weak change coalition, the interdependence of different subfields, high switching costs against low opportunity costs and accommodating on-path changes. Conducive to the reproduction mechanisms was the functional superiority of the institutional design. Institutional preferences for change were weak and opportunity costs resulting from possible institutional alternatives low, as actors regarded the new institutional setting as an appropriate solution to the problems of budgetary politics. Financial perspective and IIA overcame the self-blocking interdependence among subfields and institutionalised on-path changes, which eased pressure for change before it grew into a potential threat for the institutional path. This meant that, although the key characteristics of the 1988 institutional path remained stable, the institutional setting experienced a high number of small adaptations.[9] The new institutional setting was set outside the treaty provisions, largely as a soft-law agreement, and not legally enforceable. This left the treaty provisions as a fallback option and made the setting dependent on the satisfaction of all participants.

At the renegotiation points, each participant was able to block renewal of the institutional setting until its demands were met. Although this veto-power was a potential threat, it also ensured that the institutional setting was regularly adapted and that pressure was eased before it grew into a threat for the whole setting. Moreover, the package character of decisions on the financial perspective and the interinstitutional agreement provided ample opportunities for settling on a compromise. The weight of the whole institutional setting lay on actors' shoulders when they renegotiated the financial perspective. As failure to settle their differences would have signalled a breakdown of the path, the functional superiority and the dependence on participant satisfaction made the institutional setting strong and fragile at the same time: strong, because it ensured actors' satisfaction; fragile, because it would break down when it failed to satisfy *all* participants.

It is difficult to assess the extent to which compliance with the institutional setting was only interest-based, as contended here, or mainly based on a norm of appropriateness, where budgetary actors did not question the existence of the path, and almost automatically renewed it (Laffan 2000b). Judging from the empirical evidence, it seems that the impact of such norm-oriented behaviour can only have been marginal, because the logic of interest produced similar behaviour. If norms had an effect on actors they only strengthened the already dominating behaviour. Moreover, the one case in which interests and norms were in conflict, i.e. the 1999 dispute over the interinstitutional agreement during the adoption process and the following budgetary procedure, when Parliament complied with the rules of the interinstitutional agreement against strong distributive incentives, the empirical evidence for norm-oriented behaviour is rather weak. Instead, empirical material demonstrates that internal disunity of the EP and pressure from the member states on MEPs led to compliance. In contradiction to a norm-based explanation, senior MEPs, such as Mr Bourlanges and Mr Colomb-I-Naval, voted against the IIA, although these MEPs should have been most vocal for compliance, as they had experienced a decade of successful interinstitutional agreements.

11 Summary of the findings and update of the theoretical explanation

Concluding Part II of the book, this chapter summarises the empirical findings of the preceding two chapters and updates the theoretical explanation introduced in Chapter 8. The key objective of Part II was to answer the following question: What determines stability and change in institutional settings in EU budgetary politics? Chapter 8 put forward the argument that a combination of reproduction mechanisms stabilises an institutional setting; major changes occur only when these reproduction mechanisms lose force (see Figure 11.1). The empirical chapters demonstrated the high explanatory value of this argument and the detailed propositions that followed from it. Stability of the pre- and post-1988 institutional settings was based on a combination of four reproduction mechanisms, namely bargaining power, interdependence of subfields, switching- (relative to opportunity-) costs and the ability to accommodate pressure for change in minor adaptations. The comparison between the final breakdown of the 1970 institutional setting and the continuous stability of the 1988 institutional setting revealed that the specific combination of reproduction mechanisms present in the 1988 setting was better equipped to sustain stability. The reliance on small changes to accommodate pressure for change and the emphasis on the overall satisfaction of participants gave this setting a 'functional superiority' over the 1970 institutional setting, the stability of which was based on containing pressure for change, rather than accommodating it. The empirical chapters also illustrated that informal change was more likely to take place than formal change because actors were unwilling to bear the high switching costs, which a formal change would have entailed, and the change coalition did not have the power to enact formal change. Thus, as much as the 1970 setting relied on bargaining power and high switching costs, the informal nature of the 1988 institutional setting facilitated the breakdown of the 1970 institutional setting.

On the basis of the empirical material presented, the assessment of the 1970 institutional setting and its possible breakdown, which Scharpf put forward shortly before the 1988 reform in his seminal article on the 'joint-decision trap' in EC (budgetary) politics, becomes strikingly accurate, if not prescient. He wrote:

> By way of summary, it is now possible to define the 'joint-decision trap' more precisely. It is an institutional arrangement whose policy outcomes have an inherent (non-accidental!) tendency to be sub-optimal – certainly when

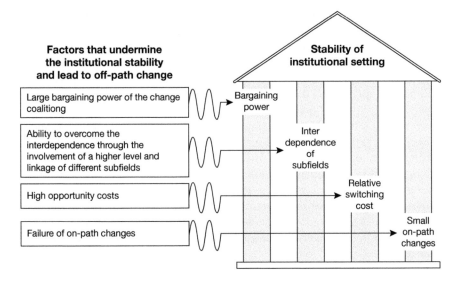

Figure 11.1 Explanation of institutional stability and change.

compared to the policy potential of unitary governments of similar size and resources. Nevertheless, the arrangement represents a 'local optimum' in the cost-benefit calculations of all participants that might have the power to change it. If that is so, there is no 'gradualist' way in which joint-decision systems might transform themselves into an institutional arrangement of greater policy potential. In order to be effective, institutional change would have to be large-scale, implying the acceptance of short-term losses for many, or all, participants. That is unlikely, but not impossible (Elster 1979). And, of course, the system might be jolted out of its present equilibrium by external intervention or by a dramatic deterioration of its performance which would undermine even its 'local optimality' for crucial participants.

(1988: 271)

Scharpf's prediction of non-gradual change neatly matches the theoretical and empirical arguments presented in this part of the book. First, the bargaining position of the 'participants that might have the power to change' was decisive for the stability, as well as the breakdown of the institutional and distributive setting of EC budgetary politics. Second, change would have been impossible unless it was 'large scale' and spanned the different subfields of budgetary politics. Third, 'external intervention' and 'dramatic deterioration of its performance' undermined stability because it made the opportunity costs of continuing with an increasingly inferior setting greater than the switching costs involved in a reform. In the case of the 1970 institutional setting, as well as the 1988 setting, the reproduction mechanisms applied as a combination and allowed change only as they lost force.

In this concluding chapter, I discuss the extent to which my rational choice explanation requires an update. My explanation is built on three assumptions: (1) a logic of expected consequences and bounded rationality; (2) material self-interest; and (3) explicit and codified institutions. From the empirical evidence presented in the two preceding chapters, I contend that these assumptions worked fairly well as proxies for actors' preferences and choices. However, the implications of these assumptions and the resulting propositions need to be clarified in three respects. First, bounded rationality means that actors make institutional choices under limited information. Over time, actors may gain new information and, consequently, revise their strategies and choices. This process can be described as learning. Second, the prominent role that the Commission president, Jacques Delors, played in facilitating the 1988 reform suggests that not only institutional structures and composite actors, but also individual politicians make a difference in certain situations. Third, the explanatory value of the propositions presented depends on a clear definition of the institutional path, even though such a clear definition is sometimes difficult to make. These three issues are discussed in further detail in the sections that follow.

Relevance of learning

The assessment of the institutional setting of the 1988 reform as functionally superior rings the alarm bells of social scientists, such as Paul Pierson, who criticise institutionalists for reverting to functional explanations whenever they face a situation of low levels of conflict and institutional stability (Pierson 2000b, 2004). This does not mean that Pierson categorically rejects the notion of functionally superior settings. Yet, he embeds it in an analytical framework that describes effective institutional designs as a special case of institutional choices. Pierson predicts that this special case is likely to occur only when actors are instrumental and farsighted. They need to have the necessary knowledge and sufficient willingness to adopt effective institutional settings. Two mechanisms that are decisive in generating knowledge and willingness are 'competition' and 'learning' (Pierson 2000b: 488). Competition turns the ability to improve institutional settings into a question of survival; successful institutional settings provide examples of effective rules that actors can copy onto their institutional setting. In politics, competition between rules is limited because institutional settings often do not have direct competitors and tasks and performance of institutions are difficult to compare. Learning is equally complicated. It is based on the notions of discourse and open access to information. Often ideas and frames are important, as they enable actors to relate different proposals to their interests and existing knowledge (see for example Hall 1991 and Garrett and Weingast 1993).

Pierson (2000b: 495) distinguishes between two phases, namely 'institutional origins' and 'institutional evolution', and specifies conditions that are favourable to functionalist explanations. In the first phase, actors must have a strong instrumental orientation and long time-horizons, and unintended consequences should be improbable. In the second phase, the environment has to promote competition or learning, revisions must be easy, and institutional development should not be heavily path-dependent.

In contrast to Pierson, this book does not seek to explain the design of the institutional settings. Although it is likely that the reproduction mechanisms of the 1988 institutional setting impacted on its actual design,[1] the explanation presented here concentrated on stability and change in institutional settings. Nevertheless, Pierson's analysis is relevant for the book, because it shows that the stability of the 1988 institutional setting resulted, in part, from actors' ability to learn from past experience. Learning affected the 'institutional origin' and the 'institutional evolution' of the 1988 institutional setting.

Institutional origin Given the high costs of continuing with an inferior institutional setting and the momentum that the single market project had initiated, actors were willing to enact a reform and followed an instrumental orientation. The most important actor in the reform discussion was the Commission, under its president Jacques Delors, who – standing above national interests – took an instrumental perspective (see next section). He presented a proposal that tried to learn from past experience, responding to failures in earlier reform attempts and copying the successful multi-annual structure of new spending programmes onto the whole budget. Delors skilfully framed his reform package so that political actors not only saw their interests served, but also felt that the budgetary reform was an automatic follow-up to the adoption of the Single European Act (Laffan 2000b: 57). The linkage with the completion of the single market in 1992 extended actors' time-horizon and made them willing to subordinate short-term interests to the long-term objective. Moreover, the relatively detailed specification of the financial perspective and the interinstitutional agreement limited the probability of unintended consequences.[2]

Institutional evolution The design of the 1988 institutional setting enabled actors to regularly adopt improvements. Although the five to seven year-cycle of the financial perspective fixed the key parameters of the institutional setting for the medium term, a complete review of the rules was institutionalised at the renegotiation points. Moreover, the setting was flexible enough to allow for the adoption of additional interinstitutional agreements between renegotiation points, e.g. the agreements on the delineation of budgetary and legislative powers. The de-politicisation of budgetary politics and the rule of experts created a climate that was more conducive to policy learning than had been the case during the 1980s.

The role of Jacques Delors

The explanation of institutional change presented here builds mainly on the analysis of composite actors and their preferences and choices. Thereby, individual politicians are seen as representatives of composite actors, implementing strategies that maximise the preferences of their organisations. In short, the institutional structures are assumed to shape the preferences of individual participants in the political process. This does not mean that actor-centred institutionalism denies the fact that, sometimes, personal capabilities and orientations of individual politicians exceed their institutionalised role and have a significant impact on bargaining processes and the outcome of negotiations.

In the case of the EU budgetary politics, Jacques Delors was a good example of an individual politician who made a difference (see on Delors' style of leadership, Drake 1995; Fligstein 1998). As the previous two chapters amply illustrated, the manner in which Delors presented his reform proposals and steered the negotiations process not only heavily influenced the design of the new institutional setting, but also facilitated the emergence of institutional change. Delors' control over the reform agenda and, most importantly, his manipulation of dimensions seems to come close to what William H. Riker identifies as 'heresthetical strategies' (Riker 1986). These strategies enabled Delors to steer budgetary actors towards the reform option. As president of the Commission, Delors greatly intensified the role that the Commission played as institutional entrepreneur. Overall, I would therefore agree with an assessment that Iain McLean makes in his analysis of the impact of individual statesmen and –women. Applying Riker's theory of manipulation to British politics McLean notes (2001: 231):

> Once in a while there comes a politician who sees further than the others. Such a politician can see opportunities where others do not, in opening up or closing down political dimensions.

The 1988 institutional setting: a completely new path?

A key building block in this explanation of institutional change was the definition of the 1988 institutional setting as a new path that broke with the main elements of the 1970 institutional setting by creating:

- A revenue system that replaced national contributions from member states with European 'own-resources' based on a fixed percentage of VAT revenue, customs duties and agriculture levies.
- A distinction between compulsory and non-compulsory expenditure, which gave each of the two arms of the budgetary exclusive authority over one of the two groups and (at least *de jure*) excluded the Commission from the second half of the budgetary procedure.
- A separation between expenditure and revenue sides, which allowed for the adoption of spending decisions regardless of revenue constrains, and denied the link between national contributions and budgetary returns.

In Chapter 8, I already conceded that distinctions between paths might be blurred for three reasons: first, a new path can be built on a set of reproduction mechanisms similar to those that stabilised the previous path; second, off-path changes can occur in a step-wise process, in which reproduction mechanisms do not break down all at once; and third, hybrid forms of institutional settings may evolve where new paths coexist with a heritage of previous institutions.

These 'blurring' factors came into full play in the case of the 1988 reform. The new institutional setting was based on the mechanisms of bargaining power, interdependence and switching costs, which had already applied in the case of the 1970 setting. Moreover, the UK rebate introduced an important element of the new path four years prior to the 1988 reform in the form of the Fontainebleau agreement. What at the time might have appeared as a drastic on-path change, turned out to be a stepping stone towards radical off-path change in 1988. Finally, the new institutional setting did not replace the 1970 budget treaty, but only corrected and supplemented it. A more encompassing path definition could therefore characterise the 1988 reform as an example of (successful) on-path change.

I reject such an encompassing path definition on methodological grounds. For the path dependence approach to have explanatory value, a restricted path definition is necessary. In the case of the 1988 reform, the new paths clearly initiated new rules, namely:

- A revenue system that was linked to GNP, which constituted a return to national contributions; and an exception for the UK, which accepted the concept of net-contributions.
- The fusion of compulsory and non-compulsory expenditure into one large multi-annual budget plan, which all three institutions adopted and jointly revised.
- Annual ceilings that limited spending decisions for all areas of spending; and decisions by spending Councils that exceed the ceilings were prohibited and only possible after the revision of a financial perspective.

The new path was not completely new. Yet, it was sufficiently novel to be characterised as new path. Moreover, its drastic effect on the level of conflict justifies the characterisation of the 1988 reform as 'off-path change'.

At the end of this chapter, it can be concluded that the rational choice explanation presented in Chapter 8 is able to account for many of the empirical developments behind the stability and change of institutional settings in EU budgetary politics. An update of the explanation is necessary only in the form of three clarifications. First, the assumption of bounded rationality entails the possibility that actors with limited information learn from past experience and update their strategies. Second, although institutional structures and composite actors are the main elements of the rational choice explanation, the personal capabilities and orientations of an individual politician make a difference in exceptional cases. Third, a clear definition of the characteristics that constitute an institutional path is essential for the analysis of path dependence, even if the particular definition may be vulnerable to criticism and rivalled by an alternative definition of a more encompassing path.

12 Conclusions

Why did the European Union experience a stark variation in the level of conflict between the late 1970s, when budgetary disputes dominated European politics, and the 1990s, when actors were able to settle upon budgetary agreements without major conflict? I argued that the problematic institutional design of the 1970 budget treaty was the primary contributing factor to high levels of conflict in the 1970s and 1980s. The treaty provisions, which gave the Community its 'own-resources' and a largely supranational budgetary procedure, were particularly problematic with respect to the exclusion of distributive and institutional interests of new member states and the EP. In addition, the scope of interpretation allowed the actors to challenge the dominant interpretation of the treaty provisions. In addressing these problems, a far-reaching reform in 1988 induced a sudden reduction in the level of conflict. It supplemented the treaty with an institutional framework for multi-annual budget plans, as well as clear rules for the budgetary procedure. The two pillars of this reform, the financial perspective and the interinstitutional agreement, were successfully renewed twice; in 1992/93 and 1999.

The book revealed that the conflict-reducing institutional reform was possible in 1988 because several mechanisms that had previously stabilised the institution had lost force. Among these factors were: (1) a reduction in the bargaining power of the coalition of member states that had enacted the 1970 treaty; (2) the rise of an entrepreneurial Commission that managed to link reform efforts in the different subfields of budgetary politics; (3) an increase in the costs of continuing with the inferior setting; and (4) the apparent inability to accommodate pressure for reform through small institutional changes. The new institutional setting has remained stable, largely satisfying the interests of participating actors and able to adapt to political and economic changes in a way that the previous institutional configuration had not.

The arguments of the book were developed from a rational choice-institutionalist approach, which assumes that actors seek to maximise their material self-interest, make rational and strategic choices and interact within a setting of codified rules. For EU budgetary politics, this approach and its assumptions proved to be of high explanatory value. In addition, however, the empirical evidence also revealed that non-codified institutions, such as norms and trust, can affect actors' behaviour, that actors' rationality is often bounded, and that, under certain circumstances, individual politicians are able to 'manipulate' actors' choices. These observations do not stand in contrast to the devised rational choice-institutionalist explanations, but they did necessitate a marginal redefinition of the original assumptions.

Complementing the detailed summaries of the findings in Chapters 7 and 11, this concluding chapter goes beyond the boundaries of my original research perspective. First, I will assess to what extent recent and current developments in EU politics, namely the negotiations on the new financial perspective and the adoption of the European Constitution, challenge my propositions on budgetary conflict and institutional change (based largely on Laffan and Lindner 2005). Second, I will link the results of the book to further aspects of institutionalist research, in particular the relevance of non-institutional factors for the level of conflict and institutional stability and the endogeneity of institutional change .

Another renewal

The financial perspective for 2007 to 2013

The negotiations of the new financial perspective take place against the background of the accession of 10 new member states and economic difficulties in many of the old member states. The EU experienced in May 2004 the most extensive enlargement in terms of territory and number of new members. Yet, in terms of economic wealth and prosperity, the new member states feature significantly below the current EU average and drastically increase the heterogeneity within the EU. The new member states have entered the EU with the expectation of gaining sizeable economic and budgetary benefits from EU membership. At the same time, most old member states, in particular the large Euro area members, Germany and France, are experiencing a period of low growth rate and strong pressures on their national budgets. Their failure, in subsequent years (2002–2004), to meet the terms of the Growth and Stability Pact, which commit members of the Euro area to compliance with the Maastricht criteria, significantly limits their willingness to accept increases of the EU budget. As predicted in the book, increased heterogeneity and economic crises create the potential for intensive conflict.

Despite the potential for intensive conflict, evidence of the current negotiations on the new financial perspective suggest that the tensions between the different distributive positions of member states do not fundamentally challenge the conflict-managing capacity of the post-1988 institutional setting even if the showdown at the failed summit in June 2005 conveyed a different image.

First, conflict is clearly challenged into the designated fora for renewing the financial perspective. Similar to previous enlargements, the new member states accepted accession treaties in 2003 that granted less than favourable budgetary conditions for their membership in the EU. None of these states received any mitigation of their budgetary contributions. Yet, the knowledge that they would be participating in the negotiations for the renewal of the financial perspective as equal partners only several months after accession prevented the occurrence of bad feelings among new member states. They knew that, in contrast to the case of the UK in the 1970s and early 1980s, they would not need to fight to establish their distributive demands on the political agenda, but they would have full veto-power to block a potentially disadvantageous agreement on a new financial perspective.[1]

Second, the existing institutional setting seems to be sufficiently robust to ensure an orderly renewal of the financial perspective. The negotiations for the new financial perspective began in early 2004 with a proposal by the Commission: 'Building our common future – policy challenges and policy means of the enlarged Union 2007–2013' (Commission 2004a). As the title of the proposal suggested, the Commission emphasised the need to give the EU the resources to match its political priorities. Rather than fighting over details of future budget allocations, the Commission sought to engage member states in a debate over the priorities of the EU.

Although the European Constitution was still negotiated when the Commission presented its proposal and many of the priorities raised in the debates over the Constitution featured in the proposal, a link between the renewal of the financial perspective and a new integration project/far-reaching treaty change did not exist. In this respect the negotiations over the new financial perspective resemble much more the ones over the Agenda 2000 than the negotiations over the Delors I or Delors II packages (with their respective links to the Single Market/Single European Act and EMU/Maastricht Treaty). At the same time, the ratification process of the Constitution might slightly complicate negotiations as the Netherlands' staunch insistence in budgetary austerity before and after the failed referendum illustrated. This had also been the case for the negotiations over the Delors II package and the ratification of the Maastricht Treaty.

The Commission proposal entailed the following features (Commission 2004a,b; see also Appendix No. 2):

- an overhaul of the expenditure headings and an emphasis on three new budgetary priorities: the Lisbon strategy, the creation of an area for freedom, security and justice, and the strengthening of the visibility of the EU's external actions;
- no significant change of agricultural expenditure based on the agreement between Heads of State or Government in 2003 which sets expenditures for market measures and direct payments until 2013, capping them at 2006 levels;
- an institutional agreement that allows for more flexibility between the different headings;
- an increase of the spending level from currently 1.0 per cent of the EU's GNI to an average spending level of 1.14 per cent over the period covered, but no change of the 'own-resources' ceiling of 1.24 per cent of GNI; and
- an adjustment to the 'own-resources' system in form of a generalised correction mechanism that would modify and extend the 'UK rebate' to other countries.

Negotiations have been conducted by successive presidencies on the basis of the Commission proposal. A number of cleavages have emerged:

Net-contributors versus net-beneficiaries In December 2003 the Heads of State or Government of Germany, France, Britain, the Netherlands, Austria and Sweden issued a joint letter to the Commission President requesting that the Union's budget should not exceed the present level of spending. Not surprisingly, these net-contributors greeted the Commission's proposal very unfavourably. By contrast, governments from beneficiary member states, such as Spain and Portugal, endorsed the Commission's proposal and stressed the importance of pursuing the objective of 'economic and social cohesion'.

Old versus new beneficiaries of regional expenditure The Commission's proposal sought to strike a balance between spending for the new member states and the interest of current net-beneficiaries of cohesion policy. Already expenditure allocated to a member states is capped at 4 per cent of GNI. Yet, current beneficiaries want to prevent an abrupt ending of transfers to their poor regions and demand compensation should their regions lose out as a result of transfers to the new member states. Germany opposes this kind of compensation, whereas Italy, Spain and Portugal insist on the need to maintain transitional support until 2014. Within Germany there are however tensions on this issue between the Berlin government and the five new *Länder*. The new member states fear that when the net-contributors insist on a zero-growth approach, these compensation payments would be financed from cuts in transfers to the east.

UK rebate versus a generalised correction mechanism The UK government strongly opposes any attempt to abolish the UK rebate through replacing it with a generalized mechanism, which is favoured by many of the other net-contributors. The pressure on the UK government is considerable because the case for maintaining the UK rebate is weak. In contrast to the situation of Fontainebleau 1984, the EU budget is no longer dominated exclusively by agricultural expenditure, and the UK has become one of the strong economies in Europe. The failure of the June 2005 summit is partly linked to this issue. The Luxembourg Presidency – in need of a political success after the failure of the referendum in France and the Netherlands – pushed too hard for an agreement and thereby pushed the UK into a corner. In such a position, the UK was neither willing nor able to agree.

New budgetary priorities versus the status quo The Commission's attempt to establish new budgetary priorities that would refocus the budget towards the provision of public goods, such as, for example, competitiveness or security, is met with scepticism among member states. Although most of them subscribe, in general, to the political objectives, member states fear that the new budgetary priorities may impinge on their core distributive demands, namely an increase in regional expenditure (for most net-beneficiaries) and a zero-growth approach (for many of the net-contributors).

The EP against the Council The EP wants to be more involved in the negotiations than in previous renewals of the financial perspective. It has established a temporary committee on the financial perspective that will present a separate proposal for a multi-annual budget plan. Thus, it seems that the EP will not simply follow the traditional pattern of negotiations whereby the EP approves the Council's financial perspective in exchange for institutional concessions for the annual budgetary procedure.

Agriculture reform against keeping the 2002 agreement Italy argues that the demands of net-contributors can only be met when the EU embarks on a substantial reform of the CAP. This issue divides net-contributors. While most net-contributors generally favour CAP reform, France has made clear that it would veto any attempts to reopen the agreement of Heads of State or Government on agricultural expenditure. New member states, in particular Poland, also have little interest in reducing farm spending.

Despite these cleavages it seems very probable that an agreement will be reached. Maruhn and Emmanouilidis (2005) predict that the outcome of the negotiations will be very much in line with previous rounds of renewals (for a similar assessment: Durand 2005). They assume that member states will adopt a new financial perspective that is of an incremental nature and that reflects the key distributive interests of the member states. The overall expenditure ceiling will probably lie between the demands of the net-contributors and the proposal of the Commission. The agreement on agriculture expenditure will not be reopened. Transfers to 'old' beneficiaries will only gradually be reduced, while the core of regional policy will, nevertheless, be oriented towards new member states. The proposed new budgetary priorities, in particular the proposed reallocation of resources towards Lisbon objectives, will not leave much of a mark of the financial perspective. On the revenue side, the UK will probably accept some minor modifications, although no significant worsening of its current level of compensation is likely to be adopted. In line with the 1988 reform, the 'own-resources' will continue to be increasingly similar to national contributions rather than true independent sources of income for the EU. Parliament will gain some distributive concessions and the Council will prevent the adoption of measure that would allow for increased flexibility between the different expenditure headings.

Overall, the negotiations for new financial perspective do confirm the propositions of the book. The financial perspective provides an institutional setting that contains conflict and ensures ordered budgetary decision-making. Moreover, the system of seven-year budget plans continues to produce a high degree of budgetary incrementalism, in which the key distributive interests of member states are respected and radical changes avoided.

Remaining on the path

The European Constitution

Although the budgetary procedure, for the first time since 1975, featured prominently in the debates over treaty reform, the final outcome of the negotiations on the European Constitution did not entail major changes. Instead the Constitution presents a budgetary procedure that remains close to the current budgetary decision-making process. In fact, the main novelties of the 'new' budgetary procedure are taken from the rules and procedures that are currently laid down in the inter-institutional agreement. In this respect, the Constitution institutionalises existing informal arrangements among budgetary actors.

Concerning the financial perspective, the Constitution makes the adoption of a multi-annual budget plan obligatory and thus, changes the way that the financial perspective is legally codified. Under the Constitution, the binding force of the financial perspective will no longer be based on the political willingness of actors to cooperate, as laid down in the interinstitutional agreement, but on the legal force of primary law. The institutionalisation of the financial perspective was regarded as the minimum reform that the drafters of the Constitution were expected to enact. Given the objectives of the constitutional process, namely to update and to streamline the treaty, the contrast between the treaty provisions and current practices was simply too pronounced in this area of the budgetary decision-making for the drafters of the Constitution to ignore. Proposals to go beyond merely institutionalising the current interinstitutional agreement, in particular the introduction of qualified majority voting (QMV) for the adoption of the multi-annual budget plan, were strongly disputed and, in the end, failed. On the revenue side, the Constitution confirmed the existing unanimity requirements.

With regard to the annual budgetary procedure, changes appear at first glance to be more far-reaching. Figure 12.1 illustrates the new budgetary procedure. The distinction between compulsory and non-compulsory expenditure is eliminated. The Council and the European Parliament meet at a Conciliation Committee to agree on a Joint Text that is then adopted by the Council and the European Parliament in separate readings. The Constitution does not specify the order of the readings after the Conciliation Committee, but, in analogy to the codecision procedure, Figure 12.1 assumes that the Council will vote first. Parliament has the right to reject the overall budget. What looks different from the current procedure is, in fact, by and large an institutionalisation of the current practice. As Chapter 10 illustrated, the interinstitutional agreement already gives the EP some say over compulsory expenditure through the *ad hoc* conciliation procedure; and the equivalent to a Conciliation Committee is already in place.

The only change in the substance of decision-making procedure, which the Constitution introduces, concerns the right of the EP and the Council to veto an agreement in the Conciliation Committee. While currently the procedure continues even if the conciliation meeting fails, the Constitution stipulates that the Commission would need to present a new proposal for a Draft Budget (DB). Granting the Council the right to withdraw its consent to the budget was introduced to keep a delicate balance of legitimacy between the powers of the EP and of the Council.

Overall, the drafters of the Constitution seem to have settled on a reform of the current budgetary procedure only to the extent that proven rules and procedures from outside the treaty are introduced into the Constitution. A change of the institutional path did not take place. This result is consistent with the propositions on institutional stability and change presented in the book. The bargaining power of the change-resistant actor coalition prevented any attempts to introduce more

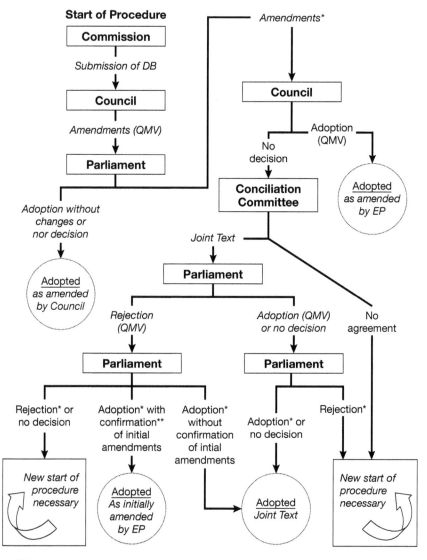

* With the majority of members
** With ³/₅th of votes and majority of members

Figure 12.1 The annual budgetary procedure in the Constitution (Article III-404).

far-reaching revisions, such as the introduction of QMV for the adoption of the financial perspective or the further extension of the budgetary powers of the EP. Moreover, switching costs for the adoption of a more far-reaching change were seen as too excessive and the opportunity costs of continuing with the current setting as negligible. The institutionalisation of the informal status quo constituted a treaty adaptation with seemingly minimal distributive effects. That it took place was mainly due to expectations from outside the budgetary realm: the drafters of the Constitution were expected – as a minimum result of their exercise – to present an updated version of the current treaty, which would bring treaty provisions in line with current practices. The current institutional setting remains on the path. The questions of whether and when the Constitution will enter into force are less of a direct relevance for EU budgetary politics.

Beyond institutions

The relevance of non-institutional factors

Although the book emphasised the role of institutions for the level of conflict, it did not advance a deterministic explanation, which denies the relevance of non-institutional factors. Chapter 2 introduced two sets of factors that did not result from the institutional setting of the budgetary procedure: first, environmental factors, such as the heterogeneity among member states and economic and agricultural crises; and second, actor-related factors, such as the difference in preferences, the intensity of preferences and the internal unity of actors. Environmental factors affect the level of conflict often through their impact on actor-related factors. For example, an economic recession increases the pressure on national finance ministers and strengthens their determination to reduce their national net-contributions to the EU budget or to defend net-benefits. This fuels budgetary disputes at the European level and complicates negotiations in the Council over the annual budget. Non-institutional factors play an important role, in particular when they take high values. In an extreme case, strong heterogeneity among member states and political dynamics at the domestic level can intensify the preferences of a national government to the extent that the level of conflict explodes, even though the institutional setting may provide tools for keeping conflict at a manageable level.

Through increasing the level of conflict, strong non-institutional factors also affect the stability of the institutional setting, because high levels of conflict have an impact on the reproduction mechanisms that Chapter 8 identified, in particular when conflict concerns not only distributive outcomes, but also the institutional setting.

• *Bargaining power of the dominant actor coalition* High preference intensity strengthens the bargaining position of the change coalition. Determined actors from the change coalition will be able to issue far-reaching and credible threats or simply disobey the existing rules.

- *Interdependence of subfields* Strong conflict among budgetary actors increases the likelihood that the European Council becomes involved and that disputes in the subfields are linked into one major round of negotiations.
- *Switching costs relative to opportunity costs* High levels of conflict boost the opportunity costs of an alternative institutional setting with less conflict.
- *Small change* Strong reform pressure makes it unlikely that small change can accommodate demands for institutional and distributive change.

The impact of high levels of conflict on the stability of the institutional setting reveals an additional link between Part I and Part II of the book. So far, I argued that because the institutional setting influences the level of conflict (Part I) and reproduction mechanisms determine the stability and change of the institutional setting (Part II), reproduction mechanisms affect *ceteris paribus* the level of conflict. Yet, as I have just demonstrated, levels of conflict also impact on the reproduction mechanisms. This establishes a feedback effect, where the level of conflict influences the stability of an institutional setting. In the extreme case, when non-institutional factors have such a strong impact that they completely marginalise the influence of institutional factors on the level of conflict, the distinction between Part I and Part II of the book becomes irrelevant. Institutions are sucked into the conflict between actors and lose their coercive force.

However, I contend that the book convincingly proves that such an extreme case is unlikely. Institutions play a strong intervening role concerning the level of conflict and the level of conflict does not directly impact on institutional stability and change. The case of the 1970 institutional setting illustrates that, even though the level of conflict was high and budgetary actors like the Parliament and the British government displayed strong determination, the institutional setting was stable for almost 15 years. Although the institutional setting had played a significant role in fuelling high levels of conflict, actors were, for a long time, unable to settle upon a new institutional setting.

Moreover, I claim that the impact of institutions on the level of conflict and on their own stability has been even stronger in the case of the 1988 institutional setting. This setting is able to remain stable against wide variation in the intensity and nature of non-institutional factors. First, the conflict-reducing effect of the 1988 institutional setting is strong. Actors that have intensive preferences have the bargaining power to block negotiations at the renegotiation point, which enables them to demand far-reaching concessions; the package deal character of the final agreement offers a variety of non-budgetary concessions that facilitate a settlement. Second, the institutional design does not determine the distributive outcomes to the same extent that the 1970 institutional design did. The renegotiation points give actors the flexibility to accommodate reform pressure through small changes in the institutional setting, in particular as all subfields of budgetary politics are up for renewal. Given the veto-power of the individual actor and the soft-law status of the institutional setting, actors have to find a compromise even if individual actors have intensive preferences.

These results on institutional stability and the impact of non-institutional factors match the latest research in rational choice institutionalism, which has just been developed in response to criticism against rational choice and which I will present in the following section.

Endogenous change

Self-reinforcement and self-destruction

It is often argued that rational choice institutionalism fails to provide convincing explanations of institutional change, because it does not sufficiently combine the focus on the development of institutions over time with a perspective on their effects. Hall and Taylor (1996: 952), for example, criticise in their seminal article rational choice institutionalism for its inadequacy 'as a framework for explaining the origins of institutions'. In their view, rational choice explanations assume that institutions are the result of discrete bargaining episodes, during which actors voluntarily and deliberately adopt a set of rules in order to achieve a set of objectives. The adopted rules constitute an equilibrium institution (Shepsle 1989). Within this framework, it is difficult, so Hall and Taylor argue, to explain why actors deviate from the equilibrium other than in reaction to exogenous shocks.

Institutionalists, such as Paul Pierson and Kathleen Thelen, make a similar argument (Pierson 2004, 2000b; Thelen 1999; Streeck and Thelen 2005). They demand that institutionalist research should take a more long-term, process-oriented perspective. Institutions are not exclusively the result of discrete bargaining episodes but also arise from non-institutional factors and a changing environment. In order to understand the timing and direction of change, research has to span an extended period of time and should combine the analysis of the effects of institutions with a focus on institutional stability. In doing so, it can detect the feedback effects that actors' behaviour within rules have on rule change.[2]

In this book, I have tried to overcome the alleged tensions between a rational choice approach and a focus on historical developments. In this respect, the book is in line with recent work of a key representative of rational choice institutionalism, the economic historian Avner Greif, who introduces, in his forthcoming book *Institutions: Theory and History* and in a recent *American Political Science Review* article with David D. Laitin, a fruitful combination between the two traditionally separated perspectives (see Greif n.d. and Greif and Laitin 2004). The result is a set of terminologies and hypotheses that neatly match the theoretical approach and empirical results presented in this book.

Greif seeks to explain why and how institutional settings influence the rate of their change. He focuses on the self-enforcing power of institutions that allows them to be stable. Specifying the temporal dimension of institutional stability, he distinguishes between those self-enforcing institutions that are, over time, also 'self-reinforcing' and those that turn out to be 'self-destructive'. In a nutshell, his argument states:

> In terms of the analytical framework, for an institution to *prevail*, it has to be *self-enforcing*, but for it to *perpetuate* over time, it has to be *(weakly) self-reinforcing*.

> A self-reinforcing institution is one whose implications increase the set of para-
> meters in which the regularity of behavior associated with it is self-enforcing.
> Conversely, an institution is self-undermining or self-destructing when its
> implications decrease the set of parameters underpinning its self-enforceability.
>
> (n.d.: VII-24, emphasis in original)

The 'parameters', he mentions, are similar to the non-institutional factors that I introduced in the previous section. They denote aspects, such as preferences, economic prosperity or number of actors. In rational choice analysis these factors are usually assumed to be stable. Yet, Greif notes that over time they can change either *endogenously* as a result of the performance of institutions or *exogenously* through external developments. The key difference between self-reinforcing and self-destructing institutions is their ability to deal with these changes. While self-reinforcing institutions widen the range of parameters that they can accommodate, self-destructing institutions become increasingly sensitive towards parameter change. Greif presumes that:

> A past institution, by reinforcing or undermining itself, can have an indirect
> influence on its rate of change by determining how large an external shock
> must be to render the behavior associated with it obsolete. But an institution
> can also influence its rate of change directly, leading to its own demise without
> exogenous change.
>
> (n.d.: VII-18)

Applying Greif's ideas to my research on budgetary politics, institutional settings of 1970 and of 1988 were both self-enforcing. They both relied on reproduction mechanisms that made them prevail over a period of time. The key difference between the two settings lies in the distinction between self-reinforcing and self-destructing. As I showed in the book, the 1970 institutional setting can be characterised as self-destructing. It led to its own demise: on the one hand, *indirectly* through its inability to deal with the strong distributive demands of new member states (i.e. the UK, Spain, and Portugal). On the other hand, it did so *directly* through inducing high levels of conflict between the institutions and accelerating the increase of agricultural expenditure (at times of decreasing revenue). Although the setting prevailed over a period of almost 15 years, it did not accommodate changes in the non-institutional factors and, thus, failed to perpetuate its existence.[3]

In contrast, the 1988 institutional setting classifies as self-reinforcing. As I have argued above, the institutional setting has been adaptive enough to apply to a variety of situations and preference intensities and to absorb changes in the environment due to its reproduction mechanisms: the unanimity rule, the package deal character and the soft-law status bestow the financial perspective with the propensity to perpetuate itself over time. Its rules have remained stable even though new member states joined the EU in 1995 and 2004 and net-contributors have repeatedly voiced strong distributive demands since the mid-1990s. Moreover, the stability of the 1988 institutional settings reveals the interesting fact that small institutional changes can prevent the (self-)destruction of an institutional setting. It is, therefore, necessary to distinguish small (on-path) changes from large (off-path) changes, as I did in Part II of the book. While the first are often conducive for stabilising an institutional setting against shifts in non-institutional factors, the latter radically alters the constitutive characteristics of an existing institutional setting and initiates a new one.

Applying Greif's framework in a forward-looking manner, one could speculate about the future development of the 1988 institutional setting. While overall I would predict that the setting will enjoy further years of institutional stability and low levels of conflict, there are two elements of the institutional setting that might, in the medium term, challenge its perpetuating nature: the unanimity rule for the adoption of financial perspective and the institutionalisation of the interinstitutional agreement through the European Constitution.

The unanimity requirement for the adoption of the financial perspective is a relevant element of the 1988 institutional setting. It ensures that the distributive interests of all member states are respected and it contributes significantly to the legitimacy of the multi-annual framework. At the same time, the unanimity rule produces budgetary incrementalism. The existing distributive order changes only gradually and far-reaching reforms are avoided. Currently, the positive effect on legitimacy seem to outweigh the loss in the efficiency and it is questionable whether, given the present state of integration, an alternative balance between supranational and intergovernmental elements of the budgetary procedure would currently be desirable (Enderlein and Lindner 2005; Enderlein *et al.* 2005).

However, indirectly and directly the unanimity requirement may threaten the stability of the institutional setting. First, the accession of further member states, such as Bulgaria, Rumania and Croatia may complicate negotiations. Even more so, the possible accession of Turkey, as a very large and relatively poor country, is likely to challenge the ability of the system to generate unanimous agreements. Second, continuous budgetary incrementalism contributes to building up a reform-backlog that might lead to a situation where the EU finds it impossible to maintain consensus for avoiding drastic changes in its expenditure policies. Realising the limits of the unanimity rule, member states may for the adoption of the financial perspective for 2014 to 2020 decide by unanimity to introduce QMV for the adoption of the financial perspective. The Constitution entails provisions for such a decision. Failing to agree on such an on-path change, the stability of the institutional setting might be threatened.

The institutionalisation of the financial perspective as an obligatory multi-annual budget framework in the European Constitution takes away the soft law status of the 1988 institutional setting. As mentioned above, actors regarded this change simply as a confirmation of the institutional status quo. However, as the book revealed, the soft law status of the financial perspective actually had a positive effective on the stability and the conflict-reducing capacity of the post-1988 institutional setting. Thus, transformation of the financial perspective into hard law and the removal of the old treaty procedure with the maximum rate of increase as a fall back option for the EP might turn out to be one of 'these marginal changes' that 'can equally be self-undermining' (Greif and Laitin 2004: 650). Although, in practice the institutionalisation does not alter the routine of adoption of financial perspectives, it may affect the actors' general attitude towards the institutional setting. While the soft law status make actors aware of the high costs and consequences of non-compliance and non-cooperation, there is the danger that cooperation and compliance will be taken for granted rather than regarded as the product of a conscious effort. The conflict-reducing capacity of the 1988 institutional setting may lose some of its grip.

Overall, budgetary conflict and institutional change will continue to maintain a dynamic relationship in EU budgetary politics. In this respect, this book is far from a plea for conflict-prevention or for institutional stasis. Conflict is positive because it prevents stagnation, stimulates interest and reveals preferences intensity. It is the function of political decision-making procedures to ensure that conflict is used productively and that it has constructive rather than destructive consequences. This means that procedures have to allow for conflict at designated fora and within accepted rules. At the same time, there are clear limits to engineering procedures. Institutions evolve over time and their stability is not necessarily a proof for the fact that they are in tune with the interests of the actors involved. This book sought to reveal generalisable mechanisms of the interaction between conflict and change that – although embedded in the empirical context of this study – will hopefully also be of use and relevance to researchers and students of other policy fields and different political systems.

Appendix No. 1

The EU budget in figures

Figures A1.1 to A1.4 illustrate key facts of the EU budget and its development over time:

- The EU budget massively increased over the last 40 years, not only in totals but also as share of the Community's GDP and as expenditure per capita.
- The EU budget (as expenditure per capita and as per cent of GDP) is still very small compared to national budgets.
- The EU is not engaged in (large scale) defence, education or classic welfare policies. 80 per cent of the budget is spent on the regional policy operations and the Common Agricultural Policy. Regional policy expenditure tripled over the last 15 years.
- The EU budget is financed mainly by a uniform percentage rate of the VAT assessment base and the 'fourth resource', which is calculated on the basis of member states' Gross National Product in market prices.
- The EU budget does not have a budget deficit.

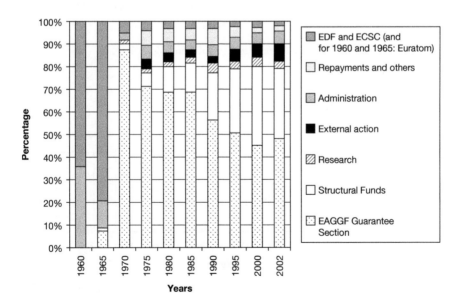

Figure A1.1 Community expenditure from 1960 to 2002 by policies.

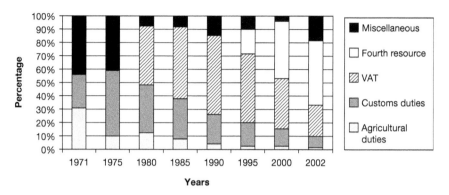

Figure A1.2 'Own-resources' by revenue sources from 1971 to 2002.

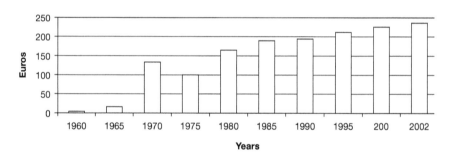

Figure A1.3 Expenditure per capita from 1960 to 2002 (in 2002 prices).

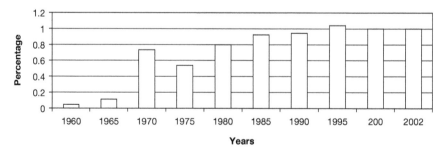

Figure A1.4 Expenditure as percentage of the Community's GDP from 1960 to 2002.
Source of all tables: European Commission (2003a).

Appendix No. 2
Financial perspectives

Parliament, Commission and Council adopt the financial perspective as part of an interinstitutional agreement, after Heads of State or Government in the European Council have settled on a financial framework.

The financial perspective distinguishes between *appropriations for commitments* and *appropriations for payments*. These two categories are linked to the differentiation between commitments and payments. Commitments are expenditure that is entered in the annual budget, but spans a period longer than the respective financial year. Commitments 'commit' the Community to expenditure in this and subsequent years. Payments are expenditure that is entered in an annual budget and that concerns only the financial year of the annual budget. This differentiation is made not for all budget lines. Appropriations for commitments are, therefore, the sum of commitments and of non-differentiated budget lines. Appropriations for payments are the sum of payments and of non-differentiated budget lines (for a more detailed analysis, see Strasser 1992: 50–52).

Table A2.1 Financial perspective 1988–1992 (in EUR million – 1988 prices)

	1988	1989	1990	1991	1992
Appropriations for commitments:					
1 EAGGF GUARANTEE SECTION	27500	27700	28400	29000	29600
2 STRUCTURAL FUNDS	7790	9200	10600	12100	13450
3 POLICIES WITH MULTIANNUAL ALLOCATIONS	1210	1650	1900	2150	2400
4 OTHER POLICIES	2103	2385	2500	2700	2800
of which: non-compulsory expenditure	1646	1801	1860	1910	1970
5 REPAYMENTS AND ADMINISTRATION	5700	4950	4500	4000	3550
of which stock disposal	1240	1400	1400	1400	1400
6 MONETARY RESERVE	1000	1000	1000	1000	1000
TOTAL of appropriations for commitments	45303	46885	48900	50950	52800
TOTAL of appropriations for payments	43779	45300	46900	48600	50100

Table A2.1 (Continued)

	1988	1989	1990	1991	1992
Appropriations for payments as % GNP	1.12	1.14	1.15	1.16	1.17
Margin	0.03	0.03	0.03	0.03	0.03
Own-resources ceiling (% of GNP)	1.15	1.17	1.18	1.19	1.20

Source: Interinstitutional Agreement (OJ L 185, 15 June 1988).

Table A2.2 Financial perspective 1992–1999 (in EUR million – 1992 prices)

	1993	1994	1995	1996	1997	1998	1999
Appropriations for commitments:							
1 COMMON AGRICULTURAL POLICY	35230	35095	35722	36364	37023	37697	38389
2 STRUCTURAL FUNDS	21277	21885	23480	24990	26526	28240	30000
3 INTERNAL POLICIES	3940	4084	4323	4520	4710	4910	5100
4 EXTERNAL ACTION	3950	4000	4280	4560	4830	5180	5600
5 ADMINISTRATIVE EXPENDITURE	3280	3380	3580	3690	3800	3850	3900
6 RESERVES	1500	1500	1100	1100	1100	1100	1100
TOTAL of appropriations for commitments	69177	69944	72485	75224	77989	80977	84089
TOTAL of appropriations for payments	65908	67036	69150	71290	74491	77249	80114
Appropriations for payments as % GNP	1.20	1.19	1.20	1.21	1.23	1.25	1.26
Margin	0.0	0.01	0.01	0.01	0.01	0.01	0.01
Own-resources ceiling (% of GNP)	1.20	1.20	1.21	1.22	1.24	1.26	1.27

Source: Interinstitutional agreement (OJ C 331, 7 December 1993).

Table A2.3 Financial perspective 2000–2006 (in EUR million – 1999 prices)

	2000	2001	2002	2003	2004	2005	2006
Appropriations for commitments:							
1 AGRICULTURE	40920	42800	43900	43770	42760	41930	41660
2 STRUCTURAL OPERATIONS	32045	31455	30865	30285	29595	29595	29170
3 INTERNAL POLICIES	5930	6040	6150	6260	6370	6480	6600
4 EXTERNAL ACTION	4550	4560	4570	4580	4590	4600	4610

Table A2.3 (Continued)

	2000	2001	2002	2003	2004	2005	2006
5 ADMINISTRATION	4560	4600	4700	4800	4900	5000	5100
6 RESERVES	900	900	650	400	400	400	400
7 PRE-ACCESSION AID	312	312	312	312	312	312	312
TOTAL appropriations for commitments	92025	93475	93955	93215	91735	91125	90660
TOTAL appropriations for payments	89600	91110	94220	94880	91910	90160	89620
Available for accession			4140	6710	8890	11440	14220
Appropriations for payments as % of GNP	1.13%	1.12%	1.18%	1.19%	1.15%	1.13%	1.13%
Margin	0.14%	0.15%	0.09%	0.08%	0.12%	0.14%	0.14%
Own-resources ceiling (% of GNP)	1.27%	1.27%	1.27%	1.27%	1.27%	1.27%	1.27%

Source: Interinstitutional Agreement (OJ C172, 18 June 1999).

Table A2.4 Commission proposal for Financial Perspective 2007 – 2013 (in EUR million)

	2006 (a)	2007	2008	2009	2010	2011	2012	2013
Appropriations for commitments:								
1 SUSTAINABLE DEVELOPMENT	47582	59680	62800	65800	682400	70660	73715	76790
1a Competitiveness for growth and employment	87910	12110	14390	16680	18970	21250	23540	25830
1b Cohesion for growth and employment (b)	38791	47570	48410	49120	49270	49410	50175	50960
2 PRESERVATION AND MANAGE-MENT OF NATURAL RESOURCES	56015	57180	57900	58120	57980	57850	57825	57810
of which: Agriculture – Market related expenditure and direct payments	43735	43500	43670	43350	43030	42710	42506	42290
3 CITIZENSHIP, FREEDOM, SECURITY AND JUSTICE	1381	1630	2015	2330	2645	2970	3295	3620

Table A2.4 (Continued)

	2006 (a)	2007	2008	2009	2010	2011	2012	2013
4 The EU as a global partner (c)	11232	11400	12180	12950	13720	14500	15115	15740
5 Administration (d)	3436	3675	3815	3950	4090	4225	4365	4500
Compensations	1.041							
Total appropriations for commitments	120690	133600	138700	143100	146700	150200	154320	158500
Total appropriations for payments (b)(c)	114740	124600	136500	127700	126000	132400	138400	143100
Appropriations for payments as a % of GNI	1.09%	1.15%	1.23%	1.12%	1.08%	1.11%	1.14%	1.15%
Margin	0.15%	0.09%	0.01%	0.12%	0.16%	0.13%	0.10%	0.09%
Own-resources ceiling (% of GNI)	1.24%	1.24%	1.24%	1.24%	1.24%	1.24%	1.24%	1.24%

(a) 2006 expenditure under the current Financial Perspective has been broken down according to the proposed new nomenclature for reference and to facilitate comparisons.

(b) Includes expenditure for the Solidarity Fund (EUR 1 billion in 2004 at current prices) as from 2006. However, corresponding payments are calculated only as from 2007.

(c) The integration of European Development Funds in the EU budget is assumed to take effect in 2008. Commitments for 2006 and 2007 are included only for comparison purposes. Payments on commitments before 2008 are not taken into account in the payment figures.

(d) Includes administrative expenditure for institutions other than the Commission, pensions and European schools. Commission administrative expenditure is integrated in the first four expenditure headings.

Source: European Commission Press Release (IP/04/189), 10 February 2004.

Appendix No. 3

Net-contributions and net-benefits of member states

Budgetary balances, i.e. the differences between payments made by a member state to the EU budget and expenditure made by the EU in that member state, are very difficult to calculate (see Deffaa 1997; Commission 1998: 66–69). Figures A3.1, A3.2 and A3.3 are each based on a different method of calculation, as data is not available for the complete period and each method. Figure A3.1 builds on the concept used by the Court of Auditors; while Figures A3.2 and A3.3 reflect the concept used by the European Commission. In Figure A3.2, the sum of all payments to the EU budget (including the corrections related to the UK rebate) is subtracted from the sum of the expenditures for agricultural, regional and internal policies ('operational expenditure'). Figure A3.3 is also based on operational expenditure but the payments from the traditional own-resources (i.e. customs and agricultural duties) are excluded. As administrative expenditure is not attributed to member states in these figures, Belgium and Luxembourg have a negative budgetary balance, although their economies benefit greatly from the EU institutions that are located on their territory.

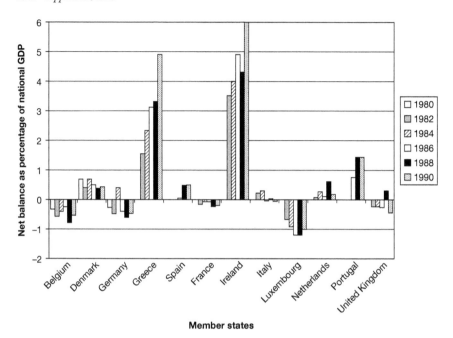

Figure A3.1: Net-contributions and net-benefits of member states (1980–1990).
Source: Tsoukalis (1993: 271) based on Court of Auditor annual reports.

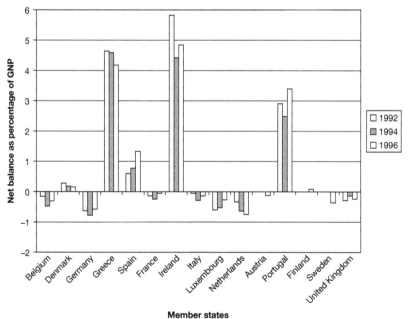

Figure A3.2: Net-contributions and net-benefits of member states (1992–1996).
Source: European Commission (1998: 114).

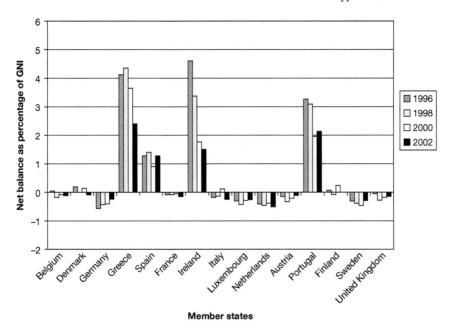

Figure A3.3: Net-contributions and net-benefits of member states (1996–2002).
Source: European Commission (2003b).

Notes

1 Introduction

1 The term 'European Community' is used in this work solely with reference to the European Union before the Maastricht Treaty. General discussions over European integration or budgetary politics at the European level will always be treated with the terms 'European Union' or 'EU budgetary politics', even if this is, strictly speaking, accurate only for the post-1994 period.

2 As from 2002, the concept of GNI has replaced the concept of gross national product (GNP) in the area of the EU budget. For the period before 2002, this book still refers to GNP.

3 The book concentrates on the process of adopting budgets and does not cover the stages of budgetary implementation and discharge. However, I include supplementary and amending budgets, which Parliament and Council adopt when major revisions of the current budget become necessary during the implementation process.

4 The EP's 'margin of manoeuvre' entitles it to add to the draft budget adopted by the Council an amount in non-compulsory expenditure equivalent to half the annual rate of increase.

5 Side-payments could also take the form of concessions in other policy areas. Yet, side-payments through the budget have an advantage, in that benefits are directly available and match the exact 'price' of the concession (for a discussion on 'issue linkages' and 'side payments' see Weber and Wiesmeth 1991; Sebenius 1983; Tollison and Willett 1979). Folkers (1994, 1998) regards the budget's role as facilitator of further integration as the key normative justification of the EU budget. He calls this the 'compensation function' of the EU budget, because the beneficiaries of further (economic!) integration compensate the losers in an extension of EU competencies.

6 A review of existing literature is included, where appropriate, in the theoretical and empirical analysis of the chapters that follow.

7 For analytical literature on budgetary processes, see: Hyde (1992); LeLoup (1988); McCaffrey (1999); Meyers (1994); Rubin (1997); and Wildavsky and Caiden (1997). For comparative analysis of the effects of different budgetary procedures see: von Hagen and Harden (1994) and Sturm (1989).

8 Although budgetary politics has a clear zero-sum character, cooperation in the budgetary procedure is often a positive-sum game, because budgetary deadlock would bring EU politics to a standstill and would, thus, endanger benefits in other policy areas.

9 For the distinction between 'soft' and 'hard' primary sources and their reliability, see Moravcsik (1998: 80-81). See Ross (1995) for an example of participatory observation in the EU context and a discussion of the advantages and disadvantages.

10 During one long-term and two short-term stays at the Commission, the EP and the Council I got first-hand insights into the work of politicians and officials in the

budgetary decision-making process. In particular, a traineeship at the Commission in autumn 2000 gave me the chance to undertake participatory observations in meetings at all levels of the budgetary decision-making process for the 2001 budget. Although I decided not to use this material directly for one of my case studies (which I selected on the basis of their relevance for the research design rather than the material available), the experience of these observations gave me an understanding of the details and the atmosphere of EU budgetary politics.

2 A rational choice-institutionalist explanation of conflict in EU budgetary politics

1 Although all these elements take effect primarily through the characteristics of the problems, they might also impact the orientation and capabilities of actors.
2 The major idea behind Figures 2.2 and 2.3 is similar for the above-mentioned reputation game. Short-term distributive effects are weighed against longer-term effects on the reputation.
3 If we assume that one actor's institutional gains are another's institutional losses, the short-term time horizon of actor B is a burden for her negotiation position in future rounds, because she made institutional concessions that limited her ability to achieve distributive benefits in the future.
4 Different modes can be combined. Institutions often entail a structural dimension that characterises the organisational environment and a procedural dimension which concerns the actual decision-making.
5 Strictly speaking, the benefits from the budget are not part of the policy environment, but a direct result of the institutional setting. Yet, it makes sense to mention the impact of net-benefits at this point.
6 In a coordination problem, a very rich actor (that will benefit heavily from the integration decision) might be willing to pay off a poor member state in order to gain benefits. Here, heterogeneity is beneficial.
7 New members not only affect the characteristic of the problem, but they also change the actor constellation, which may in turn influence the level of conflict.
8 Exception: the more regional policy becomes a prominent feature of the budget, the more the Council seeks to keep this element of non-compulsory expenditure constant.
9 This is a similar argument to Tsebelis (1995): he contends that the larger the distance of ideal points, the smaller the probability of intersecting indifference curves.
10 The maximum rate of increase of non-compulsory expenditure is a percentage of the non-compulsory expenditure of the current year that indicates the upper limit of increase of the non-compulsory expenditure of the coming year. The Commission calculates this figure on the basis of indicators that are given in the treaty. It can be modified only by a joint-agreement between the EP and the Council (see Chapter 1).
11 The pay-off for the No Budget-solution may vary between the two players. I assume here that both have the same preferences concerning the status quo. However, there might be an argument that the Council has a higher interest in overcoming the status quo because it gains directly from the money. On the other side, reputational costs of being responsible for having caused a non-agreement might affect both players equally.
12 Most obvious variant of opportunistic interpretation is based on the vague distinction between compulsory and non-compulsory expenditure. In increasing the base for the maximum rate of increase by classifying compulsory expenditure of the budget of the current financial year as non-compulsory expenditure, the EP increases the amount of non-compulsory expenditure possible for next year's budget.
13 When assessing the impact of the financial perspective, I include all elements of the 1988 reform, and its subsequent renewal, most importantly the interinstitutional agreement.

14 The Council promised the EP that it would accept any maximum rate of increase of non-compulsory expenditure that the EP demanded annually, as long as it remained within the ceilings of the categories.

15 Assuming that the EP favours a higher budget and the Council a lower budget. It is mainly the EP that feels the constraining effect of the financial perspective. However, it is also possible that the Council wants to go beyond the financial perspective in an area, like agricultural expenditure, and that the EP insists on the application of the financial perspective.

16 Great Britain introduced this system in 1999. From 1979 to 1999, it relied on a constituency-based system which made MEPs slightly more receptive to the demands of their voters.

17 Before 1979, the problem of reelection was exclusively reduced to the problem of reappointment by national parliaments. Although this entailed a clear dependence on the national party leadership, or more precisely on the parliamentary group in the national party, MEPs were less dependent on their position as MEPs because they already had a more prestigious and powerful position as members of their national parliament.

18 An additional actor in the EP is its president who, after the second reading, declares the budget as finally adopted.

19 Although absenteeism dominated in the 1980s more than today, it is still a relevant feature of the Parliament (Scully 1997).

20 Decisions to increase the own-resources have to be ratified by national parliaments.

21 Legally speaking, treaty changes are adopted by Heads of State or Government and own-resources decisions are adopted by the Council. Yet, it is the European Council which politically provides the forum for taking the political decisions on these issues.

22 Member states also differ in their institutional preferences and time horizons. Although they share a general emphasis on a strong Council, they support institutional reforms that increase their chances to gain preferred budgetary changes, e.g. Southern member states might support a stronger role of the EP because EP and Southern member states share the interest in regional policy. The time horizon determines the priority that a member state gives to its institutional preferences. Differences in time horizon can reduce unity among member states because member states may disagree over whether to prioritise distributive over institutional interests. As divergence over distributive objectives is higher than over institutional ones, unity in the Council is the highest when all member states share the same long time horizon.

23 Moravcsik (1997, 1998) sees domestic politics determining national government's preferences. In contrast to the focus on the impact of functional divisions that this chapter takes, he assumes that national governments speak with one voice and that the institutional structure of the international level does not play a significant role.

24 The correlation between proximity of elections and time horizon is mediated by (1) the salience of European politics and annual budgetary decision-making; and (2) the probability that a government will be reelected.

25 Although the Commission might, in exceptional circumstances, be able to refuse implementation and take the EP or Council to Court, such an act would need to be warranted by an actual breach of the EU law.

26 Given the complicated appointment procedure that, over the last decade, strengthened the involvement of the EP, conflict-reduction seems to be a dominant strategy for a Commissioner that wants to be appointed.

3 Obstructing decision-making

1 The figure builds on four indicators: actors' inability to abide by the budgetary timetable as laid down in the treaty (including the enactment of the one-twelfth rule), actions taken before the European Court of Justice (against the EP, Commission, or

Council), rejection of the general budget or a supplementary and amending budget by the EP, and member states' refusal to pay their share of the enacted budget.

2 Strictly speaking, the refusal to pay took place in 1979. Yet, it relates to failure to enact an uncontested budget in 1978 and is therefore counted to 1978. A similar counting system is applied in the following figures on conflict in the annual procedure.

3 Bieber (1982) regards the attitude of the Council as embedded in (and to some extent sparked by) the institutional legacy of the Community. The treaties of Rome did not make any specific references to the expenditure side. Instead, they assumed that the budget would simply result from the legislative decisions of the different spending Councils. At the same time, they introduce a 'balance budget rule' an upper limit to expenditure (Ackrill 2000). The reason for these provisions was the reluctance of the founding fathers to mention explicitly distributive objectives of European integration. They feared that this would have endangered the ratification of the treaties.

4 The role that the European Council played in annual decision-making was quite ambivalent. Officially it stood outside the procedure. Yet, unofficially it was a frequent reference point for the Budget Council and the Parliament. The Budget Council followed the European Council when Heads of State or Government made specific financial decisions concerning the budget. At the same time, when the European Council adopted general declarations that were in line with the EP's interests in deepening integration, the Budget Council ignored them ('cheap talk' Cram 1997). Parliament had a similarly dialectic attitude towards the European Council. Although it used the declarations of the European Council as a reference point, it rejected the interference of the European Council when it came to concrete financial decisions, as for example the setting of annual amounts for the regional fund in the 1978 budget.

5 I use the term 'legalising' in this context to illustrate that the Council accepted the distributive side of the Parliament's opportunistic interpretation. The Council nevertheless kept its position on the institutional question of classification. This meant that the Council increased the maximum rate of increase, which following the Parliament's interpretation would not have been necessary.

6 The impression of the insufficiency of the new institutional setting was so widespread that even the Council was tempted to give it official recognition. In its resolution for the 1976 budget, the EP demanded a change in the treaty, arguing the treaty had proven unsuccessful. The Italian Council President-in-Office acknowledged that the present budgetary procedure was complicated and unclear and did not rule out improvements for the future (EC Bull. 12–75: 81).

7 The year 1978 was also the first time that Parliament and Council applied the 1975 treaty for a full budgetary cycle. Accounts of the budgetary procedure for the 1979 budget can be found in Strasser (1979); Sopwith (1980: 335–340); Bywater (1980); and Isaac (1980: 325–334).

8 The novel character of the crisis made participants believe that the intensive institutional conflict over the 1979 budget had marked a unique 'historical' moment. Budget Commissar Tugendhat stated in the final debate on 24 April 1979: 'This has been a historic budget procedure, this has been a budget procedure which the constitutional historians and the lawyers will be writing about for a long time' (p. 36). He did not know that the 'fame' of the procedure would not last long, because budgetary crises were to become the norm in the coming years.

9 It confirmed the annual figures agreed by the European Council for a period of three years in 1977.

10 The French governments strongly criticised this attitude. In a press release, the French 'Conseil des ministres' commented on the second reading: 'Au cours des cette session, la France s'est opposée à ce que certains Etats membres contraignent le Conseil à entériner des propositions de l'Assemblée européenne qui sortent des limites que les traités communautaires lui imposent' (quoted in Strasser 1979: 246).

11 Debate on 12 December 1978 p.36.

12 Although the EP was certain that its position was legally justified, the remarks by Mr Dankert, first speaker for the socialist group in the budget debate and later president of the Parliament, disclosed an interesting dialectic in the EP's position. Addressing the Commission, which supported the Council's interpretation, he said: 'I am not concerned with juridical interpretation: a juridical interpretation often follows political reasoning. One interpretation is contained in the political argument put forward by Mr Bangemann and the other in the political arguments of the Council. The Commission's political argument seems to follow those of the Council very closely. Perhaps the lawyers will later decide that one interpretation is best, but it seems to us that the Treaty offers sufficient latitude for an interpretation which enables the Commission to support the Parliament in its struggle over the Regional Fund.' (Debate on 12 December 1978, p. 43).

13 The British conservative, Mr Rippon, told colleagues in his speech shortly before the vote: 'I would therefore put it to those who think as I do that we should accept the budget as it has been in effect accepted by the Council, thereby avoiding a conflict. In that case, I would want to continue to vote against these amendments, even though they involve no additional expenditure' (Debate on 14 December 1979, p. 195). Some of the socialists also voted against the amendments.

14 The UK's support of France's and Denmark's refusal to comply with the budget as adopted by the EP may appear paradoxical given that it was the UK that had prevented the Council from rejecting the increase of the Regional Fund. However, this move results from a Labour government policy manoeuvre: after the British government had defended its distributive interests in the vote on the Regional Fund, it was then, at the beginning of 1979, under pressure from the Labour left, which insisted that the powers of the EP should be strictly curbed. So, with national and European elections that year, the government abruptly shifted its ground and joined France and Denmark (*Financial Times*: 6 February 1979).

15 In this arrangement, the member states *de facto* agreed that the Council would only approve of amendments that would exceed the maximum rate if a majority voted explicitly in favour of an increase of maximum rate. (EC. Bull. 3–1979: 87–88). Only the Dutch delegation did not sign this internal agreement because the Dutch Parliament had joined the EP in its condemnation of a unilateral interpretation of the treaty by the Council (Strasser 1979: 250, Fn 42; also see Chapter 9 of this book).

16 Although in the above-mentioned case of the 1979 budget the EP had to decide between short-term or long-term gains and opted for long-term, institutional gains.

17 Läufer (1990b: 129/130) makes a similar point. He argues that conciliation meetings did not have a significant effect during that time because the conciliation before the second reading in the Council was often too late.

18 The chairman of the Committee on Budgets, Mr Lange, and others senior members of the Committee, such as Mr Notenboom, Mr Dankert and Mr Bangemann, continued as MEPs.

19 Many of them were members of the Committee on Agriculture, came from the groups of French and the Irish (partly also Danish) MEPs or were members of the liberals and the European People Party. As Thöne (1982: 192) reveals, most members of the Committee on Agriculture had strong personal links to the farming community. Overall, the strength of the agricultural lobby within Parliament was not surprising. Given the enormous importance of the European agricultural expenditure for the farming Community, farming association had a very strong interest to influence the selection of candidates for the European Parliament.

20 The blocking minority lay at 19 votes. In total, Italy (10), Greece (5), and Ireland (3), weighed in with 18 votes (Strasser 1982: 315).

21 The opportunistic interpretation was (as in the case of the 1983 budget) motivated by institutional, as well as distributive objectives - the EP wanted to participate in the negotiations on the intergovernmental level.

22 The case study is based on the Läufer 1983, 1990b: 132–142; Läufer and Siebert 1988: 164–206; Strasser 1982; EC-Bulletins: in the EP Parliament and documents from the archives of the Council and the EP.

23 The Council was not fully united on the question of how to react (Strasser 1982: 340/341). Finally, the Belgian Presidency brokered a compromise among the majority of member states. Yet, two delegations, presumably Greece, Ireland or Italy, rejected the declaration and, out of distributive interests, stood by the EP's interpretation.

24 This is also relevant for an explanation of the relatively peaceful 1983 budget procedure. Much of the conflict potential focused on the rejection of the supplementary budget No. 1/1982 and was therefore exhausted.

25 Concerning the distributive importance, Fugmann (1992: 401) shows that the average increase that the EP adopted in the second reading in comparison to the result of the second reading in the Council (between 1980 and 1983) was around half a per cent of the overall budget.

26 Only 69 of the 410 MEPs had already been members of the old Parliament (Pöhle 1982: 181).

27 Table 3.9 does not include the 1988 budget, because this budget was adopted within the framework of the financial perspective in spring 1988.

28 The representative of the Spanish delegation mentioned in the interview that Portugal also supported the bloc frequently (yet not always, as the Portuguese government wanted to underscore its independence from the voting behaviour of its large neighbour) and that the Netherlands joined from 1987 the anti-CAP coalition. Moreover, he said that Italy was largely 'out of the picture'. Due to internal coordination problems between the Italian finance minister and his delegation, Italy often did not have a clear position and was a relatively ineffective blocking partner.

29 The following case study is based on Läufer 1987; Wallace 1987; Nicoll 1988a; Cova 1986a,b; Corbett *et al.* 2003a,b; debates in the European Parliament; EC-Bulletins and documents from the Secretariat General of the Council.

30 Since the Iberian accession on 1 January 1986, 23 votes constituted a blocking minority.

31 It only just stayed within the maximum rate in the case of the commitments (8.09 per cent), with a slightly more comfortable margin for payments (7.37 per cent).

32 See the dialectic reasoning in the Resolution (Doc A2–190/86, Article 10): The EP 'regards that its amendments are being within the maximum rate but notes that there is disagreement between the two arms of the budgetary authority on this question; invites, therefore, the Council to agree on the basis of its view on classification, to the increase in the maximum rate of increase'.

33 For the payment appropriations the compromise remained and went directly up to the maximum rate - the Council offered the EP the full amount it wanted - inscribed as 'negative reserve'. Only Britain voted against the compromise arguing that budgetary discipline had been breached (see also Agence Europe 14 Feb 1987 No. 4489: 5).

4 Facilitating decision-making

1 The 1991 budget is another outlier, albeit at a much lower scale, as I will show below. Unfortunately, the rough indicators of Figure 4.1 do not reveal the differences between these two outliers.

2 The situation was peculiar: as a new interinstitutional agreement had not yet been adopted, the ceilings of the financial perspective did not bind the EP. The revision was part of the concessions that Council granted the EP in the negotiations for the interinstitutional agreement (which were completed in October 1993).

3 An exception to this was the Italian government during the adoption of the own-resources decision in 1988 and 1995. Both times, the Italian government tried to gain concessions after the European Council had already adopted the financial perspective (interview with a representative of a national delegation).

4 In contrast to legislative committees, the Budget Committee had a particular autonomy because it depended to a much lesser extent on the assistance of the Council's legal service (interview with official from the secretariat general of the Council).

5 A former representative of a national delegation said that, between 1988 and 1996, readings in the Council never lasted longer than two hours.

6 The exception was a dispute in the procedure for the 1989 budget over the distinction between privileged non-compulsory and non-privileged non-compulsory expenditure. The Council argued that only the former would be exempted from the application of the maximum rate of increase (see Chapter 10). The EP rejected the distinction. In the end, the Council accepted that the interinstitutional agreement did not leave scope of interpretation on this issue and that the ceilings had *de facto* replaced the maximum rate of increase (Nicoll and Lentz 1989; Läufer 1989; Verschraegen 1989).

7 However, the EP did not fully give in. It adopted a budget for 1992 that did not include the aid to the Soviet Union. This strategy paid off and the Council agreed to a revision in spring 1992. Yet, this revision was financed through redeployments of savings from other headings and did not increase the overall ceiling of the financial perspective.

8 The following case study is mainly based on Fernandez-Fabregas and Lentz (1995), Deffaa and Zangl (1995), monthly EU-Bulletins, internal papers of the secretariat general of the EP, a EP report on the procedure for the 1995 budget (European Parliament 1995), debates in Parliament, and interviews with practitioners (i.e. officials from the secretariat general of the EP, the rapporteur, the chairman of the Committee on Budgets and Commission officials).

9 The 1993 financial perspective entailed an increase in the own-resources ceiling from 1.20 per cent to 1.21 per cent. In 1994, the Council still had not adopted the necessary decision to put the increase into practice. The reason for the delay was the veto of the Italian government, which tried to gain concessions on the unrelated issue of milk quotas (see for the argument put forward by government in justification of its veto: Agence Europe 9 September 1994, No. 6311: 1). Once adopted, the decision of the Council had to be ratified by national parliaments.

10 Issues of classification had gained specific importance as budget experts prepared themselves for the intergovernmental conference, which was due to start in early 1996. They hoped that they might get the issue of institutional reform of the budgetary procedure on the agenda.

11 In this new procedure, the EP and the Council would discuss the structure and classification of compulsory expenditure shortly before the first reading in the Council.

12 The theoretical centrepiece of the 'institutional attack' was the argument that the compulsory nature of an item would not derive from the item itself, but from the implicit character of the legislation. The classification of compulsory would be restricted to those items relating to legislation that imposes an obligation vis-à-vis third parties without any margin of discretion being left during implementation (European Parliament 1995: 2).

13 In an unusual step, the Committee on Budgets made Mr Wynn rapporteur for the 1995 budget, although he had already been rapporteur for the general budget in the previous year. Therefore, he was ideally equipped to pursue the institutional attack after having had the experience of first attempts in the budgetary procedure of the previous year.

14 This was relevant because it touched on the question whether the Council would give its consent to a rise in the maximum rate of increase. Although the Council had *de facto* always accepted the new maximum rate of increase when below the ceiling of the financial perspective, it still held to the legal position that, in accordance with the treaty, a new maximum rate had to be set for the increase of non-compulsory expenditure. As this required that EP and Council agree on the exact scope of the expenditure classified as non-compulsory expenditure, the Council's consent was - in the particular case of the 1995 budget – much in doubt.

15 Mr Wynn asked the president-in-office (EP debate 13.12.1994: 23): 'The question I

need put to Mr Haller is: if the Council agrees, is it saying that when the President of Parliament signs the budget on Thursday, that it will be illegal? If Mr Haller does not wish to make a statement on that, I would like to ask him this: if the Council stays silent on that question, will it challenge this budget in the Court of Justice?' and president Haller answered: 'Madam President, the Council will of course undertake the necessary examination. That is all I can say.'

16 The French government saw its vested agricultural interests in danger and was, anyway, one of the member states least sympathetic to expansions of Parliamentary rights.

17 The following case study is based on Deffaa (2000), monthly EU-Bulletins, internal papers of the secretariat general of the EP and the Commission, debates in Parliament, and extensive interviews with officials and politicians.

18 In contrast to the German SPE's support, the German EPP members rejected the financial perspective and were eager to show that the German red-green government had failed to achieve a good result for Germany. This was also the case for some other EPP members with left-wing governments.

19 It is unclear the extent to which rejection remains as an option within the institutional setting of the financial perspective. Although legally still an option, it would probably be regarded as a breach of the interinstitutional agreement.

5 Blocking intergovernmental relations

1 See overview of all presidency conclusions in Centre Universitaire d'Enseignement du Journalisme (2002).

2 This high degree of institutionalisation reflects the state of European integration. Member states fear the impact of supranational budgetary decisions on their national budgets. As the power to tax is regarded as an important aspect of national sovereignty, member states codify the details of the Community's 'own-resources' in a quasi-treaty document.

3 In the intergovernmental realm, the 'implementing' and 'enacting coalitions' of the institutional setting are identical. Thus, the step from distributive to institutional decisions is a small one.

4 John Lambert in *The Sunday Times*, 27 January 1973 (quoted in George 1998: 68).

5 Later an agreement was reached and the British government was able to follow this up securing the assignment of regional policy to one of the two British consumers (Denman 1996: 244).

6 Wilson called a general election in October 1974, which brought a majority for his government in Parliament.

7 The then Under Secretary in the Foreign Office who was in charge of the Community, Michael Butler (1986: 93), explains in his autobiography: 'I toured the Community capitals in April 1974 with Alan Bailey of the Treasury to prepare the negotiations and was told everywhere that nothing could be done about the expenditure side; that we should have to rely on Community policies being created in new areas and expenditure going to the UK. There was just a hint that something might temporarily be done about our above-average gross contribution. And so we went for a correction on the gross contribution side.'

8 Given the strong resistance against the concept of net-contributions, it is surprising that the financial mechanism also entailed a link to the net flow of Community budget cash between member states. It limited the payments under the mechanism to an amount not exceeding cash transfers from EC budget to the member state in question (Emerson and Scott 1977: 222).

9 A key problem seems to have been the North Sea oil, which changed the British balance of payments between exports and imports. The correction mechanism had stated that eligible member states had to have a negative balance of payments.

10 The 1979 agricultural prices were decided after British and Italian general elections. The new British minister accepted a flat rate increase (Neville-Rolfe 1984: 291).

11 When Prime Minister Callaghan discussed the results of the Paris summit in March 1979, the then Leader of the Opposition, Margaret Thatcher, criticised the Prime Minister's strategy at the European summit. She asked the Prime Minister: 'Does he agree that it would be more to Britain's advantage if he and his colleagues dropped their abrasive and critical attitude towards our Common Market partners and behaved genuinely as partners, in which case we might get some of the problems solved? (. . .) Would it not be better if, instead of that criticism, he were more cooperative?' (Thatcher database 79_076). In retrospect, this statement seems almost grotesque.

12 Other pillars of Thatcher's strategy were the withholding of British payments into the EC budget, which Thatcher put forward as possible, although legally, problematic option (Thatcher 1993: 79; Howe 1994: 182) and the 'disruption' of European Council meetings by continuously raising the issue of net-contribution. The exit option did not exist, as Mrs Thatcher had ruled this out (Werts 1992: 231).

13 These were unanimous decisions, which meant further blocking power for Britain.

14 When the Foreign Secretary presented the May Mandate to the Prime Minister, she was initially reluctant to accept it (Howe 1994: 182; Thatcher 1993: 86). Yet, she understood that it was the best result that Britain could achieve at that time. Moreover, the Europeanists within the UK government had pushed for an agreement. They hoped that the newly adopted CAP guidelines would help to contain agricultural expenditure and that Germany would support the UK's plea for budgetary discipline.

15 When the British refused to agree to higher target prices for food, 100,000 angry farmers moved into Paris on 23 March 1982 and mounted the biggest demonstration seen in that city since May 1968 (Taylor 1983: 398).

16 *The Guardian* on 26 May 1982 spoke of a 'dim deal', which was not much different to the one offered two weeks previously, which the government had vetoed.

17 Werts (1992: 276, Fn 2447) quotes a British official, who explained that, because the Community had no money left, 'we are all together in one room and the only way out is through a door to which we have the key'. His reference is *Agence Europe* 29 March 1984: 1.

18 For the first time, Mrs Thatcher encountered an important negative side effect of her confrontational strategy against the EC. The issue began slowly to divide the Conservative Party. In the mid-1980s the divide was still marginal, in particular as anti- and pro-European Tories supported the single market project due to its free trade purposes (the anti-protectionism dimension dominated the national sovereignty dimension of European integration). Once the single market was adopted, the divide became fully apparent and split the Conservative Party (McLean 2001: 226).

19 In March 1984 Ministers of Agriculture had reached a provisional agreement on limiting milk production and on reducing the level of the monetary compensation amounts. They also adopted a small overall reduction in farm prices and cuts in diary quotas. This allowed the British government to maintain that it had not agreed to an increase of the own-resources without some indication that the Community was in earnest about reining in CAP expenditure (George 1998: 157).

20 Yet, it was clear that the financial dimension of this concession was limited by the increasing relevance of VAT share of the Community's own-resources.

21 As Taylor (1983: 401) argued: 'the value of Britain's net-contribution is around 3.5 per cent of the total value of the British budget in the early 1980s. (. . .) In other words, the sums involved, though not negligible, are fairly minor in proportion to other items of expenditure in Britain, and in comparison with the total budget in Britain.'

6 Accepting intergovernmental burden sharing

1 The veto-power is strongest when the new financial perspective entails an increase of revenue because such an increase can only take place after a unanimous decision in the Council. When the revenue ceiling remains unchanged, a member state still has a veto-power over the financial perspective. Yet, the other member states can go ahead with the annual budgetary procedure out-voting the vetoing member state. Thus, decisions on the financial perspective take place in the 'shadow of majority voting' (Scharpf 1997), when no increase in the revenue ceiling is involved.

2 In the 1980s, member states partially recognised Germany's large financial burden. They limited Germany's share of the costs of the UK rebate (Wagner 2001: 215; Strasser 1992: 369).

3 Unification had induced a bubble of economic growth in the old Länder and increased the imports. This accelerated the GNP- and tariff-based own-resources payments to the EU budgets in the early 1990s (Bundesbank 1993).

4 The *Financial Times* (5 December 1991) wrote: 'Mr Kohl must know that Spain has a good case, just as he knows that the German piggy bank has been emptied by eastern Germany. But since he is himself the main source of the treaty on political union, Mr Kohl is hoist by his own petard.'

5 The link to the Maastricht Treaty was made explicit in the title of the proposal: 'From the Single Act to Maastricht and Beyond: The Means to Match Ambitions' (Com(92) 2000; Supplement 1/1992 - EC Bull.).

6 The German finance minister, Theo Waigel, demanded that the efforts of consolidating national budgets, which net-contributors pursued in their drive to fulfil the convergence criteria for EMU, was to be taken into account. Given the burden from German unification and the aid to Eastern Europe it was not acceptable, said Mr Waigel, that German contributions, as had been proposed by the Commission, would increase by 5 billion ECU within the following five years (Wolf 1992: 315).

7 Despite resistance in the national parliament and strong distributive demands, Britain used ratification less strategically (than Spain) as it held the presidency at the second half of 1992 and was therefore interested in a successful conclusion of the negotiations.

8 Jacques Delors reminded Germany of this promise when he emphasised in an interview with a German newspaper, that Germany did not bear the costs of unification alone, but that other member states indirectly carried much of the burden (*Süddeutsche Zeitung* 10 December 1992).

9 At the Edinburgh summit, Heads of State or Government had agreed on an increase of own-resources for the years after 1995. After the Council had transformed this agreement into legislation, national parliaments had to ratify the decision. The Bundestag supported the increase with a large majority.

10 Although the opposition endorsed the government's stance on the German problem, it claimed that senior members of the parties in government, in particular the Bavarian Prime Minister Edmund Stoiber, had stirred populism against net-contributions. This despite the fact that their own government was responsible for the situation (see the speech of Mr von Larcher, MP; *Deutscher Bundestag* 16 February 1995: 1421–1422).

11 As Chapter 4 illustrated, this strategy was a success; the rate of increase of annual budgets decreased significantly from 1995.

12 Wagner (2001: 211, Fn 24 and 220) notes that from an economic self-interest point of view, the political activities of the Länder on the issue did not make much sense, as they were not directly affected in their share of the national tax revenue by German contributions to the EU budget. Such an analysis ignores two important factors. First, large contributions to the EU from the national purse crowded out other federal expenditure that benefited the Länder directly, such as investment programme or active labour market policies. Second, members of the Länder governments had political ambitions on the national level. Not only did the Länder governments constantly try to

make sure that the Länder would be recognised as a key factor in Germany's approach towards EU, but the prime ministers of Bavaria and Lower-Saxony, Edmund Stoiber and Gerhard Schröder, also sought to enhance their national profiles by criticising Chancellor Kohl for not sufficiently defending the national interest.

13 A report of the EP secretariat general presents a detailed analysis of both models (*European Parliament* 1998).

14 This 'schizophrenia' of defending the CAP and pressing for budget discipline had always been part of the Germany's stance on budgetary questions. So far, it had not been this prominent or pressing because of the institutional separation between budgetary and agricultural negotiations. Repeatedly in the 1990s, the German agricultural minister had demanded increases in agricultural spending, in particular when German farmers had been hard hit by currency fluctuations while the finance minister preached budgetary discipline.

15 Newspapers started to characterise the new approach of the German government as increasingly 'British' (e.g. *The Economist* 9 August 1997; *Frankfurter Allgemeine Zeitung* 30 October 1997).

16 Schröder invigorated this image in government (see Schröder's speech at the SPD convention in Saarbrücken on 8 December and his speech in the Bundestag on 12 December 1998, mentioned in Wagner 2001: Fn 41).

17 Summits, other than the Berlin summit, were meetings of the G8 and the European Council which both took place in June 1999 in Cologne.

18 In contrast to other policy issues, interest groups do not much influence government's stance on the problem of net-contribution. As the costs of budgetary contribution are spread among taxpayers, there are no private actors and interest groups that are mobilised around the issue.

19 Arguing from the school of neo-realism in international relations (against its neo-liberal contender), Wagner (2001) discusses the extent to which Germany's demands for a reduction in its net-contributions was either motivated by domestic interests and the emergence of the German problem (neo-liberal argument), or by a reaction to the increased political weight and power that Germany gained after the unification (neo-realist argument). He argues that, after the Delors II package, sealed by German politicians in the mindset of the unification process, the unified Germany wanted to liberate itself from the burden of its post-war concessions and flexed its muscles over net-contributions. Wagner (2001) is right in contending that the German government made its case forcefully and with self-confidence. During the negotiations in 1998/99, it deliberately breached the implicit consensus among member states that a rebate mechanism should be extended, and angered its traditional ally France. Yet, the behaviour of German politicians reflected the politicisation of the issue in the domestic arena and the increase in power did not alter Germany's willingness to shoulder the largest burden. Overall, Wagner fails to make a convincing case that interest in power, rather than domestic gains, motivated German politicians. In the end, he himself concedes that 'the available evidence does not allow discrimination between power politics and gain-seeking policy' (Wagner 2001: 223).

20 In the time between renegotiation points, the German government could concentrate on building a coalition for an approach of budgetary discipline in the annual budgetary procedures. It was successful in reducing annual budget well below the ceiling of the financial perspectives (see Chapter 4).

21 This incrementalism induced, as a negative side-effect, political and economic costs of postponing or diluting necessary reforms, such as the reform of the CAP and preparations for the accession of new member states.

22 It seems likely that the membership in the enacting coalition of the financial perspective carried a normative obligation for Germany to comply with the distributive and institutional framework - similar to the normative justification that Britain found in the exclusion from the enactment of the 1970 treaty for its conflict strategy.

23 The 1988 and the 1999 financial perspectives were adopted under German presidency, while the 1992 financial perspective was accepted under the British. When planning the negotiations for a new financial perspective (at the Cardiff summit in 1998) governments agreed on the German presidency and did not want to leave the conclusion to the Finish, which succeeded the German presidency in 1999.

24 This was the case, in the Maastricht Treaty and the Amsterdam Treaty, where the Dutch held the presidency at the decisive meetings, as well as the European Constitution that was adopted under Irish Presidency. It stands in contrast to the Nice Treaty under the problematic French presidency and the failure of the Italian Presidency to conclude the negotiations on the European Constitution.

7 Summary of the findings and update of the theoretical explanation

1 Non-institutional factors, such as heterogeneity among member states, the occurrence of economic crises (including the developments on the agricultural markets) and the intensity of preferences also influenced the potential of conflict.

2 It soon became obvious that the rationale behind the distinction between compulsory and non-compulsory expenditure was nothing more than an attempt by member states to contain parliamentary powers.

3 In a vote on the budget treaty, the EP accepted the proposed budgetary procedure because it knew that the alternative to the budgetary powers on offer was 'no budgetary powers'.

4 Richardson and Jordan's account on 'negotiated order' is inspired by Heclo and Wildavsky's study of the spending community in Whitehall (Heclo and Wildavsky 1974).

8 A rational choice-institutionalist explanation of institutional change in EU budgetary politics

1 A shorter version of this part of the book was published as Lindner (2003).

2 Institutions are sets of rules. They can be characterised along the three dimensions (Abbott *et al.* 2000; Stone Sweet *et al.* 2001): (1) *obligation* refers to the degree that actors are legally bound by the rules; (2) *precision* indicates the extent that the rules are unambiguously defined; and (3) *delegation* denotes the involvement and authority of a third party in the process of application and interpretation of the rules.

3 I do not discuss disobedience here. Yet, disobedience works similar to unilateral interpretation. It is an attempt to undermine a rule with the possible effect that a rule that is generally not complied with, will lose force.

4 Alternatively, they might lobby the group of actors, which enacted the original set of rules, to adopt formal change.

5 The term 'formal change' does not mean that other changes cannot be formalised and legally codified. It is called formal change because it alters the existing high level of formalised and binding rules, mentioned above.

6 Problems do not only arise at the decision-making level but also on the cognitive level ('bounded rationality'). The complexity of politics and the short-term orientation of politicians set hurdles for learning. Major reforms only play out in the long run and are therefore less attractive for politicians that seek to present immediate successes to their voters. This is also the case when institutional choices entail significant uncertainties. Risk averse political actors may prefer a predictable status quo to an institutional reform with uncertain consequences (Genschel 1997).

7 With the here presented distinction of necessary and sufficient condition, I go further than True *et al.* (1999). They stress the sequential nature of the adoption of policy issues by the higher-level authority, which could be seen as standing in contrast to my interpretation.

8 Knight (1992, 1995) also mentions this form of change. The dominant actor constellation has an interest in the change because the distributive implication of the existing institutional setting have changed and no longer reflect the dominant actor's bargaining power.

9 Some reproduction mechanisms are more prone to incremental change, such as mechanism of large switching costs, than others where pressure builds up and gets discharged in off-path change, e.g. mechanism of institutional interdependence. Abrupt radical changes are often associated with a dynamic of acceleration (like positive feedbacks in punctuated equilibria): once a change is initiated, a momentum is triggered that extends change beyond the boundaries that might have been expected.

9 Resisting reform

1 The 1975 budget treaty altered the 1970 treaty. The changes concerning the decision-making procedure were not far-reaching (Strasser 1992: 32–34; Rossi 1997: 28). It was introduced because member states had committed themselves in 1970 to a review of the treaty two years after its ratification.

2 The joint declaration on the conciliation procedure from 1975 was an exception. The Council had been willing to fix a code of conduct for parliamentary consultation in cases of legislative acts with financial implications.

3 Lawyers had strongly argued for interinstitutional agreements between the EP and the Council as a successful strategy to resolve conflict over the interpretation of the treaty (Bieber 1981, 1984).

4 Participants in the negotiations were: the Belgian foreign minister, Leo Tindemans, and members of the Council secretariat general (for the Council); the EP president, Piet Dankert, the chairman of the Budgets Committee, Erwin Lange, and members of the EP secretariat general (for the EP); and the president Gaston Thorn and Budget Commissioner Christopher Tugendhat (for the Commission).

5 Shortly after the signing of the joint decision, Dewost and Lepoivre (1982) emphasised that the willingness of institutions to make the new joint decision work would be essential for its success.

6 An internal agreement that the Council adopted in reaction to the institutional dispute with the EP over the 1979 budget was an initial step toward rules on budgetary discipline. It concerned only non-compulsory expenditure, because the bargaining power of the member states favouring increases in non-compulsory spending was relatively small and the conflict with the EP united member states on the issue. However, the impact of the agreement was limited. EP succeeded in increasing non-compulsory expenditure well above the maximum rate of increase (building in parts on the support of the member states that benefited from the rise in expenditure).

7 The British government had failed to gain support for a legally binding commitment to budgetary discipline (Neville-Rolfe 1985: 39). The adopted agreement was a 'Council conclusion' rather than a regulation; a number of member states emphasised that they would not feel bound by the agreement.

8 The 'necessary condition' of overcoming interdependence was already fulfilled in the negotiations for the joint declaration in 1982. Here, the presidents of all three institutions had settled upon an agreement (see above). However, the 'sufficient condition' was not fulfilled because other subfields were not involved.

9 This is in line with the 'schizophrenia' between Germany's position on budgetary discipline and its stance of CAP expenditure mentioned in Chapter 6. The contradiction between the two positions resulted from the functional divisions in the government and the EU decision-making processes, as well as the strength of the German CAP lobby.

10 The Commission's proposal for a multi-annual budget plan with clear ceilings for different categories got some of its inspiration from a report that a group of academics

had produced following an invitation from the Commission and the Centre for European Policy Studies (Spaventa *et al.* 1986; interview with Commission official). At least equally important for laying the intellectual groundwork for the Commission's budget proposal was the report 'Efficiency, Stability and Equity' by Tommaso Padoa Schioppa (1987) and his collaborators (Delors 2004 emphasises the report's relevance).

11 Even during the negotiations on the Single European Act, when the costs of changing the treaty would have been relatively small, member states decided not to alter the treaty provisions on the budgetary procedure. The Commission had proposed reforms, but was supported by only one member state (Strasser 1992: 35).

12 With its conflict strategy, EP increased the political costs of the existing institutional setting deliberately.

13 Even the EP began to doubt whether it would gain any political benefit from continuous conflict (interview with official from secretariat general of the EP).

14 Delors regarded the adoption of the 1988 reform as the greatest achievement of his 10 years in office (Delors 1994: 231).

15 The Commission's reform proposal was called 'Making a success of the Single Act' (Com (87) 100).

10 Initiating a new institutional path

1 The bargaining power of the EP concerning the distributive framework was not without ambivalence. As the ceilings of the financial perspective lay above the maximum rate of increase for most of the seven years, MEPs' distributive incentive to return to the treaty was limited. Where the ceilings were below, as in the case of the 1994 budget, the bargaining power of the EP was stronger and it gained minor distributive concession towards the ceilings (Cammarata 1995: 44).

2 As was illustrated in Chapter 4, the maximum rate of increase exceeded the ceilings of the financial perspective in 1998. This made the threat of the EP credible.

3 The EP was less successful in the case of the financing of the common and security policy. The interinstitutional agreement from July 1997 granted the EP fewer codecision powers than it had demanded (Commentaire J. Megret 1999 *et al.*: 28–29; interview with assistant to MEP).

4 Observers, such as Godet (2000: 294), regarded the 1999 interinstitutional agreement as a bad deal for the EP on distributive grounds. Commission officials interviewed shared this view and voiced their astonishment that the EP had accepted and subsequently obeyed the interinstitutional agreement.

5 On the revenue side, the degree of institutionalisation was stronger and the effect of the institutional design on distributive outcomes was felt more directly.

6 In response to the demands of the net-contributors, the Commission had proposed co-financing for the CAP (Commission 1998). This would have been a more comprehensive on-path change. France blocked these proposals. Proposals for radical off-path changes in the form of a system of true own-resources, as the Commission had also contemplated in its own-resources report from October 1998, were not put forward, because it was clear that they would not gain any support among member states (Commission 1998).

7 Of these policy reforms probably the most far-reaching was the MacSharry-reform of the CAP in spring 1992 (Fennell 1997: 169–171). As it took place several months before the adoption of the Delors II-package, it might be regarded as counterexample to the importance of interdependence. Such an analysis, however, would fail to recognise the budgetary motivation of the reform. In addition to outside pressure from the negotiations at the Uruguay round, the Commission had produced the MacSharry-initiative because it sought to ensure compliance with the ceiling of the financial perspective and wanted to begin the negotiations for its renewal (Patterson 1997: 152–161).

8 Parliament and Council also decided against repeated demands of the Commission to further institutionalise the interinstitutional agreement. The Commission had proposed to remove the temporal character of the agreement and to establish a permanent soft-law agreement. Parliament and Council seemed to prefer a situation in which the commitment to the interinstitutional agreement had to be renewed every time a new financial perspective was due.

9 These on-path changes demonstrate that stability does not necessarily equal institutional inertia!

11 Summary of the findings and update of the theoretical explanation

1 As the discussion on informal versus formal change already revealed, the design of the 1988 institutional setting certainly reflected the bargaining power of the change coalition, attempts to combine the different subfields and actors' interest in keeping the switching costs low.

2 Actors agreed on a high level of specification because they were ensured that the soft-law character of the reform allowed reversibility.

12 Conclusions

1 Similarly, the annual procedure for the 2005 budget did not witness an immediate increase in the level of conflict. Although as in previous years the EP tried to pressure the Council into fully endorsing Parliament's budgetary priorities, both arms did, in the end, peaceably adopt an annual budget for 2005. The accession of new member states did not significantly shift the pattern of interinstitutional relations between the Council and the EP.

2 Such a holistic approach reunites (rational choice) institutionalism with one of its pioneers, the Nobel-laureate Douglas C. North. Much of North's work focuses on the (economic) performance of institutions and the impact of it on their stability (e.g. North 1990).

3 While Greif assumes that institutional change is likely to proceed gradually (n.d.: VII–46), I found that change can also occur relatively abruptly after a long period of stability.

Bibliography

Offical publications

Centre Universitaire d'Enseignement du Journalisme (2002) Les Conseils Européens de 1975 à 1999, http://cuej.u-strasbg.fr/forma/euroj/euro_ser/cons_43_63/43_63_sce.html (accessed 20 October 2002).

Deutsche Bundesbank (1993) 'The financial relations of the Federal Republik of Germany with the European Communities since 1988', Monthly Report, November, pp. 61–78.

Deutsche Bundesbank (1999) 'Neuere Tendenzen in den Finanzbeziehungen Deutschlands zur Europäischen Union', Monthly Report, July, pp. 59–74.

Deutscher Bundestag (1995) Plenary debate on 16 February 1995.

European Commission (1975–2000) *Monthly Bulletin of the European Communities of the European Union*, Luxembourg: Offical Publications.

European Commission (1977) *The MacDougall Report. The Role of Public Finance in European Communities*, Brussels: European Commission.

European Commission (1987): 'The Single Act: A new frontier for Europe', Communication from the Commission, COM (87) 100.

European Commission (1992) 'From the Single Act to Maastricht and beyond: The means to match our ambitions', Communication from the Commission, Com (92) 2000.

European Commission (1995) *European Union Public Finances*, Luxembourg: Official Publications.

European Commission (1998) 'Agenda 2000. Financing the European Union. Commission report on the operation of the own-resources system', *EU-Bulletin*, Supplement 2/98.

European Commission (2000) *The Community Budget: The Facts in Figures*, Luxembourg: Official Publications.

European Commission (2002) *European Union. Public Finance*, Luxembourg: Official Publications.

European Commission (2003a) *Financial Report 2002*, Luxembourg: Official Publications.

European Commission (2003b) Allocation of 2002 EU operating expenditure, http://europa.eu.int/comm/budget/pdf/agenda2000/allocrep_en2002.pdf (accessed 23 February 2005).

European Commmission (2004a) 'Building our common future – policy challenges and Budgetary means of the enlarged Union 2007–2013', Communication from the Commission, COM(2004) 101 final.

European Commission (2004b) 'Financing the European Union: Commission's report on the operation of the own-resources system', COM(2004) 505 final – Volumes I and II.

European Parliament (1974–2000) Plenary debates.

European Parliament (1979) 'Purse-strings of Europe. The European Parliament and the Community Budget', London: The London Information Office of the European Parliament.

European Parliament (1986a) Resolution on the draft general budget of the European Communities for the financial year 1987, Doc. A2–190/86, OJ, C 7, 12 January 1987.

European Parliament (1986b) Resolution of the decision of the Council of 13 February taken on the basis of the Commission's rectifying letter of 9 January 1987 concerning the financial year 1987 of the Community, OJ, C 76, 23 March 1987.

European Parliament (1996) Report on the Budgetary Procedure. Financial year 1995, Brussels: European Parliament.

European Parliament (1997) Report on the Budgetary Procedure. Financial year 1996, Brussels: European Parliament.

European Parliament (1998) 'Reform of the own-resources system and net positions in the EU budget', Directorate-General for Research, Working Document, Budget Series, BUDG–100 EN, Luxembourg: European Parliament.

Länder (1997) Finanzbeziehung der Bundesrepublik Deutschland zur Europäischen Union, Working Party Report of the Conference of Finance Ministers of the German Länder, June 1997. Bundesratsdrucksache 904/97 of 28/11/1997.

Official Journal of the European Communities (1982) Joint Declaration on various measures to improve the budgetary procedure, C 194, 28 July 1982.

Official Journal of the European Communities (1988) Interinstitutional Agreement on Budgetary Discipline and Improvement of the Budgetary Procedure, L 185, 15 June 1988.

Official Journal of the European Communities (1993) Interinstitutional Agreement on Budgetary Discipline and Improvement of the Budgetary Procedure, C 331, 7 December 1993.

Official Journal of the European Communities (1999) Interinstitutional Agreement on Budgetary Discipline and Imporvement of the Budgetary Procedure, C 172, 18 June 1999.

Samland, D. (1999) The evolution of Headings 1–5 of the Financial Perspective, 1993–1999, Committee on Budgets, European Parliament, http://www.europarl.ep.ec/committees/budg/fourthleg/menu_eu.htm (accessed 20 March 2001).

Archival documents

Documents from the secretariat general of the Council:

Council documents 11074/81: Draft minutes of the 741st meeting of the Council held in Brussels on Monday and Tuesday 23 and 24 November 1981.

Verbatim of the interinstitutional meeting on 28 May 1982.

Extract of the discussion of a meeting of the Council, a delegation from the European Parliament and the Commission in the setting of an interinstitutional trialogue on budgetary matters, Luxembourg 22 June 1982. Draft minutes.

Data base of speeches, statements, and documents of Margaret Thatcher:

Document 79_076 : Statement as Leader of the Opposition in the House of Commons, March 1979.

Press

Agence Europe, The Times, Financial Times, The Independent, The Guardian, The Economist, Neue Züricher Zeitung, Frankfurter Allgemeine Zeitung, Süddeutsche Zeitung, Der Spiegel, Le Monde, Figaro, Das Parlament.

Oral sources

Fifty-three interviews with 40 interview partners from the European Commission, the European Parliament, the Council, national permanent representations, the German Bundesbank and national ministries of finances (detailed list of interview partners is available from the author).

Books and articles

Abbott, K.W. and D. Snidal (2000) 'Hard and Soft Law in International Governance', *International Organization*, 54, 3, pp. 421–456.

Abbott, K.W., R.D. Keohane, A. Moravcsik, A-M. Slaughter and D. Snidel (2000) 'The Concept of Legalization', *International Organization*, 54, 3, pp. 401–419.

Ackrill, R. (2000) 'The European Union Budget, the Balanced Budget Rule and the Development of Common European Policies', *Journal of Public Policy*, 20, 1, pp. 1–19.

Aggarwal, V.K. (1998) *Institutional Design for a Complex World. Bargaining, Linkages, and Nesting.* Ithaca and London: Cornell University Press.

Ardy, B. (1988) 'The National Incidence of the European Community Budget', *Journal of Common Market Studies*, 26, 4, pp. 401 – 429.

Arthur, W.B. (1994) *Increasing Returns and Path Dependence in the Economy.* Ann Arbor: University of Michigan Press.

Attali, J. (1995) Verbatim, volume 2, *Chronique des années 1986–1988*. Paris: Fayard.

Baché, J.-P. (1999) 'Agenda 2000: les enjeux et les résultants de la negotiation sur le cadre financier pour la période 2000–2006', *Revue du Marché commun et de l'Union européenne*, 429, pp. 372–379.

Baché, J.-P. and P. Jouret (1992) 'Le budget de la Communauté après Maastricht', *Revue du Marché commun*, 359, pp. 559–572.

Bangemann, M. (1979) 'La procédure budgétaire de 1979: l'équilibre nécessaire de la répartition des pouvoirs entre le Conseil et le Parlement', *Revue du Marché commun*, pp. 169–184.

Bates, R.H., A. Greif, M. Levi, J-L. Rosenthal and B. Weingast (1998) *Analytical Narratives.* Princeton, NJ: Princeton University Press.

Begg, I. (1999a) 'Reshaping the EU Budget: Yet another missed opportunity?', South Bank University: *South Bank European Paper* 5/99.

Begg, I. (1999b) 'The new EU Budget deal: good politics, bad economics?', *Economic Outlook*, April, pp. 13–18.

Begg, I. and N. Grimwade (1998) *Paying for Europe.* Sheffield: Sheffield Academic Press.

Begg, I. (2004) 'Future Fiscal Arrangements of the European Union', Common Market Law Review, 41, pp. 775–794.

Beyers, J. and G. Dierickx (1998) 'The Working Groups of the Council of the European Union: Supranational or Intergovernmental Negotiations?', *Journal of Common Market Studies*, 36, 3, pp. 289–317.

Bieber, R., A. Bleckmann, F. Capotorti and D. Nickel (eds) (1981) 'Kooperation und Konflikt – Elemente einer Theorie des internen Organisationsrechts der EG', *Gedächtnisschrift für Christoph Sassen*. Baden-Baden: Nomos, pp. 327–347.

Bieber, R. (1982) 'Die Ausgaben der Europäischen Gemeinschaften', *Europarecht*, 17, 2, pp. 115–132.

Bieber, R. (1984) 'The Settlement of Institutional Conflict on the basis of Article 4 of the EEC Treaty', *Common Market Law Review*, 21, pp. 505–523.

Bieber, R. (1986) 'Rechtswirkung und gerichtliche Kontrolle des EG-Haushalts – Zugleich

Anmerkung zur Entscheidung des EuGH vom 3 Juli 1986, Rs 34/86 (Rat gegen Europäisches Parlament)', *Deutsches Verwaltungsblatt*, 101, pp. 961–968.

Biehl, D. (1988) 'Ein substantielles, aber begrenztes Reformpaket – Zum Brüsseler Reformgipfel', *Integration*, 11, pp. 64–74.

Bradley, K.St.C. (1987) 'Maintaining the Balance: The Role of the Court of Justice in Defining the Institutional Position of the European Parliament', *Common Market Law Review*, 24, pp. 41–64.

Brehon, N.-J. (1997) *Le budget de l'Europe*. Paris: L.G.D.J.

Brinkhorst, L. (1997) 'Demokratische Strukturen im Haushaltsrecht der Europäischen Union', *Vörträge und Berichte* Nr. 81. Bonn: Zentrum für europäisches Wirtschaftsrecht.

Bulmer, S. and W. Paterson (1987) *The Federal Republic of Germany and the European Community*. London: Allen & Unwin.

Butler, M. (1986) *Europe: More than a Continent*. London: Heinemann.

Bywater, M. (1979) 'Le budget communautaire: une perspective britannique', *Revue du Marché commun*, 230, pp. 431–434.

Bywater, M. (1980) 'Le conflit budgétaire', *Revue du Marché commun*, pp. 101–103.

Cammarata, A. (1995) 'Guerre et Paix dans les Finances Publiques Europeennes: Les Divergences d'interpretation des Accords Interinstitutionnels entre les Institutions signataire', *Affari sociali internazionali*, 4, pp. 25–57.

Carrubba, C.J. (1997) 'Net Financial Transfers in the European Union: Who Gets What and Why?', *Journal of Politics*, 59, 2, pp. 469–499.

Chevalier, J.-P. (2000a) 'L'accord interinstitutionnel du 6 mai 1999 et les Perspectives Financières 2000–2006: des nouvelles ambitions pour l'union européenne?', *Revue du Marché commun et de l'Union européenne*, 440, pp. 441–465.

Chevalier, J.-P. (2000b) 'L'accord interinstitutionnel du 6 mai 1999 et les Perspectives Financières 2000–2006: de nouvelles ambitions pour l'union européenne?', *Revue du Marché commun et de l'Union européenne*, 441, pp. 524–532.

Commentaire J. Megret (1999) *Les Finances De l'Union Européenne*, Vol. 11, 2nd edn. Brussels: University of Brussels.

Coombes, D. (1979) *The Future of the European Parliament*. London: Policy Studies Institute.

Corbett, R., F. Jacobs and M. Shackleton (2003a) *The European Parliament*, 5th edn. London: John Harper Publishing.

Corbett, R., F. Jacobs and M. Shackleton (2003b) 'The European Parliament at Fifty. A View from the Inside', *Journal of Common Market Studies*, 41, 2, pp. 353–373.

Coser, L. (1956) *The Function of Social Conflict*. Glencoe, IL: Free Press.

Coussens, W. (2004) 'Financing the EU Budget: Time for Reform', Studia Diplomatica, vol. LVII, 4.

Cova, C. (1986a) 'Nouvelles Difficultués Budgétaires', *Revue du Marché commun*, 293, pp. 1–2.

Cova, C. (1986b) 'Budget: Le Casse-Tête Européen', *Revue du Marché commun*, 302, pp. 563–564.

Cram, L. (1997) *Policy-making in the EU*. London/New York: Routledge.

Dankert, P. (1983) 'The Joint Declaration by the Community Institutions of 30 June 1982 on the Community Budgetary Procedure', *Common Market Law Review*, 20, pp. 701–712.

David, P. (1985) 'Clio and the Economics of QWERTY', *American Economic Review*, 75, May, 332–337.

De Bassompierre, G. (1988) *Changing the Guard in Brussels. An Insider's View of the EC Presidency*. New York/Westport/London: Praeger.

Deeg, R. (2001) 'Institutional Change and the Uses and Limits of Path Dependency: The Case of German Finance', Max-Planck-Institute for the Study of Society, Cologne, Discussion paper no. 01/6.

Deffaa, W. (1997) 'Deutschland –"Zahlmeister" Europa?', R. Ceasar (ed.): *Zur Reform der Finanzverfassung und Strukturpolitik der EU*. Baden-Baden: Nomos, pp. 153–160.

Deffaa, W. (2000) 'Haushaltspolitik', W. Weidenfels and W. Wessels (eds): *Jahrbuch der Europäischen Integration 1999/2000*. Bonn: Institut für Europäische Politik, pp.155–162.

Deffaa, W. and P. Zangl (1994) 'Haushaltspolitik', W. Weidenfels and W. Wessels (eds): *Jahrbuch der Europäischen Integration 1993/94*. Bonn: Institut für Europäische Politik, pp. 145–152.

Deffaa, W. and P. Zangl (1995) 'Haushaltspolitik', W. Weidenfels and W. Wessels (eds): *Jahrbuch der Europäischen Integration 1994/95* Bonn: Institut für Europäische Politik, pp. 123–130.

Deffaa, W. and P. Zangl (1996) 'Haushaltspolitik', W. Weidenfels and W. Wessels (eds): *Jahrbuch der Europäischen Integration 1995/96*. Bonn: Institut für Europäische Politik, pp. 125–130.

Delors, J. (1994) *L'Unité d'un Homme. Entretiens avec Dominique Wolton*. Paris: Editions Odile Jacob.

Denman, R. (1996) *Missed Changes. Britain and Europe in the Twentieth Century*, London: Cassell.

Delors, J. (2004) Mémoires, Paris: Plon.

Denton, G. (1981) 'How to prevent the EC budget reinforcing divergence: a British View', M. Hodges and W. Wallace (eds): *Economic Divergence in the European Community*. London: Allen & Unwin, pp. 80 –100.

Denton, G. (1984) 'Restructuring the EC budget: Implications of the Fontainebleau Agreement', *Journal of Common Market Studies*, 23, 2, pp. 117–140.

Deutsch, M. (1973) *The Resolution of Conflict. Constructive and Destructive Processes*. New Haven/ London: Yale University Press.

Dewost, J.-L. and M. Lepoivre (1982) 'La declaration commune du Parlament europén, du Conseil et de la Commission relative à différentes measures visant à assurer un meilleur déroulement de la procedure budgétaire, signée le 30 juin 1982', *Revue du Marché Commun*, 261, pp. 515–524.

Dinan, D. (1999) *Ever Closer Union: Introduction to European Integration*, 2nd edn. Basingstoke: MacMillan.

Discors, D. (1997) 'La procédure budgétaire pour 1997 et ses enjeux institutionnels', *Revue du Marché commun et de l'Union européenne*, 413, pp. 682–706.

Discors, D. (1998) 'La procédure budgétaire pour 1998, une idylle interinstitutionnelle', *Revue du Marché commun et de l'Union européenne*, 423, pp. 681–704.

Dodsworth, J. (1975) 'European Community Financing: An Analysis of the Dublin Amendment', *Journal of Common Market Studies*, 24, pp. 129–139.

Dowding, K. (2000) 'Institutionalist Research on the European Union. A Critical Review', *European Union Politics*, 1, 1, pp. 125–144.

Drake, H. (1995) 'Political Leadership and European Integration: The Case of Jacques Delors', *West European Politics*, 18, 1, pp. 140–160.

Durand, G. (2005) 'The EU Financial Perspectives: Negotiating in the Dark', Commentary, Brussels: European Policy Centre, http://www.theepc.be/en/default. asp?TYP=TEWN&LV=470&PG=TEWN/EN/detail&AI=470 (accessed 25 February 2005).

Ehlermann, C.-D. (1988) 'Die Beschlüsse des Brüsseler Sondergipfels: Erfolg einer Gesamtstrategie der Delors-Kommission', *Integration*, 11, 2, pp. 56–63.

Ehlermann, C.D. and M. Minch (1981) 'Conflicts between Community Institutions within the Budgetary Procedure, Article 205 of the Treaty', *Europarecht*, 1, pp. 23–42.

Ehlermann, C.-D. (1975) 'Applying the new Budgetary Procedure for the first time', *Common Market Law Review*, 21, pp. 325–343.

Elster, J. (1979) *Ulysses and the Sirens. Studies of Rationality and Irrationality*. Cambridge: Cambridge University Press.

Emerson, M.R. and T.W.K. Scott (1977) 'The Financial Mechanism in the Budget of the European Community: The Hard Core of the British Renegotiations of 1974–1975', *Common Market Law Review*, pp. 209–229.

Enderlein, H. and J. Lindner (2005) 'The EU Budgetary Procedure in the Constitutional Debate', Jeremy Richardson (ed.) *European Union: Power & Policy-Making*, 3rd edn. London: Routledge.

Enderlein H., J. Lindner, O. Calvo-Gonzalez and R. Ritter (2005): 'The EU Budget – How Much Scope for Institutional Reform?', *ECB Occasional Paper Series*.

Endo, K. (1999) *The Presidency of the European Commission under Jacques Delors. The Politics of Shared Leadership*. Basingstoke: Macmillan.

Falkner, G (ed.) (2002) 'The EU Treaty Reform as a Three-Level Process: Historical Institutionalist Perspectives', *Journal of European Public Policy*, 9, 1.

Farrell, H. and A. Héritier (2001) 'Formal and Informal Institutions under Codecision: Continuous Constitution Building in Europe', Max Planck Project Group – Common Goods, Bonn. *Discussion paper*.

Fennell, R. (1997) *The Common Agricultural Policy. Continuity and Change*. Oxford: Clarendon Press.

Fernandez-Fabregas, F. and J. Lentz (1991) 'Le Budget 1991 – Le déroulement de la procédure budgétaire: ses incidents et son aboutissement', *Revue du Marché commun*, 326, pp. 293–313.

Fernandez-Fabregas, F. and J. Lentz (1992) 'Le Budget 1992 – Son cadre politique et financier, son établissement: ses incidents et son aboutissement', *Revue du Marché commun*, 360, pp. 637–657.

Fernandez-Fabregas, F. and J. Lentz (1993) 'Le Budget 1993 – Le déroulement de la procédure budgétaire: ses incidents et son aboutissement', *Revue du Marché commun et de l'Union européenne*, 370, pp. 628–655.

Fernandez-Fabregas, F. and J. Lentz (1994) 'Le Budget 1994 – Le déroulement de la procédure budgétaire: ses incidents et son aboutissement', *Revue du Marché commun et de l'Union européenne*, 381, pp. 505–526.

Fernandez-Fabregas, F. and J. Lentz (1995) 'Le Budget 1995 – Le déroulement de la procédure budgétaire: son environnement, ses incidents et son aboutissement', *Revue du Marché commun et de l'Union européenne*, 388, pp. 284–314.

Fligstein, N. (1998) 'Institutional Entrepreneurs and Cultural Frames: The Case of the European Union's Single Market Program'. *Paper presented at the Ideas, Culture and Political Analysis Workshop*, Princeton University, May 15–16 1998.

Folkers, C. (1994) Die Kompensationsfunktion des Europäischen Haushalts, *Diskussions-beiträge*, Nr. 4, Institut der Europäischen Wirtschaft: Ruhr-Universität Bochum.

Folkers, C. (1998) 'Finanz- und Haushaltspolitik', P. Klemmer (ed.): *Handbuch der Europäischen Wirtschaftspolitik*. München: Verlag Franz Vahlen, pp. 561–663.

Fouletier, M. (2001) 'Refléxions sur la jurisprudence de la CJCE au regard des conflicts inter-institutionnels en matière budgétaire', *Revue Française de Finances Publiques*, 9, pp. 117–133.

Fugmann, F. (1992) Die rechtliche Struktur der Finanzverfassung der Europäischen Gemeinschaften – zugleich eine kritische Studie der Möglichkeiten der Reform der EG-Finanzverfassung, jur. *Dissertation*, Universität des Saarlandes: Saarbrücken.

Galloway, D. (1999) 'Keynote Article: Agenda 2000 – Packaging the Deal', *Journal of Common Market Studies*, 37, supplement 1, pp. 9–35.

Garrett, G.F. and B.R. Weingast (1993) 'Ideas, Interests, and Institutions: Constructing the European Community's Internal Market', J. Goldstein and R.O. Keohane (eds): *Ideas and Foreign Policy: Beliefs, Institutions and Political Change*. Ithaca: Cornell University Press, pp. 173–206.

Genschel, P. (1997) 'The Dynamics of Inertia: Institutional Persistence and Change in Telecommunications and Health Care', *Governance*, 10, 1, pp. 43–66.

George, A.L. and T.J. McKeown (1985) 'Case Studies and Theories of Organizational Decision Making', *Advances in Information Processing in Organizations*, 2, pp. 21–58.

George, S. (1998) *An Awkward Partner – Britain in the European Community*, 3rd edn. Oxford: Oxford University Press.

Giraudy, J.L. (1975) 'Le budget 1976 des "Neuf" ne traduit pas une volonté de faire progresser la construction européenne', *Revue du Marché commun*, 190, pp. 491–494.

Glaesner, H. (1981) 'Mögliche Konfliktzonen zwischen den Gemeinschaftsorganen', *Europarecht*, 16, pp. 1–22.

Glaesner, H.-J. (1982) 'Die Beziehungen zwischen Ministerrat und Europäischem Parlament – Erfolg der "kleinen Schritte"?', *Zeitschrift für Parlamentsfragen*, 13, 2, pp. 191–198.

Glaesner, H.-J. (1987) 'Anmerkungen zum Urteil des EuGH von 3. Juli 1986, Rs. 34/86', *Europarecht*, pp. 157–161.

Godet, R. (2000) 'Le nouveau "code de procédure budgétaire" et l'amélioration de la procedure budgetaire du 6 mai 1999', *Revue Trimestrielle de Droit Européen*, 36, 2, pp. 273–298.

Godley, W. (1980) 'The United Kingdom and the Community Budget', W. Wallace (ed.): *Britain in Europe*, London: Heinemann, pp. 72–85.

Goybet, C. (1984) 'Parlement contre Conseil: La fixation du budget 1985 de la CEE promet une fin d'année agitée', *Revue du Marché commun*, pp. 453–455.

Grabitz, E., O. Schmuck, S. Steppat and W. Wessels (1988) *Direktwahl und Demokratisierung –Eine Funktionsbilanz des Europäischen Paralments nach der ersten Wahlperiode*. Bonn: Europa Union Verlag.

Green, D.P. and I. Shapiro (1994) *Pathologies of Rational Choice*. New Haven/London: Yale University Press.

Greif, A. (n.d.) *Institutions: Theory and History*, Cambridge: Cambridge University Press (excerpts at: http:www.econ.stanford.edu/faculty/greif-Ireland/influence-rateofchange. pdf, accessed 22 February 2005).

Greif, A. and D.D. Laitin (2004) 'A Theory of Endogenous Institutional Change', *American Political Science Review*, 98, 4, pp. 633–652.

Greven, M.T. (2000) 'Can the European Union Finally Become Democratic?' M.T. Greven and L.W. Pauly (eds): *Democracy Beyond the State? The European Dilemma and the Emerging Global Order*. Lanham: Rowman & Littlefield, pp. 35–61.

Grossir, J. (2001) 'La procédure budgétaire pour 2001: un long fleuve tranquille?', *Revue du Marché commun et de l'Union européenne*, 449, pp. 374–393.

Guth, E. (1998) 'Haushaltspolitik', W. Weidenfels and W. Wessels (eds): *Jahrbuch der Europäischen Integration 1997/98*. Bonn: Institut für Europäische Politik, pp.155–162.

Guth, E. (1999) 'Haushaltspolitik', W. Weidenfels and W. Wessels (eds): *Jahrbuch der Europäischen Integration 1998/99*. Bonn: Institut für Europäische Politik, pp.173–178.

Guth, E. and Discors, D. (1997) 'Haushaltspolitik', W. Weidenfels and W. Wessels (eds): *Jahrbuch der Europäischen Integration 1996/97*. Bonn: Institut für Europäische Politik, pp. 119–126.

Hall, P. (1991) 'Policy Paradigms, Social Learning, and the State', *Comparative Politics*, 23, pp. 275–296.

Hall, P. and R. Taylor (1996) 'Political Science and the Three New Institutionalisms', *Political Studies*, 44, pp. 952–973.

Hayes-Renshaw, F. and H. Wallace (1997) *The Council of Ministers*. Basingstoke: Macmillan.

Heclo, H. and A. Wildavsky (1974) *The Private Government of Public Money*. Basingstoke: Macmillan.

Hemerijck, A. and K. van Kerbergen (1999) 'Negotiated Policy Change: Towards a Theory of Institutional Learning in Tightly Coupled Welfare States', D. Braun and A. Busch (eds): *Public Policy and Political Ideas*. Cheltenham, UK: Edward Elgar, pp. 168–185.

Hendriks, G. (1991) *Germany and European Integration*. New York and Oxford: Berg.

Hix, S. (2005) *The Political System of the European Union*, 2nd edn. Basingstoke: Palgrave Macmillan.

Hix, S. (2002) 'Constitutional Agenda-Setting Through Discretion in Rule Interpretation: Why the European Parliament Won at Amsterdam', *British Journal of Political Science*, 32, 2, pp. 259–280.

Howe, G. (1994) *Conflict of Loyalty*. London: Macmillan.

Hyde. A.C. (ed.): (1992) *Government Budgeting – Theory/Process/Politics*, 2nd edn. Pacific Grove: Brooks/Cole Publishing Company.

Iida, K. (1993) 'When and How Do Domestic Constraints Matter? Two-Level Games with Uncertainty', *Journal of Conflict Resolution*, 37, 3, pp. 403–426.

Iida, K. (1996) 'Involuntary defection in two-level games', *Public Choice*, 89, pp. 283–303.

Isaac, G. (1980) 'Les finances communautaires (Année 1978 – 1er semestre 1979)', *Revue Trimestrielle de Droit Européen*, 16, 2, pp. 302–353,

Isaac, G. (1984a) 'Le Processus de Décision Interne du Parlement Européen en Matière Budgétaire', R. Hrbek, J. Jamar and W. Wessels (eds): *The European Parliament of the Eve of the Second Direct Election: Balance Sheet and Prospects*. Bruges: De Tempel, pp. 690–726.

Isaac, G. (1984b) 'Le "problème" de la contribution budgétaire du Royaume-Uni', *Revue Trimestrielle de Droit Européen*, 20, 1, pp. 107–122.

Isaac, G. (ed.): (1986) *Les Ressources Financiers de la Communauté Européenne*. Paris: Economica.

Issac, G. (1994) 'L'encadrement à moyen terme des finances publiques communqutqires: l'Accord institutionnel sur discipline budgétaire et l'amélioration de la procédure budgétaire, bilan et avenir', *Revue Francaise des finances publiques*, 45, pp. 9–49.

Jachtenfuchs, M. (2002) *Die Konstruktion Europas. Verfassungsideen und institutionelle Entwicklung*. Baden-Baden: Nomos.

Janning, J. (1994) 'Bundesrepublik Deutschland', W. Weidenfeld and W. Wessels (eds): *Jahrbuch der Europäischen Integration 1993/94*. Bonn: Institut für Europäische Politik, pp. 305–312

Janning, J. (1997) 'Bundesrepublik Deutschland', W. Weidenfeld and W. Wessels (eds): *Jahrbuch der Europäischen Integration 1996/97*. Bonn: Institut für Europäische Politik, 1996/97, pp. 293–302.

Janning, J. (1998) 'Bundesrepublik Deutschland', W. Weidenfeld and W. Wessels (eds): *Jahrbuch der Europäischen Integration 1997/98*. Bonn: Institut für Europäische Politik, pp. 311–318.

Jenkins, M. (1980) 'Britain and the Community Budget; the end of a chapter', *Common Market Law Review*, 17, pp. 493–507.

Jessen, C. (1999) 'Agenda 2000', *Integration*, 3, pp. 167–175.

Johnston, M.T. (1994) *The European Council. Gatekeeper of the European Community.* Boulder/ San Francisco/Oxford: Westview Press.

Jouret, P. (1993) 'Les conclusion d'Edimbourg sur le paquet "Delors II"', *Revue du Marché commun et de l'Union européenne*, 368, pp. 391–411.

King, G., R. O. Keohane and S. Verba (1994) *Designing Social Inquiry. Scientific Inference in Qualitative Research.* Princeton, NJ: Princeton University Press.

Kitzinger, U. (1973) *Diplomacy and Persuasion. How Britain joined the Common Market.* London: Thames & Hudson.

Knight, J. (1992) *Institutions and Social Conflict.* Cambridge: Cambridge University Press.

Knight, J. (1995) 'Models, Interpretations and Theories: Constructing Explanations of Institutional Emergence and Change', J. Knight and I. Sened (eds): *Explaining Social Institutions*, Ann Arbor: The University of Michigan Press, pp. 95–120.

Kohler, B. (1978) 'Der Abgeordnete als Vertreter des Europäischen Volkes. Die Demokratietheorie vor der Bewährungsprobe', *Europarecht*, 3, pp. 333–350.

Laffan, B. (1997) *The Finances of the European Union.* Basingstoke: Macmillan.

Laffan, B. (1999) 'The Berlin Summit: Process and Outcome of the Agenda 2000 Budgetary Proposals', *ECSA Review*, Fall 1999, pp. 6–8.

Laffan, B. (2000a) 'The Agenda 2000 Negotiations: La Présidence Coûte Cher?'. *German Politics*, 9, 3, pp. 1–22.

Laffan, B. (2000b) 'The Big Budgetary Bargains: from negotiation to authority', *Journal of European Public Policy*, 7, 5, Special Issue, pp. 725–743.

Laffan, B. and J. Lindner (2005) 'The EU Budget', H. Wallace, W. Wallace and Mark Pollack (eds): *Policy-Making in the European Union.* Oxford: Oxford University Press.

Laffan, B. and M. Shackleton (1996) 'The Budget', H. Wallace and W. Wallace (eds): *Policy-Making in the European Union*, 3rd edn. Oxford: Oxford University Press, pp. 71–96.

Laffan, B. and M. Shackleton (2000) 'The Budget. Who Gets What, When, and How', H. Wallace and W. Wallace (eds): *Policy-Making in the European Union*, 4th edn. Oxford: Oxford University Press, pp. 211–241.

Läufer T. (1979) 'Das Europäische Parlament nach der Direktwahl: Positionsstärkung durch intrakonstitutionellen Wandel?', Europarecht, 14, pp. 261–276.

Läufer, T. (1981a) 'Haushaltspolitik', W. Weidenfels and W. Wessels (eds): *Jahrbuch der Europäischen Integration 1980.* Bonn: Institut für Europäische Politik, pp. 153–162.

Läufer, T. (1981b) Die Haushaltskonflikte der EG: Ratsallmacht und Parlamentsohnmacht?, *Europa-Archiv*, 18, pp. 545–552.

Läufer, T. (1982) 'Haushaltspolitik', W. Weidenfels and W. Wessels (eds): *Jahrbuch der Europäischen Integration 1981.* Bonn: Institut für Europäische Politik, pp. 189–199.

Läufer, T. (1983) 'Haushaltspolitik', W. Weidenfels and W. Wessels (eds): *Jahrbuch der Europäischen Integration 1982.* Bonn: Institut für Europäische Politik, pp. 128–140.

Läufer, T. (1985) 'Haushaltspolitik', W. Weidenfels and W. Wessels (eds): *Jahrbuch der Europäischen Integration 1984.* Bonn: Institut für Europäische Politik, pp. 131–142.

Läufer, T. (1986) 'Haushaltspolitik', W. Weidenfels and W. Wessels (eds): *Jahrbuch der Europäischen Integration 1985.* Bonn: Institut für Europäische Politik, pp. 137–148.

Läufer, T. (1987) 'Haushaltspolitik', W. Weidenfels and W. Wessels (eds): *Jahrbuch der Europäischen Integration 1986/87.* Bonn: Institut für Europäische Politik, pp. 141–153.

Läufer, T. (1989)'Haushaltspolitik', W. Weidenfels and W. Wessels (eds): *Jahrbuch der Europäischen Integration 1988/89.* Bonn: Institut für Europäische Politik, pp. 122–131.

Läufer, T. (1990a)'Haushaltspolitik', W. Weidenfels and W. Wessels (eds): *Jahrbuch der Europäischen Integration 1989/90.* Bonn: Institut für Europäische Politik, pp. 137–144.

Läufer, T. (1990b) *Die Organe der EG – Rechtsetzung und Haushaltsverfahren zwischen Kooperation und Konflikt*. Bonn: Europa Union Verlag.

Läufer, T. and C. Siebert (1988) 'Das EG-Haushaltsverfahren für 1982: Testfeld parlamentarischer Mitregierung', E. Grabitz, O. Schmuck, S. Steppat and W. Wessels (eds): *Direktwahl und Demokratisierung*. Bonn: Europa Union Verlag, pp. 164–206.

Lax, D.A. and J.K. Sebenius (1986) *The Manager as Negotiator: Bargaining for Cooperation and Competitive Gain*. New York: Free Press.

LeLoup, L.T. (1988) 'From Microbudgeting to Macrobudgeting: Evolution in Theory and Practice', I.S. Rubin (ed.): *New Directions in Budget Theory*. New York: State University of New York Press, pp. 19–42.

Levi, M. (1997) 'A Model, a Method, and a Map: Rational Choice and Historical Analysis', M.I. Lichbach and A.S. Zuckerman (eds): *Comparative Politics – Rationality, Culture and Structure*. Cambridge: Cambridge University Press, pp. 19–41.

Lindenberg, S. (1990) 'Homo Socio-oeconomicus: The Emergence of a General Model of Man in the Social Science', *Journal of Institutional and Theoretical Economics*, 146, pp. 727–748.

Lindner, J. (2003) 'Institutional Stability and Change: Two Sides of the Same Coin', B. Rittberger and J. Stacey (eds): *The Formal and Informal Dynamics of Institutional Change in the EU*, *Journal of European Public Policy*, 10, 6, Special Issue, pp. 912–935.

Lindner, J. and B. Rittberger (2003) 'The Creation, Interpretation and Contestation of Institutions – Revisiting Historical Institutionalism', *Journal of Common Market Studies*, 41, 3, pp. 445–473.

Lord, C. (1998) *Democracy in the European Union*. Sheffield: Sheffield Academic Press.

Magiera, S. (1985) 'Zur Überbrückung von Haushaltsdefiziten der Europäischen Union durch "Vorschüsse" der Mitgliedstaaten', *Europarecht*, 20, pp. 273–292.

Magiera, S. (1995) 'Zur Finanzverfassung der Europäischen Union', A. Randelzhofer, R. Scholz and D. Wilke (eds): *Gedächtnisschrift für Eberhard Grabitz*. München: Beck, pp. 409–430.

Mahoney, J. and D. Rueschemeyer (eds): (2002) *Comparative Historical Analysis in the Social Sciences*, New York: Cambridge University Press.

Majone, G. (1996) *Regulating Europe*. London/New York: Routledge.

March, J.G. and J.P. Olsen (1989) *Rediscovering Institutions – The Organizational Basis of Politics*. New York: The Free Press.

Maruhn, R. and J.A. Emmanouilidis (2005) 'Agenda 2007 – Der Konflikt um den Finanzrahmen 2007–2013', *Reform Spotlight*, 01/2005.

Maurer, A. (2000) 'The German Presidency of the Council: Continuity or Change in Germany's European Policy?', *Journal of Common Market Studies*, 38, Annual Review, pp. 43–47.

McCaffrey, J. (1999) 'Features of the Budgetary Process', R.T. Meyers (ed.): *Handbook of Government Budgeting*. San Francisco: Jossey-Bass, pp. 3–29.

McLean, I. (2001) *Rational Choice & British Politics. An Analysis of Rhetoric and Manipulation From Peel to Blair*. Oxford: Oxford University Press.

Meyers, R.T. (1994) *Strategic Budgeting*. Ann Arbor: University of Michigan Press.

Misch, A. (1987) *Das Euopäische Parlament und die Finanzpolitik der EG in den Jahren 1979–1984*. Ebenhausen: Stiftung Wissenschaft und Politik.

Møller, J. (1982) *Member States and the Community Budget*. Copenhagen: Samfundsviden-skabeligt Forlag.

Monar, J. (1994) 'Interinstitutional agreements: The Phenomenon and its new Dynmaics after Maastricht', *Common Market Law Review*, 31, pp. 693–719.

Moravcsik, A. (1993) 'Introduction. Integration of International and Domestic Theories of International Bargaining', P.B. Evans, H.K. Jacobson and R.D. Putnam (eds): *Double-Edged Diplomacy. International Bargaining and Domestic Politics*. Berkley/Los Angeles/London: University of California Press, pp. 3–42.

Moravcsik, A. (1997) 'Taking Preferences Seriously: A Liberal Theory of International Politics', *International Organization*, 51, 4, pp. 513–553.

Moravcsik, A. (1998) *The Choice of Europe. Social Purpose & State Power from Messina to Maastricht*. London: University College London Press.

Moravcsik, A. (1999) 'A New Statecraft? Supranational Entrepreneurs and International Cooperation', *International Organization*, 53, 2, pp. 267–306.

Nava, M. (2000) *La finanza europea, Stocia aualisi e perspettive della politica fiscale europea*. Rome: Carocci.

Neville-Rolfe, N. (1984) *The Politics of Agriculture in the European Community*. London: Policy Studies Institute.

Neville-Rolfe, N. (1985) 'Budgetary Discipline: Will it Work?', *European Trend*, 1, pp. 35–40.

Nicoll, W. (1985) 'The Budget of the European Community in 1984', *Revue d'integration européenne*, 8, 2–3, pp. 157–171.

Nicoll, W. (1986) 'From Rejection to Repudiation: EC Budgetary Affairs in 1985', *Journal of Common Market Studies*, 25, 1, pp. 31–49.

Nicoll, W. (1988a) 'EEC Budgetary Strains and Constraints', *International Affairs*, 64, pp. 27–42.

Nicoll, W. (1988b) 'The Long March of the EC's 1988 Budget', *Journal of Common Market Studies*, 27, 2, pp. 161–169.

Nicoll, W. (1995) 'The Budget Council', M. Westlake (ed.): *The Council of the European Union*. London: Catermill Publishing, pp.179–191.

Nicoll, W. and J. Lentz (1989) 'Le Budget 1989. Son cadre financier et réglementaire et établissement', *Revue du Marché commun*, 326, pp. 209–223.

Nicoll, W. and J. Lentz (1990) 'Le Budget 1990. Le déroulement de la procédure budgétaire: ses incidents et son aboutissement', *Revue du Marché commun*, 336, pp. 269–282.

North, D.C. (1981) *Structure and Change in Economic History*. New York: Norton.

North, D.C. (1990) *Institutions, Institutional Change and Economic Performance*. Cambridge: Cambridge University Press.

Noteboom, H.A.C.M. (1988) *Het Europees Parlement en de finacien*. s'Gravenhage: SDU-Uitgeverij.

O'Neill, C. (2000) *Britain's Entry into the European Community*. Report by Sir Con O'Neil on the Negotiations of 1970–1972, D. Hannay (ed.). London/Portland, OR: Whitehall History Publishing in association with Frank Cass.

Olson, M. (1971) *The Logic of Collective Action*. Cambridge, London: Harvard University Press.

Padoa Schioppa, T. (1987) *Efficiency, Stability and Equity: A Strategy for the Evolution of the European Community*. Oxford: Oxford University Press.

Patterson, L.A. (1997) 'Agricultural policy reform in the European Community: a three-level game analysis', *International Organization*, 51, 1, pp. 135–165.

Pierson, P. (1996) 'The Path to European Integration. A Historical Institutionalist Analysis', *Comparative Political Studies*, 29, 2, pp. 123–163.

Pierson, P. (2000a) 'Increasing Returns, Path Dependence, and the Study of Politics', *American Political Science Review*, 94, 2, pp. 251–267.

Pierson, P. (2000b) 'The Limits of Design: Explaining Institutional Origins and Change', *Governance*, 13, 4, pp. 475–499.

Pierson, P. (2004) *History, Institutions and Social Analysis.* Princeton/Oxford: Princeton University Press.

Pinder, J. (1988) 'The Delors Proposals and the Beyond – The Interests of the Sparenland and the other Partners', W. Wessels and E. Regelsberger (eds): *The Federal Republik of Germany and the European Community: the Presidency and Beyond.* Bonn: Europa Union Verlag, pp. 66–86.

Pipkorn, J. (1981) 'Legal Implications of the Absence of the Community Budget at the Beginning of a Financial Year', *Common Market Law Review*, 2, pp. 141–167.

Pöhle, K. (1982) 'Zweieinhalb Jahre direkt gewähltes Europäisches Parlament – eine beachtliche Bilanz', *Zeitschrift für Parlamentsfragen*, 13, 2, pp. 180–184.

Putnam, R.D. (1988) 'Diplomacy and Domestic Politics: The Logic of Two-Level Games', *International Organizations*, 42, pp. 427–460.

Régnier-Heldmaier, C. (1994) 'La distinction DO-DNO, instrument de lutte pour le pouvoir budgétaire', *Revue du Marché commun et de l'Union européenne*, 375, pp. 94–102.

Reich, C. (1994) 'La Mise en Oeuvre du Traité sur l'Union Européenne par les Accords Interinstitutionnels', *Revue du Marché commun et de l'Union européenne*, 375, pp. 81–85.

Reichenbach, H. (1983) 'EC Budgetary Imbalances: A Conceptual Framework', *Finanz-archiv*, 41, 3, pp. 452–462.

Revue du Marché commun (1985) 'Qu'est-ce que la discipline budgétaire', *Revue du Marché commun*, 285, pp. 132.

Richardson, J. (1996) 'Actor-based Models of National and EU Policy Making', H. Kassim and A. Menon (eds): *The European Union and National Industrial Policy.* London/New York: Routledge, pp. 28–51.

Richardson, J. (2000) 'Government, Interest Groups and Policy Change', *Political Studies*, 48, 5, pp. 1006–1025.

Richardson, J.J. and A.G. Jordan (1979) *Governing under Pressure. The Policy Process in a Post-Parliamentary Democracy.* Oxford: Basil Blackwell.

Riker, W.H. (1986) *The Art of Manipulation.* New Haven: Yale University Press.

Rittberger, B. (2005) *Building Europe's Parliament. Democratic Representation beyond the Nation-State.* Oxford: Oxford University Press.

Rittberger, B. and J. Stacey (eds) (2003) 'The Formal and Informal Dynamics of Institutional Change in the EU', *Journal of European Public Policy*, 10, 6, Special Issue.

Ross, G. (1995) *Jacques Delors and European Integration.* Cambridge: Polity Press.

Rossi, M. (1997) *Europäisches Parlament und Haushaltsrecht: Eine kritische Betrachtung der parlamentarischen Haushaltsbefugnisse.* Baden-Baden: Nomos.

Rubin, I.S. (1997) *The Politics of Public Budgeting/ Getting and Spending, Borrowing and Balancing*, 3rd edn. Chatham, NY: Chatham House Publishers.

Rubin, I.S. (1999) 'Understanding the Role of Conflict in Budgeting', R.T. Meyers (ed.): *Handbook of Government Budgeting.* San Francisco: Jossey-Bass, pp. 30–52.

Scharpf, F.W. (1988) 'The Joint Decision Trap: Lessons from German Federalism and European Integration', *Public Administration*, 66, pp. 239–278.

Scharpf, F.W. (1997) *Games Real Actors Play*, Boulder, Oxford: Westview Press.

Scharpf, F.W. (1999) *Governing in Europe. Effective and Democratic?.* Oxford: Oxford University Press.

Scharpf, F.W. (2000a) 'Institutions in Comparative Policy Research', *Comparative Political Studies*, 33, 6/7, pp. 762–790.

Scharpf, F.W. (2000b) 'Notes Toward a Theory of Multilevel Governing in Europe', *MPIfG-Discussion Paper* 00/5. Cologne: Max-Planck-Institute for Study of Society.

Schelling, T.C. (1960) *The Strategy of Conflict.* Oxford: Oxford University Press.

Schimmelfennig, F. (2001) 'The Community Trap: Liberal Norms, Rhetorical Action, and the Eastern Enlargement of the European Union', *International Organization*, 55, 1, pp. 47–80.

Schmitz, C.W. (1982) 'Rechtsprobleme im EG-Nachtragshaushaltsplan Nr. 2 für 1980 und das Verhalten der Haushaltsorgane', *Europarecht*, 17, pp. 179–192.

Schmuck, O. (1993) 'Der Gipfel von Edinburgh: Erleichterung nach einem europapolitisch schwierigem Jahr', *Integration*, 16, 1, pp. 33–36.

Schneider, G. and M. Aspinwall (eds): (2001) *The Rules of Integration: Institutionalist Approaches to the Study of Europe*. Manchester and New York: Manchester University Press.

Schneider, G. and L.-E. Cederman (1994) 'The Change of Tide in Political Cooperation: A Limited Information Model of European Integration', *International Organisation* 48, 4, 633–662.

Scully, R.M. (1997) 'Policy Influence and Participation in the European Parliament', *Legislative Studies Quarterly*, 22, 2, pp. 233–252.

Sebenius, J.K. (1983) 'Negotiation arithmetic: adding and subtracting issues and parties', *International Organization*, 37, 2, pp. 281–316.

Shackleton, M. (1990) *Financing the European Community, The Royal Institute of International Affairs*. London: Pinter Publishers.

Shackleton, M. (1991) 'The EC's Budget in the Move to a Single Market', *Governance*, 4, 1, pp. 94–114.

Shackleton, M. (1993a) 'The Community Budget After Maastricht', A.W. Cafruny and G.G. Rosenthal (eds): *The State of the European Community – The Maastricht Debates and Beyond*, Vol. 2. Burnt Mill: Longman Group, pp. 373–390.

Shackleton, M. (1993b) 'The Budget of the EC: Structure and Process', J. Lodge (ed.): *The European Community and the Challenge of the Future*. London: Pinter Publishers.

Shepsle, K.A. (1989) 'Studying Institutions – Some Lessons from the Rational Choice Approach', *Journal of Theoretical Politics*, 1, 2, pp. 131–147.

Shepsle, K.A. (2001) 'A Comment On Institutional Change', *Journal of Theoretical Politics*, 13, 3, pp. 321–325.

Siebert, C. (1988) 'Haushaltspolitik', W. Weidenfels and W. Wessels (eds): *Jahrbuch der Europäischen Integration 1987/88*. Bonn: Institut für Europäische Politik, pp. 148–156.

Simmel, G. (1955) *Conflict* New York: Free Press.

Skiadas, D.V. (2000) 'Judicial Review of the Budgetary Authority during the enactment of the European Union's Budget', *European Integration Online Papers*, 4, 7.

Snyder, F. (1995) 'Interinstitutional Agreements: "forms and Constitutional Limitations"', *EUI Working Paper Law* No. 95/4. Florence: European University Institute.

Sopwith, C. Sir (1980) 'Legal Aspects of the Community Budget', *Common Market Law Review*, 17, pp. 315–347.

Spahn, P.B. (1993) *The Community Budget for an Economic and Monetary Union*. Basingstoke: Macmillan.

Spaventa, L., L. Coopmans, P. Salmon, S. Smith and P. Bernd Spahn (1986) 'The Future of Community Finance', *CEPS Paper* No. 30. Brussels: Centre of European Policy Studies.

Stacey, J. (2001) 'Constitutional Re-engineering in the European Union: The Impact of Informal Interinstitutional Dynamics'. *Paper presented at ECSA Seventh Biennial International Conference*, Madison, Wisconsin, 31 May–2 June 2001.

Stark, J. (1996) 'Die künftige Finanzierung des EU-Haushaltes und der Beitrag des Bundesrepublik Deutschalnd', *Integration*, 3, pp. 159–163.

Stone Sweet, A. (1999) 'Judicialization and the Construction of Governance', *Comparative Political Studies*, 31, pp. 147–184.

Stone Sweet, A., Fligstein, N. and Sandholtz, W. (eds): (2001) *The Institutionalization of Europe*. Oxford: Oxford University Press.

Strasser, D. (1975) 'La nouvelle procédure budgetaire des Communautés Européennes et son application à l'établissement du budget pour l'exercise 1975', *Revue du Marché commun*, 182, pp. 79–87.

Strasser, D. (1976) 'Le Budget pour 1976. Bilan d'une procédure, perspectives pour une nouvelle anneé', *Revue du Marché commun*, 192, pp. 10–19.

Strasser, D. (1977) 'Le Budget 1977. Bilan d'une procédure, perspectives pour une nouvelle anneé', *Revue du Marché commun*, 205, pp. 127–136.

Strasser, D. (1978) 'Le Budget pour 1978. Bilan d'une procédure, innovations juridiques, perspectives pour une nouvelle année', *Revue du Marché commun*, 213, pp. 13–28.

Strasser, D. (1979) 'Le Budget pour 1979. Bilan d'une procédure. Difficultés politiques et juridiques. Perspectives pour une nouvelle année', *Revue du Marché commun*, 227, pp. 240–263.

Strasser, D. (1980) 'Le Budget pour 1980. Environnement politique et financier rejet et établissement. Première experience d'un régime de douzièmes provisoires. Analyse', *Revue du Marché commun*, 239, pp. 358–369.

Strasser, D. (1981a) 'Budget 1981. Son environnement politique et financier. La deuxième crise budgétaire. Les resultats de la procédure. Perspectives pour une nouvelle année', première partie, *Revue du Marché commun*, 248, pp. 279–311.

Strasser, D. (1981b) 'Budget 1981. Son environnement politique et financier. La deuxième crise budgétaire. Les resultats de la procédure. Perspectives pour une nouvelle année', sonconde partie, *Revue du Marché commun*, 252, pp. 561–605.

Strasser, D. (1982) 'Budget 1982. Son environnement politique et financier. Les resultats de la procédure budgétaire. Perspectives pour une année nouvelle', *Revue du Marché commun*, 258, pp. 306–364.

Strasser, D. (1983) 'Le Budget 1983. Son environnement politique et financier. Le trilogue, des deux procédure budgétaire. Perspectives pour une année nouvelle', *Revue du Marché commun*, 268, pp. 307–321.

Strasser, D. (1984) 'Le Budget 1984. Son environnement politique et financier. Son établissement et son execution, l'épuisement des resources propres', *Revue du Marché commun*, 279, pp. 322–382.

Strasser, D. (1985) 'Le Budget 1985. Son environnement politique et financier. Son rejet et établissement. La deuxième experience d'un regime de douzièmes provisoires', *Revue du Marché commun*, 289, pp. 372–444.

Strasser, D. (1992) *The Finances of Europe: The Budgetary and Financial Law of the European Communities*, 3rd edn. Luxembourg: Official Publications.

Streeck, W. and K. Thelen (2005) *Beyond Continuity: Institutional Change in Advanced Political Economies*. Oxford: Oxford University Press.

Streeck, W. and K. Thelen (2005) 'Introduction: Institutional Change in Advanced Political Economies', W. Streeck and K. Thelen (eds): *Beyond Continuity: Explorations in the Dynamics of Advanced Political Economies*. Oxford: Oxford University Press, pp. 7–39.

Sturm, R. (1989) *Haushaltspolitik in westlichen Demokratien. Ein Vergleich des haushaltspolitischen Entscheidungsprozesses in der Bundesrepublik Deutschland, Frankreich, Großbritannien, Kanada und den USA*. Baden-Baden: Nomos.

Taylor, P. (1983) 'The EC Crisis over the Budget and Agricultural Policy. Britain and its Partners in the late 1970s and early 1980s', *Government & Opposition*, 17, pp. 397–413.

Thatcher, M. (1979) Winston Churchill Memorial Lecture ('Europe – the obligations of liberty'), http://www.margaretthatcher.org/speeches/displaydocument.asp?docid= 104149 (accessed 25 February 2005).

Thatcher, M. (1993) *The Downing Street Years*. London: HarperCollins Publishers.

Theato, D.R. and R. Graf (1994) *Das Europäische Parlament und der Haushalt der Europäischen Gemeinschaft*. Baden-Baden: Nomos.

Thelen, K. (1999) 'Historical Institutionalism in Comparative Politics', *The Annual Review of Political Science*, 2, pp. 369–404.

Thöne, E.M. (1982) 'Das direkt gewählte Europäische Parlament. Ein Beitrag zur Abgeordnetensoziologie', *Zeitschrift für Parlamentsfragen*, 13, 2, pp. 149–180.

Timmann, H.-J. (1988) 'Die Interinstitutionelle Vereinbarung über die Haushaltsdisziplin vom 29. Juni 1988', *Europarecht*, 3, pp. 273–289.

Timmann, H.-J. (1989) 'Das Haushaltsverfahren 1989 – Erste Erfahrungen mit der Interinstitutionellen Vereinbarung über die Haushaltsdisziplin', *Europarecht*, 1, pp. 13–29.

Timmann, H.-J. (1991a) 'Haushaltspolitik', W. Weidenfels and W. Wessels (eds): *Jahrbuch der Europäischen Integration 1990/91*. Bonn: Institut für Europäische Politik, pp. 129–136.

Timmann, H.-J. (1991b) 'Haushaltsdisziplin und politischer Entscheidungsmechanismus in der Europäischen Gemeinschaft', *Europarecht*, 26, pp. 121–139.

Timmann, H.-J. (1992) 'Haushaltspolitik', W. Weidenfels and W. Wessels (eds): *Jahrbuch der Europäischen Integration 1991/92*. Bonn: Institut für Europäische Politik, pp. 135–142.

Timmann, H.-J. (1993) 'Haushaltspolitik', W. Weidenfels and W. Wessels (eds): *Jahrbuch der Europäischen Integration 1992/93*. Bonn: Institut für Europäische Politik, pp. 131–138.

Tollison, R.D. and T.D. Willett (1979) 'An economic theory of mutually advantageous issue linkages in international negotiations', *International Organization*, 33, 4, pp. 425–449.

Tonelli, R.M. (1981) 'Le juste retour: une loi communautaire? (IV)', *Revue du Marché commun*, 251, pp. 477–491.

True, J.L., B.D. Jones and F.R. Baumgartner (1999) 'Punctuated-Equilibrium Theory. Explaining Stability and Change in American Policymaking', P.A. Sabbatier (ed.): *Theories of the Policy Process*, pp. 97–115.

Tsebelis, G. (1990) *Nested Games – Rational Choice in Comparative Politics*. Berkley/Los Angeles/London: University of California Press.

Tsebelis, G. (1994) 'The Power of the European Parliament as a Conditional AgendaSetter', *American Political Science Review*, 88, 1, pp. 128–142.

Tsebelis, G. (1995) 'Decision Making in Political Systems: Veto Players in Presidentialism, Parliamentarism, Multicameralism, and Multipartyism', *British Journal of Political Science*, 25, 3, pp. 289–326.

Tsoukalis, L. (1993) *The New European Economy: The Politics and Economics of Integration*. Oxford: Oxford University Press.

Tugendhat, C. (1986) *Making Sense of Europe*. Harmondsworth: Penguin Books Ltd.

Ungerer, W. (1988) 'The Main Problems on the EC Agenda', W. Wessels and E. Regelsberger (eds): *The Federal Republik of Germany and the European Community: the presidency and beyond*. Bonn: Europa Union Verlag, pp. 95–107.

Van Lier, H. (1986) 'Les avances intergovernmentales au soutien des resources propres – un bilan', *Revue du Marché commun*, 294, pp. 71–79.

Vanden Abeele, M. (1982) 'The Mandate of 30 May 1980, Budget Financing and the Revitalization of the Community: An Unfinished Journey', *Common Market Law Review*, 19, 4, pp. 501–519.

Verschraegen, M. (1989) '1988–1989: Naissance et premiers pas d'une novelle mecanique budgetaire', *Revue du Marché commun*, 326, pp. 224–234.

von der Vring, T. (1996) 'Die Verteilung der budgetären Kompetenzen in der Europäischen Union', *Jahrbuch zur Staats- und Verwaltungswissenschaft*, 8, Baden-Baden: Nomos, pp. 203–224.

von Hagen, J. and I.J. Harden (1994) 'National budget processes and fiscal performance', *European Economy, Report and Studies*, 3, 315–418.

Wagner, W. (1999) 'Die Finanzverfassung der Europäischen Union', *Aus Politik und Zeitgeschichte*, B 1–2/99, pp. 32–38.

Wagner, W. (2001) 'German EU Constitutional Foreign Policy', V. Rittberger (ed.): *German Foreign Policy Since Unification. Theories and Case Studies.* Manchester/New York: Manchester University Press.

Wallace, H. (1977) 'The establishment of the Regional Development Fund: Common Policy or Pork Barrel?', H. Wallace, W. Wallace and C. Webb (eds): *Policy-Making in the European Communities.* London: John Willey, pp. 137–163.

Wallace, H. (1980) *Budgetary Politics: The Finances of the European Community*, London: George Allen & Unwin.

Wallace, H. (1983) 'Distributional Politics: Dividing up the Community Cake', H. Wallace, W. Wallace and C. Webb (eds): *Policy-Making in the European Communities*, 2nd edn. London: John Willey, pp. 81–113.

Wallace, H. (1987) 'A European Budget made in Strasbourg and Unmade in Luxembourg', *Yearbook of European Law*, 7, pp. 263–282.

Wallace, W. (1995) 'Germany as Europe's Leading Power', *The World Today*, August-September, pp. 164.

Weber, S. and H. Wiesmeth (1991) 'Issue Linkage in the European Community', *Journal of Common Market Studies*, 29, 3, pp. 255–267.

Werts, J. (1992) *The European Council.* Amsterdam: Elsevier Science Publishers.

Weidenfeld, W. (ed.): (1998) *Deutsche Europapolitik. Optionen wirksamer Interessenvertretung, Münchner Beiträge zur Europäischen Einigung*, Volume 2, Bonn: Institut für Europäische Politik.

Wildavsky, A.B and N. Caiden (1997) *The new politics of the Budgetary Process*, 3rd edn. New York: Longman Classics Series.

Wolf, A. (1992) 'Deutschland', W.Weidenfeld and W.Wessels (eds): *Jahrbuch der Europäischen Integration 1991/92.* Bonn: Institut für Europäische Politik, pp. 310–320.

Index